THE BOTTOM LINE
MONEY

BOOK

How to Earn More...Keep More... And Invest More Wisely

Bottom Line Books

Bottom Line® Books publishes the advice of expert authorities in
many fields. The use of a book is not a substitute for legal,
accounting or other professional services. Consult a competent
professional for answers to your specific questions.

Library of Congress Cataloging in Publication Data
Main entry under title:

The Bottom Line Money Book

    1. Life skills—United States.   I. Bottom line personal
ISBN 0-88723-180-2

Bottom Line® Books is a registered trademark of
Boardroom® Inc.
55 Railroad Avenue, Greenwich, CT 06830

Printed in the United States of America

Happiness is positive cash flow.

—Fred Adler
Fulbright & Jaworski, LLP

Contents

Chapter 1
Financial Fitness
How to Hold on to What You've Got

Chapter 2
Better Tax Strategies
Don't Pay More than You Have To

Chapter 4

Investing in Your Future

Make Your Money Grow

Chapter 3

Banking & Credit

Keep Your Money Safer

Chapter 5

Mastering Health Care

Hold on to Your Family's Health and Your Savings

Chapter 6

Home Finance

Make the Most of Buying, Selling and Living in Your Home

Chapter 7

Automotive Expertise

Keep Down the Costs of Your Car

Chapter 8

Paying for College

Plan for Your Child's Higher Education

Chapter 9

Estate Planning

How to Keep the Most for Your Family

Chapter 10

Dollar Stretchers

Get the Most for Your Money

Chapter 12

Travel

Go Far on a Little

Chapter 11

Retirement

Live Well without Working

Chapter 13

Much Better Business

Working for Yourself

Financial Fitness

How to Hold on to What You've Got

Jonathan Pond's Techniques to Simplify Your Financial Life

The busier you are, the more difficult it is to manage your family's finances. While everyone recognizes the importance of saving and investing, keeping up with the paperwork and the markets on top of limiting expenses such as commissions and fees can be overwhelming. Here are some simplification basics.

REDUCE THE NUMBER OF YOUR BROKERAGE ACCOUNTS

Most people have far too many of them. It is not unusual for middle-income individuals to have three or more. Many people also have several IRA accounts—some with full-service brokers and a few others with a discount broker.

Reasons: Some people use a full-service broker for long-term investments and research data, and a discount broker for frequent trading. Others try to give broker friends and relatives some business.

Problem: In addition to costing more in expenses, a large number of accounts can cause you headaches at tax time. Most brokerages and funds are good about sending out tax statements in early January, but if you neglect to account for one of them, the IRS will ask you to pay up later.

Solution: Determine which type of broker you use most often, full-service or discount. Then pick one and close out the other accounts. It really doesn't pay to maintain more than one account, especially if you're like the average investor and trade only a few times a year. By consolidating your brokerage accounts, you're also likely to get better service. The larger your account, the more attention you will receive from your broker.

SET UP A SIMPLE RECORD-KEEPING SYSTEM

Too many well-intentioned organizational attempts fail because they are overly ambitious or too complicated to maintain. A good, basic system includes the following.

1 A folder or box for all incoming bills that need to be paid.

2 A folder for material that will support this year's tax returns, such as bank, brokerage and mutual fund statements, life insurance, homeowner's and car insurance records, and stubs and canceled checks proving you've paid your bills.

3 A folder for all of your home-improvement records over the years. This folder will come in handy when you sell your home and need to offset the gains realized on the sale.

4 Accordion folders for the past four-years' tax returns and the paperwork that supports those returns.

5 A three-ring binder with an inventory of your household possessions, in case you suffer a major loss from theft or disaster. Include a video or photographs of your residence and possessions.

Important: Use a safe-deposit box to store the binder and the video, along with those things that are irreplaceable or hard to reconstruct, such as birth, marriage and stock certificates. List your spouse and children as the co-owners of the box. If you store valuables in your box, such as jewelry or coins, add safe-deposit box insurance to your homeowner's or renter's policy.

HAVE YOUR MONEY AUTOMATICALLY INVESTED

You'll never miss the money if it is taken out of your paycheck before you even see it.

Strategy: You can arrange to have your employer deposit part of your check into a mutual fund or see if the mutual funds of your choice can take preset sums from your checking account each pay period.

The sooner you get your money into investments with good potential returns, the sooner it begins to grow. In addition, investing automatically forces you

Prepare an Annual Projection of Your Retirement Income and Expenses

This may not seem like it belongs on a list of ways to simplify your financial life, but a goal of simplification is to help you sleep better. Most people are so worried about whether they'll have enough money to retire that they are afraid to face the issue at all. This type of planning is not that difficult to do. There are plenty of free worksheets available from mutual funds.

Here's how: To be conservative, I suggest using an inflation rate of 3.5% and a life expectancy of 95 years in preparing these projections. While most people will discover that they need to save a bit more for retirement each year than they do now, they will also find that they're coming pretty close to meeting this projection.

The median income of American households in 1995 was $34,076.
Source: U.S. Census Bureau

to dollar-cost average and lowers your average purchase price over time.

Most people are accustomed to investing automatically if they participate in a 401(k) plan. You can do the same thing on your own with an IRA.

Here's how: See if your favorite mutual fund will have your bank transfer about $39 a week, or $167 a month, to your IRA. By the end of one year, you will have made the maximum $2,000 contribution.

Time is Money

The sooner you begin saving, the more you will have when you retire.

A lump sum of $10,000 earning 8% for	Can add up to	$2,000 invested yearly, earning 8% for	Can add up to
10 years	**$21,590**	10 years	**$31,291**
20 years	**$46,610**	20 years	**$98,844**
30 years	**$100,630**	30 years	**$244,692**

REDUCE YOUR NUMBER OF MUTUAL FUNDS

Most investors need only four stock funds: a growth fund, an equity-income or a growth-and-income fund that owns dividend-paying stocks, a small-company fund and an international fund. This mix gives you the best exposure to stock-investing categories but is still a small enough number to be manageable.

REDUCE YOUR NUMBER OF CREDIT CARDS

For some people, it's still a badge of honor to whip out a wallet filled with credit cards. Many people have six or more: an airline card, a few gas cards and several department store cards.

Reality: At most, all you need are two cards: a charge card, such as American Express, for when you don't want to worry about bumping up against a credit limit, and a low-interest MasterCard or Visa for everyday expenditures. This way, you will have only one or two bills to pay each month and, in most cases, lower annual fees.

Robert Ortalda, Jr.'s Tips on How to Live Within Your Means

Although baby boomers are supposed to be America's most affluent demographic group, they are not as affluent as they think they are.

Thanks to the hyperinflation of the 1970s and 1980s and credit card debt of the 1990s, boomers have suffered a decline in their real earning power over the last 20 years, even though their wages seem to have been increasing.

Yet boomers want to be free of overdue bills and in a position to put money aside for what they want now or in the future. Here's how to avoid life's big spending traps.

RECOGNIZE THAT DEBT IS EASIER TO TAKE ON THAN TO PAY OFF

Credit cards are the major factor behind most consumer debt. The problem is that there is no longer any social stigma to spending more than you make. Overspending is now socially acceptable. As a result, there's nothing external that tells us to stop.

I'm not advocating that you give up all your credit cards. They can be beneficial when their use is planned and controlled. But you should know how much you can afford to pay back before you ever whip out the plastic.

Prepare an Outline of Your Financial Holdings for Your Heirs

It's a thoughtful thing to do and will simplify their lives during a stressful time. This is called a letter of instructions.

Here's how: Use a three-ring binder to summarize where important documents are kept, what assets and investments you own and where they are held. Include names and phone numbers of contacts at brokerages, banks and insurance companies, as well as how to access information from key accounts over any voice-automated systems, which are becoming increasingly popular. Also include a copy of your estate attorney's letterhead stationery so that your heirs will know whom to call.

Some people also write investment instructions to their spouse or guardians who may not be financially savvy. The instructions should provide an overview of your strategy, explaining such things as what each account is for and which investments to sell first if necessary.

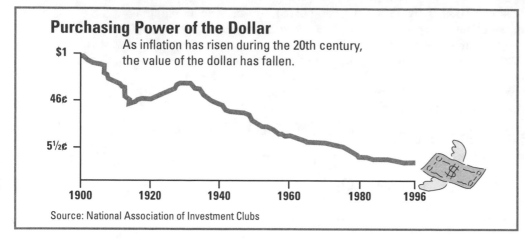

Purchasing Power of the Dollar

As inflation has risen during the 20th century, the value of the dollar has fallen.

$1

46¢

5½¢

1900   1920   1940   1960   1980   1996

Source: National Association of Investment Clubs

Be careful about using automated teller machine (ATM) cards. In the past, people had to manage their money carefully because they had to use cash for all purchases. There was no question about when they reached their limit and what they couldn't afford.

With ATM machines, however, cash is only a few buttons away. It's also easy to borrow from ATMs if you go beyond your means.

BEWARE OF HOME EQUITY LOANS

These are tricky because they make good tax sense. They are one of the few loans that are tax deductible.

Caution: You can use the loan to clear the balances on your credit cards, but that may tempt you to charge them up again. If you do, you'll have two sets of monthly payments, the credit cards and the second mortgage payments, while you used to have only one.

BEWARE OF SPENDING UNEXPECTED INCOME THREE TIMES OVER

Most people spend occasional bonanzas, at least mentally, several times before they actually get them.

Example: You just got a $5,000 bonus. In your mind, you've already spent it on renovating the bathroom, buying a bike and taking the family on a vacation. But your spouse has spent it, too—on different things. And both of you forgot to factor in the extra taxes you'll owe on the money, since a bonus is added to your gross income on your W-2 form.

Solution: Whenever you receive a windfall, whether it's from a bonus, from a spouse working an extra job or from an inheritance, make a joint list of the items on which you intend to

spend the money. Be sure to deduct taxes from the windfall before you spend it.

CREATE A BUDGET THAT LEAVES ROOM FOR UNUSUAL EXPENSES

Most people don't have trouble drawing up a budget that provides for spending on food, housing and transportation.

The problem is with intermittent expenses, such as taxes, insurance, car repairs, gifts and family vacations. Just because these bills aren't due every month doesn't mean they don't occur periodically.

The goal is to estimate what they will come to on an annual basis, and to then divide that figure by 12 so you can set aside enough money each month to handle them.

RECOGNIZE THAT FOLLOWING A BUDGET IS A JOINT VENTURE

Typically, one partner or the other takes the lead in preparing and monitoring the family budget, even though both agree on overall goals.

Key to success: Avoid a budget plan that clamps down on one person. It's crucial that each partner be allowed to spend some money on what is important to him or her.

Example: The wife thinks that photography is an

Financial Records Disposal Alert

A garbage can fraud ring stole more than $10 million in dozens of states by recovering canceled checks, deposit slips and credit card receipts from trash receptacles, using the account information to create phony identification papers, then cashing counterfeit checks, filing false tax returns and even staging auto accidents to collect on fraudulent claims.

Self-defense
Shred or burn personal financial records and receipts except for tax records— do not just throw them out.

important hobby, but her husband feels she's no good at it and should stop. It would be a big mistake to draw up a budget that cuts out her spending on photography altogether. She is likely to become resentful and make sure she finds other ways to spend the money.

Save Your Next Pay Raise

You didn't have the money before, so you won't miss it now.

Strategy: Have the extra amount deducted from your checking account and deposited into an investment account.

Shrewder Spending

Prioritize expenses by keeping close track of them and labeling each one A, B, C or D.

A: necessities like groceries and rent or mortgage, and savings.

B: important items, clothes and gifts.

C: nice-to-have things like trips and meals at restaurants.

D: enjoyable but worthless items, such as knick-knacks and checkout-line magazines.

If you need to save income, find the money by cutting C and D expenses.

Beware Falling Raises
The average pay raise for salaried exempt employees has been decreasing since 1990.

Source: Hewitt Associates

Six Months to Financial Fitness

It's no wonder that we're all so worried about money. We're living longer, retiring earlier and expecting more out of our retirement. At our high rate of spending and low rate of saving, 75% of us will retire with less than half of what we need. The key is to do something about it now.

Here's a money diet to put you on the right track.

MONTH 1
GET ON THE FINANCIAL SCALES

Total Assets
- Total Liabilities
= NET WORTH

Create an overview of where you stand financially by creating net worth and cash flow statements.

Net worth
Set up separate folders for your bank, investment and retirement accounts, credit cards, and any real estate and cars that you own. Make up a worksheet. On the left side, list the fair market value of your assets.

Example: Estimate conservatively what you could sell your house for today (not what you would like to get for it).

Add up the numbers. The result is your total assets. On the right side, list your liabilities, including mortgages, credit card balances, car loans and other debt. The result is your total liabilities.

Your net worth: Subtract your total liabilities from your total assets.

Cash flow
Once you have calculated your net worth, determine how you are spending your money on a regular basis.

Here's how: Set up another worksheet. On the left, write the 12 months on separate lines, starting with the current month and going in reverse chronological order.

Make two headings at the top of the page: Total Monthly Deposits (credits) on the left side and Total Monthly Withdrawals (debits) on the right side.

Step 1: Gather your bank statements for the last 12

months. Under each column on the worksheet, fill in the deposits and withdrawals, month by month. Add up the columns to get your yearly credits and debits.

Step 2: Subtract from both columns the annual amount withheld for Social Security and any income taxes paid by check in the past 12 months. This process provides you with a more accurate indication of your spendable income and those expenses over which you have control. Add to both columns all other nontax expenses withheld from your paycheck, such as company insurance premiums and company parking space costs.

Step 3: On the credit side, add savings and retirement-plan contributions withheld. On the debit side, either add or subtract the increase or decrease in the amount of your consumer debt during the past 12 months.

Step 4: Examine the results: your after-tax annual income and total annual expenses. Income must exceed expenses, or you're heading for financial trouble.

Strategy: Track your weekly expenses in detail for the next five months to find out where your money goes. Write down every cent you spend in a small notebook or on the back of your ATM receipts. Don't try to do anything about the pattern at first. Most people take at least two months to begin to change their spending habits.

The Growing Middle Class

Over the past few years, the percentage of all U.S. families whose net worth (in 1995 dollars) falls into the lowest and highest categories has decreased, while the median net worth has increased.

Net Worth	1992	1995
Less than $10,000	27.0%	25.8%
$10,000-24,999	10.4	10.0
$25,000-49,999	11.4	11.6
$50,000-99,999	15.3	16.9
$100,000-249,999	20.7	21.3
$250,000 and more	15.2	14.4
Median family net worth	**$52,800**	**$56,400**

Source: Federal Reserve Bulletin, January 1997

MONTH 2
SET LONG-TERM GOALS

If you don't figure out your long-term financial goals, you will almost always fail to reach them, because short-term needs are always so demanding.

Strategy: Set up a new worksheet with four headings: Annual Pretax Income, Annual Expenses, Goals and Estimated Cost of those goals in current dollars. Here are some common goals.

College for your kids

The cost per child now is around $10,000 a year at a public school, and $25,000 at a private college. Multiply the annual cost by the number of years in college, for a range of $40,000 to $100,000, and by the number of children. Like everything else, college costs increase with time: the annual increase is about 6% to 8%. The good news is that most students are eligible for some type of financial aid.

A worry-free retirement

Multiply your current annual expenses by 0.8% (If you make $50,000 a year, that's $40,000). This is about what you will need annually to retire comfortably. Ideally, your investments should be able to provide you with this annual retirement allowance while continuing to grow with inflation.

A home of your own

With a down payment of 20%, the most expensive house you can buy is about 2.5 times your gross annual household income.

Insurance

If you die or become disabled and have a spouse and a child, your family will need 70% of your current income, or 50% if you

just have a spouse. If you become disabled, you will also need about 70% of your current income. Start researching policies now.

MONTH 3
REDUCE EXPENSES AND DEBT

This is the first month you're going to make changes. Don't make unrealistic spending cuts at first. Pick four or five problem areas, such as restaurants, clothes and hobbies. Work on reducing a couple of expenses each month.

Get in the habit of smart spending, making decisions when you spend. Ask yourself, "Is what I'm getting today worth the money I lose for my family's and my future goals?"

Start reducing debt
Avoid making only small minimum payments on credit cards. It can take up to ten years to pay off your current balance.

Strategy: If you charge $30 for dinner, deduct that amount from your checkbook when you get home. Pay the full amount on your credit card bill when it arrives. This strategy will make you think twice about casually dining out. Also, ask credit card companies to reduce your interest rates and forgo fees.

Pay automatically
Have regular expenses, such as insurance premiums, deducted automatically from your paycheck or bank account.

MONTH 4
TAXES AND INVESTMENTS
Review every item on last year's return to see how

you can reduce your taxes.
● Keep track of deductions, especially those for cash expenditures, such as mileage, faxes, photocopies and charity. It all adds up.
● Contribute the maximum to tax-deferred retirement plans.

● Consider your investment strategy. If you're intimidated by the market, start with an index mutual fund, one that conservatively invests in stocks in the S&P 500. You can move on to other kinds of mutual funds later.

MONTH 5
INSURE THE FUTURE

The best financial plan can be ruined if catastrophe strikes. You have to protect your income and assets with insurance.

Disability
Buy as much disability insurance as you can afford.
Key: Be sure the policy provides benefits until you reach age 65 or for life, and that it covers you if you can't work at your own occupation.

Life insurance
The rule of thumb is to have coverage that equals five to seven times your annual income. A term policy is often best for people in their 30s who have young children and need a lot of coverage but don't have a lot of money for premiums. Term insurance will cover you for a set number of years but gets more expensive each time you renew the policy. Cash-value insurance is ideal for those who can afford coverage for 20 years or longer. Part of cash-value premiums grows tax-deferred.

Homeowner's insurance
This should cover what it would cost to replace your home and personal property now.

Automobile insurance
Liability coverage is key, so make sure you have enough. For both comprehensive and collision coverage, take the highest deductible with which you feel comfortable. Consider dropping comprehensive and collision if your car is more than 5 years old and has lost most of its value.

Estate planning
If you don't have a will, a power of attorney and a living trust, see an estate attorney. Preparation costs range from $500 to $2,000 or more, depending on the

complexity of your estate. If you already have these documents, review them and make any changes needed to bring them up to date.

MONTH 6
REVIEW WHAT YOU'VE DONE

Write out your accomplishments. Redo net worth and cash flow worksheets using your current information, and compare the results with those from six months ago. You'll feel better knowing you're in control of your money and financial life. That provides the motivation to make your money diet an automatic part of your life.

Take Control of Your Assets in Seven Days

The only way to truly achieve financial security is to live beneath your means. That will give you the extra money you need to pay off debts and begin to save.

Some people think it is impossible to save today. But even in these crazy times, it is not only possible, but essential, to be financially responsible. And it's not as difficult as you may think.

Here's a seven-day plan for getting control of your money. All it takes is 20 minutes a day for one week.

DAY 1
ORGANIZE YOUR FINANCIAL RECORDS

If you want to dig yourself out of a financial hole, you must figure out how you got there. That means calculating how much money you earn and where it goes. As a first step, gather the following records.

- Recent pay stub.
- Latest tax return.
- Most recent bank statement.
- Checkbook.
- Current credit card bills.

The pay stub will tell you how much you bring in from work, and the tax return will tell you how much you get from investments and other sources of income.

The bank statement and checkbook will tell you where you are spending the bulk of your money. The credit card bills will tell you how much additional money you spend that is not being covered by your paycheck.

DAY 2
FIGURE OUT WHERE YOUR MONEY GOES

Once you have compiled your financial statements, you are ready to prepare a summary of your monthly expenses.

Make a list of all your expenses, right down to the smallest item. Pay particular attention to exactly where the cash goes. There's often a lot of room to cut back in this area.

If necessary, keep a journal for a day or two and write down every purchase you make. You will quickly realize that you waste a lot of money, and that there are many ways to save.

DAY 3
CATEGORIZE YOUR EXPENSES

Slot them into one of the following three categories.

- Regular payments that you have to make, such as for the mortgage and utilities.
- Expenses you must incur but that could be reduced, such as those for food, clothing and transportation.
- Expenses you could eliminate entirely, such as eating at restaurants, going to concerts and buying lottery tickets.

In the last two categories, you will find many areas in which you can cut back.

DAY 4
DEVISE A PLAN FOR LIVING BENEATH YOUR MEANS

You have to reduce your monthly expenses so that you spend less than you take in. How much should you cut back? If you are adding $500 a month to paying off your credit card balance, then you have to cut $500 a month from your spending just to stop your finances from deteriorating.

Even if you manage to do that, you are still not making progress. You must cut more than $500 to get your current debt under control and start building your savings. Make a list of all the expenses that you are eliminating and how much you hope to save.

DAY 5
DEVELOP A DEBT-REDUCTION STRATEGY

Now that you have figured out how to spend less than you earn, what should you do with the extra money you are saving?

First, pay off your debts. Start with the debts that charge the highest interest rates. These are usually the credit card bills. Set target dates for when you want each debt to be completely paid. Don't be too ambitious or you will set yourself up for failure.

DAY 6
ESTABLISH A SAVINGS PLAN

If you don't have any money saved, plan to begin saving while reducing your debts. This should not mean that you end up paying off your debts more slowly.

Financially, that doesn't seem to make sense. It's better to pay off credit card debt at 20% interest than to save money that earns 4% or 5%. But psychologically, it's a real boost to get some savings under way. In addition, your savings will be helpful in case you lose your job or become ill.

Investing a Little Can Earn You a Lot
A $50 monthly investment earning 8% a year will turn into almost $50,000 over a 25-year period.

5 yrs	10 yrs	15 yrs	20 yrs	25 yrs
$3,674	$9,147	$17,302	$29,451	$47,551

Source: Oppenheimer Funds

DAY 7
START AN AUTOMATIC INVESTMENT PLAN

It's not only time to think about saving for an emergency, but also about investing for the future.

Call your bank, credit union or a mutual fund company and arrange an automatic investment plan. With this type of plan, money will be deducted directly from your paycheck or bank account every month and put into an investment account.

To arrange for this, you will have to commit to investing $50 or $100 every month. This money can become the basis of your retirement portfolio or your child's college fund.

After you've completed this seven-day plan, you will feel much better, you will get back on track financially and, most importantly, you will not lapse into your old spendthrift ways.

Terry Savage's Financial Strategies For Working Couples

Few two-income couples take full advantage of their financial power, and they don't concentrate on making their money work for them.

Think about it. If you both were living separately, you would each have rent or mortgage payments, phone and utility bills, and it wouldn't be as much fun to dine at home.

So don't spend all of your double income; use it to your advantage.

TIP **Smarter Saving Strategy**

Investors who systematically put aside a certain amount each month over a period of years should remember to increase the amount each year to make up for inflation. $100 a month, which was a fairly significant sum 25 years ago, is not adequate today to build a retirement nest egg. If you assume an inflation rate of 4%, the value of the money you've saved will be cut in half in 18 years. If you accumulate $100,000, it will be worth only $50,000 after inflation.

ATTITUDES ABOUT MONEY

There are two types of people: savers and spenders. For better or worse, they tend to marry each other. The result is often conflicting views of money and how it should be spent and invested.

To make matters more stressful, both adults in dual-income households usually are aggressive about having their way.

Result: It's easy to find yourself trying to control each other's financial behavior in ways that generate conflict.

Solution: Sit down with your partner and confront your money attitudes. Then discuss how best to handle your finances. Take a close look at your overall financial picture.

Ask yourselves:
- How much of your respective incomes do you want to save?
- What are your savings goals (vacation, new car, down payment on a house, college for the kids or retirement)?
- Should you be accountable to each other for all of your spending, or should you each have a private account?
- How many credit cards will you use? Will you cut up all but one of your cards and take a weekly cash allowance?

Another way to limit the amount of damage done by reckless spending habits is to set up separate accounts for portions of your earnings. Pay your household expenses out of one joint account.

Remember: Depending on your state of residence, you may be responsible for your spouse's debts, and your spouse's bill-paying habits could affect your credit report.

SHARE FINANCIAL CHORES

In many households, the financial chores are divided. One person pays the bills and balances the checkbook while the other invests and organizes the taxes. However, it is far better if both of you understand and are responsible for all aspects of your finances. After all, you never know when you'll have to take over the entire job of financial management.

Added benefits: If the spender had to balance the checkbook and pay the bills, he or she might not be so willing to buy impulsively. If the person who han-

A saver and a spender can balance each other out.

dles the checkbook understood more about investing, that person would probably better understand why it is so important to make out that monthly check to the mutual fund to save for college or retirement.

RECONCILE TAX STRATEGIES

Spouses often have different views about how to handle their income taxes and organize their records, especially if they prepare their own tax returns.

Example: You may be an aggressive filer who claims every deduction, while your spouse may be more conservative for fear of triggering an audit.

Important: If both of you sign the return, both of you are liable for any mistakes, disallowances (when the IRS disallows a deduction) or penalties.

Strategy: Seek professional tax-filing help. Find a CPA who makes both of you comfortable. It may be worth the extra expense to give you peace of mind about your taxes.

RETIREMENT ACCOUNTS

IRAs offer a tremendous opportunity to save for your future. You may each deduct a $2,000 contribution to an IRA if neither of you is covered by an employer-sponsored retirement plan, such as a 401(k).

Even if you do participate in such a plan, you still might be eligible to deduct some IRA contributions, or make nondeductible contributions to Roth IRAs depending on you income level. Check with your tax adviser. Even better than an IRA is a company-sponsored 401(k) plan. Try to contribute the maximum amount allowed, especially if your company matches your contributions.

Important: Some couples leave retirement planning to the highest earner. That causes two problems.

1. The couple doesn't save enough to meet their retirement needs.

2. One of them may be at a big disadvantage if they ever divorce.

Strategy: If you can't afford to contribute the maximum amounts to two company savings plans, concentrate all your savings in the plan that offers the best deal.

Example: If your spouse's employer matches employees' retirement contributions but your employer does not, you might consider having your spouse contribute more. Nevertheless, each of you should have savings in your own name.

LIFE INSURANCE NEEDS

If both of you are working, you might need additional life insurance to replace some of the income that would be lost if one spouse died.

That means you must figure out how much supplemental income you would need, especially to cover long-term expenses such as mortgage payments or college costs. Comparison shop for the least expensive term life insurance from a highly rated company.

Helpful: Get term insurance quotes from SelectQuote (800-343-1985) and TermQuote (800-444-TERM).

Alternative: If you don't have a policy, consider buying a first-to-die whole-life policy. It will insure the life of the person who dies first and might be as much as 40% cheaper than buying separate policies for each of you.

Important: Make sure that the policy can be converted to cover a surviving spouse without a new physical exam.

HEALTH INSURANCE

Be careful about tampering with your health insurance. Since both of you have jobs, you may be able to save some money on your coverage. For example, you might opt out of one partner's plan and let the other plan cover you both.

Warning: Such a move could leave you vulnerable if the covered spouse stops working.

Strategy: Compare the two plans and figure out how much you could save by dropping one of them. If the savings are considerable, find out if you can temporarily drop one and then get back into it later without being subject to restrictions for preexisting conditions.

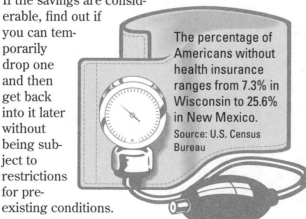

The percentage of Americans without health insurance ranges from 7.3% in Wisconsin to 25.6% in New Mexico.
Source: U.S. Census Bureau

If not, consider keeping both health insurance plans, despite the extra cost.

LIVING ON ONE INCOME

Just because both of you are working now doesn't mean your family will always have two incomes. One of you may decide to take time off to change careers, raise children or go back to school. There is also the very real risk that one of you will lose your job at some point in the future.

Bottom line: Being a two-income family gives you power, leverage and maneuverability. Change your attitudes about spending and saving. Think of spending less now not as a penalty, but as a form of deferred consumption with a real bonus: the interest or gains you can earn on the money you save.

Remember: If you don't see the money, you won't spend it. Start automatic monthly deductions from your paycheck or checking account into a stock or money market mutual fund. Let your money work as hard for you as you work for it.

Rainy-Day Money is a Necessity

How much you need depends on your age, health and job outlook. The traditional advice is to have three to six months' worth of living expenses in cash. But that may be too much if you can easily borrow against assets with a home-equity line of credit or brokerage margin account, or if you have cash-value life insurance. It may also be too much cash for two-income households, unless you are spending both incomes, since it is unlikely both earners would lose their jobs at the same time. Do keep more cash on hand if your work is seasonal, you own a business, you have one income and your job may be at risk, or you are facing disability or severe illness.

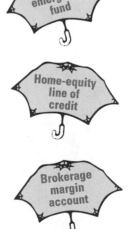

Cash emergency fund

Home-equity line of credit

Brokerage margin account

Cash-value life insurance

Carol Keeffe Tells How to Get What You Want in Life

You don't have to make more money to get more of what you really want. What it takes is better money management, some creativity and a clear sense of your own values.

I know. I've practiced what I preach and found that it really does work.

It works whether you have money problems or not. After all, haven't we all met people who have a lot of money coming in but are never able to afford the things they want?

Fifteen years ago, my financial life was a mess. My husband and I had two young children, and we spent every cent we earned—and then some.

We had no savings and owed a total of $7,000 on seven different credit cards. At the time, we earned

It's not how much you're making, but how you're managing it that counts.

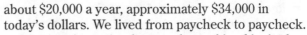

about $20,000 a year, approximately $34,000 in today's dollars. We lived from paycheck to paycheck.

My transformation began when a friend invited me to a three-part personal finance workshop at a nearby community college. It opened my eyes.

The instructor discussed the importance of establishing a financial foundation.

I immediately realized that my family had no financial foundation. I also knew that the problem wasn't the amount of money we were making but how we were managing it. We had things backwards. Our financial attention had been focused exclusively on trying to pay off our bills and not focused on making our income do what we really wanted, and needed, it to do. A few simple steps helped me change my focus, and can help you, too.

1. PREPARE A BUDGET

Properly motivated for the first time in my life, I bought a recordkeeping handbook called *The Family Living Account Book*. This booklet made recording expenses easy and helped me to see clearly what habits I wanted to change.

Example: The month that expenses for our aquarium totaled $120, we found a new home for our fish.

2. MAKE SURE THAT YOU HAVE A FAMILY FOUNDATION

Everyone should establish an emergency fund as a financial buffer for emergencies. This fund should be relatively liquid and not used for daily expenses.

3. SET SPECIFIC, ACHIEVABLE FINANCIAL GOALS

What are your true, heartfelt priorities? A special trip? A gift for yourself, a child or a grandchild? New furniture?

My first goal was a family trip to Disneyland.

Strategy: Label a jar or a box Disneyland or New Zealand, for instance, and fill it with your loose change, found money and impulse payments. Impulse payments? That's when you pass the jar or box and just happen to toss in $2, $5 or $25. Add regular monthly payments as well. Periodically take this money to the bank.

HOW TO SAVE MORE EFFECTIVELY

Poor spending habits waste 20% to 30% of many people's discretionary income.

Strategy: Begin saving at least $1 a day (including weekends) plus all pocket change. When buying, pay in cash to remind yourself that you are really spending money. Ask for cash discounts, especially on major purchases. Do things for yourself for which you might pay others, like lawn work and car washes.

4. MAKE SURE THE MONEY IS IN A SEPARATE ACCOUNT

I can't emphasize this enough. Part of what turned my life around was learning to set up separate accounts for emergencies, long-term savings and goals.

A single savings account doesn't work for many people. I used to make my deposit into the account and mentally divide the money into different categories: $87 for our family reunion in Wisconsin, $122 to remodel the kitchen, $43 for a love seat. The theory was that all the goals would soon be reached.

That was the theory. When the bank statement arrived, I'd mentally register the total amount, $252, without considering my goals.

Then I'd either buy something, confident that I could afford it because I had money in the bank, or an emergency would arise and I'd pay for new tires or furnace repairs. My one savings account never quite took me where I wanted to go.

Now, however, I always reach my goals. As I see money accumulate in a goal account, a snowball effect occurs. Each week, the goal seems more attainable, and I have more incentive to increase my contributions and no desire to raid the account.

Today, when an emergency occurs, I tap the emergency account. And when a new need arises, I simply open up a new account.

5. SAVE UP FOR BIG TREATS

When you start accumulating money for important goals, you no longer want to fritter away $2, $5 or $50 on something you really don't care about.

First, you'll realize that a lot of small expenditures can quickly add up.

Example: Let's say you spend $2.75 on a bagel and cappuccino

Little Treats Add Up

One bagel	$1.00
+ one cup cappuccino	+ 1.75
	=$2.75
Every day for a year	x 365
Total cost	$1003.75

every day. Over the course of a year, that's more than $1,000! You'll begin snatching up money you used to fritter impulsively and take it home for your dream jar. Try it and see.

Note: We often give ourselves small rewards because we're feeling down or deprived. My family's "Oh, poor me, I must reward myself" mentality that made us squander money was transformed into "Disneyland, here we come!"

6. AVOID PAYING DOWN DEBT TOO FAST

If you do nothing but pay off debts, life soon seems to be little more than a struggle.

When you use all excess funds to pay off credit card debt, you never build up an emergency fund. So when the vacuum cleaner breaks, you have to use credit cards again.

Result: Debt doesn't decline and you never accumulate any savings.

Strategy: Pay only the minimum on different debts, directing the difference towards savings.

Note: Many money experts frown on this approach because the interest you pay on credit cards or any other debt is so much higher than what you earn on savings. Another criticism is that it can take years to pay off the debt.

Both views are valid but they both miss the bigger picture. The amount I lost in interest ended up working well for me psychologically as I watched our savings grow larger.

7. FOCUS ON WHAT MATTERS

I focused on what I really wanted in life because my goal accounts were now earning interest.

When I quit concentrating exclusively on digging myself out of debt and began focusing on the things I valued most in life, dreams started coming true and bills dwindled—all with the money I already had. You can do it too!

How Much Should You Save?

Do not put too much money aside for a rainy day. The common recommendation—to keep enough cash for six months' worth of living expenses—forces you to hold significant amounts of money in very low-interest locations like savings accounts.

Strategy: Keep enough cash to handle small-scale disasters, such as the need for a new refrigerator or major car repairs. Put the rest of the rainy-day money into a good stock fund.

Reason: The fund should provide good returns, eventually being worth far more than you need to live for six months. In case of personal disaster when stocks are down, tap home equity or get a credit card cash advance, then repay the loan by selling shares of the fund after the market recovers.

How Reformed Spendthrift Mary Hunt Keeps Spending Under Control

The best way to keep spending under control is to stay away from places that tempt you to buy what they sell. Here is what I do to keep my over-zealous spending in check.

DON'T SHOP IN PRETTY PLACES

I rarely go into malls, but recently I had no choice but to venture into one. We were leaving on a trip, and I had to buy shirts for my husband.

Where to Find Cash Fast

Don't pull out your high interest-rate credit card when you need a large sum of cash quickly. There are much smarter sources to tap first.

Negotiate a home-equity line of credit. You win two ways with a home-equity loan: rates are low and the interest you pay on it is tax-deductible. Take the time to shop around for the best deal. Competition is forcing banks to lower their borrowing costs.

Caution: You can lose your home if you are not careful about repaying the loan.

Borrow from your IRA. You can withdraw money from your IRA once a year, as long as you put the entire amount back into an IRA account at the end of 60 days.

Borrow from parents and friends. If you are borrowing less than $10,000, the money can be treated as a gift and will not be taxed. If, however, you want the money to be treated as a loan, you must work out a payback schedule and pay a reasonable rate of interest.

Caution: Borrowing from parents, friends or relatives can strain your relationship.

Borrow from your 401(k) plan. In general, you can borrow from 401(k) plans to pay college tuition or medical costs, or to make the down payment on a house. The money must be repaid in five years. Check with your 401(k) plan administrator at work because rules vary.

Obtain a margin loan through your stockbroker. They usually carry very low interest rates because your stocks and bonds are used as collateral.

Drawback: The IRS does not allow you to deduct the interest payments.

Cash in your certificates of deposit. The only penalty you pay is forfeiting three or six months' worth of interest.

Exception: People who hold long-term, high-yielding CDs from years ago should probably look for some other source of cash.

I owe my broker $

401(k)

IRA

CD

When I arrived at the mall, I parked close to the men's department so I wouldn't have to walk through much of the store. I made a beeline for the shirts, racing past a handbag display as fast as I could and not stopping for even a minute to look at them.

I use these strategies all the time. When I have to make a purchase, I pick my shopping centers and malls very carefully. Basically, I shop in the least attractive stores, those I don't enjoy very much.

I also avoid supermarkets as much as I can. When I have to go into one—every three or four weeks to stock up—I go with my husband, who is not a compulsive shopper.

The Price Club is an ideal place for me to shop. The one closest to us is not air-conditioned. The lights are dim, it's certainly not pretty, I buy in bulk and I pay in cash. I don't bring a checkbook or credit cards, which means I have to do some advance planning to have the right amount of cash with me.

My rule is to pay cash as often as I possibly can. This forces me to control impulse purchases. I always have to plan ahead how much cash to carry with me, and that means I am much more likely to be in control. Therefore, I am not as influenced by what I see.

TIP **Here is what I ask myself before I buy anything that costs more than $20.**

- Do I really need it?
- If the answer is yes, can I afford to pay for it with cash?
- If I can, do I already own something that would serve just as well? (This question alone saves me plenty of money.)
- If I don't have anything that will do the job, do I know for a fact that I have found the best value? Have I really checked around enough to know?

If the prospective purchase passes all of these checkpoints, I still wait at least 24 hours before making the purchase.

The result is that I often wind up not buying the item, and not regretting it either, simply because it would be too much trouble to go back the next day to get it.

FIND THE FUN IN SAVINGS

The funny thing about saving money is that eventually you begin to find gratification in it and start putting extra money aside for investments. That new, delayed gratification takes away some of the hunger for instant rewards.

I still work at it. I want my temperament, which is compulsive and out to impress everybody, to work for me as a saver the way it worked for me as a spender. I used to feel that spending money was the only way to feel significant.

Combine business with pleasure and save.

I've made great progress. Now, we eat out at restaurants far less often than we used to, and when we do eat out, we often share dishes. I find splitting food is less wasteful than asking for doggie bags and taking home leftovers, which wind up spoiling in the refrigerator.

Since my husband and I both travel for our jobs, we try to combine vacations with business travel as often as we can. That cuts the after-tax cost of our trips. And we always plan how much cash to take with us. We restrict our use of credit cards to an absolute minimum.

BEAT THE CATALOG TEMPTATION

I did a lot of personal reflection to figure out precisely where I got the most excited about spending.

The answer is when I bought from catalogs. I also discovered that my greatest pleasure came from the looking and ordering. The process of looking through the catalogs and dreaming that I could have anything I wanted was more satisfactory than receiving the goods.

Now, when catalogs arrive at my home, I look through them and carefully select all the things I think I need. I fill out the order form, add the sales and delivery charges, and total the bill. Then, I write the amount on the outside of the envelope and put the order and the envelope in my desk drawer for seven days. Usually, when I take it out of the drawer a week later, I look over the order and throw it out. I've already had my thrill.

ADMIRE, NOT ACQUIRE

My other great discovery was that I don't have to own things to enjoy them. I used to go to Nordstrom and admire the beautiful china, crystal and silverware, or go to shops where the sheets were $400 each. I would feel that I needed these things.

The reality is that I do not need them. I do need to enjoy them, however.

Strategy: Now I go into those stores without my handbag, as if I were going to a museum to admire beautiful things. I continue to enjoy them without spending money to buy them, store them, clean and polish them, and buy insurance to protect them.

TAKE THE BIG-PURCHASE TEST

I have even given up owning my own car. Fortunately, my husband and I work near each other, so we drive to work together. If I absolutely need a car for a few days for a business trip, I rent one. We've found we can manage quite well with only one car, and it's a sacrifice I find myself willing to make while we build up our savings. There are so many better ways to use $10,000.

Eliminate a nonessential car and save $10,000.

Strategy: When struggling with the decision of whether to spend or save money, try this.
- Pretend your monthly payments on your home or car are $500 higher.
- Every month, put that $500 into the bank, a mutual fund or some other savings. Never miss a payment.
- After six months, evaluate how you feel about having to make that $500-per-month payment. If it was a struggle, was the sacrifice worth what you might buy with the money? Did some unexpected expense come up that made it very difficult, maybe even impossible, to put away that $500? Think about what the implications would be if you missed a mortgage or car-lease payment.

After taking this test, you will be in a better position to make the decision as to whether or not you should commit yourself to that big expense.

SHARE SPENDING SECRETS

A lot of excessive spending is done secretly. Mine certainly was.

Fortunately, big spenders often marry people who want to save. But the spenders too often wind up in charge of the finances and cover up their out-of-control spending. To stay in control, try the following.
- Put the spouse who is more inclined to save in charge of the bank account and checkbook.
- Confess your spending weakness to those close to you, even to your friends and neighbors. Tell them that you are making every effort to get control of your spending problem. Once you are open about it, you will find that other people's knowledge of the problem will help you help yourself.

— I'm a secret spender!

Michael Stolper Tells How to Become a Millionaire

My wealthy clients became rich by saving their money, not by spending it. Here are three strategies that anyone can use to become affluent.

1. Weigh all purchases carefully. Ask yourself whether you can get almost the same satisfaction by spending less on any product or service. By questioning all your purchases, you will make fewer costly ones.

2. Invest discretionary income. While the temptation is to spend extra money on small rewards, you are better off putting the money in a good stock mutual fund. The money will keep pace with inflation, and you will have something saved for a rainy day.

3. Don't let major expenses sneak up on you. Get a head start on funding life's big expenses (college tuition and retirement) long before you're hit with them. Calculate what your needs will be, and create savings rituals to meet them.

How Amy Dacyczyn Avoids the Big Money Traps

Being a tightwad is a mindset that can help anyone reach his or her goals, whether you earn a lot of money or just a little. Here's how my family avoids the big money traps that keep most people from realizing their dreams.

NOT SAVING ENOUGH MONEY

For the first seven years of our marriage, my husband and I had a combined annual income of less than $30,000. Despite this, we set three goals that we would not compromise: buy a house, have lots of kids and avoid putting those kids in day care.

Over the course of seven years, we saved $49,000 for a down payment on our house and began having our six children.

People are surprised that my husband and I still save 20% of our annual income. We save our money instead of buying a lot of luxury items because we know that life is unpredictable. The mistake most people make is assuming that their current income will continue forever.

Reality: It is easy to lose a high-income, middle-management job today and never be able to replace that salary. Job burnout is also common, but many people must stay at jobs they dislike because they are financially trapped.

Strategy: Ask yourself what you would do if you lost your job or experienced other major life changes. That will help give you the motivation you need to start thinking about new saving and spending habits.

TIP Before You Toss Your Old Bills Away

Keep any utility bill showing a deposit until the deposit is credited back to your account. This applies to bills from telephone and cable-TV companies and any other firms that require deposits when starting service.

LIVING ON THE FINANCIAL EDGE

Many people have to borrow money when a financial crisis occurs. My husband and I have never had that problem, in part because we save aggressively. Even though we're doing better today than when we started out, we always have money in the bank to handle unforeseen problems.

Strategy: Motivate yourself to spend less money by setting a goal. It could be retiring early, buying a house, becoming a one-income family, building up an emergency fund or paying off debt.

When you have a goal, spending less money does not feel like deprivation. It feels like you are moving toward your goal, and that is very satisfying.

In 1995, American women working full-time earned only **71%** of what their male counterparts were making.

Source: U.S. Census Bureau

MISUSING A BUDGET

It is important to keep track of your spending, but I'm not a big fan of strict budgets.

Reason: You almost always feel you have to spend every penny that you budget for each of your spending categories instead of trying to conserve extra funds.

Example: Someone who has allocated a total of $150 for groceries each week will spend $150—even if he or she could have spent much less.

Strategy: Set spending limits in different categories. Then experiment with lower levels of spending until you reach a level that is uncomfortable. When that happens, you can bump up your spending by a notch.

Example: For the first years of our marriage, my husband and I kept reducing our food budget by shopping more and more carefully, even though we continued to have more children.

SPENDING ON IMPULSE

Why did Imelda Marcos go out and buy thousands of pairs of shoes? Like other impulse buyers, she was looking for an adrenaline rush. The trouble is, the rush doesn't last long.

When I was single, I would go to three movies a day on the weekends, looking for that one movie that would give me the feeling I was craving. I finally realized that it wasn't worth the time or the money. One movie would have been just fine.

Critique Yourself

Before you buy something, ask yourself if you can accomplish the same task with things that you already own. Is the product you're eyeing something you only need occasionally? In that case, maybe you can borrow or rent it.

If you do buy a big-ticket item, such as a major appliance, a power tool or a car, do plenty of research to make sure you are getting the best value. If possible, wait—you may find the item on sale or find a used one.

PAYING TOO MUCH FOR CONVENIENCE

Often, people justify making an expenditure because it frees them to devote more time to their work and make more money. But many people trade too much of their hard-earned salaries for unnecessary things.

Strategy: Figure out how much you earn, after deducting expenses and taxes, for one hour of labor. Then try to calculate how much you would save by forgoing certain expenses or doing things yourself.

BRIBING YOURSELF

Whatever you do, don't spend money to reward yourself for working at a job you hate.

Examples: One woman told me she bought a $2 cappuccino every day on her way to work because it helped her cope with the fact that she hated her job. I told her that if she would do things like make coffee for herself at home and bring it to work in a thermos, she might save enough money so that she wouldn't have to work as many hours.

Other people take vacations or buy fancy cars because they don't like the way they have to spend their time at work.

Remember: Every extravagant expenditure means that somewhere in your life, you will have to give up some freedom.

Money Lessons from Warren Buffett

Only a handful of Americans have Warren Buffett's kind of money, but we can all learn from the rumpled billionaire's humble lifestyle. Here are Buffett's secrets of simple living and an ever-growing net worth.

- **Don't waste money on housing.** Like many of us, Buffett spends more time at work than he does at home. As a result, he still owns the house he bought in the mid-1950s for around $31,000.
- **Never pay full price.** Buffett only buys things that deliver great value and are on sale, so he buys Coca-Cola by the case and his suits off the rack.
- **Stay on top of your finances.** Buffett writes his company's annual letter to shareholders and reportedly does his own income taxes.
- **Don't waste money on status or power trips.** Buffett's car is several years old, and he drives it himself.
- **Read as much as you can.** Buffett reads or skims about 100 magazines, newspapers and annual reports each month. He believes reading teaches you a great deal about human nature and helps develop a sixth sense for spotting investment trends early enough to profit from them.

SOURCES

Sources are listed in the order in which their contributions appear. A source may have contributed part or all of an article or a series of articles.

Jonathan D. Pond, Financial Planning Information, Inc.

Robert Ortalda, Jr., CPA, author of *How to Live Within Your Means and Stay Financially Secure*

William Britt, Internal Revenue Service

Susan Gregory, editor of *Out of the Rat Race*

Tod Barnhart, author of *The Five Rituals of Wealth: Proven Strategies for Turning the Little You Have into More than Enough*

Ginger Applegarth, Applegarth Henderson Advisors

Jonathan D. Pond, Financial Planning Information, Inc.

Sheldon Jacobs, editor of *The No-Load Fund Investor*

Terry Savage, author of *Terry Savage's New Money Strategies for the '90s*

Alexandra Armstrong, Armstrong, Welch & MacIntyre, Inc.

Carol Keeffe, author of *How to Get What You Want in Life with the Money You Already Have*

Loren Dunton, National Center for Financial Education

Jonathan Clements, financial writer for *The Wall Street Journal*

Mary Hunt, publisher of *The Cheapskate Monthly*

Lewis J. Altfest, L. J. Altfest & Co.

Michael Stolper, Stolper & Co.

Amy Dacyczyn, publisher of *The Tightwad Gazette*

Robert Hagstrom, Lloyd, Leith & Sawin

Better Tax Strategies

Don't Pay More Than You Have To

Commonly Ignored Deductions

Claim every deduction you are entitled to on your tax return. That means taking time to review these frequently overlooked deductions. You may have to reduce the amount of certain itemized deductions if your income exceeds certain amounts.

CHARITABLE CONTRIBUTIONS

1. Out-of-pocket costs
- Driving costs incurred for church, synagogue, school, scouting or other volunteer activities. You can take a deduction of 14¢ per mile plus other cash expenses such as tolls and parking.
- Scout leader's uniforms and other special clothing bought for charitable work that aren't suitable for normal wear.
- Travel costs, including meals and lodging, when you travel away from home to perform a service for a church or charity.
- Appraisal fees for charitable deductions.
- Purchases donated to charity. If you bake goods and donate them to a church fair you can deduct the cost of the ingredients.
- Dues paid to organizations such as The National Geographic Society and the Smithsonian Institution, to the extent they exceed the value of subscriptions received in return.
- When you buy holiday cards or similar items from a charity, you can deduct the excess of the amount you pay over the value of the items you receive.
- When you attend a charitable event, you can deduct the excess of the amount you paid for a ticket over the value of the meal or entertainment received. Many charities will itemize this for you.
- If you make a payment to a college or university for the right to buy tickets to sporting events, you can deduct 80% of the payment.

2. More charitable tax breaks
- Make cash charitable contributions just before December 31. That way you keep use of your money for almost the full year but still get a full deduction for your gift.
- Contribute long-term capital gains property, such as stock shares, instead of cash when possible. You get a deduction for the full market value of the gift while avoiding ever having to pay tax on its appreciation.
- Donate surplus personal items. Clean out your closets, garage and attic, and donate items you no longer need to Goodwill, the Salvation Army, or a similar group. The deduction you get will be a " found" tax savings.

Important: Charitable contributions of $250 or more must be documented by a written acknowledgment from the charitable recipient to be deductible. Moreover, if the gift is one of property rather than cash, the acknowledgment letter must also give a description of the property that is sufficient to identify it. You must obtain this acknowledgment letter before you file your return, or your deduction may be disallowed.

If you donate money to charity through payroll deductions, don't forget to claim a corresponding deduction on your return.

MISCELLANEOUS EXPENSES

The following items qualify as Miscellaneous, and are deductible to the extent that their total exceeds 2% of your Adjusted Gross Income (AGI).

IRS Income and Outlays

These pie charts show the relative sizes of the major categories of Federal income and outlays for fiscal year 1996.

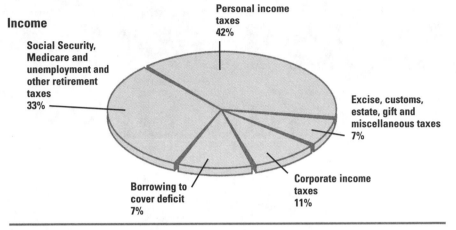

Income

- Personal income taxes 42%
- Social Security, Medicare and unemployment and other retirement taxes 33%
- Excise, customs, estate, gift and miscellaneous taxes 7%
- Borrowing to cover deficit 7%
- Corporate income taxes 11%

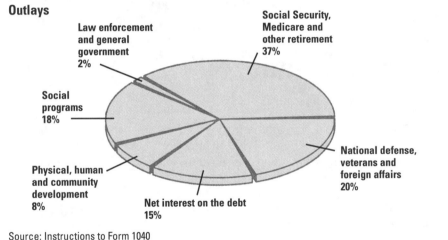

Outlays

- Law enforcement and general government 2%
- Social Security, Medicare and other retirement 37%
- Social programs 18%
- National defense, veterans and foreign affairs 20%
- Physical, human and community development 8%
- Net interest on the debt 15%

Source: Instructions to Form 1040

Strategy: Estimate total expenditures for such items during the beginning of each year. If you think you'll be over the 2% of AGI limit, double up by prepaying expenses for the following year whenever possible. If you won't be over the 2% limit, defer paying as many of these expenses as possible until the following year so you'll have a better chance of getting over the limit the next year.

1. Employee business expenses

If you are an employee, you can deduct some work expenses that your employer does not reimburse.

- Uniforms and other special work clothes not suitable for general wear.
- Office supplies, furnishings and decorations that you purchase yourself, like pens and paper.
- Tuition and fees for educational courses or professional seminars that improve your work skills.
- The unreimbursed costs of business travel.
- Subscriptions to professional journals and magazines.

Total Miscellaneous Expenses
− 2% of your AGI
= Deductible Miscellaneous Expenses

- Dues to professional or trade organizations, or unions.
- Rental costs for clothes, such as tuxedos, worn to business functions.
- Dry cleaning costs incurred on business trips.
- Medical examinations required by an employer or otherwise required for work. Deducting them as a business expense lets you avoid the 7.5% of Adjusted Gross Income (AGI) deduction threshold that generally applies to medical expenses.
- Tips paid to waiters, coatroom attendants and others in relation to business meals and entertainment are 50% deductible.
- Job hunting expenses incurred when looking for a new job in your current line of work, even if your job search is not successful. Included: Employment agency fees, resume preparation and printing costs, the cost of travel to job interviews, postage, phone calls, meal and entertainment expenses (50% deductible) and so on.

2. Tax, accounting and legal fees
- Tax return preparation fees.
- Fees paid to an accountant or lawyer for tax advice.
- Fees paid to a lawyer related to the tax-planning aspects of your will or estate plan.
  Key: Get an itemized bill from your lawyer that breaks out fees for tax advice from fees for non-tax-related legal advice.
- Books and periodicals devoted to tax planning.
- Professional fees incurred fighting a tax dispute with the IRS.
- Legal fees incurred to collect taxable income, as when negotiating to collect alimony or suing to collect interest due on a debt, or dividends due on an investment.

3. Investment expenses
- Safe-deposit box fees are a deductible investment expense when the box is rented to hold securities and other investment-related items.
- IRA trustee fees are a deductible investment expense when you pay them by separate check instead of having them automatically deducted from your account.

- Expenses created from obtaining investment advice for investments producing taxable income are deductible, including the cost of books and periodicals, travel to meet your broker and phone calls to your investment adviser.

MEDICAL EXPENSES
Medical expenses are deductible only to the extent that they exceed 7.5% of your Adjusted Gross Income (AGI).

The courts have allowed deductions for central air conditioners, elevators, escalators, extra bathrooms, garages, swimming pools and the removal of lead paint, when such improvements have been required for medical purposes.

The deductible amount equals the cost of the improvement minus any increase in market value that it adds to the house. You can also deduct portable equipment, such as air conditioners and dehumidifiers, that is needed for a medical reason.

Total Unreimbursed
Medical Expenses
− 7.5% of your AGI

= Deductible Medical
Expenses

Often overlooked:
- The extra cost of special diets and food preparation above and beyond the cost of normal food.
- Transportation to and from the doctor's office.
- Treatment for drug or alcohol abuse.
- The cost of removing lead paint that poses a health hazard.
- Contact lenses, eyeglasses, hearing aids, false teeth, orthopedic shoes and the like.
- Contraceptives bought with a prescription.

Moving Deduction
You can deduct the expenses you incur when moving to a new location if your new main job is at least 50 miles farther from your former residence than your old main job was. Job-related moving expenses now are deducted as an adjustment to income, so you can deduct them even if you do not itemize your deductions, but claim the standard deduction instead.

Deductions in the Workplace

Too often, employees neglect to make the most of the tax-favored benefits their employers provide for them.

1. FLEXIBLE SPENDING ACCOUNTS (FSAs)

An FSA is a kind of savings account that you can use to pay medical or dependent-care expenses with pre-tax dollars.

How it works: At the beginning of the year you elect to contribute a portion of your pay into an employer-sponsored medical or dependent-care FSA. Funds from the FSA can then be used to pay the corresponding types of expenses. Because the FSA pays bills with pretax dollars, big savings result.

Example: If you are in the 40% tax bracket (federal and local combined), you need $1.67 of taxable salary to match the after-tax buying power of $1 spent through an FSA.

In spite of these savings, studies show that employees consistently contribute too little money to their FSAs.

Reason: Money contributed to an FSA is forfeited if not spent by year-end, so many employees fear contributing too much.

In reality, though, it's easy to consume money that remains unspent in a medical FSA during the last few weeks of the year, by scheduling doctor or dental appointments, stocking up on your prescription drugs for the coming year, buying eyeglasses or contact lenses and so on.

2. 401(k) SAVINGS PLANS

These tax-favored savings plans provide multiple benefits. The amount you contribute is deducted from your taxable pay, so your income tax bill is reduced. In addition, investment returns earned are tax-deferred. Because they compound before taxes are taken out, your savings grow faster than they would in a taxable account earning the same rate of return.

Strategy: Cut taxes and build future wealth by making the largest contributions permitted.

3. IRAs

Salary income may also entitle you to make a deductible contribution to an IRA of up to $2,000, or $4,000 if you have a nonworking spouse.

You are eligible to deduct your IRA contribution on your income taxes if one of the following is true.

a) You or your spouse is not an active participant in a qualified retirement plan.

b) You and your spouse is an active participant in a retirement plan but your 1998 Adjusted Gross Income is under $50,000 on a joint return or $30,000 on a single return.

c) If one spouse is an active participant, the other can deduct up to $2,000 provided the couple's AGI is no more than $150,000.

If you are eligible to make an IRA contribution, don't wait until the April 15 due date of your tax return to do so. Make it as early as possible to maximize the tax-deferred investment returns in your IRA account.

Important: Those with AGI up to $150,000 on a joint return or $95,000 on a single return can fully fund a nondeductible Roth IRA. Even if your AGI prevents you from making deductible contributions or nondeductible Roth IRA contributions, you may still fund a nondeductible regular IRA.

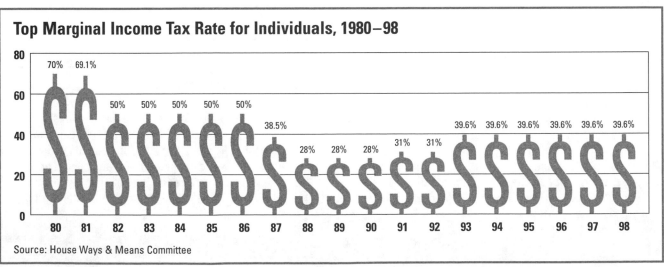

Top Marginal Income Tax Rate for Individuals, 1980–98

Year	Rate
80	70%
81	69.1%
82	50%
83	50%
84	50%
85	50%
86	50%
87	38.5%
88	28%
89	28%
90	28%
91	31%
92	31%
93	39.6%
94	39.6%
95	39.6%
96	39.6%
97	39.6%
98	39.6%

Source: House Ways & Means Committee

How Tax Deferral Works to Your Advantage

Assume you are single and in the 36% bracket. You put $10,000 of after-tax money into each of two investments, both compounded monthly and earning 5%. One is tax-deferred and one isn't.

Taxable Plan
You pay tax on all earnings annually

for example	
$10,000	original investment
+ 16,289	30 years of earnings after annual taxes paid

=$26,289 Value after taxes

Tax-deferred Plan
You pay no tax on earnings until you withdraw

for example	
$10,000	original investment
+ 34,678	30 years of tax-deferred earnings
= 44,678	pre-tax value
− 12,484	federal taxes on withdrawal

=$32,194 Value after taxes

**TAX SAVINGS
$5,905**

Tax Opportunities Not to Be Missed

1. STATE AND LOCAL TAXES

Don't overlook any payments of state and local taxes that are deductible on your federal return.

Key: When computing this deduction, you'll probably look at your W-2 wage withholding statement and estimated tax payment stubs to find the amount of local taxes paid during the year. But these won't include any tax that you paid in April as a balance due for the previous year, and such a payment is deductible on your current return.

**IRS FORM
W-2**

Hint: Go through your checkbook to find every check written for state and local taxes, including property taxes, during the current calendar year.

Also, refunds of state and local taxes received during the current year are not included in taxable income on your federal return if you derived no federal tax benefit from the state or local tax payment when it was made.

Example: In 1997 you overpaid your state taxes, and in 1998 you received a refund of the overpayment. On your 1998 federal return, the refund

a) Is taxable to you if you deducted the state tax payment on your 1997 federal return.

b) Is not taxable to you if you took the standard deduction on your 1997 federal return, and so did not claim an itemized deduction for state taxes. Nor is it likely to be taxable if you were subject to the **Alternative Minimum Tax (AMT)** in 1997, and thus received no benefit from the deduction for local taxes.

2. KIDDIE TAX

In 1998 you can avoid filing multiple tax returns for children who have less than $7,000 of investment income by including their income on your own tax return. Use **IRS Form 8814**.
Caution: If children's income is reported on your return, the children may lose the ability to claim tax-saving personal exemptions for themselves on state tax returns.

**IRS FORM
8814**

Also, reporting children's income on your return will increase your Adjusted Gross Income (AGI), and thus may reduce deductions on your return that are subject to AGI-related limitations, such as deductions for casualty losses, medical expenses and miscellaneous expenses.

Consider the implications before choosing how your children should file.

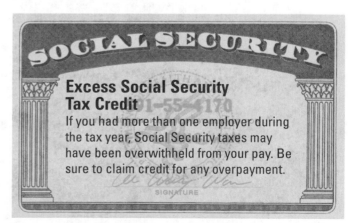

Excess Social Security Tax Credit
If you had more than one employer during the tax year, Social Security taxes may have been overwithheld from your pay. Be sure to claim credit for any overpayment.

3. INVESTMENT DEDUCTIONS

- **Early withdrawal penalties.** If you cashed in a Certificate of Deposit or other time deposit before maturity and paid an early withdrawal penalty, you can deduct the penalty even if you do not itemize your deductions.
- **Prepayment penalties.** If you incurred a prepayment penalty on a loan, the penalty qualifies as interest that may be deducted under the rules applying to investment, business or mortgage interest, whichever is appropriate. A penalty incurred on a consumer loan is not deductible.
- **Bond premiums.** If you bought a bond for more than its face value because it pays a high interest rate, you can deduct the premium you paid over the period of years until the bond's maturity. Specific rules for claiming the deduction vary according to when the bond was purchased, so check with your tax adviser.
- **Losses on tax-exempt bonds.** Only the *interest* on municipal bonds is tax-free. If you sold a tax-exempt bond at a loss (or gain), you have a deductible capital loss (or taxable gain).

4. INVESTMENT INTEREST

A deduction for investment interest is allowed to the extent that you have investment income, but long-term capital gains are no longer included in investment income for purposes of computing this deduction. If you find your interest deduction is limited by this rule, you can:

a) Elect to have a portion of your long-term capital gains taxed at normal rates, so they are counted among investment income, or

b) Carry over your excess deduction for investment interest until next year.

Work through the figures both ways to see which option is best for you.

Home mortgage points are deductible by the buyer, even when they are paid by the seller.

5. PROPERTY TAX DEDUCTIONS

- **Mortgage Points.** Finance fees or points incurred on a mortgage used to acquire a home are deductible by the home buyer. The IRS recently ruled that this is true even if the seller pays the points because the cost of the points is presumed to be passed through to the buyer in the sale price. This IRS ruling is retroactive, so if you bought a home in a deal involving seller-paid points within the last three years, you may be able to file an amended tax return to deduct them and claim a tax refund.

Points incurred when you refinance a home cannot be currently deducted as a lump sum, but must be deducted at an even rate over the life of the loan. However, if you refinance a home for a second time, any remaining undeducted points from the first refinancing may be deducted immediately.

Average Itemized Deductions

In the chart below, you can see how your deductions in three key categories compare with those of other taxpayers with similar adjusted gross incomes (AGIs). These are the unofficial averages of deductions reported on 1996 federal income tax returns (the most recent available). Of course, any deductions you take must be based on your actual expenses.

Adjusted Gross Income Ranges	Medical Expenses	Taxes	Interest	Contributions
$15,000 to $20,000	$4,988	$2,039	$5,742	$1,449
$20,000 to $25,000	3,749	2,125	5,325	1,215
$25,000 to $30,000	4,211	2,320	5,166	1,349
$30,000 to $40,000	2,990	2,700	5,511	1,410
$40,000 to $50,000	4,506	3,310	5,915	1,507
$50,000 to $75,000	5,854	4,342	6,783	1,793
$75,000 to $100,000	7,421	6,260	8,244	2,289
$100,000 to $200,000	21,557	9,433	10,916	3,692
$200,000 or more	—	38,366	20,570	36,054

Source: *IRS Statistics of Income Bulletin*

Which Form Should I Use?

You can use this simple form if you fit the following criteria.

IRS FORM
1040-EZ

- Single or married filing jointly.
- Under age 65 and not blind.
- Claim no dependents.
- Taxable income less than $50,000.
- Income only from wages, salaries, tips, unemployment, scholarships, fellowships and interest of $400 or less.
- Received no advance EIC (earned income credit) payments.
- Owe no household employment taxes.
- No itemized deductions, credits or adjustments.

Source: *Your Federal Income Tax*, Internal Revenue Service Publication 17

You can use this middle-length form if you fit these criteria.

IRS FORM
1040-A

- Income only from wages, salaries, tips, IRA distributions, dividends, pensions and annuities, social security and railroad benefits, unemployment, scholarships, fellowships and interest of $400 or less.
- Taxable income less than $50,000.
- No itemized deductions.
- Your only adjustment to income is IRA contributions.
- Your only taxes are the amount from the Tax Table, household employment taxes and EIC payments.
- Your only credits are for child and dependent care expenses, the elderly or disabled, adoption credit, and the EIC.

You must use this form if you fit any of the following criteria.

IRS FORM
1040

- Taxable income over $50,000.
- Itemized deductions.
- Self-employed.
- Received income that cannot be recorded on form 1040EZ or 1040A.
- Sold or exchanged capital assets or business property.
- Claim adjustments other than IRA contributions.
- W-2 shows uncollected taxes.
- File form 2119, 2555, 2555EZ, 4563, 4970, 4972, 5329, 8271 or 8814.

- **Taxes on real estate bought or sold.** If you bought or sold a house or other property during the past year, review the allocation of deductible real estate taxes between buyer and seller.

  Often, the final tax liability for the year isn't known at the time of sale, so an estimate is used. If the actual final tax bill for the year is greater than the estimate, you may be entitled to a deduction larger than that shown on the real estate closing statement.

  Moreover, if real estate taxes for a year are paid after year-end, the seller has the choice of deducting his or her share of the taxes in either the year of the sale or in the year in which the tax was paid, whichever produces the greatest benefit.

  The situation is different for the buyer, who may deduct the taxes he or she pays only in the year actual payment is made. Deductibility rules differ on a state-by-state basis depending on whether taxes are paid in the current year or in the following year.

- **Personal property taxes.** Local taxes based on the value of personal property are deductible.

Who Uses Paid Preparers?

1040	72.0%
1040A	17.6%
1040EZ	3.5%

6. SELF-EMPLOYED MEDICAL EXPENSES

Self-employed people may be able to deduct in 1998 up to 45% of the amount they pay for health insurance on themselves and their families. You cannot, however, take the deduction for any month in which you were eligible to participate in a subsidized health plan.

7. OTHER DEDUCTIONS

- An interest deduction is available for penalties paid on premature savings withdrawals and mortgage prepayment penalties.
- Securities and debts that became worthless during the year are deductible. Review your portfolio to be sure none are overlooked.
- Gambling losses are deductible to the extent that

you have gambling winnings. So record your losing wagers on lottery tickets and the like to shelter any winnings you have from tax.

- Get a possible tax deduction by donating a used car to the National Kidney Foundation (NKF). The car doesn't even have to run—it can be sold for parts—and the NKF will arrange to have it picked up. Call for more information: 800-488-2277.

Lock in Your Gains

Lock in investment gains this year while deferring tax on the gains until next year by selling short against the box.

Here's how: Say you own shares of a stock that you think have topped in value. Instead of selling the shares you own, you can make a short sale—have your broker sell borrowed shares of the stock for your account. You get the full proceeds from the sale now. After year-end you repay the broker by giving him or her your shares of the stock, and that is when your gain is taxed.

Caution: New rules can turn short sales into income in the year you enter into them (rather than in the year you close them out). Be sure to discuss this with your tax adviser.

U.S. vs. Foreign Taxes

Despite bitter complaints, Americans pay comparitively less in taxes than many other developed countries.

Country	Total tax revenues as a percentage of gross domestic product
France	44.1%
Germany	39.3%
Canada	36.1%
United Kingdom	34.1%
Japan	27.8%
United States	27.6%

Tax Savings from Your Old Returns

It may pay to review your old tax returns. If you find a deduction or other tax-saving strategy that was overlooked during the past three years, you can file an amended tax return **(IRS Form 1040X)** to obtain tax refunds.

If you underreported tax owed in a prior year that could result in a back tax bill and penalties, filing an amended tax return can correct the mistake and help

You Can Deduct Destroyed Property That Was Uninsured

Personal property destroyed by flood or earthquake and not covered by insurance can be deducted on your income tax, even if receipts also have perished. To calculate the deduction, find out how much it costs to replace each item. Calculate depreciation by dividing the number of years you owned the item by the number of years you expected to own it. Multiply the result by the replacement cost and subtract this result from the replacement cost.

you avert tax penalties that might be imposed if the IRS discovers the underreporting.

Here's what to look for in your old tax returns.

ERRORS ON INCOME FORMS

Errors often occur with regard to the **1099 Forms** that are filed by banks and brokers to report payments of income made to individuals.

Such forms may report incorrect amounts, they may arrive too late to be included in your return or they could be overlooked when you tally up income amounts on your return.

IRS computers match these forms with tax returns, and any discrepancies are likely to bring extra attention to your tax return—so be sure the numbers on the forms and your returns agree.

Here's how: If you failed to report income shown on a late-arriving or temporarily misplaced 1099

Records the IRS Receives Automatically

Record	What It Reports
1098	Mortgage interest payments
1099-B	Capital gains & barter proceeds
1099-DIV	Dividend income
1099-G	Unemployment pay & state tax refunds
1099-INT	Interest income
1099-MISC	Rent, royalties & free-lance income
1099-R	Retirement plan income
1099-S	Real-estate transaction proceeds
K-1	Partnership, S corporation & trust income
W-2	Employee pay & withheld taxes
W-2G	Gambling winnings

form, you can file an amended tax return that includes it.

If you copied the numbers from an incorrect 1099 form onto your tax return and later discovered the error, you can ask the issuer for a corrected 1099 form and then file an amended tax return.

BAD DEBTS AND WORTHLESS SECURITIES

You can claim a loss deduction for bad debts and securities that become worthless, but the deduction must be claimed for the year in which the debt goes bad or the security becomes worthless.

Special rule: You can use amended tax returns

Form Fact
All 1099 forms are supposed to be mailed to taxpayers by January 31. As soon as they arrive, check that the numbers reported on them are correct—and that you have received all the 1099 forms you are expecting. If you find any errors, act quickly to have them corrected before April 15.

to claim deductions for bad debts and worthless securities up to seven years back, instead of only three.

Whether or not a debt or security is completely worthless may be unclear. Often, as in cases involving litigation, the date on which a debt or security became worthless is determined only after the fact, perhaps after the normal three-year statute of limitations on tax returns has run out. Thus, the Tax Code allows extra time to claim such deductions.

Opportunity: Review your portfolio before year-end, especially if you have received investments through inheritances or gifts. You may find loss deductions that were previously overlooked.

CASUALTY LOSSES

If you suffered a casualty loss during an event that results in your area being declared a federal disaster area, you get a special tax break: You have the choice of deducting your loss either in the year it occurs or in the prior year.

Example: If you suffered such a loss during 1998, you can wait and deduct it on the return that you will file for 1998 or file an amended return to deduct the loss on the return you filed for 1997.

By filing an amended return to claim the deduction for the prior year, you can speed up your refund, since you don't have to wait for the current year's return to be filed and processed. The choice of years also may give you a larger deduction, since casualty losses are deductible only to the extent that they exceed 10% of your Adjusted Gross Income (AGI). You increase the amount of your deduction by taking it in the year when your AGI is lower.

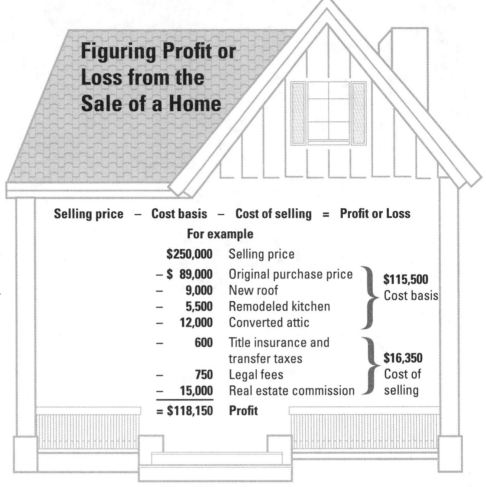

Figuring Profit or Loss from the Sale of a Home

Selling price — Cost basis — Cost of selling = Profit or Loss

For example

$250,000	Selling price
– $ 89,000	Original purchase price
– 9,000	New roof
– 5,500	Remodeled kitchen
– 12,000	Converted attic
– 600	Title insurance and transfer taxes
– 750	Legal fees
– 15,000	Real estate commission
= $118,150	**Profit**

} $115,500 Cost basis

} $16,350 Cost of selling

HOUSE SALES

If you sold your home before May 7, 1997 and filed **IRS Form 2119** *Sale of Your Home* to defer gain on the sale, and then fail to buy a replacement residence within the two-year replacement period, your gain is taxable in the year during which the sale occurred. You will have to file an amended return to report the gain for the year when the house was sold.

Key: Deferral of gain is mandatory when a taxpayer is eligible for deferral, and, in most cases, home sellers will want to defer gain. But a home seller who had large net investment losses during the year of the sale may want to recognize gain, because the losses can be used to offset the gain and shelter it permanently from tax.

Thus, a home seller may intentionally fail to qualify for tax deferral by failing to buy a replacement residence before the deadline, then file an amended return to report the gain in the past year.

RETIREMENT CONTRIBUTIONS

Get a retroactive deduction by making deductible retirement plan contributions after year-end, but before you file your tax return for that year.

● An IRA contribution can be made as late as the filing due date.
● A Keogh contribution can be made by a self-employed individual as late as the extended due date of the tax return, if the Keogh account was opened by December 31.

If you had self-employment income but failed to set up a Keogh plan by year-end, you can still make a deductible retirement contribution from self-employment income by opening a Simplified Employee Pension (SEP) account before the extended due date of your return.

Bonus: You'll receive an additional tax benefit from your contribution, in that investment income earned

FILING

File an amended tax return by using **IRS Form 1040X**. Form 1040X is a one-page form on which you simply note the changes to be made to your original tax return. You do not need to attach a copy of your entire original return, but it's a good idea to attach copies of the particular pages or schedules that are being corrected.

The deadline for filing an amended tax return is three years after the date on which your original return was filed, or two years after the date on which you paid the tax, whichever is later. If you filed early, you have three years after the due date of the return.

IRS FORM
1040-X

AUDIT RISK

Amended returns are reviewed carefully by the IRS, so filing an amended return may expose you to extra audit risk. In the case of routine error corrections, the risk is slight, but a Form 1040X that dramatically cuts your tax bill for the year is likely to undergo more serious scrutiny.

On the other hand, filing an amended return does not give the IRS extra time to audit your original return. Thus, some advisers recommend that an amended return won't increase audit risk to the original return if it is filed just before the return's three-year statute-of-limitations period runs out.

Do a Makeover on Your Taxes

September is a good time to look for tax-saving opportunities for the next year. Enough of the year has passed to estimate your income and basic deductions for the year and enough still remains for you to take tax-saving actions.

WHERE TO START

First look at last year's tax return. Compare your items of income and expenses for the current year to those of last year. Factor in the major changes that have occurred in your financial situation during this year—investment gains or losses, a raise in pay, the birth of a child, or a child who is no longer a dependent—and you'll get a basic picture of your current tax liability.

CARRYOVERS

Be sure to note any deductions that were disallowed on your last year's tax return that can be carried forward and deducted in the following year.

Examples:

● Capital losses in excess of the $3,000 deduction limit.
● Investment interest in excess of investment income.
● Unused passive losses—losses from investment partnerships.
● Charitable contributions that exceeded applicable deduction limits.

MATCH CAPITAL GAINS AND LOSSES

Count the gains and losses realized so far this year, and the unrealized gains and losses still in your portfolio.

a) If you have taken net capital gains this year,

Figuring Capital Gains and Losses

You can determine your gain or loss by subtracting your cost basis from the proceeds of a sale. The cost basis is your total cost for the item, including its original price and the expenses of buying, holding and selling it, such as commissions and the costs of investment transactions. If you receive an asset as a gift, your cost basis is the same as the giver's was. If you inherit an asset, however, your cost basis is the asset's market value on the date of the giver's death.

PROCEEDS	The amount you get when you sell your asset
− **BASIS**	The original cost of the asset, plus the cost of buying, holding and selling it
= **GAIN OR LOSS**	

consider taking some losses on bad investments by year-end in order to offset the gains and shelter them from tax.

b) If you've taken net losses so far this year, take gains by year-end so they'll be offset by the losses.

SHIFT INCOME TO CHILDREN

Children under age 14 can have up to $1,400 of investment income in 1998 before being subject to the "kiddie tax." You can reduce the family tax bill by shifting assets that generate that much income to each child.

Here's how: Open an investment account for the child through your bank or broker under the Uniform Gift to Minors Act (UGMA) or the Uniform Transfers to Minors Act (UTMA).

Children age 14 or older aren't subject to the "kiddie tax," so you can shift larger amounts of income to them. To avoid gift tax, the assets transferred should be limited to $10,000 per child per year, or $20,000 if the transfer is made jointly by husband and wife.

MAKE INTEREST DEDUCTIBLE

If you are paying a lot of high-rate consumer interest, such as on credit cards, consider paying off your consumer debts with a home equity loan or line of credit. Interest paid on up to $100,000 of such borrowing is deductible, and you may obtain a lower rate of interest as well.

Bonus: Interest on borrowing in excess of $100,000 that's used to finance an investment is deductible as investment interest. An individual borrowed more than $100,000 against his home and lent the proceeds to an investment partnership, of which he was a member. The IRS allowed the interest deduction.

TIP

Defer Investment Income

Buy Treasury bills or short-term certificates of deposit that mature after year-end in order to postpone receipt of taxable income into the next year.

PREPAY LOCAL TAXES

State and local income and property taxes are deductible on the federal return for the year in which they are paid, even if the payment is credited to another tax year. By prepaying local tax bills by December 31, you may be able to obtain a deduction on your federal tax return. But don't prepay if you're subject to the AMT since state and local taxes are not deductible for AMT purposes.

Do You Owe Estimated Taxes?

It's not always simple to figure out how much tax you owe, even if you have money withheld on a W-2. If you pay too little throughout the year, you could end up owing a good deal in taxes and penalties on April 15.

You may have to pay quarterly estimated taxes if you have income that is not subject to withholding tax and you match any of the following criteria.

● You are self-employed.

● You are retired and receive income in addition to Social Security.

● You have investment income.

● You receive unemployment or alimony payments.

● The additional tax you owe when you file exceeds the IRS limit.

● Withholding and credits are less than 90% of the current year's tax or 100% of the previous year's tax (higher for some high-income taxpayers).

● Your tax situation has changed suddenly due to divorce, windfall, loss of dependent or other circumstance.

Caution: If you are in an AMT situation, prepaying state and local taxes may not be advised since you will lose the benefit of these payments.

WITHHOLDING AND PREPAYING

Make a new estimate of your final tax bill for the current year that includes the new tax strategies you plan to use.

Useful: Try one of the new computerized tax-return preparation programs now on the market. You can plug in different numbers to see the dollar impact on your tax bill. Use this estimate to make sure you are paying enough tax through wage withholding and quarterly payments to avoid underpayment penalties.

IRS FORM
W-4

Through a combination of withholding and quarterly estimated payments, you must pay at least 90% of your tax bill for the year, or 100% of the prior year's tax bill, whichever is less.

IRS FORM
1040 ES

However, if your Adjusted Gross Income for the previous year exceeded $150,000, you must pay the lower of 90% of the current year's taxes or between 100% and 112% of the prior year's taxes (depending on the year). You may also incur a penalty for underpaying taxes in a particular quarter—for instance, if you took a large investment gain and didn't make a corresponding estimated tax payment.

If you find that you have underpaid your taxes to date, make up the shortfall by increasing wage withholding instead of making an estimated tax payment.

Reason: Withholding is treated as taking place at an even rate over the year, even when it is increased late in the year. So by increasing withholding, you can retroactively make up a tax shortfall for an earlier quarter and avoid a penalty.

In contrast, if you make up the tax shortfall with an estimated payment, you may still owe underpayment penalties for earlier quarters.

Tax-Free Income Loopholes

Not all the money you receive is taxable income, even though the IRS might like you to think it is.

GAIN ON THE SALE OF YOUR HOME

You're not taxed on gain up to $250,000 ($500,000 on a joint return) from the sale of your principal residence. You qualify for this exclusion if you owned and used the home for two out of five years before the date of the sale, regardless of your age.

Retroactive effective date: The new exclusion amounts apply to profits on homes sold on or after May 7, 1997.

Mostly winners: Most people who sell their homes will be winners under the new law, although tax is still owed on joint gains over $500,000.

LIFE INSURANCE PROCEEDS

The beneficiary receives the proceeds of life insurance policies free of tax. But the decedent's estate may be liable for estate tax on the proceeds.

Gifts and Inheritances

You do not pay income tax on money or property you receive as a gift or inheritance. Any gift tax owed is the responsibility of the person who gave the gift. In the case of an inheritance, federal estate tax is paid by the decedent's estate, not by the beneficiaries.

If you inherit property that has increased in value, such as the family home, you receive it at its stepped-up estate value. This allows you to avoid tax on the gain. When you sell the property, you use its stepped-up value, rather than the original cost, to calculate your taxable gain, another big benefit.

BORROWED MONEY

You can borrow up to $50,000 from your company pension plan tax-free.

Reason: Borrowing is not treated as a taxable transaction.

GRANTS FOR EDUCATION

Scholarships and fellowship grants are tax-free provided you are a degree candidate and the money is used strictly for tuition, fees, books, supplies and required equipment. (Grants for room and board are taxable.)

Voided Debt
If a debt you owe is canceled, the amount of debt forgiven might become taxable income to you.

EMPLOYEE AWARDS

Awards of tangible personal property (not cash) for length of service or safety achievements, up to $400 per employee or $1,600 if the employer has a qualified plan, are tax-free. (Awards for suggestions to an employer are generally taxable.)

DAMAGES

Damages received in a lawsuit due to personal injury or sickness and certain kinds of discrimination are tax-free.

ROLLOVERS

No tax is payable on a lump-sum payout from a company pension plan directly transferred into an IRA within 60 days.

PROPERTY SETTLEMENTS

Settlements between spouses in a divorce are not taxable to the recipient. However, the recipient takes over the tax cost (basis) in the property and will be taxed on any gain when the property is sold.

CHILD SUPPORT AND ALIMONY

Child-support payments are tax-free to the recipient. Alimony is generally taxable, but it can be tax-free if the parties agree.

MUNICIPAL BOND INTEREST

Generally, the interest is exempt from federal income tax and sometimes from state and local tax as well.

Exception: Interest from certain "private activity" municipal bonds is subject to the AMT. Also, municipal bond interest is taken into account in figuring your income level to determine whether any of your Social Security benefits are taxable.

AMT Alert
The alternative minimum tax, or AMT, prevents taxpayers who benefit from special credits and deductions from paying too little or no taxes. You may have to pay the AMT if your taxable income with adjustments is above a certain level ($45,000 for married filing jointly and $33,750 for single or head of household.

RETURN-OF-CAPITAL DIVIDENDS

Some companies pay dividends that are considered a return of your investment in the company. These are wholly or partially tax-free. However, your tax cost in the stock has to be reduced by the amount of untaxed dividends.

LIFE INSURANCE POLICY DIVIDENDS

These are generally considered a partial return of the premiums you paid and are not taxable. You don't have to pay tax on these dividends until they exceed the accumulated premiums paid for the policy.

ANNUITY PAYMENTS

The part of an annuity payment that represents the return of your investment in the annuity contract is not taxed. Pension and IRA distributions that represent any non-tax-deductible contributions are also not taxed.

EDUCATION SAVINGS BONDS

Interest on U.S. Series EE savings bonds issued after December 31, 1989, is tax-free to many taxpayers if the bonds are later redeemed to pay for education expenses.

Limits: This exclusion is not available for taxpayers with income in excess of certain annually determined amounts.

ALSO TAX-FREE

- Workers' compensation.
- Social Security payments if your income is less than $32,000 if married filing jointly, or $25,000 if filing singly.
- Federal income tax refunds. (However, any interest the IRS pays on a late refund is taxable.)
- State income tax refunds, provided you did not itemize deductions on your federal tax return for the previous year. If, however, you itemized your deductions for the year, your state refund is taxable. State refunds are not taxable if you were subject to the AMT the previous year and got no tax benefit for your state tax payments.
- Disability payments from accident or health insurance policies paid for by the taxpayer are generally not taxable. But they're usually taxable if your employer paid the premiums.
- Foreign-earned income. In 1998 the first $72,000 of salary earned in another country is excluded from U.S. tax if you were a resident of that country for the entire tax year. Some of your housing expenses are also excluded from U.S. tax.
- Certain fringe benefits from your employer.
  Examples: Health and accident insurance, pension plans, up to $50,000 of life insurance coverage, child- and dependent-care expenses, legal services under group plans, supper money, employee discounts and transit passes not exceeding $65 per month.
- Reimbursed medical expenses not claimed as itemized deductions.
- Reimbursed travel and entertainment expenses that you adequately account for to your employer (unless the reimbursement is included on your W-2 form).
- Amounts received for insurance reimbursement up to the amount of your original cost for the property that was lost or damaged.

The Importance Of Careful Records

Keep a household inventory that lists your assets, their value and your tax cost (basis) in them. You may need it to make an insurance claim, or to take a casualty or theft-loss deduction for losses that are not insured.

Recent case: A woman suffered the loss of valuable jewelry and silver coins that she had inherited, but she had no inventory of the stolen items or of their value when she inherited them. So she couldn't support her loss deduction when it was challenged by the IRS.

Split decision: The Tax Court was convinced by police reports that a serious theft had occurred. It allowed a deduction half the size of the one claimed.

Tax Records to Keep

- Investment costs, earnings and sales.
- Capital gains and losses.
- Charitable donations.
- Tax-free interest on state and local bonds.
- Mortgage and home-equity loan interest.
- Home purchase and home-improvement expenses.
- Job-related expenses.
- Tip income.
- Home-office expenses.
- Self-employment income and expenses.
- IRA contributions and withdrawals.

Family Loan Loophole

Family loans can be written off if they are not repaid, even if they are not fully documented. The IRS used to regard these loans as gifts unless they were formalized and accompanied by standard loan paperwork. But the Tax Court now says all that is required is minimal evidence that loans have been made to family members in the past, and that some have been repaid. Canceled checks, deposit slips or bank records will be considered adequate evidence. Bad loans cannot be deducted until proven uncollectible. It is not necessary to start a lawsuit if you have reasonable grounds for believing the debtor doesn't have assets or the ability to repay your loan.

Tax-Saving Opportunities for Everyone

You don't have to be rich—or own your own business—to have tax-shelter opportunities. Cut your tax bill by making the most of these tax-saving ideas that are available to everyone.

WITHHOLDING

Each year, review the amount of tax withheld from your pay.

a) If you overpay withheld taxes, your personal cash flow will be reduced throughout the year, and you'll wind up making an interest-free loan to the government until you receive your refund.

b) If you underpay, you'll owe a surprise tax bill on April 15 and may owe underpayment penalties. Remember, you are entitled to file a new W-4 form with your employer to claim as many withholding allowances as you are entitled to.

Even when your income stays the same from year to year, your tax liability may change sharply if you get married or divorced, have a child, buy a house and obtain a mortgage-interest deduction, have investment gains or losses, or receive sideline income.

Be sure to file a new W-4 to adjust your withholding accordingly.

INVESTMENTS

Manage your investments in order to earn the greatest after-tax return.

Opportunities:

● Stock shares and mutual fund shares offer a double tax advantage.

1) A capital gains tax rate of only 20% applies when gains arise on shares that are held for more than 18 months and then sold.

2) Shares benefit from tax deferral, since capital gains aren't taxed until the shares are cashed in. In the meantime you can benefit from their appreciation in value by borrowing against them.

Note: In the case of mutual funds, you will be taxed on any gains associated with sales of stock by the manager of those funds.

● Interest on U.S. Treasury securities is exempt from state and local taxes.

● Interest on municipal bonds may be totally tax-exempt.

Important: The worst thing you can do is be undecided about how to invest your money. By leaving it in a conventional savings account, you'll receive only a low interest rate that is fully taxed. After taxes, you may not even keep up with inflation.

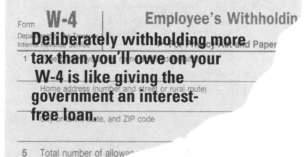

Deliberately withholding more tax than you'll owe on your W-4 is like giving the government an interest-free loan.

CHILDREN

Your children can serve as a valuable tax shelter.

a) Children under age 14 can receive (in 1998) $700 of investment income tax-free, and another $700 that is taxed at only a 15% rate. So you can cut your family's taxes by putting assets that produce up to $1,400 of income annually in a young child's name.

Young children can also benefit from owning capital assets, such as stock shares, that they will cash in after reaching age 14.

b) Children age 14 or over can receive in 1998 up to $25,350 of income taxed at only a 15% rate.

Your Gain on Tax-Free Investments

Your tax bracket		15.0%	28.0%	31.0%	36.0%	39.6%
Tax-free yield*	5%	5.88	6.94	7.25	7.81	8.28
	6%	7.06	8.33	8.69	9.37	9.93
	7%	8.24	9.72	10.14	10.93	11.59
	8%	9.41	11.11	11.59	12.50	13.25

For an investor in the 31% bracket, a tax-free yield of 7% earns the equivalent of a 10.14% taxable yield.

$$\frac{\text{Tax-free yield}}{100 - \text{Your tax rate}} = \text{Equivalent taxable yield}$$

For example

$$\frac{7}{100 - 31} = 10.14\% \quad \text{Equivalent taxable yield}$$

* Source: *The Ernst & Young Tax-Saving Strategies Guide 1994*

Tax-Free Is Not Risk-Free

Municipal bond funds provide tax-free income, but principal is at risk as interest rates rise.

Self-defense: Invest in funds holding shorter-term bonds. The less time until a bond matures, the less it reacts to interest-rate changes.

Long-term alternative: Stick with low-yielding growth stocks if you can handle the short-term risks and do not need current income from investments.

Last-Minute Opportunities Checklist

There's still time to take steps to cut your tax bill before year-end. Consider these last-minute tax-saving strategies.

FAMILY TAXES

Use your annual gift tax exclusion to make as many gifts as you wish, of up to $10,000 each, to children and grandchildren. The limit is $20,000 per gift when you make the gift jointly with a spouse.

● Such gifts reduce your future taxable estate, especially if the gift property will appreciate in value.

● You can use gifts to reduce the family's income tax bill by giving income-producing assets to children who are in a lower tax bracket than you are.

Caution: When giving assets to a child, remember the child will become the real owner of the gift property and may use it in a manner that is contrary to your wishes.

Example: A bank or brokerage account opened for a child under the Uniform Gift to Minors Act (UGMA) or the Uniform Transfers to Minors Act (UTMA) becomes the property of the child when he or she reaches the age of legal majority, age 18 or 21 in most states. The child then obtains full legal control over the property.

Self-defense: When planning gifts of large amounts of money, consult with an attorney to set up a trust that controls how gift amounts may be spent.

SELF-EMPLOYED CITIZENS

Persons with self-employment income can use these tax-cutting strategies.

1. Open a Keogh retirement plan, and make deductible contributions to it. The plan must be established by December 31 to accept contributions for that year, although the contributions do not have to be made until the extended due date of your tax return.

2. Postpone income by delaying invoices so income won't come in until after year-end.

3. Accelerate deductions by paying discretionary expenses, such as for business supplies, before year-end.

4. Use the expensing election that lets you deduct the cost of up to $18,500 in 1998 of new business equipment (computers, furniture and so forth) placed in service before year-end.

Medical opportunity: The IRS lets a self-employed individual obtain a full deduction for family medical bills by hiring his or her spouse as an employee and adopting a benefit plan that reimburses employees for family medical bills.

The IRS says such an arrangement is a legitimate employee benefit program, the cost of which is deductible, even when the business owner's family is the primary or only beneficiary.

Requirement: The spouse must be a real employee who receives wages and be treated as such for purposes of employment taxes, unemployment insurance, workers' compensation and so forth. And the program must cover all employees.

By acting to establish such a program by year-end, you may be able to deduct family medical expenses incurred over the whole year. So consult with your tax adviser about the idea now.

MUTUAL FUND TRAP

Beware of buying shares in a stock mutual fund during the last weeks of the year. Mutual funds are required to remit capital gains they have earned during the year to shareholders through a year-end dividend. This dividend is taxable and is taxed to the shareholder of record on the dividend date. So if you

buy mutual fund shares just before the dividend date, you may also buy a capital gains tax bill.

Hint: Learn the fund's dividend date from its prospectus or from your investment adviser and don't buy any fund shares until after the dividend date.

Valuable Tax-Saving Compensation Ideas For Executives

Here are some of the best strategies to provide executives with the most valuable benefit packages possible at the least after-tax cost.

DEFERRED COMPENSATION

Voluntary programs under which executives defer receiving part of their pay until a later year can be used to reduce personal tax bills.

● By electing not to receive a portion of pay until a later year, executives avoid current taxation of the deferred pay.

● If deferred pay ultimately is received when recipients are in a lower tax bracket than they are now—such as after retirement, or after a lowering of tax rates—they will owe less total tax.

● Interest that is credited to deferrals compounds on a pretax basis, providing employees with the same benefit of tax-deferral for investment returns that is provided in a qualified plan. Savings grow faster than they would in a taxable account earning the same return.

There's more than one way to provide extra benefits for key executives.

Split Dollar Insurance

Deferred Compensation

SERPS

Health Insurance

Disability Insurance

the company may deduct the payment.

Caution: The company's obligation to pay deferred compensation is merely contractual, so payments may be at risk if the company is unable or unwilling to pay them when they become due.

However, trust arrangements can be used to increase the security of deferred-pay programs.

1. Rabbi trusts

A rabbi trust can be currently funded with amounts needed to finance deferred compensation. Money in a rabbi trust can be used only to pay deferred compensation, and may be placed under the control of a third-party trustee, to assure that management won't spend it on something else and that the money won't disappear during a corporate reorganization or hostile takeover.

But a rabbi trust does not offer 100% security. That's because trust assets remain the property of the company, so if the company becomes insolvent, they will be within the reach of creditors.

2. Secular Trusts

A secular trust can be used to provide full security for deferred pay by placing the funds used to finance it beyond the reach of the company's management and creditors.

Catch: Because receipt of the future benefit becomes a certainty, the tax treatment changes. The executive is taxed immediately on the benefit, even though it won't be received until a later year. And trust earnings are currently taxed as well.

But when the benefit is paid out in the later year it is tax-free (since it has already been taxed).

Plus: The company gets an immediate deduction for its contribution to a secular trust. This is a major economic benefit, since otherwise the company can't claim its deduction until years later when it actually pays the benefit. And this tax saving can be shared with executives in a way that helps them pay their SERP-related tax bills.

Example: A company plans to make a $10,000 payment to a SERP funded by a secular trust for an executive in the 40% tax bracket. It will pay $4,000 cash to the executive for him to use to pay his tax

Caution: An election to defer pay must be made before the pay is earned, and the IRS interprets this to mean before the year in which pay is earned. So companies with deferred compensation programs should have their executives make appropriate elections before year's end.

SERPs

Supplemental Executive Retirement Plans (SERPs) are increasingly being provided to highly-paid executives whose qualified-plan benefits are restricted by tax law changes.

Advantages: Deferred compensation programs are not governed by qualified-plan rules. Thus, they can be provided to selected employees, and arrangements with individual employees can be custom-designed to meet particular needs.

Deferred pay generally is not taxable to the employee until it is actually paid out, and at that time

Benefit for High Earners

Qualified-plan benefits cannot be based on more than $160,000 of compensation in 1998 (down from $235,840 under old law). But a SERP can provide benefits based on compensation in excess of the $160,000 limit.

bill, and deposit $6,000 in the secular trust. The company can deduct the full $10,000 right away.

Key considerations:
- Rabbi trusts are best used with voluntary deferral programs since they preserve the desired tax deferral for employees.
- Secular trusts are best for SERPs that provide benefits on pay in excess of the $160,000 limit, because payment of the benefit is certain.

Other methods of securing benefits generally haven't been approved by the IRS.

SPLIT-DOLLAR INSURANCE
Split-dollar insurance is a flexible form of insurance the cost of which the company and executive share in a mutually advantageous manner, and which can be provided to employees on a selected basis.

How it works:
The company acquires a cash-value insurance policy on an executive's life and pays most of the premium, with the executive paying a portion equal to the cost of a term insurance policy with the same benefit. Or the company can pay the whole premium and include the term-equivalent cost in the executive's taxable compensation.

Key: The company recovers its entire investment in the policy
a) From policy proceeds if the executive dies, or
b) From the policy's cash value if the policy later is distributed to the executive.

So if the company pays one $10,000 premium on a $1 million policy and the executive then dies, the company recovers its $10,000 and the employee's beneficiary collects $990,000.

Example: Say the company buys a $1 million policy on a 35-year-old executive, paying a $10,000 annual premium. After ten years the arrangement is terminated; perhaps the executive is leaving the business. At that point the company has paid $100,000 into the policy which has a cash value of $140,000.

The company then gets back its $100,000, and the policy with its $40,000 cash value is transferred to the executive.

Advantages:
- The company has provided ten years of insurance benefits to the executive at no cost (other than the time-value of money).
- The executive emerges with the $40,000 value of the policy, the policy remains in force with premiums and benefits based on his age and health ten years earlier, and commissions and expenses on the policy have already been paid. The executive would be unable to buy a new policy on such favorable terms.

Key: The accumulating cash value of a split-dollar policy grows on a tax-deferred basis, and can be used creatively to fund many other kinds of benefits, such as a SERP. If an employee stays with the company for the long term and the arrangement is kept in place, borrowing against cash value can be used to pay policy premiums, eliminating any future cost of the arrangement to the company.

DISABILITY INSURANCE
During their working years, employees are much more likely to become disabled than to die, yet people who have adequate life insurance often lack disability insurance. Corporate group disability policies often do not provide sufficient benefits to meet the needs of top executives, so extra coverage may be a valuable benefit.

Tax angle:
Alternative tax treatments exist for disability premiums and benefits.

1. Premiums can be paid for employees as a tax-free benefit, but then any benefits received by an employee under the policy will be taxable income.

> **The number of people with disability insurance has almost doubled in the past ten years, and is still growing.**

2. Premiums can be included in employee income and taxed, after which any benefits received under the policy will be tax-free.

Planning: People naturally are reluctant to incur a tax bill they can avoid, but it can be advantageous to pay a tax on disability premiums in order to collect tax-free benefits later.

Reason: Most disability policies provide a benefit equal to about 70% of income. For individuals in a 30% tax bracket or higher (federal and local combined), a 70% disability benefit taken tax-free provides as much or more after-tax cash as 100% of regular salary when needed the most: during a family financial crisis.

HEALTH INSURANCE

To control rising health care costs, most companies are increasing the share of costs paid by employees through limitations on coverage and increases in co-payments and deductibles.

Opportunity: Generally, medical benefits must be provided to employees on a nondiscriminatory basis. But a quirk in the tax law lets special medical benefits be offered to selected employees, provided the benefits are funded through insurance, rather than direct payment.

Example: A company's major medical plan excludes benefits for psychiatric treatment. The company can provide coverage for such treatment to certain employees on a selective basis if it funds the coverage by buying an insurance policy covering psychiatric illness, instead of having the plan pay out such benefits directly.

Riders to the company's insurance coverage may provide other valuable medical benefits to key employees, perhaps covering copayments and deductibles. Consult with the firm's insurance adviser.

Maximize Your Deductions

The tax law imposes strict limits on personal deductions. But creative tax planners have found ways to get around these limits.

With a little careful planning, you can turn nondeductible expenses into tax deductions.

Parent Plus

Get a double tax benefit by making a charitable contribution on your dependent parents' behalf. The payment counts both toward calculating support and as a charitable deduction.

DEDUCT MEDICAL EXPENSES OF DEPENDENTS

Even though you may not be able to claim a personal exemption for your contribution to the support of relatives because they had a gross income of $2,700 or more in 1998, you can still deduct any medical expenses that you pay on their behalf.

IRS FORM 2120

Key: You must provide more than one-half of the relative's support.

Strategy: Instead of giving your relative cash to pay medical bills, pay the bills yourself. This may give you a deduction.

Whoever is claiming a dependency exemption for a parent under a multiple support agreement **(Form 2120)** with other relatives should also pay the dependent's medical expenses.

Reason: In determining qualification for the exemption, the payment of medical expenses is treated as part of the dependent's support. The payment is also deductible as a medical expense.

Impact: You get a double tax benefit for the same payment, a dependency exemption and a tax deduction.

Another way to get a double benefit is to make a charitable contribution on your parents' behalf. The

HELP WANTED
MUST BE UNDER 18

Hire Your Kids

Instead of paying your child a nondeductible allowance, put him or her to work as a bona fide employee in your business. The wages are a deductible business expense.

Bonus: If your business is not incorporated, you don't have to pay Social Security tax on wages paid to a child who is under 18.

payment is included in calculating support. You also get a charitable deduction.

TURN HOBBY LOSSES INTO DEDUCTIONS
Expenses for activities that are primarily sport, hobby or recreation are not deductible. To convert these nondeductible expenses into allowable deductions, the activity must be changed to an activity carried on for the production or collection of income. This is not hard to do if you keep accurate records. Factors that the IRS considers include the following.
● A profit in at least three of the immediately preceding five years.
● Activity considered businesslike in nature.
● The extent of your knowledge and expertise and the manner in which you use them.
● Your success in conducting other types of related activities.

TAKE EMPLOYEE BUSINESS-EXPENSE DEDUCTIONS
Most unreimbursed employee business expenses come under the category of "miscellaneous itemized deductions" and, as such, can only be deducted to the extent that they exceed 2% of your Adjusted Gross Income (AGI).

Loophole I: Have your employer reduce your salary by the amount you normally spend during the year on business expenses, say $1,000. Then have your employer reimburse you directly for the $1,000 of expenses. That way, you get a deduction for the full $1,000 of expenses through the salary reduction.

Caution: The salary reduction may affect your pension contributions.

Important: Be sure to adequately account for the expenses to your employer. If you don't, you could be required to pick up the entire amount of the reimbursement as ordinary income.

Loophole II: Impairment-related work expenses (for anyone who is physically or mentally handicapped) are not subject to the 2%-of-AGI limit on miscellaneous itemized deductions.

Loophole III: Beat the 2% floor on deductibility of employee business expenses by filing **Schedule C**, *Profit or Loss from Business*, where there is no such limitation. To qualify for reporting your expenses on Schedule C, you must fit into one of the following categories.

a) Self-employed individual or independent contractor.

b) Statutory employee. This is a category of worker that includes full-time outside salespeople or life insurance agents, commission drivers and home workers. Statutory employees are entitled to file Schedule C even though Social Security tax has been withheld from their paychecks and they have been issued W-2 forms.

c) Qualified performing artist. To qualify in this category, a taxpayer must have performed services in the performing arts for at least two employers in the tax year, had performing arts-related business expenses in excess of 10% of performing arts gross income, and had an AGI of $16,000 or less. Performing arts expenses can be deducted even though deductions are not itemized.

DEDUCT PASSIVE LOSSES
The passive loss rules generally limit the deductibility of losses from passive activities to the amount of income derived from such activities. Passive activities are defined as those activities involving the

Real Estate Loophole
If you or your spouse actively participates in real estate activities for at least 750 hours a year, losses from real estate activities can be deducted against other income without limitation.

conduct of a trade or business in which the taxpayer does not materially participate. Material participation in a trade or business activity means satisfying any one of a variety of tests.

Loophole: IRS regulations for self-charged interest permit the matching of interest income (normally portfolio income) directly against passive losses to the extent that the loss includes self-charged interest through the entity by an S corporation shareholder or partner.

Credit Card Interest Could Be Deductible

When tax law changes made personal interest nondeductible, most people stopped deducting interest paid on personal credit cards. But deductibility of interest is determined by the purpose of the debt and the use of borrowed funds. It is not determined by whether a charge card is used. So some credit card interest may still be deductible.

Examples: If you buy business equipment, such as a computer, for your sideline business and bill it to the personal credit card, the related interest is deductible. And if you use a credit card to finance an investment, interest may also be deductible.

Strategy: Simplify records by keeping a separate card for deductible charges.

Filing Separately Doesn't Mean "I Don't Love You"

The most favorable way for a married couple to file their taxes is not necessarily a joint tax return. The tax rate for couples who use the married filing separately status may be higher, but the tax bill could still be lower.

It is always better to file a joint return when only one spouse has income. But when both spouses have income, a separate return may result in a lower combined tax bill.

On a joint return, it's the combined AGI of you and your spouse that counts when figuring the medical or miscellaneous threshold. On a married filing separately return, it's the AGI of the spouse who incurred the expense that counts. It may be easier for one spouse alone to meet this threshold, especially when one spouse makes much more.

UNDERSTAND THE MARRIAGE PENALTY

People often hear this expression and make the mistake of thinking that the married filing separately status is more favorable than joint status because of the marriage penalty.

Reality: In most cases, the final tax bill for two single people living together will be lower than that of a married couple who files separately, even though each individual has the same income as the corresponding person from the other pair. A married couple filing separately is therefore subject to the marriage penalty because that couple pays more taxes than two single people with the same income.

ALLOCATE DEDUCTIONS

When considering which status to use, keep in mind that some expenses, even though they are joint, can be entirely deducted by the spouse who will reap the most tax benefit.

Examples:
- State taxes paid can be allocated between spouses in any proportion you choose.
- Dependent children can be claimed by either parent.

MARRIED FILING SEPARATELY? **MARRIED FILING JOINTLY?**

Couples in which only one spouse is working should always file a joint return, but if both spouses are working, filing separately might allow more miscellaneous and medical deductions, and save more money.

  OR

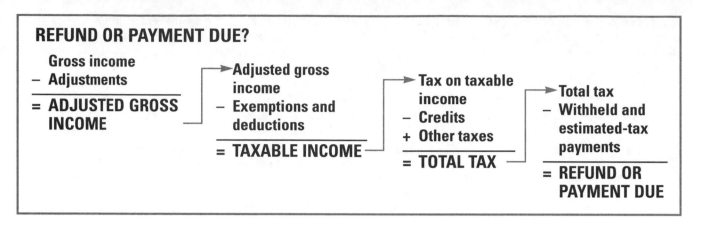

REFUND OR PAYMENT DUE?

Gross income
– Adjustments
= **ADJUSTED GROSS INCOME**

→

Adjusted gross income
– Exemptions and deductions
= **TAXABLE INCOME**

→

Tax on taxable income
– Credits
+ Other taxes
= **TOTAL TAX**

→

Total tax
– Withheld and estimated-tax payments
= **REFUND OR PAYMENT DUE**

CONSIDER NON-TAX REASONS

There are other factors that may affect your decision to file a separate return. You may have a rocky marriage or could be separated and living apart from your spouse. Sometimes one spouse doesn't want the other spouse to know how much income there was over the year, despite the tax consequences. If you don't think your spouse is reporting all of his or her income and you don't want to be liable for future tax consequences, file a separate return.

Inheritance Loopholes

To maximize the tax advantages of receiving an inheritance, consider the following information.

THE RECIPIENT DOESN'T PAY ESTATE TAX

Estate tax is paid by the estate; to the recipient, an inheritance is estate-tax-free.

THE RECIPIENT DOESN'T PAY CAPITAL GAINS TAX

This is because of a tax break known as step-up-in-basis. The recipient takes an inheritance over at its value on the estate tax return, not the property's cost to the decedent.

Example: You receive by inheritance a house that cost the decedent $20,000 and that's now worth $150,000. You pay no tax when you receive the house by inheritance. And if you immediately sell it for $150,000, you pay no capital gains tax.

Reason: Your tax cost is considered to be the property's value when the decedent died (or six months later if the estate chooses that date). Since the house was sold for the same price at which you inherited it,

you pay no capital gains tax. If you sell the house for more than $150,000, you'll have to pay taxes on the excess capital gains.

SELLING PROPERTY AT A LOSS

If you sell inherited property at a loss, you'll get a tax deduction for the loss.

Suppose you sell the house in the above example for $120,000. You'll have a deductible $30,000 capital loss, subject to annual deduction limits. (Capital losses are deductible dollar for dollar against capital gains and up to $3,000 of ordinary income each year. Excess losses can be carried forward to subsequent tax years.)

Deduct Extra Dependents

If you are supporting adult children or grandchildren who live with you—and who have no income—they qualify as dependents.

This entitles you to a $2,700 dependency exemption in 1998 for each child or grandchild on your tax return, if you are below certain income levels.

IT CAN PAY TO GIVE UP AN INHERITANCE

In some situations, a great deal of estate tax can be saved when a beneficiary disclaims (gives up) an inheritance.

Example: A wife leaves $500,000 to her husband, who has an estate of $10 million. No estate tax would be owed on the wife's death because of the unlimited marital deduction. But on the husband's death, the extra $500,000 would be taxed to his estate at 55%. The tax would be $275,000. That tax could be saved if, on the wife's death, the husband were to disclaim the $500,000 inheritance and let it pass to the couple's children or other beneficiaries. The gift would not be taxed in the wife's estate because of her exemption equivalent ($625,000 in 1998, increasing to $1 million by 2006).

THE QTIP

Sometimes a life interest in an inheritance will qualify for the unlimited marital deduction.

Example: Property in which a spouse is given only an interest for his or her life may qualify for the unlimited marital deduction as Qualified Terminable Interest Property, or QTIP. If it qualifies, the property will pass to the surviving spouse estate-tax-free. It will

IRS FORM 706

be included in the surviving spouse's estate at death. One of the requirements for qualification as QTIP property is that the executor make an unequivocal election on **IRS Form 706, Schedule M**, to have it qualify.

INCOME TAX VS. ESTATE TAX

If the estate is in a higher tax bracket than the decedent, it pays to take the deductions for estate administration expenses and losses on the estate tax return rather than on the income tax return. The deductions produce a bigger tax benefit because the rate is higher.

Example: If the estate is in the 55% bracket and the individual in the 31% bracket, it would pay to take the deductions on the estate tax return rather than on the income tax return.

Before Mailing Your Tax Return

☐ Recheck the arithmetic.

☐ Include your name, address and Social Security number on the first page of the return. If you use the IRS pre-addressed label, correct any wrong information.

☐ Write your name and Social Security number on every page and on every form you send to the IRS.

☐ Attach copy B of your W-2 form.

☐ Sign and date the return. (Both spouses must sign a joint return.)

☐ Make a copy of the return.

☐ Include every form.

☐ Remember that payment of any tax due is made with **Form 1040 V** (payment voucher), which is mailed to an address different from where your tax return is mailed.

☐ Address the return to the Internal Revenue Service Center for your state. Many tax experts say that using the IRS envelope will speed up your refund check.

☐ Mail the return on or before April 15. Use certified mail. Otherwise the IRS may not accept proof of filing.

CHOOSING A TAXABLE YEAR FOR TAX SAVINGS

Estates can have a fiscal year, any year of the executor's choosing, rather than a calendar year. Choosing a fiscal year can extend the time the beneficiary has before reporting the income earned on estate assets.

Example: Suppose the executor chooses a March 31 fiscal year. Any income earned from the date of death to March 31 will be taxed to the beneficiaries in the later year. The income earned from April 1 to the following March 31 will not be taxed until the beneficiaries file their returns for the following year.

INHERITING STOCK

If the decedent owned stock in a C corporation that had high retained earnings, the stock can be redeemed income-tax-free by the estate. The redemption is treated as a capital gain. There is no income tax payable because the value of the stock is stepped up to its value on the date of the decedent's death.

Normally, if you take money out of a corporation's retained earnings without liquidating the corporation, the money is taxed as a dividend.

INCOME IN RESPECT OF A DECEDENT

Generally, when you inherit assets they are subject to the step-up-in-basis rule. Your tax cost is stepped up to the asset's date-of-death value. However, this does not apply to income that was earned by the decedent but was not paid before death.

This after-death income may be subject to both income tax in the recipient's hands and to estate tax. There is, however, a deduction on the estate tax return for the income tax paid.

PENSION DISTRIBUTIONS

Pensions are treated the same as income in respect of a decedent and are subject to double taxation.

Lump-sum pension distributions payable on death may qualify for five- or ten-year averaging, which greatly reduces the income tax on the distribution. The part of a distribution that relates to pre-1974 participation in a pension plan may qualify for tax-favored capital gains treatment.

PENSION DISTRIBUTION

A surviving spouse can elect to roll over a pension distribution into an IRA and defer the payment of income tax.

Estate Tax Audits Are Common

IRS audits of estate tax returns are much more common than income tax audits. Large estates and estates including family-owned businesses are almost sure to be audited. In examining an estate, the IRS scrutinizes what the executor reports. It also checks the decedent's income tax returns for interest and dividends to be sure all stocks and bonds are reported on the estate return; sends appraisers to value artworks, antiques and jewelry; and checks insurance records to find out how any property was valued.

Shrewd Tax Planning For Children's Summer Jobs

Here's how to make the most of your children's summer income by paying as little as possible of it to the IRS.

TAX ADVANTAGE

Children's earned income is not subject to the kiddie tax, so, unlike a child's investment income, the earned income of a child under age 14 is not taxed at the rate paid by the child's parents.

This means that children of all ages can take advantage of the standard deduction to pay zero tax on up to $4,250 of their income in 1998. And income that they earn in excess of this tax-free amount is taxed at the child's tax rate, starting at only 15%.

Bonus: Tax-free earnings can be increased to $6,250 if the child makes a $2,000 deductible contribution to an IRA. Although tax rules require that a person have earned income to make an IRA contribution, and require $2,000 of earnings in order to

**Children can earn up to $6,250 tax-free annually
if they put $2,000 into an IRA.**

make the maximum IRA contribution, they do not require that the contribution be made with the child's earned income.

Thus, a child's IRA contribution can be funded with $2,000 received as a gift from a parent or grandparent, allowing the entire tax-free $6,250 to be saved for college or put to some other purpose.

Starting IRA contributions when a child is in his or her teens provides a tremendous financial payoff due to the power of tax-deferred compounding of interest over time.

Example: A child who begins at age 15 placing $2,000 each year in an IRA that earns 8% annually will reach age 65 with $1,148,000 in the IRA account.

By contrast, someone who doesn't begin saving $2,000 annually until age 25 will have less than half as much at age 65, only $518,000, even though he or she saved only $20,000 less.

Even better, forego the IRA deduction and make contributions to a Roth IRA. Then, withdrawals after

age 59½ that have been in the account for at least five years will *all* be tax free.

WITHHOLDING

No income tax withholding is required from the summer wages of a child who owed no income tax last year, expects to owe no tax this year, and who has no taxable investment income.

Such a child can claim exempt status on the W-4 form that is filed with the employer when he or she begins work. That way, the child's paychecks will not be reduced by income tax withholding.

Caution: If your dependent child has any taxable investment income, even $1, withholding will be required if the child's annual wages will total more than $700.

Strategy: A child with investments can avoid having current investment income by investing in appreciating assets, such as Series EE savings bonds or nondividend-paying growth stocks, or in tax-exempt securities.

When withholding is required from a child's wages, it may be minimized by asking the employer in writing to withhold tax on a part-year employment basis. This option may be available when the child will be employed for periods totaling no more than 245 days (about eight months) during the year.

Benefit: Part-year withholding tables recognize that income will not be received year-round, and permit the withholding of somewhat less tax than standard withholding tables.

Catch: The part-year withholding method is optional for the employer, who must voluntarily agree to it.

BEST BREAK

If you own a business or sideline business, you can hire your own children.

Payoff: You can deduct the wages you pay your children at your own high rate, while they pay tax on their wages at their own low, or zero, tax rate. As a result, the family's overall tax bill can be reduced.

The Tax Court has allowed deductions for wages paid to children as young as age 7 when the taxpayer

Value of an IRA at age 65, based on $2000 annual contributions, earning 8% annually

Age 65

$1,148,000 **$518,000**

Start at age 25

Start at age 15

Why It Pays to Open an IRA Early

The values of two IRAs at age 65, based on $2,000 annual contributions earning 8% annually, differ dramatically.

has been able to show that the child performed real work and was paid a reasonable wage for it.

Examples: Wages were deductible when paid to young children who performed clean-up duties around a family-owned trailer park, and to a doctor's young children who took phone messages and performed simple office tasks to assist in the practice.

No Social Security taxes are owed on the wages paid to a child under age 18 who is employed by a parent's not-incorporated business, and no federal unemployment taxes are owed on wages paid to such a child who is under age 21.

Bonus: By hiring your child, you may avoid paying employment taxes that you would owe on a non-family member doing the same task, and the child avoids employment taxes that would be subtracted from his salary if he worked for someone else.

Computers and The IRS

Your computer can become a valuable tool this filing season, letting you obtain IRS tax forms and publications without taking a trip to stand in line at the local IRS office or waiting for the IRS to send them to you by mail.

Moreover, the IRS says that revised tax forms reflecting currently pending tax law changes will become available electronically before paper forms are printed—enabling you to file a return that reflects the law changes earlier.

The IRS On-Line

World Wide Web
IRS Forms: **http://www.ustreas.gov**
IRS Information: **http://www.irs.ustreas.gov**
Digital Daily:
http://www.irs.ustreas.gov/plain/cover.html
On-line filing information:
http://www.irs.ustreas.gov/prod/elec_svs/ol-txpyr.html

Internet
IRS Forms: **ftp.fedworld.gov**
IRS Information: **ftp.irs.ustreas.gov**

Telnet
IRS: **iris.irs.ustreas.gov**

Other On-Line Tax Information
These pages and groups offer information to help you navigate your tax returns.

World Wide Web
Directory of state tax websites:
http://www.uni.edu/schmidt/state.html
Directory of tax preparers by location:
http://www.cctax.com/ccsearch.htm

Usenet Groups (good for specific questions)
misc.taxes
misc.taxesmoderated
alt.irs.class-action

TIP **Family Business Trips**
You can bring a spouse on a business trip and still deduct most of the trip's cost. That's because you can deduct the full cost you'd have incurred traveling alone.

Examples: You can deduct the cost of a single hotel room (a double costs a little extra), the cost of a car you'd have rented alone (even if your spouse uses it) and the full cost of a single airfare (even if you get a discount for family travel). Of course, you do not get a deduction for your spouse's separate expenses, such as meals, which you would not have incurred traveling by yourself.

Little-Known Expatriate Retiree Tax Facts

Retiring to a foreign country does not let you avoid paying U.S. taxes. Unlike most other countries, the U.S. taxes its citizens regardless of where they live.

Exception: U.S. citizens can earn up to $72,000 in 1998 tax-free while residing overseas and receive a tax-free housing allowance. This exclusion applies only to wages, salaries and self-employment income, not to investments, annuities and pensions.

Problem: The IRS has admitted that there's no effective way to enforce tax laws on expatriates and that it has no way of tracking down Americans living abroad who do not file returns.

Bottom line: If you're not willing to repudiate your U.S. citizenship, moving abroad does nothing to avoid U.S. taxes—unless you're willing to break the tax law.

Big Tax Savings For Home Owners

The new tax law on home sales really is tax simplification. It will give people a lot more freedom and flexibility in selling their homes than before.

Also, the new law will relieve a lot of people (but not all) of record keeping—because every time you move, you start with a clean slate.

TAX-FREE PROFITS

The new law allows couples to exclude from income a gain of up to $500,000 on the sale of a principal residence. Single people are allowed to exclude gains of up to $250,000. This replaces the previous once-in-a-lifetime tax exclusion on capital gains of up to $125,000 on home sales.

The new law also: Abolished the requirement that you be age 55 or older to take an exclusion.

Abolished the rollover/deferral rules, which allowed taxpayers to avoid capital gains tax on the sale of a principal residence as long as it was replaced with a new one costing as much—or more—within two years of the sale.

Generally allows people to take an exclusion each time they sell a principal residence.

Since the majority of people who sell their principal residence do not end up with a gain of more than $500,000, all profit they realize will be tax free.

You can now take such a tax-free gain as often as every two years. But in order to be eligible, you are required to have owned and lived in the home for two of the last five years.

The old law generally created pressure on home owners to trade up when they moved so as to defer tax. Now they can sell freely.

Mostly winners: Most people who sell their homes will be winners under the new law, although there will also be some losers—mainly people who have

gains of more than $500,000, thanks to a lifetime of trading up and rolling over gains.

Retroactive effective date: The new exclusion amounts (and other changes in the tax rules on home sales) apply to profits on homes sold on or after May 7, 1997.

NEW OPPORTUNITIES

Opportunity: For empty nesters. A lot of people are downsizing today. Often they are empty nesters who want to move into condos because they want to travel more or they just don't want all the work of maintaining a big house and grounds once the kids are away at school.

Previously, the choice these people faced was to pay a large capital gains tax on selling the big house or to wait until they were 55 years old to get the $125,000 exclusion. Things change dramatically for them under the new law.

Example: A couple in their late 40s have two children in college and a $600,000 home in which they have a $200,000 cost basis. They can now sell the home, pay no capital gains tax, and use some of the $600,000 to buy a condo and pay for the kids' educations, and still have some money left over to invest for retirement.

Opportunity: For people who get a new job or are transferred to a new town. In the past, most people moving from a high-cost housing market, like New York or San Francisco, to a low-cost market like Evansville, Indiana, or Austin, Texas, spent a lot for a new house because they would rather buy a bigger home than they needed than pay a nickel of taxes to the IRS.

New strategy: Now they can buy what they actually need and invest their surplus profits. If the financial markets continue to outperform the real estate market as they have in recent years, these people would then have enough to buy even nicer houses, should they move back to a high-cost locale.

Opportunity: For people who want to sell and not buy a new home. People who are temporarily out of the home-ownership market are real winners under the new law.

Example: A few local employers send employees overseas, generally for a few years. Often the employees rented out their homes while they were away. Reason: If they sold their homes, paid a capital gains tax, and invested the balance, they might not have enough to buy equally nice houses when they returned home. Now, a better strategy for employees sent overseas for a few years is to sell and be 100% invested in the market.

Opportunity: For people who remarry after divorce or widowhood…there will now be far more flexibility. People who are divorcing will have more flexibility, too.

Tax considerations will no longer dictate personal choices. For years, when two older people were getting married and combining households, they saw their clergyman, then saw their accountant to find out what to do about selling the extra home. Do we sell before or after we are married? The answer depended on individual circumstances. If both were over age 55, we had to ask if either had used the one-time $125,000 exclusion. If so, then the other needed to sell before the wedding or forfeit his/her right to the exclusion. Now people planning to remarry don't have to worry about that anymore. They can sell whenever is most convenient, before marriage or after, and if they want to sell both homes and buy a

new one—unless they have very large gains—that will generally make sense, too.

NEW TRAPS AHEAD

That is not to say everyone will be a winner. There are still some tax traps for home owners.

Trap: Big gains. Some Americans—particularly wealthy or older, middle-class people who have assiduously traded up in housing every few years, taking advantage of appreciation and the old roll-over rule—will have capital gains of more than $500,000 when they sell their homes. Anything over $500,000 will be subject to capital gains taxes, but the new law caps that tax at 20% for the time being.

Strategy: There are two ways to lessen the capital gains tax bite. One is to keep careful records of all home improvements because those costs become part of the house's tax cost and lessen the gain. The other is to realize loss positions in a securities portfolio and use those losses to offset the house gains.

Some people hate to sell at a loss because only $3,000 of net capital losses can be used against ordinary income each year. But if a taxpayer has a taxable capital gain on a home, portfolio losses, if made available, can offset the gain dollar for dollar.

Transition rule for big gains: People who sold their homes after May 6, 1997, and before August 5, 1997, can choose whether to use old or new rules in reporting their gain. This exception also applies if the sale was made after August, 5, 1997, but a binding contract was in effect on that date. Impact: People with a big gain on a sale between those dates could use the old deferral rules if they bought another house for an equal or greater amount.

Trap: Renting out the home. Often people who were transferred out of town and were not sure the move would be permanent or people who tried to sell a house and were not happy with any offers they received converted their homes to rental properties. Then they could claim depreciation on the homes.

New law: Any taxes avoided because of depreciation deductions over the years will be recaptured when the home is sold. This is an incentive to simplify your life. Sell the house and pocket the profit tax free when it is time to move. Forget about becoming a landlord.

Bottom line: The traps in the new law are small compared with the opportunities. Most people will benefit significantly when they sell.

The cost of any permanent improvement to your home can be added to its basis

Of course, this includes major items such as room additions and kitchen remodeling. But it also includes small-ticket expenditures that can add up to big dollars over a lifetime.

Examples: New doorbells, upgraded wiring or plumbing, new or improved outlets and fixtures, permanently installed carpeting, storm windows and doors, even decorations such as birdbaths.

Helpful: Have a simple shoebox file in which you keep receipts for every expenditure made on your home, with brief explanatory notes attached. These can add up to big amounts over the years to save future tax dollars. Also, fix-up expenses incurred as you prepare to sell your home can be added to its tax basis.

Caution: These new rules do not apply to vacation homes or rental properties, both of which involve a separate morass of tax rules.

HOME-EQUITY BORROWING
You can extract tax-free cash from your home without selling it by borrowing against its appreciation in value or against the equity you have obtained in it by paying down the mortgage.

Such borrowing is tax-favored and can save you money. The interest you pay on up to $100,000 of home-equity borrowing is deductible as home mortgage interest. Of course, you can borrow as much as you'd like against your home, but interest paid on borrowing in excess of $100,000 is not deductible. Be sure you have sufficient itemized deductions, and that your tax benefit is high enough to make this worthwhile.

REVERSE FINANCING
An increasingly popular option for extracting cash from a home is reverse financing, or a reverse mortgage.

With this, a lender pays an amount to you each month for a specified period of time, at the end of which the lender will own a portion (or all) of the house. The house can then be sold with any appreciation in its value being shared by you (or your estate) and the lender.

Tax aspects: When reverse financing is set up as a loan, payments to you are tax-free to the extent that they are payments of loan principal rather than interest. Such a deal can also be set up as an installment sale, in which case a portion of each payment is tax-free as a return of principal, and a portion is long-term capital gains subject to a tax rate of just 20% (10% if you are in the 15% tax bracket when installment payments are received).

SECOND HOMES
If you are interested in buying a vacation home to enjoy during your retirement years, you should know that mortgage interest incurred on a second residence is deductible, and a boat or vehicle can qualify as a residence provided it has living facilities.

To qualify a second home as a residence, you must make personal use of it for more than 14 days during the year, or more than 10% of the number of days that you rent it out to others, whichever is greater.

DEDUCT MOVING EXPENSES
If you intend to live in another part of the country during retirement, you may be able to deduct your moving expenses if you work in the new area after relocating. You may work either as an employee or as a self-employed individual.

Rules:
- If you get a job as an employee, you must work full-time for 39 weeks during the year after you move.
- If you are a self-employed individual, you must work full-time for 78 weeks in the following 24 months.
- You do not have to have your new job before you relocate.
- Your new place of work must be at least 50 miles farther from your old residence than your old residence was from your former place of work.
- You qualify for the moving expense deduction if either you or your spouse meet these conditions.

Get Cash from Your Home Without Selling It

Home Equity Loans
The amount you can borrow is based on, and secured by, your home's market value minus what you owe on your mortgage. The interest you pay on loans of up to $100,000 is tax-deductible.

Reverse Financing
A reverse mortgage is a loan you take against the value of your home. You can receive regular payments or take money when you need it, eventually reducing your equity to zero.

How to Cut Your Property Tax Assessment

Many home owners unnecessarily pay too much in property taxes. But by learning how the property tax system works, you may be able to lower your property tax bill yourself, without paying big legal fees. A reduction in a tax assessment can produce thousands of dollars in tax savings. Here's what you really need to know.

Local tax jurisdictions typically allow only a short window of time, such as 15 to 30 days, in which to formally file a property tax appeal. You should prepare your case for a tax reduction before that window arrives.

TYPICAL CALENDAR

Months 1 to 5
Prepare case.

Months 5 to 8
Seek informal hearing with assessor about your assessment and possibly get an adjustment without a formal appeal.

Month 8
Proposed tax notice arrives.

Month 9
Appeal deadline.

Month 10
Tax rates that apply to assessments are set.

Month 11
Final tax bill arrives.

TAX DUE

The tax calendar varies for different jurisdictions, so the first thing to do is learn the dates and deadlines that apply in your jurisdiction for challenging assessments and filing appeals. Your jurisdiction's property tax year may begin on any month of the calendar year.

Procedures for contesting an assessment vary in each jurisdiction, so contact your local assessor's office for details.

> ### Hidden Tax Increases
> When local authorities announce that there will be "no tax rate increase" or "no increase in tax assessments" in the current year, it does not necessarily mean that there will be no tax increase in the current year.
>
> That's because when tax rates remain the same, the government can collect more tax by raising assessments, and vice versa.

HOW PROPERTY TAXES WORK

Your property taxes are determined by a two-step process.

1. First, local authorities assess the value of all properties within the jurisdiction.

2. Second, they impose a tax rate on the total assessed value that is sufficient to collect enough revenue to meet the needs of local government.

It's important to realize that your house's assessed value for property tax purposes is not the same as its market value.

Market value: The market value of your home is the price you could expect to obtain for it on the open market. An appraisal of your home obtained from a bank, Realtor or insurance company will tell you its market value.

Assessed value: The assessment on your home is a tax value as determined by a government official. Usually it is a percentage of your home's market value. Thus, a home with a $100,000 market value may have an assessed value of $80,000.

State guidelines impose this percentage on the local tax assessor. If the state mandates an assessment-to-market-value ratio of 85%, a house with a market value of $100,000 should be assessed at $85,000.

HOW TO CUT YOUR TAX BILL

1. Find assessment errors

The government can't assess every house every year, so it conducts mass assessments. Your assessment is the average assessment that the local authorities think is appropriate for homes like yours in your area. Thus, the first way to reduce an assessment is to point out particular factors that differentiate your house from other houses in a way that reduces your home's relative value.

Examples:
- **Physical deterioration.** Faults in your home such as a cracked foundation or leaky roof reduce your home's value.
- **External deterioration.** This can include an increase in the local crime rate or the location of undesirable facilities (prison, airport, highway) near your home.

Reasons for a Tax Break
- Assessment value errors.
- Reduced market value.
- Technical errors on your assessment.
- Low appraisal norms in your area.

- **Functional obsolescence.** Your home may have a poor layout or other design problems—a lack of windows or out-of-date kitchen facilities. Be prepared to document these problems when meeting with an appraiser.

2. Determine market value

Weak real estate market prices can also provide justification for a reduced appraisal.

a) The most direct way to document your home's market value is to find comparable sales. Look for homes similar to yours that have been sold in your neighborhood or nearby in recent months.

Here's how: First, visit the assessor and ask for a copy of your property record card. This will contain the description of your house that's used for assessment purposes. Then seek out sales of homes with similar descriptions. Visit a broker and ask for a list of the previous year's sales, or look up the information yourself in records kept at the local assessor's office, courthouse, library or on your county computerized tax roll.

Tactic: Watch local newspapers to learn of sales of homes similar to yours, then look up a detailed description of the sold properties in the appraiser's office and save them for next year.

Important: You must have hard evidence of what comparable homes have sold for. Match property descriptions with actual sales prices as recorded in public documents.

b) A second way to document the value of your home is to produce independent appraisals of its value that have been recently obtained. If you recently refinanced your home, the lender probably required an independent appraisal of the home's value. You can present this to the local assessor as evidence of value.

3. Technical errors

When you obtain the property record card that describes your home from the assessor, examine it for errors. Mistakes in the recorded square footage or number of rooms may inflate your assessment, as may other errors.

4. Check appraisal norms

Federal National Mortgage Association appraisal norms say that no house can be assessed for more than 115% of the highest sale price received for a home in the area in the past year.

Opportunity: Assessors' computers are programmed to automatically assess homes by square footage, even if this produces a value above the 115% figure. If you have a large-square-footage house with an assessed value over the 115% amount, you may be entitled to a reduction.

The Biggest Tax Traps

The Tax Code is filled with quirky rules that can trip up unwary taxpayers. Here are some tax traps you will want to look out for and avoid.

TRAP

AVOIDANCE

TAKING RETIREMENT PLAN DISTRIBUTIONS TOO LATE

The Tax Code says that you must start withdrawing money from regular IRAs by April 1 of the year after the year in which you turn 70½. Otherwise you'll owe a 50% penalty on the amount which you should have taken out but didn't.

If you turn 70½ in 1998, you must make a withdrawal by April 1, 1999. You must also make a second withdrawal by December 31, 1999, for the 1999 tax year.

NOT CHOOSING YOUR IRA PLAN BENEFICIARY CAREFULLY

If your spouse is named beneficiary and then predeceases you, all IRA plan money is paid out and taxed when you die.

Instead of naming a spouse, name a child as your beneficiary so the money is paid out over a long time and continues to build up tax-free.

Caution: The beneficiary you choose cannot be changed for purposes of calculating minimum distributions after April 1 of the year after you turn 70½.

OWING TAXES ON PENSION DISTRIBUTIONS

When you take a 401(k) or another retirement plan distribution as a lump sum and then put it into an IRA yourself, your employer must withhold 20% for taxes. If you don't deposit the full amount, replacing what was withheld with your own money, you will owe tax on the difference.

Example: You take $100,000 from your retirement plan. The company gives you $80,000 and withholds the balance for taxes. You have to come up with $20,000 out of your own pocket to avoid taxes on the distribution. (You'll get this money back as a tax refund in the following year.)

Ask your employer or plan sponsor to transfer the $100,000 directly into the IRA, not cut a check to you. If the money is directly deposited, the company is not required to withhold 20% for taxes.

DONATING APPRECIATED PERSONAL PROPERTY

If the charity cannot use the property and sells it, your deduction will be limited to your cost basis, not the fair market value of the property.

Example: You donate art, which you bought for $100 and is now worth $1,000, to the United Way. The United Way sells the art and keeps the cash. Your charitable contribution deduction is only $100.

Make sure the donation will be used appropriately by the charity. That way you'll get a deduction for the full fair market value of your gift.

Example: Artwork that is donated to a museum.

TRAP	AVOIDANCE
DONATING DEPRECIATED PROPERTY TO CHARITY When you do so, you forfeit your loss deduction.	Sell the property yourself and donate the cash. **Example:** You own stock worth $500 but you paid $1,000 for the shares. If you sell them, you receive $500 cash and you can take a $500 loss deduction on your tax return. When you donate the cash, you get a $500 charitable deduction.
PREPAYING TOO MUCH IN STATE TAXES Many people project their state tax liability and then prepay it in December with the balance due in April. But too big a deduction could create AMT liability. Then you would lose your deduction for state taxes entirely.	Project AMT as well as regular income taxes and watch how juggling your expenses and deductions could affect the AMT.
PAYING TOO MUCH IN TAXES ON MUTUAL FUND SHARES When mutual funds declare dividends each year, most investors opt to have the money reinvested in additional shares rather than taking it in cash. But from the IRS's point of view, you received cash dividends and then bought more shares, so you owe tax in the year the dividends are declared. Then you will probably pay tax again, when the shares are sold.	Add all reinvested dividends to your cost basis in the shares when it is time to calculate your taxable gain. **Example:** You paid $1,000 for shares that are now worth $10,000. If you reinvested dividends of $2,500, your gain is not $9,000. Instead, add the $2,500 of reinvested dividends to your $1,000 cost basis and then subtract the total from $10,000.
INVITING IRS SUSPICION OF YOUR W-4 When you claim ten or more exemptions on your W-4 form, your employer must report it to the IRS. The IRS may then take a closer look at your exemptions.	Be prepared to justify yourself with proper documentation of the reasons for your exemptions.
LETTING TOO MUCH INCOME BE TAXED IN A TRUST Many people used to set up trusts because the trust income tax rate was much lower than the individual income tax rate. That has changed, and now trusts in 1998 pay tax at the top rate of 39.6% at only $8,350 of income. By contrast, individuals don't get to the 39.6% top rate until they reach $278,450 of income.	Have the trust distribute income and pay taxes on the beneficiary's return.
PAYING TOO MUCH TAX ON ALIMONY PAYMENTS Alimony payments are deducted by the payer and are taxable income to the recipient. Other types of payments are not. But the deduction route is not necessarily the best way to go because the former spouses combined might pay more tax.	You can choose whether each year's payments are to be considered taxable alimony based on the former spouses' projected tax situations that year.

Taxes on Household Workers

A separate tax form is required by anyone who paid a household worker $1,100 or more during 1998. The new form, **Schedule H of Form 1040**, must be filed to report both the employee's and the employer's share of Social Security tax, Medicare tax and income tax, in addition to the federal unemployment tax that has been taken out of the employee's pay. Before filing this form you must obtain an Employer Identification Number (EIN) from the IRS. You can get an EIN quickly by filling out **Form SS-4**, and then calling your local IRS office.

Home Buyer's 90-Day Tax Trap

An IRS rule says that after purchasing a home you have just 90 days to obtain a mortgage against it that qualifies as a home acquisition mortgage on which interest is fully deductible. If you miss the deadline, your mortgage interest may not be deductible. This can pose a costly trap if you buy a second home using a home-equity loan against your primary residence, figuring you'll later replace the home-equity loan with a mortgage against the second home, a tactic that's pushed by quite a few lenders.

Senior Citizen Property Tax Cut

Property tax cuts are often available to people in special circumstances. Many communities offer tax abatements to people over age 65. Others allow senior citizen tax deferrals—taxes are due after the house is sold.

Tax Trap in Jointly Held Property

Owning property in joint tenancy can be expensive from an income tax standpoint.

Tax rule: The tax cost (basis) of property owned at a person's death receives a new tax cost: The fair market value on the date of the person's death.

Example: Joe owned Public Co. stock that he purchased for $2,000 more than 25 years ago. When he died, the stock had a value of $100,000. In his will he left it to his sister Mary, who sells it for $103,000. Mary pays income tax only on $3,000.

Now suppose the same stock was held in joint tenancy, each paid half the purchase price, and Mary sells it for the same $103,000. Her tax cost is $51,000. Why? According to the tax law, she owned half of the property with a tax cost of $1,000, while Joe's half became hers with a new tax cost of $50,000. Mary must pay income tax on $52,000 ($103,000 minus $51,000).

Important: If you own property in joint tenancy with your spouse, review both the estate and income tax consequences. One half the property is included in the estate of the first spouse to die, regardless of who paid for it. Thanks to the unlimited marital deduction, you can change the form of holding property without incurring any current gift tax.

Beware of Joint Tenancy

Suppose your spouse left you stock worth $100,000 that was bought in 1983 for $2,000, and you're selling it for $103,000.

Without Joint Tenancy

$ 103,000	Cost at sale
− 100,000	Your cost basis
= $ 3,000	Your taxable gain

With Joint Tenancy

$ 103,000	Cost at sale
− *51,000	Your cost basis
= $ 52,000	Your taxable gain

*The cost basis of the half that became yours was established at your spouse's death ($50,000), but the cost basis of the half that was your original share is still what it cost at purchase ($1,000).

Tips for Better Filing

FILING SAFETY

When you mail your tax return to the IRS this April, be sure you correctly fill out the certified mail receipt you will keep as proof of filing. When a taxpayer miscopied two digits of an envelope number onto a receipt and the numbers didn't match, the court rejected the receipt as proof of filing.

PAYING BY CHECK

When paying the IRS, be sure to write your Social Security number on the front of the check, along with the notation "income tax," so the check can be traced if it goes astray. Make the check out to Internal Revenue Service, not IRS. If a check written to IRS gets lost, the letters can easily be changed to MRS, and the check cashed improperly.

WHEN YOU CAN'T PAY YOUR TAXES

If you can't pay the tax shown on your tax return, ask to pay off the balance through monthly installments.

Here's how: Fill out **IRS Form 9465**, *Installment Agreement Request*, and staple it to the front of your tax return. This allows you to obtain an extended payment period of up to 36 months. The IRS is required to respond to your request within 30 days. If you owe less than $10,000, you shouldn't have a problem obtaining a payment extension, although the IRS will add interest and penalties to your monthly payments. If you owe more than $10,000, you will have to file a financial disclosure statement and negotiate the details of your payment schedule with the IRS.

IRS FORM 9645

Tax-Filing Traps and How to Avoid Them

Certain legal income tax deductions are red flags to tax professionals. They attract the IRS's attention and are likely to trigger an audit.

Reason: Through long experience, the IRS has found that many of these deductions are abused. As a result, IRS agents are more likely to say "Show me" when these red flags appear on a return.

If you plan to take any of these deductions or have any of these red flags, be sure you have the paperwork to back them up.

1. HOME-OFFICE DEDUCTION

This is one of the IRS's favorite targets. In fact, the IRS has gone to court repeatedly, winning support for its tough stand in rejecting taxpayers' deductions.

To take depreciation on a portion of your home, or deduct a portion of your rent, for the space you use as a home office, you must be able to show that the room is used regularly and exclusively for business, and that it is the principal place of your business. People who take work home at night are not eligible for this deduction.

2. TRAVEL AND ENTERTAINMENT EXPENSES

Many entrepreneurs and even employees find it necessary to entertain prospective customers to win business. The IRS knows that a lot of these people tuck personal bills in with their business receipts.

For this reason, only 50% of the cost of meals can be written off, down from 80% in the past.

To make sure your legitimate tax deductions stand up, keep carefully organized and documented

Secret Bank Accounts

The government of the Bahamas recently committed itself to continuing bank confidentiality and secrecy laws. The Bahamas does not share tax or financial information with other countries. Banking information can be revealed only on the order of the Supreme Court in a criminal case, and tax rules of foreign countries are not considered criminal. Banks also are financially sound; foreign parents of local banks are required to guarantee the liabilities of their subsidiaries, and such banks include Citicorp and Royal Bank of Canada.

Also: There is no Bahamian income tax. But, of course, American taxpayers are required to report their worldwide income.

receipts and a diary stating the business purpose of all entertainment.

3. INTEREST DEDUCTION

Although home mortgage interest is generally 100% deductible and investment interest is deductible to the extent it is matched by investment income, personal interest, interest paid on personal debts such as credit cards and car loans, is not deductible.

The IRS, however, suspects that taxpayers fudge sometimes.

Examples: Someone who incurred margin debt on a brokerage account to buy a car might list it as investment interest, or someone with a sideline business who properly files **Schedule C** to report the income might try to deduct interest on a personal debt as a business expense.

If you take this deduction, be sure you have the paperwork to back it up.

4. MISCELLANEOUS ITEMIZED DEDUCTIONS AND CASUALTY LOSSES

Items such as professional or union dues, unreimbursed business expenses, safe-deposit box rentals or job-hunting expenses are miscellaneous itemized deductions on **Schedule A.** They can be taken only if they exceed 2% of your Adjusted Gross Income (AGI).

The IRS tends to eagle-eye deductions in schedule categories that do not have minimums. These categories include:

- **Schedule C:**
  Personal business.
- **Schedule E:**
  Rental income.
- **Schedule F:**
  Farm income.
  Casualty losses are deductible only if they exceed 10% of AGI, and there is no deduction for the first $100 of each casualty.

Except in disaster areas, claiming a casualty loss is almost like putting a label on the return that says "Audit me."

5. AVOIDING SELF-EMPLOYMENT TAXES

Both employees and employers must pay Social Security and Medicare taxes.

Self-employed individuals essentially have to pay both sides of these two taxes. The income, even a few thousand dollars of sideline consulting income, is reported on Schedule C and **Schedule SE** for the

Audit Triggers

To the IRS, all tax returns are not created equal. High income and certain clues of underreporting make it more likely that the IRS will audit a return. Here are some "red flags" that increase your chances of an audit.

- Alimony paid or received.
- Amended returns claiming significant refunds.
- Deductions for bad debt.
- Evidence of unreported income.
- Extensive business deductions.
- Foreign investments.
- Large deductions for rental property.
- Large deductions out of line with income.
- Low reported income for normally high-paying types of jobs.
- Tax shelters.
- Unusual or suspicious entries.

self-employment tax of up to 15.3%.

If maximum Social Security tax has been withheld on salaried income, that will not be owed on Schedule SE, but Medicare tax will.

Caution: Sometimes taxpayers list the income on the front of the IRS Form 1040 under Other Income, (Line 21) and do not file Schedule SE. Line 21 is for such things as prizes or jury pay, not for self employment income.

6. HIGH INCOME

Although fewer than 1% of all taxpayers are audited, if your income is above $50,000, you are four times as likely to be audited as someone whose income is between $10,000 and $25,000 and who takes the standard deduction.

Your best defense against an audit is a carefully prepared return with all calculations double-checked and neat, and detailed records in your files in case you are called to substantiate any deductions.

Beware of IRS Undercover Agents

In one sting, the IRS was able to prosecute tax-cheating restaurant owners after IRS agents posed as prospective restaurant buyers and got the owners to reveal that they kept two sets of books: one for tax purposes and the other showing real cash flow. In other cases, IRS agents have posed as doctors, lawyers, reporters and even members of the clergy.

Dangerous IRS Surprises

An unpleasant surprise from the IRS can be unsettling to your peace of mind and your finances. But, with some inside knowledge of how the IRS works, you may be able to resolve surprise problems happily—or keep them from arising at all.

SURPRISE! THE IRS IS ABOUT TO TAKE YOUR PROPERTY

The IRS is supposed to give you ample warning before seizing or placing a lien on property or a levy on your wages or bank account. But if you receive a surprise notice that the IRS is about to take such a collection action, don't assume it is a mistake.

- A **levy** on wages or a bank account requires an immediate response or the IRS will take your money 21 days after issuing the levy notice.

Audits by Income	
Income	**% of Returns Audited**
Under $25,000	0.71%
$25-50,000	0.58%
$50-100,000	0.88%
$100,000+	4.03%
Schedule C	
Under $25,000	2.24%
$25-100,000	2.41%
$100,000+	3.91%

Tax Evaders Beware

More tax evaders will go to jail under new federal sentencing guidelines. Offenses drawing new scrutiny include claiming phony deductions, omitting taxable income and failure to file. But people who come forward voluntarily after failing to file tax returns or pay taxes in recent years will generally not be prosecuted, though they will still owe the taxes, plus interest and penalties.

Defense: Immediately call the IRS Problem Resolution Officer (PRO), the taxpayer's representative within the IRS. Normally you must first try to resolve a problem twice through regular distribution channels before going to the PRO, but with a levy there is no time to spare. Tell the PRO that you didn't receive the required prior notification about the levy, and ask for a stay of its enforcement until it is explained to you and you have a chance to respond.

Your Money or Your Property

In fiscal year 1995, the IRS filed 799,000 notices of liens on property and over 2.7 million notices of levies on property. In addition, IRS revenue officers made 11,000 seizures of property.

Source: *Internal Revenue Service Data Book 1996*

- A **lien** is not so time-sensitive because the IRS is not threatening to take your property. The lien merely registers a claim against it at the county courthouse. The IRS will send you a copy of the lien when it is filed.

Response: Read the copy of the lien, and write back to the IRS collection office that originally filed it explaining any mistake it has made. The Tax Code requires the IRS to remove an erroneous lien within 90 days of being informed it is erroneous.

Important: If you don't receive a release-of-lien form in 90 days, check with your county courthouse to be sure it has been lifted. If it hasn't, contact the PRO for assistance.

- A **property seizure notice** always includes the name and phone number of the IRS Revenue Officer handling the case. Quickly call the Revenue Officer directly to obtain an explanation of the problem. If the Revenue Officer isn't available and doesn't return your call within one day, call the same number and ask for the officer's manager. If the manager isn't helpful, call the PRO.

SURPRISE! IRS NOTICES TO YOU WERE LOST IN THE MAIL

An IRS notice to you is valid even if you never received it. All the IRS is required to do is send its tax notices to the last-known address it has for you. Usually, this is the address on the latest tax return that you filed.

Self-defense: Whenever you move, file **IRS Form 8822**, its official change-of-address form, using registered mail. After you've done so, the IRS must send tax notices to your correct address. If it can't produce proof that it has done so, its notices will be considered invalid.

Trap: Forwarding of mail overseas is very unreliable. Therefore, if you move abroad for several months or longer, use Form 8822. Have IRS notices sent to a U.S. address, such as that of a relative or professional adviser, where you can be sure they will be handled properly.

SURPRISE! YOUR REFUND IS MISSING

You can check the status of an overdue refund by calling the IRS's Automated Refund Information telephone line (800-829-4477) or the number for your locality listed in the back pages of the instruction book to your tax return.

When you call, know the first Social Security number shown on your return, your filing status and the exact dollar amount of the refund you requested.

SURPRISE! THE IRS NEVER RECEIVED YOUR RETURN

Normally your tax return is deemed "filed when mailed," but this is true only if your return is received by the IRS.

If the IRS never received the return, or says it never received it, your return may be deemed not filed even if you know you put it in the mail. Similarly, if the Postal Service delivers your return to the IRS late, you may incur late-filing penalties.

Key: The postmark on the envelope containing your tax return determines its time of filing. But it is risky to rely on the postmark as proof of timely filing because it may be illegible or the mailing envelope may be lost—especially if a tax dispute arises years after the return was filed. And, if the return is lost in the mail, there won't be any envelope or postmark.

Self-defense: Always mail important tax documents by certified or registered mail. The Tax Code specifies that a certified or registered mail receipt is the only acceptable proof of timely filing other than a postmark. Receipts from express-delivery services, postage meter date stamps and other kinds of evidence are not satisfactory.

Important: The mailing receipt that you get when you pay the postage is your proof of filing, not the return receipt that comes back from the IRS. So if you have the mailing receipt, you have proof of filing even if the return receipt never comes back to you.

TIPS

- Never send two different tax filings to the IRS in one envelope. The IRS may lose the envelope, and then you won't have a mailing receipt for one of the filings.
- Keep the canceled checks that you sent to the IRS with your tax returns and copies of refund checks you've received. They may serve as proof that you filed, although they don't prove timely filing.
- Always be careful to send tax filings to the correct IRS office. A filing sent to the IRS at the wrong address may result in your return being considered late, and incur the related penalties.

SURPRISE! YOUR TAX PAYMENT IS LOST OR MISCREDITED

The best way to handle this problem is to prevent it. Write all the information that the IRS needs on the

check: your Social Security number, the type of tax being paid and the number of the corresponding tax form, the period for which the payment is being made and so on.

Reasons:
- If your payment is miscredited, your returned check has both the IRS's endorsement on the back and your designation of the tax being paid on the front, and is proof that the tax was paid. You can photocopy both sides of the check and send it to the IRS to resolve the matter.
- If the check is separated from the tax return, the IRS will still be able to process it.

SURPRISE! AN IRS "SPECIAL AGENT" APPEARS

If an IRS representative appears at your home or office and identifies him or herself as a "special agent," beware. Special agents are criminal investigators.

What to do: The agent will say whether he is investigating someone else or you.

a) If someone else is being investigated, cooperate as you would with any other law enforcement officer.

b) If you are being investigated, say you don't want to talk until after you get counsel. Then contact a lawyer who handles criminal tax matters. Don't depend solely on advice from your accountant or bookkeeper. Neither is qualified to give advice on legal matters.

SURPRISE! AN UNEXPLAINED TAX BILL ARRIVES

Never ignore an unexplained tax bill assuming it is a mistake that the IRS will correct on its own. When IRS computers mark an account as owing a tax bill, even if done erroneously, they begin moving forward in the collection process until somebody stops them. Failing to clear up the problem quickly can lead to a cascade of subsequent problems.

Example: You elect to apply your 1997 tax refund toward your first-quarter estimated payment for 1998, but the IRS decides you're not entitled to the refund. You won't get credit for the estimated payment, so you will have underpaid for the first quarter, which will cause you to be underpaid for subsequent quarters as well. You'll incur penalties for each until you realize what's going on.

What to do: Call the phone number on the IRS notice to find out what the problem is. If you can't get through on the phone (most tax notices come from IRS Service Centers that are designed to process paper filings rather than answer calls), write to the address on the notice and ask for an explanation. Send the letter certified or registered mail for your records.

Once you understand the problem, you'll probably have to write to the IRS again to resolve it. An IRS agent needs some kind of paper in hand to justify an action, such as a copy of a canceled check to credit your account with a payment.

Solution: Help the IRS resolve your problem by including in your letter all the information that is needed to handle it. Remember that the agent who opens your letter will know nothing about your case. If the agent has to pull your records from IRS files, further delays will result. So include a full explanation of the problem and photocopies (not originals) of all relevant documents, such as canceled checks and relevant pages of your tax return.

If any further tax notices arrive in the mail, don't ignore them thinking that you have handled the problem. Send them copies of your earlier reply.

Important: Keep a record of all your contacts with the IRS, including copies of correspondence and the names of people with whom you speak.

IMPOSSIBLE PROBLEMS

If a problem with the IRS bureaucracy just won't go away—your refund check never arrives or a payment is never credited to your account—you can take your case to the PRO. The PRO has the power to cut

---

Call for Tax Forms and Assistance

IRS Tax Information:
800-829-1040
IRS Form Hotline:
800-829-3676
IRS Information for the Hard of Hearing:
TDD 800-829-4059
IRS Automated Refund Information:
800-829-4477
IRS Tax Fax Service:
703-487-4160 (call from the handset of a fax machine)

---

through IRS red tape to solve taxpayer problems.

Generally, you must try to solve a problem twice on your own through normal channels before going to the PRO, one reason for keeping a record of all your contacts with the IRS.

A listing of PRO numbers can be found by calling 800-829-1040.

What Happens if You Don't Provide the IRS Your Records?

The IRS has the authority to examine books, records and other documents used to prepare your income tax return. Generally, a written request is made by a revenue agent for those records he believes are relevant to the examination of your tax return. If the request is overly broad, explain to the revenue agent why it would cause a burden to comply. For instance, the revenue agent has requested every personal check you have written during the past three years but you throw away your checks after one year. The agent can force you to reconstruct your records for the missing two years.

In the event a compromise is not possible, the revenue agent can issue an administrative summons that compels the production of the records sought. Failure to comply with the summons provides the IRS with the ability to seek enforcement of the summons in federal court. If a judge orders you to produce disputed records and you continue to fail to do so, the judge can hold you in contempt of court. You could go to jail.

Refund Claim Trap

When a tax-filing date falls on a weekend or holiday, it is deferred until the next business day.

Example: April 15 was a Saturday in 1995 so tax returns weren't due until April 17.

Trap: This does not similarly defer the deadline for claiming a tax refund, even though the deadline is defined as being three years after the filing date.

Case: When a couple filed a refund claim on April 16, three years after a return filing date that had been deferred to April 17, they lost their refund.

How to Negotiate with The IRS and Win

When you have a tax problem, don't presume that the IRS holds all the cards. While there are mountains of tax rules and regulations, there's also some wiggle room built into the system. Taxpayers always have some room to maneuver; you just have to know where that room is and how far the IRS can go.

Taxpayers can represent themselves or use professionals to negotiate for them.

Caution: Always use a professional in criminal matters. Penalties may include going to jail.

Trap: By representing yourself, you run the risk of making incriminating statements.

The ins and outs of negotiating with the IRS depend upon the type of issues at hand. Among these are the following.

AUDITS AND APPEALS

In the initial stages of an audit, you are contacted by an IRS agent. The agent's job is to gather all the facts and apply these to the IRS interpretation of the law and regulations.

At this stage, you can tussle with the agent over the facts.

Example: If the agent finds that your documentation of an expense is inadequate, the expense will be disallowed because the law requires that taxpayers keep adequate records.

Reality: Few taxpayers' records meet this high standard, something that the IRS recognizes.

Negotiating strategy: Maximize deductions. Show the auditor that you have made a good faith attempt to keep adequate records, even if you cannot document every penny. The auditor can use discretion to accept other, less well-documented deductions.

Here's how: Before the audit, organize your receipts and canceled checks by type of deduction. Then attach an adding machine tape that shows how you came up with the figure claimed on your tax return.

Negotiating strategy: Make mutual concessions. Let's say that you have a very strong issue on your return, one for which you have almost all of the necessary documentation. You also have an issue that is much weaker. You might concede the weaker issue in return for the IRS dropping the stronger one entirely.

Negotiating strategy: Ask to see the auditor's supervisor. When you cannot work satisfactorily with the IRS agent assigned to your case, you have the right to see the agent's supervisor. This right is listed in **IRS Publication 1,** *Your Rights as a Taxpayer.* If the supervisor is more fair and open-minded than the agent, you may have a better chance of resolving your case at this level.

When you get nowhere with the supervisor, the next step is to take your case to the IRS Appeals Division.

Caution: You have only 30 days after the revenue agent's report is issued to file your appeal.

Negotiating strategy: Take into account the "hazards of litigation." The appeals officer is allowed to negotiate with taxpayers based on the hazards of litigation. This means the odds are that the IRS will prevail if your case goes to court.

Example: If the IRS decides that you have a 50% chance of success in court, it can settle for one-half of the disputed amount.

The Tax Regulations Just Keep Growing

Pages of tax regulations	
1954	1,288
1986	6,248
1994	7,800+

Criminal Investigations

What's the worst that can happen if you lie on your taxes? You can be convicted of criminal tax fraud and go to jail, as 1,387 people did in 1995.

Region	People investigated	People sent to prison
Northeast	1,056	469
Southeast	983	357
Midstates	840	297
Western	819	264
U.S. Total	3,698	1,387

Source: *The Internal Revenue Service Data Book 1995*

The odds of settling your case in the Appeals Division are very high. The Appeals Court settles nine out of ten cases without litigation.

Negotiating strategy: Present your case in writing to the appeals officer before your face-to-face meeting. That way, he has a chance to think about it and the meeting can be devoted to discussing the differences between your positions.

Include all relevant information. There's nothing to be gained by holding back essential information as a bargaining chip. Be professional in your presentation, not emotional. If your case moves to litigation, you may have another chance to negotiate a settlement with the IRS attorney assigned to direct the case through this stage.

Exception: Some IRS attorneys take the position that you had a chance to settle with the appeals officers and that their job is only to litigate.

COLLECTIONS
Negotiating strategy
Make early initial contact. Contact the IRS collections division as soon as you know that you will not be able to pay your tax bill. Being up front about your financial situation helps build credibility that shores up your negotiating position.

Let's say that you can't pay your taxes immediately when you file your return on April 15. You can request an extension to pay the taxes due. These are short-term deferrals of up to six months.

If that is too short, you can negotiate an installment agreement that lets you defer paying taxes for up to several years. The IRS doesn't make it too easy for taxpayers to do this, however.

How to negotiate an installment agreement
Submit **Form 9465** with your tax return or immediately afterwards. The form asks for information such as how much tax is due and how much you propose to pay monthly. Send it to the IRS service center where your return was filed.

How much should you pay monthly? While deferring the tax bill as long as possible seems to make sense, try to pay off the total as soon as you are able.

Reason: Penalties plus interest of about 9% will greatly increase the amount you owe. (This figure fluctuates from quarter to quarter.)

The IRS will ask you to complete **Form 433**, *Collections Information Statement*. That asks you to describe your monthly income and expenses, plus your assets and liabilities. The agency uses this to determine how much it can reasonably ask you to pay.

Negotiating strategy: Make installment agreements. The IRS is much more likely to accept installment agreements now than it was just a few years ago.

Reason: The agency is under severe pressure to collect as much of its accounts receivables as possible from the general public.

Another option: You can negotiate an offer in compromise. This lets you pay a reduced amount of money to the IRS in full payment of your debt.

Here's how: Submit your request using **Form 656**, which lays out information such as all of your assets and liabilities, and prospects for future income.

Odds of acceptance: The IRS received 29,087 offers in compromise in a recent year. It accepted 14,047.

How to Deduct Nondeductible Expenses

Interest on personal debt is not deductible. This includes interest on car loans, college loans, credit cards, revolving charge accounts, installment purchases, and late-paid taxes. But interest on home-equity loans of up to $100,000 is fully deductible.

Strategy: Take out a home-equity loan on your first or second home, and use the proceeds to pay off personal debt. Your interest payments will then be deductible. You will have converted nondeductible personal interest payments into deductible mortgage interest.

Likelihood of Audits by Region

Where you live could influence whether or not the IRS examines your tax return. The distribution of 1996 IRS audits indicates a disparity in audit rates by region.

Region	Percent of Region's Returns Examined
Philadelphia	0.41%
Nashville	0.45%
Baltimore	0.55%
Hartford	0.59%
Fort Lauderdale	0.69%
Manhattan	0.74%
Dallas	0.93%
Las Vegas	1.02%
San Francisco	1.42%
Los Angeles	1.57%

Recent Taxpayer Victories

These taxpayer victories over the IRS may help you save on your tax bill as well.

REFUND OF ANOTHER'S TAXES ALLOWED

The U.S. Supreme Court has ruled that a person who is compelled by practical necessity to pay someone else's tax bill can sue the IRS for a refund of the taxes later. This decision overrules the IRS's long-held position that only the person who legally owes a tax can sue for its refund.

Facts: Lori Williams' divorce settlement gave her sole ownership of the family home, but before the divorce was final, the IRS put a lien on the home to collect taxes owed by her husband. Lori couldn't sell the home with the lien on it, so she paid her husband's tax bill. Then she sold the home and sued for the refund.

Supreme Court: Lori had no alternative but to pay the tax she didn't owe, so her refund suit is allowed.
U.S. v. Williams, U.S. Supreme Court.

Free Tax Clinics

There are free tax clinics designed to help people who are in trouble with the IRS but who cannot afford a lawyer, or who have found that hiring one would cost more than the disputed tax. At least 16 law schools sponsor free clinics. Some help only the poor, but others accept people of any income level who have tax bills that do not justify paying legal fees.

In addition, two accounting-school clinics (operating with IRS sanction) counsel and represent taxpayers headed for audits. The clinics are at the University of North Texas in Denton and the University of South Florida in Tampa. Call your local university to see if it provides these services.

FAMILY DEBT IS DEDUCTIBLE

A father advanced $35,000 to his daughter to help her open a business. When the business failed and she couldn't repay the loan, the father claimed a bad-debt deduction. The IRS noticed that the loan's terms had never been written out or documented. Therefore, it concluded that the money really was a gift, not a loan, and denied the deduction.

Tax Court: The deduction was allowed. Both parties involved had intended the arrangement to be treated as a loan. The father had made several similar loans to other family members, all of which had been repaid on time. This clearly indicated that family members recognized their undocumented loans as being genuine.

Loy E. Bowman, TC Memo 1995-259.

IRS MUST ASSIST INFORMATION REQUEST

A couple fighting a tax dispute filed a Freedom of Information Act request with the IRS demanding that it produce voluminous data on all similar tax cases dating back to 1978. The IRS refused, saying that the request was too broad and meeting it would be "prohibitively expensive." The couple then modified the request by asking the IRS to start with only the "most current" materials. The IRS still refused.

Court of Appeals: The IRS cannot refuse to comply with a Freedom of Information Act request simply because it is burdensome. Instead, the IRS must cooperate with the couple to draw up a manageable request that it can meet.

Michael Ruotolo, CA-2, No. 94-6236.

IRS PAYS, AND PAYS AGAIN

Carol Davis defeated the IRS in court, and the IRS was ordered to pay the legal fees she had incurred during the dispute. Then the IRS appealed the fee award.

Decision: The award was upheld, and the IRS had to pay the legal fees Carol incurred during the appeal as well.

Carol Davis, D. Colo., No. 93-C-1173.

IRS MUST EXPLAIN PENALTIES

The IRS added penalties to Robert Fisher's tax bill for taking improper deductions. He claimed the penalties should be waived because he had taken the deductions on the advice of competent tax counsel. But both the IRS and Tax Court sustained the penalties without explanation.

Court of Appeals: The IRS "cannot make a taxpayer haul it into court to discover the rationale for its decision." Rather, it must explain itself. The Tax Court was at fault, too, because it couldn't have reviewed an explanation the IRS had never given.

Robert D. Fisher, CA-10, No. 93-9029.

IRS SHOULD HAVE CALLED THE LAWYER

Before leaving on a trip, a couple informed the IRS that they wouldn't be reachable and then hired a lawyer to deal with the IRS for them. They failed, however, to give the lawyer a power of attorney for tax matters.

The IRS then sent a tax deficiency notice to the couple's home. They didn't receive it until after the deadline for responding had passed, but the IRS said the notice was valid because the couple hadn't properly authorized the lawyer to represent them and had left no other forwarding address.

Court of Appeals: The IRS knew the couple had left home and had hired the lawyer. It should have simply asked the lawyer to get the power of attorney. The notice was deemed invalid.

Anthony Teong-Chan Gaw, DC Cir., No. 93-1619.

RUSHED WIFE IS INNOCENT

Sallyanne Cook had a graduate degree and worked a full-time job. The IRS tried to hold her liable for taxes and penalties on a fraudulent joint return that her husband had prepared and she had signed, arguing she was too sophisticated in financial affairs to escape liability as an "innocent spouse."

Sallyanne's defense: Her husband had their return prepared by a CPA without consulting her and had handed it to her to sign on the morning of the day it was due as she was leaving the house for work. She had asked some questions about it in the few moments before she left and had been assured that everything was proper before she signed it.

Tax Court: Sallyanne had met her obligation to make "reasonable inquiries" in the little time she had, so she was an innocent spouse and wasn't liable for the taxes.

Cecil H. Cook III, TC Memo 1995-247.

$500,000 CHARITABLE DEDUCTION ALLOWED

A person who owned a tract of land created a conservation easement that limited the way the land could be developed and claimed a $500,000 charity deduction for the easement. The IRS argued that he never intended to develop the land. The IRS also said that the land's market value hadn't been reduced by the easement, so no deduction should be allowed.

Court: Before-and-after valuation was insufficient. The easement sharply limited the ability to earn income from the land through development and exploitation of hunting and fishing rights. A $500,000 valuation for the easement was reasonable, and a corresponding deduction allowed.

Charles R. Schwab, TC Memo 1994-232.

RIGHT TO SILENCE

Your Fifth Amendment right not to give evidence against yourself applies if you think you are the target of an IRS criminal investigation, even if no charges have been made against you.

Case: Eugene J. Peters refused to give his records to the IRS after it brought criminal charges against persons with whom he'd had dealings. He had seen IRS agents peering into his house through his living room window, and IRS agents had warned him he "had better" have his tax papers in order.

Court: Peters had reasonable grounds to fear that the IRS was preparing a criminal case against him, therefore he did not have to produce his records.

Eugene J. Peters, C.D. Calif., No. CV94-0622 JGD.

EXPERT ADVICE SAVES PENALTY

A person who improperly took large deductions escaped having penalties added to his tax bill by showing that he had relied on the advice of a tax lawyer and an accountant who had reviewed the deductions and concluded they were proper. The individual had filed his return in good faith, so penalties would not be added.

George S. Mauerman, CA-10, No. 93-9009.

LATE-FILING PENALTIES

Penalties were lifted when a taxpayer showed that she had given her records to a professional return preparer on time and he had misplaced them (putting them in the trunk of a car that his grandson drove to California).

Court: This was a reasonable excuse for not filing until the preparer recovered the records.

Elizabeth A. Gravett, TC Memo 1994-156.

BANK RECORDS ARE CONFIDENTIAL

If a bank releases your financial records to the IRS without receiving a subpoena first, you can sue the bank for damages plus the legal fees and expenses incurred in bringing your suit.

Case: A bank gave a couple's financial records to the IRS in response to an IRS agent's informal request. The couple sued the bank and recovered more than $83,000 in damages and expenses.

Peggy J. Neece, CA-10, No. 93-5127.

UNSIGNED JOINT RETURN IS VALID

The IRS rejected a couple's joint return because the husband signed his wife's name on it instead of having her sign it herself. The IRS then tried to collect tax at higher separate-return tax rates.

Court: The husband had signed his wife's name to the return with her permission, since she had been out of town tending a sick relative when the return was prepared. Because the wife had intended to file a joint return, the return was valid even though she hadn't signed it.

Frank G. Boyle, TC Memo 1994-294.

"FINAL" ISN'T FINAL

A new refund request can be made even after reaching a "final" settlement of a year's disputed tax bill with the IRS, provided the new claim is unrelated to the prior dispute and settlement agreement. Thus, a taxpayer could file a new refund claim even after signing a final settlement agreement that specifically stated the taxpayer would file "no claim or refund, for the year" in the future.

Tyco Laboratories, Inc., D. N.H., No. 93-362-M.

EXTENSION SAVED

An individual filed an extension for his tax return, estimating that he owed no more taxes for the year and making no payment with it. When it turned out that he still owed more than $90,000 in taxes, the IRS revoked the extension and imposed late-filing penalties.

Court: The individual's accountant had underestimated the tax still due because full records for the year weren't yet available, which was why the extension had been requested. The extension had been filed in good faith, so it was valid.

Paul E. Harper, E. D. Okla., No. CIV-94-073-S.

UNFAIR TACTIC

Vince S. Han refused to give the IRS extra time to audit his return, so it quickly assessed taxes and refused his request to have his case heard by the IRS Appeals Division, forcing him to go to Tax Court. There he won a complete victory on the merits of his case and asked the Court to make the IRS pay his legal fees. The IRS said it didn't have to pay because Han hadn't "exhausted his remedies" before going to Tax Court. It said that if he had given the IRS the extra time it had requested, he could have gone to Appeals.

Court: The law does not require a taxpayer to extend the statute of limitations when the IRS can't build a case within three years. The IRS had forced a meritless case into Court and had to pay the resulting costs.

Vince S. Han, TC Memo 1993-386.

NO RECEIPT, NO CASE

The IRS sent a deficiency notice to Clayton J. Powell's old address after he had moved. It said the notice was valid even though he never got it because he hadn't told the IRS of his move.

Problem: The IRS couldn't find the certified mail return receipt showing that the notice was undeliverable.

Court: If the IRS ever had the receipt, it would have been informed that Powell had moved and been required to try to find him, which it made no attempt to do. And if the IRS never had the receipt, it had no proof that the notice had been delivered. Either way, the notice was invalid.

Clayton J. Powell, CA-4, No. 89-1489.

Sloppiness Isn't Fraud

A taxpayer delivered "a sack" of records to his accountant each year when it was time to prepare his tax return, and his taxes were regularly underpaid due to the poor paperwork. The IRS treated the consistent underreporting as fraud and assessed taxes and penalties going back several years.

Tax Court: Negligence isn't fraud. The individual had demonstrated no organized plan to evade taxes. The IRS could not assess back taxes for years protected by the statute of limitations.

Gong Yok Tsun Chin, TC Memo 1994-54.

SOURCES

Sources are listed in the order in which their contributions appear. A source may have contributed part or all of an article, or a series of articles.

Rebecca S. Whitmore,
Price Waterhouse, LLP

Sylvia Pozarnsky,
Ernst & Young, LLP

Kerry M. Kerstetter, CPA,
Editor of *The Kerstetter Letter*

Nadine Gordon Lee,
Ernst & Young, LLP

Barry Salzberg,
Deloitte & Touche, LLP

Sylvia Pozarnsky,
Ernst & Young, LLP

Barry Salzberg,
Deloitte & Touche, LLP

Sylvia Pozarnsky,
Ernst & Young, LLP

Martin M. Shenkman, Esq.,
author of *The Complete Book of Trusts*

Nadine Gordon Lee,
Ernst & Young, LLP

Barry Salzberg,
Deloitte & Touche, LLP

Sylvia Pozarnsky,
Ernst & Young, LLP

Randy Bruce Blaustein,
Blaustein, Greenberg & Co.

Robert A. Pedersen,
KPMG Peat Marwick

James E. Pickett,
Coopers & Lybrand, LLP

Edward Mendlowitz,
Mendlowitz Weitsen, CPAs

Pamela D. Johnson,
TC Memo 1995-412

Randy Bruce Blaustein,
Blaustein, Greenberg & Co.

Nadine Gordon Lee,
Ernst & Young, LLP

Anthony Ogorek,
Investment adviser

Nadine Gordon Lee,
Ernst & Young, LLP

Alan A. Nadel,
Arthur Andersen, LLP

Edward Mendlowitz,
Mendlowitz Weitsen, CPAs

Kerry M. Kerstetter, CPA,
Editor of *The Kerstetter Letter*

Laurence I. Foster,
KPMG Peat Marwick

Edward Mendlowitz,
Mendlowitz Weitsen, CPAs

Randy Bruce Blaustein,
Blaustein, Greenberg & Co.

Robert Runde, author of
The Common Sense Guide to Estate Planning

Marc Britton and Larry B. Scheinfeld, KPMG Peat Marwick, LLP

Carole Gould, author of *The New York Times Guide to Mutual Funds*

James Glass, Esq.

Bob Carlson, author of *Bob Carlson's Retirement Watch*

Lisa N. Collins
Harding, Shymanski & Co., PC

Henry Willen Sanchez, ASA,
Willen Sanchez Associates Inc.

Martin Nissenbaum,
Ernst & Young, LLP

Laurence I. Foster,
KPMG Peat Marwick

Paul Kamke, CPA

Randy Bruce Blaustein,
Blaustein, Greenberg & Co.

Paul B. Ledford, S.D. Ind.,
No. IP 90-2169-C.

Eric Tyson, MBA, author of
Taxes for Dummies

Frederick W. Daily, author of
Stand Up to the IRS: How to Handle Audits, Tax Bills and Tax Court

James Smith,
Bahamas Central Bank

Julian Block, author of *It's Not What You Make—It's What You Keep*

Martin E. Pollner, Loeb & Loeb

Pete Medina, Ernst & Young, LLP

Howard Berman,
Arthur Andersen, LLP

Lisa N. Collins
Harding, Shymanski & Co., PC

Banking & Credit

Keep Your Money Safer

When to Open a New Bank Account

Break up your bank-held savings accounts, including retirement accounts, when balances exceed $100,000. The Federal Deposit Insurance Corporation (FDIC) will insure only up to $100,000 per ownership category (eg. single or joint accounts) in any one institution. The limit applies per bank, not per account, so move amounts in excess of $100,000 to another institution.

Exception: Retirement accounts such as IRAs and Keoghs are insured separately from all other accounts for up to $100,000 per bank. For more information, contact Consumer Affairs, FDIC, 550 17th St. N.W., Washington, D.C. 20429, 800-934-3342.

How a Husband, Wife and Two Children Can Have FDIC-Insured Accounts Totaling $1,400,000

Individual Accounts:

Husband	$100,000
Wife	$100,000
Child Number One	$100,000
Child Number Two	$100,000

Joint Accounts:

Husband and Wife	$100,000
Husband and Child Number One	$100,000
Wife and Child Number Two	$100,000
Child Number One and Child Number Two	$100,000

Revocable Trust Accounts:

Husband as Trustee for Wife	$100,000
Husband as Trustee for Child Number One	$100,000
Husband as Trustee for Child Number Two	$100,000
Wife as Trustee for Husband	$100,000
Wife as Trustee for Child Number One	$100,000
Wife as Trustee for Child Number Two	$100,000
	$1,400,000

The same grouping of insured accounts can be arranged for a grandfather, grandmother and two grandchildren.

Source: Federal Deposit Insurance Corporation

The Secrets to Cheaper Checking Accounts

Service charges at financial institutions, especially at large banks and those which have been taken over, have risen as much as 400% over the last ten years. Checking accounts have become particularly expensive for consumers.

If you have a checking account at a big bank, making some phone calls to comparison shop can save you $100 or more, year after year. Here are some great alternatives to expensive checking accounts.

1. CREDIT UNIONS

Credit unions charge much lower service fees on their share-draft (checking) accounts. They also have much lower balance requirements (sometimes as low as $250), charge less for checks and overdrafts, and have higher interest rates on NOW accounts.

More than 60 million Americans belong to credit unions, and many more are eligible to join. To find out which credit unions might accept you as a member, call 800-358-5710.

2. SAVINGS & LOANS

S&Ls may not offer quite as good a deal as credit unions, but they're usually much cheaper than large banks. The huge banks really don't care about keeping you as a customer. But a small, local S&L (or very small bank) does, and may even custom design an account for your needs—if you ask.

Negotiate: It's not as difficult as most people think to negotiate with a financial institution. If you can, use your past history as a good bank customer as leverage. When possible, link your request for special consideration to a pending transaction. Say, "I'm about to deposit $3,000. I assume that entitles me to free checking."

Note: The smaller the institution, the easier it

will be to negotiate because your business is needed.

Important: To avoid an overdraft fee, ask the S&L or bank to alert you whenever you're about to be overdrawn. Also, ask that you be allowed to make a same-day deposit to square the account. Keep asking until you find a sympathetic bank officer. If that doesn't work, speak to the vice president of operations at your bank.

3. DIFFERENT BANK ACCOUNTS

Some big banks offer cheaper accounts for senior citizens, students and people with disabilities, but they usually don't advertise them. You have to ask to get the deal. Credit unions and S&Ls may also offer special accounts. Often there are also special deals like paying only 10¢ or 15¢ per check if you write no more than five checks per month.

4. STOCKBROKERS' CASH-MANAGEMENT ACCOUNTS

You get free checking for an annual fee of $100 or $125. Some deep-discount brokers may charge lower fees. If you're paying high monthly fees now, this could be a good deal. Of course, it's only sensible if you find the convenience of the account's other features to be a major benefit. Otherwise, you can pay lower overall fees somewhere else.

5. MONEY-MARKET ACCOUNTS & MUTUAL FUNDS

These are great alternatives for people who write only a few large checks each month. In many cases, there may be a limit on the number of checks per month, or a minimum of $250 to $500 per check, or both.

Most people think it's impossible to negotiate with a financial institution. It's not.

It's your money, and you're lending it to the bank. The bank makes a profit from your money. You're entitled to a good deal.

6. CHECKS FROM PRIVATE COMPANIES

You can save about 50% by ordering checks directly from private companies. These checks meet all national standards. Call Checks in the Mail (800-733-4443) or Current (800-533-3973) for more information.

How to Get Your Bank to Reduce Fees

Nearly every fee charged by your bank is negotiable. It's also easy to request better terms.

KEY STEPS

Step 1: Before you call your bank, find out what other banks charge. Competition among banks throughout the country is intensifying. As an increasing number of banks aggressively seek new customers, yours is more likely to go out of its way to hold onto you, especially if you have consistently paid your bank bills on time.

Step 2: Simply tell the bank representative what you want. Many people are afraid to negotiate, or they're afraid of being rejected. In most cases, however, there's actually very little hard-core negotiating involved. You're usually talking to someone who fields hundreds of similar requests each week. Banks usually provide their representatives with guidelines on the deals they can make.

Important: Point out your loyalty by mentioning how long you've been a customer and how many accounts you have at the bank. Also talk about loans you've paid off.

Step 3: If you're dissatisfied with the bank's first offer, politely hint that you are considering taking your business elsewhere. In some cases, banks resist your initial request in order to determine how serious you are about leaving—or whether your knowledge of its competitors is genuine. Now is the time to refer to all the bank offers you have been receiving in the mail or have spotted in ads.

Prevent Checking Account Fraud

Never give your account number—or the numbers printed along the bottom of your checks—to anybody, including anyone claiming to work for your bank. Give account numbers only to businesses you know are reputable. Report lost or stolen checks immediately. Properly store or destroy canceled checks and keep new ones in a secure place.

TIP How to Lower Your Checking Fees

Buy your bank's stock. Many people have trouble meeting the minimum balance for free checking—often between $1,000 and $6,000. However, you may be able to convince the bank to give you special treatment if you ask to have your investment in the bank's stock included.

Strategy: Call the manager of your branch first, then corporate headquarters if you don't get satisfaction.

Important: Avoid toll-free numbers, where operators are not authorized to make exceptions.

OTHER STRATEGIES

● Consider opening an additional savings account or investing in a CD. Some banks will negotiate only with customers who already have established different types of accounts with the institution. The promise of more business may persuade the representative to give you a better deal. Point out that a better rate will encourage you to do more business with the bank, which will ultimately mean higher profits for the institution.

● Ask about direct payment options. Many lenders will lower car loan rates by as much as one percentage point if you agree to have payments automatically removed each month from one of your accounts. Other banks give better savings rates if you have your paycheck directly deposited.

● Ask to have loan fees waived. Whether the transaction is a mortgage or a home equity loan, the bank is going to make a lot of money from your business. As a result, it can afford to let several hundred dollars' worth of fees slide—if it thinks you'll go elsewhere for the mortgage.

Example: When you refinance a mortgage, consider doing the deal with your existing bank, instead of with another lender. You may get discounts on the title search, the bank's attorney fees, the application fee and the appraisal fee.

● Repeat your request if you're turned down. In some cases, the person with whom you're speaking may deny your request because he does not appreciate your value to the bank. Just go over the person's head. Don't be embarrassed about being persistent. It's your money, and you're lending it to the bank.

How to Get a Better Deal: Just Ask

When persons posing as Certificate of Deposit shoppers went to 25 banks and asked if they could get rates above posted rates, 11 of the banks said "yes." The average extra yield obtained was just over half a point. Results were even better when the shoppers approached credit card issuers. Of 38 banks called, 84% waived their annual fee, lowered their interest rate or did both when asked if a better deal could be had.

A Better Fee System

Avoid a bank checking account that charges a monthly fee when your account drops below a certain limit for one day. Instead, find an account for which monthly fees are determined by the average daily balance.

Don't Be Outsmarted By Your Bank

Have you ever noticed that people will go out of their way to get an extra eighth of one percent on a CD, and then pay their banks much more than that in fees they have been told are unavoidable?

Reality: Banks don't want you to know their fees and interest rates are negotiable. Often all you have to do is ask.

Strategy: Learn the chain of command at your bank. If you encounter a bank employee who won't negotiate fees, ask to speak with his or her boss. Most senior personnel would prefer you to be happy with the bank, especially if you are a good customer.

Here is how to minimize your ATM fees, your overdraft charges and the penalties for falling below the bank's minimum balance requirements.

1. USE A SMALL BANK

Your bank should be one of the smallest in your area. A big bank won't go the extra mile for you because it doesn't feel it needs your business. A small bank will be flexible because it needs satisfied customers in order to attract new customers and grow.

2. DON'T USE ATMs

Not only can they be costly, they prevent you from establishing important personal relationships with bank officers. Those cordial relationships can help you get better rates and terms on future bank loans and services.

3. AVOID MINIMUM BALANCE CHARGES

Many banks will waive minimum balance requirements if you insist.

4. PLAN BEFORE YOU BORROW

Go into the bank and update your personal financial statement every six months or so, even if you don't need a loan. Strike up conversations with the people who help you.

Reason: You want at least one teller, one loan officer and one bookkeeper to know your face. Then, if you need a loan based only on collateral, you're much more likely to get it if the bank's employees are familiar with you—and your credit history.

HOW BANKS CAN DETERMINE INTEREST

Assume a 5% interest rate	June 1 Start with	June 10 Withdraw	June 30 End with
Day-of-deposit: All of the money earns interest every day it's in the account.	$3,000	$1,000	$2,000.00 + $9.58 interest
Average daily balance: You earn interest on the average balance for the period.	$3,000	$1,000	$2,000.00 + $9.58 interest
Lowest balance: You earn interest only on the smallest balance of the entire period.	$3,000	$1,000	$2,000.00 + $8.33 interest

5. REFUSE UNNECESSARY PRODUCTS

Banks are intimidating to average consumers, who are afraid to question what is put in front of them.

Example: Most people are so happy to get a car loan, they're afraid to refuse the hugely overpriced credit life and disability insurance the bank often adds to the loan. Even worse—they don't realize that because the insurance cost has been added to the loan, the premium is subject to a finance charge.

Watch Out for Sneaky Fees

Paying More for Checking

Bank fees significantly outpaced inflation from April 1993 to April 1995.

Percent Increase

22%
Regular checking accounts

14%
Interest-bearing checking accounts

5.5%
Inflation

Source: U.S. Public Interest Group

Bank fees are rising on ATMs and checking accounts, for a wider range of services and for account infractions.

Example: Some banks now charge customers up to $18 a year for ATM cards, as well as fees for accounts that slip below a set amount even for just one day.

Self-defense: Request your bank's fee list. Limit using your ATM card to no more than once a week.

Benefit: You'll live by your budget.

Safe-Deposit Boxes Aren't So Safe

They are not insured by the Federal Deposit Insurance Corp. The FDIC insures only money deposited in bank accounts. Your homeowner's insurance, however, may cover safe-deposit box contents if it has an off-premise clause. But even policies with such a clause may not cover jewelry and collectibles.

Solution: Ask about adding a rider to your policy to cover such irreplaceable items.

Important: Always insure valuables for their replacement cost—not the purchase price.

When Your Bank Changes Hands

If your bank changes hands, be sure to find out the new owner's policies. Banks pay different interest rates, provide services such as checking accounts at different costs, have different fees, such as overdraft charges, and have different policies, such as check-hold periods. If you do not like the policies of the new bank, look elsewhere.

What Not to Keep in Your Safe-Deposit Box

Do not keep cash, savings bonds or securities in safe-deposit boxes. Theft is on the rise as robbers distract guards, make wax impressions of master keys and return with copies to loot boxes. Because it's impossible to prove that currency was in the box, your loss may not be covered by the bank.

Solution: Keep cash in a fireproof home safe. Also keep savings bonds and securities at home—but keep copies at the bank for proof of ownership.

Debit Card Users Alert

WATCH OUT FOR PHONY GUARDS

Crooks have been known to pose as bank guards to steal customers' ATM Personal Identification Numbers (PINs) and clean out their accounts.

Here's how: The crook buys a jacket that looks like the ones worn by security guards, attaches a phony badge and posts an out-of-order sign on the ATM. When a customer comes, the phony guard explains that the machine is temporarily out of order, but that the bank is giving customers a small amount of cash manually. He looks at the ATM card, gets the account number and PIN, gives the customer $100 in cash and then cleans out the account when the victim leaves.

Self-defense: Never give your PIN to anyone.

STOLEN ATM CARD DANGER

Stolen bank ATM cards can lead to greater liability than stolen credit cards.

Difference: Liability for unauthorized charges on a credit card is limited to $50. But the same limit applies to ATM cards only if the loss of a card is reported within two days. After that, liability rises to $500. And if you don't report the loss of the card within 60 days after your next bank statement is mailed to you, liability may become unlimited.

Important: Always know where your ATM card is and examine every bank statement to be sure all charges are proper.

ATM CREDIT REPORT PROBLEM
If your card is stolen or lost and money is removed from your account, you're likely to bounce some checks before straightening things out. The bounced checks may show up as late payments on your credit reports, causing problems when you apply for a loan.

Note: Debit cards do not help build a credit record or fix a bad one because credit reports contain information on borrowing, not on bank account activity.

Slash Your Credit Card Costs

This year has been a good year for credit card holders. Issuers continue to fill mailboxes with some very good offers. Here's how to find the best credit card for you.

FIND OUT WHAT YOU ARE PAYING
If you took out a credit card with a low introductory rate during the past year or so, the rate you are paying now is most likely much higher.

Teaser rates usually go up after six months to a year, and the jump can be dramatic—from 6.9% to 18.9%, for example. Your current rate must be listed on your credit card statement.

Check to make sure the interest rate is not in the high double digits. If it is, switch to a card with a lower rate, or request a lower rate from that same issuer. You probably won't get the introductory rate again, but you should get one that's competitive.

DEMAND A BETTER DEAL
Five years ago, it was unheard-of for a credit card company to give a lower rate to a customer who asked for one. Now it's commonplace. If you pay your bills on time, an issuer may lower your rate by 2% to 5% at your insistence.

Here's how: Call the customer service department and politely tell the representative you are going to close your account because of the high interest rate. Then say you would consider keeping it if the issuer were to give you a lower rate. If the first person you speak with is not helpful, ask to speak to a supervisor. Don't be intimidated. The credit card business is extremely competitive, and most issuers are struggling to keep customers.

OPEN YOUR MAIL
Save all the credit card offers you receive over several months. Then go through them carefully. While most aren't worth the paper on which they're printed, there are some gems, especially for short-term loans.

Example: One bank offered a Visa Gold card with a six-month introductory rate of 8.9% for balance

If your current credit card company won't give you a competitive rate, look for a better deal.

transfers, no annual fee and no fee for balance transfers. And the transfers were treated as purchases, not cash advances, so they carried a 25-day grace period. That's a better rate than any bank or credit union in the area offered for an unsecured loan.

Caution: If you use an introductory rate to pay off balances on higher-rate credit cards, keep in mind that you'll have to either pay off the balance within six months, switch to another card at that time or pay a hefty rate after the introductory period ends. If

How Credit Cards Compare

Five low-rate national credit card issuers as of March, 1997

Institution	Interest Rate	Annual Fee	Grace Days
Bank One, Columbus, NA Columbus, OH 800-436-7920	16.3%V*	None	25
Capital One Richmond, VA 800-952-3388	4.9%F*	$29	25
Crestar Bank Richmond, VA 800-368-7700	5.9%F*	None	25
FCC National Bank Wilmington, DE 800-766-4623	16.15%V*	None	20-25
Federal Savings Bank Little Rock, AR 800-374-5600	9.35%V*	$33	25

F=Fixed rate, V=Variable rate

*Interest rate at time of printing. Many rates go up after six or 12 months.

you're not willing to put the time into finding a new card, you're better off choosing a card that has a slightly higher, but more stable rate.

CONSOLIDATE

The average cardholder carries balances on six or more credit cards. Consolidating several high-rate balances into a low-rate card can save $200 or more in interest charges.

Example: If you have a $2,500 balance on a MasterCard that charges 18% and you also have a Visa card with a 14% interest rate, transfer the balance from your higher-rate card to the lower-rate one and you'll save $103 in interest the first year.

Here's how: Call the credit card company to which you want to transfer your balances (in this case, the VISA issuer) and ask for instructions. Some issuers will do it for you. You fill out an authorization form, and the issuer will pay off the balance you specify on another card.

Others will send you convenience checks, which look just like personal checks. You simply write a check to pay off another credit card. The amount of the check or balance transfer will appear on your next statement, often as a cash advance.

Caution: Be sure the interest rate for transferred balances isn't higher than the advertised rate. Also watch for steep cash-advance fees for balance transfers—these can be as much as 2% of the amount you transfer. Many issuers will waive the fees if you insist. Also, look for cards that offer interest-free 30-day grace periods on balances transferred over.

RACK UP THE FREEBIES

The frequent-flier cards that are offered by almost all major airlines typically give cardholders one frequent-flier mile for every dollar charged on the card. Rebate cards usually earn rebates toward products from the sponsoring company.

Caution: These cards are often expensive, with high annual fees and interest rates. In most cases, you'll have to charge thousands of dollars each month to earn anything significant, and you must pay your bill in full or you'll overpay in finance charges.

Strategy: If you do get a rebate or frequent-flier card, and you're disciplined enough to pay the bill in full each month, use the card everywhere it's accepted. This includes less traditional places, such as grocery stores, post offices, movie theaters and even when paying utility bills. These small purchases will help you rack up miles or rebates more quickly.

Example: The Continental Airlines Marine Midland Gold MasterCard (800-446-5336) gives one frequent-flier mile on Continental Airlines for every dollar you charge. If you use the card for everything and pay the bill in full each month, in just over one year you will have earned enough miles to get a free round-trip domestic ticket, which justifies the $75 annual fee you are paying. If, like most consumers, you only charged $200 a month on the card, it would take about eight years to earn a free ticket. And if you carried a balance, the 18.4% interest rate (prime rate plus 9.9%) would easily wipe out the benefits of any miles you earned.

PAY MORE TO SAVE MORE

While credit cards with no annual fees are common these days, don't completely rule out the idea of paying an annual fee if you carry a balance and the fee buys you a really low rate.

Example: Wachovia Bank (800-842-3262) offers the Prime for Life program, where your interest rate will always equal the prime rate. The annual fee is steep—$88—but if you transfer a large balance, you'll offset the fee with the interest savings. Transferring a $4,000 balance from a card charging 17%, for example, will save you $322.27 in finance charges the first year (using a prime rate of 9%).

READ THE FINE PRINT

Before you transfer a balance, check the new card's fine print. Card issuers know that most people don't sift through the fine print on their credit card offers.

Scan the Disclosure Box

Every card solicitation must carry a box that spells out the main cost factors: interest rates and grace periods. Don't stop there, though. Read the fine print below the box, where you'll often find more details about the interest rate, grace period and fees for balance transfers or cash advances.

APPLY FOR ONE CARD ONLY

Ensure you'll qualify for cards you want in the future by applying for only one new card at a time now.

Problem: Some people use a shotgun approach, applying for many cards at once. They use this strategy hoping that they'll be approved by at least one of the companies.

Trap: Future lenders and credit card companies may deny you credit when they see such activity in your credit reports. The shotgun strategy is a red flag that signals a high probability of financial irresponsibility. It doesn't matter whether or not such irresponsibility applies in your case.

NOTIFY THE CREDIT BUREAUS

If you decide to cancel your old card, ask the new card issuer to report to all three credit bureaus that you have closed your old account and opened the new one. Otherwise, your credit report will continue to list all the old accounts, including their maximum credit lines. This could lead a lender to reject a credit or mortgage application because you have too much

credit available—even if you never use it.

Order your credit reports approximately six weeks later to be sure that the new card issuer has made good on its promise.

Credit bureaus:
- Equifax: 800-685-1111
- TRW: 800-687-7654
- TransUnion: 316-636-6100

Protect Yourself from Credit Cards

The growing number of new credit, charge and debit cards and the dizzying array of special offers from the companies that issue them are leaving many people confused about how to manage their wallets.

Cards are much more convenient to use than cash and checks—and now they promote a greater variety of perks and discounts that encourage people to apply for more accounts than they really need.

Fact: The average person owns eight to ten cards and carries balances on most of them, even though many of the basic services that these cards provide overlap.

The result is widespread uncertainty over which types of cards best suit an individual's needs, and how to best use the ones the individual already owns.

CREDIT CARDS

More than 6,000 different financial institutions issue bank cards such as MasterCard and Visa. Discover, which is issued by Greenwood Trust Co., is also a bank card. Retail cards are issued by stores.

Problem: More than two-thirds of Americans use their credit cards as personal loans, carrying balances from month to month and making hefty interest payments. Many people who carry balances do not realize that they are almost always charged interest on all new purchases immediately. Therefore, you could be paying interest on purchases you intend to pay off completely at the end of the month, such as groceries, gasoline and meals.

Strategy: You only need two credit cards. Use one with a low interest rate, 12% or less, for purchases you want to pay for over time. Use a second bank credit card—one that charges no annual fee and has a grace period during which time you are not

Look Out!

Carrying a large balance on your credit card is like accepting a 20% interest rate on a personal loan. The monthly payments are small, but you pay much more in the long run.

charged interest on new purchases—for items that you plan to pay for in full each month.

CHARGE CARDS

American Express, Diner's Club and most gasoline cards require you to pay the bill in full each month. These cards are useful for those who want the convenience of plastic but don't want to run up large debts.

Charge cards, however, are not accepted in as many locations worldwide as credit cards.

DEBIT CARDS

With a debit card, the price of your purchase is deducted from your checking or savings account either immediately or within a few days, depending on the type of card you own.

Some ATM cards (which are a type of debit card) now can be used to make purchases at gas stations and retail stores.

MasterCard and Visa both offer debit cards through banks, credit unions and other financial institutions. They look similar to credit cards and can be used anywhere that credit cards like MasterCard or Visa are accepted.

Some people prefer to use debit cards because they don't want to carry around a lot of cash or spend more money than they have in their checking accounts.

Both MasterCard and Visa offer on-line debit cards that deduct money from checking accounts immediately. MasterCard's is called Maestro and Visa's is called Interlink. Both also offer off-line programs which can take a few days to make the deductions. MasterCard's is called MasterMoney and Visa's is Visa Check Card. All of these debit cards are available from many local banks.

Drawback I: Fees for debit cards can be costly. Your bank may charge an annual fee of $12 or up to $1.50 every time you make a purchase with a debit card. In addition, merchants who accept the card

may charge transaction fees from 50¢ to $1.50.

Drawback II: Debit cards are not covered by the same consumer protection laws as credit cards. If you pay for something with a debit card and there's a problem with the merchandise, you can't refuse to pay the charge under the Fair Credit Billing Act. That law only covers credit and charge cards. And since the money has already been deducted from your account, it can be more difficult to get a refund.

Solution: Unless you hate paying bills, use a credit or charge card instead of a debit card and pay the bill in full.

SECURED CREDIT CARDS

For anyone who can't qualify for a credit card because of bankruptcy or previous credit problems, or because they haven't established credit, a secured credit card could be the answer.

Here's how: You deposit between $250 and $400 in a savings account as a security deposit. In return, you get a MasterCard or Visa with a credit line that is equal to your deposit. The secured card looks and works just like a conventional credit card. No one will know it's not except you and the bank.

Strategy: Avoid banks that charge high up-front fees. Also, check out the program's reputation in advance with the Better Business Bureau to make sure there haven't been many complaints.

Make sure that your payments will be reported on a regular basis to all three major credit bureaus since one of the purposes of the card is to help you rebuild your credit rating.

Banks Offering Secured Credit Cards
as of March, 1997

American Pacific Bank
Aumsville, OR, 800-610-1201
Deposit: $400-$15,000
Interest Rate: 17.4%, F
Keeps your secured status confidential.

Bank of America
Phoenix, AZ, 800-243-7762
Deposit: $500-$5,000
Interest Rate: 19.15%, V
Reports your secured status to credit bureaus.

First Consumers National Bank
Beaverton, OR, 800-876-3262
Deposit: $100+
Interest Rate: 19.8%, F
Keeps your secured status confidential.

People's Bank
Bridgeport, CT, 800-262-4442
Deposit: $500-$1500
Interest Rate: 16.9%, F
Reports your secured status to credit bureaus.

Prudential Bank
Atlanta, GA, 800-774-4944
Deposit: $7,000-$70,000
Interest Rate: 10.25%, V
Reports your secured status to credit bureaus.

F=fixed rate, V=variable rate

Source: Bankcard Holders of America

REBATE CARDS

These cards are offered by a variety of companies, from auto makers to computer software firms. They provide cash rebates, discounts on goods and services or free merchandise. In most cases, the amount of the rebate is tied to how much you charge on the card each year.

Drawbacks: If you're like most people and charge less than $200 a month, you won't earn much of a rebate. In addition, these cards charge higher interest rates than other bank cards, making them an expensive choice for cardholders who carry balances. They are only worthwhile if you charge several thousand dollars each month and pay the bill in full each month.

Example: The Citibank Ford Visa and Citibank Ford MasterCard offer 5% rebates on every purchase, up to $700 per year. The rebates can be used toward the purchase or lease of a new Ford car or truck. Interest rates on these cards vary but there is usually no annual fee. If you charged an average of $200 per month, your rebate in one year would be only $120. To earn the maximum annual rebate of $700, you would have to charge $14,000 in one year.

AFFINITY CARDS

Many charities, professional organizations and membership organizations offer members credit cards stamped with their logos. The sponsoring organization usually receives a donation of part or all of the first year's annual fee, plus a percentage of purchases made on the card. One-half of 1% is common.

Strategy: Accept an affinity card only if the interest rate, annual fee and other terms are competitive with regular bank cards.

FREQUENT-FLIER CARDS

Most airlines are tied into credit card programs that allow you to earn frequent-flier miles. In general, you earn one frequent-flier mile for every dollar charged on the credit card.

Those who charge at least $2,000 a month can usually earn a free round-trip domestic ticket in a year. If you're a big spender and can pay the bill in full each month, one of these cards could pay for next year's vacation.

Trap: Annual fees on these cards are usually expensive. If you carry a balance, any free ticket you earn could wind up costing you more in extra interest charges than the actual price of the ticket.

Celebrity Card Scam

Beware of the new credit cards that have images of celebrities, celebrity artwork or stadiums. These cards are designed to attract fans who may overlook their drawbacks.

Strategy: Before applying, call the issuer and ask about the interest rate after the introductory period expires, whether there are restrictions and if there are fees for not using the card frequently enough.

Example: United Airlines Mileage Plus Visa, issued by FCC National Bank in Wilmington, DE, earns one frequent-flier mile for each dollar in purchases charged, with 20,000 miles required for a free round-trip domestic ticket. The annual fee is $60 to $100. You would have to charge $2,084 each month to earn a free ticket in one year.

Strategy: If you are already earning frequent-flier miles from business travel or other tie-ins, you can use this type of card to top off your miles.

The most flexible programs are American Express's Membership Rewards (800-297-6453), which allows you to earn miles on any of five U.S. and seven international airlines' frequent-flier programs, and Diner's Club Premier Rewards (800-234-6377), which allows you to earn miles on any U.S. airline with a frequent-flier program.

These cards charge no interest because you must pay the bill in full. Both have steep annual fees, but if they help you get a free ticket, they may be worth it. To compare costs and benefits, send for a Rebate/Frequent-Flier Cost Benefit Guide ($5) from Bankcard Holders of America, 524 Branch Dr., Salem, Virginia 24153.

Beware "Fixed-Rate" Credit Cards

The rates on fixed-rate cards stay fixed only until the issuer feels like changing them—which it can do by giving 15 days' written notice to cardholders.

Important: Fixed-rate cards may not even offer the best rates. If you carry a balance, pay your bills on time and if your credit record is good, you may qualify for a variable-rate card with a better rate.

Tricky Credit Card Traps

The next time you want to switch credit cards in an attempt to get the lowest possible interest rate, watch out. A growing number of card issuers have been quietly adding penalties and restrictions to their accounts in an effort to make up for lost revenues.

Solution: Forget what appears on the outside of a promotional envelope or in an advertisement. Instead, read the disclosure box that, by law, must appear on the back of all credit card applications. Unfortunately, fewer than 10% of all consumers read these boxes. Those who don't can end up paying unexpected fees if they violate their agreements.

Look out for these disclosure box red flags.

1. NO MENTION OF A GRACE PERIOD

More than 90% of credit card issuers offer a grace period of about 25 days, meaning you have 25 days to pay for your purchase before being charged interest.

Self-defense: Stay away from any card whose application doesn't mention a grace period. You will pay interest on all charges—even if you pay the card's bill in full each month. That's because interest starts the day you make a purchase.

2. HIGH ANNUAL FEES

It's easy today to find a no-fee credit card with a decent interest rate, or a low-fee card with a very good interest rate.

Key question: If the issuer charges a high annual

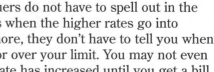

fee, are there enough benefits you can use to justify paying the high rate?

3. TOO-LOW INTEREST RATES

If the interest rate is lower than 10%, chances are it's an introductory rate: one that's offered for only a short time. The card issuer must disclose how long the rate lasts and what the new rate will be. A 7% rate that jumps to 18.9% after six months is a bad deal, unless you're sure that you'll have all of the charges paid off before the introductory rate expires.

Strategy: If the difference between a card's introductory rate and its long-term rate is greater than six percentage points, look elsewhere for a better deal.

4. PENALTY INTEREST RATES

Some disclosure boxes may tell you that a higher interest rate goes into effect if you fail to meet the requirements of your account. Those requirements are not always spelled out as clearly as they should be.

Violation of these standards usually includes making a late payment or exceeding your credit limit. Limits are most often exceeded when staying at hotels, which charge you after you leave.

Examples: Some new Visa or MasterCard applicants who fail to pay on time or exceed their credit limits may have their rates raised to 21.65%.

In some cases, there are more obscure provisions. Your interest rate can be raised if the bank decides you've become a poor credit risk. Some banks monitor credit files semiannually.

Important: Issuers do not have to spell out in the disclosure boxes when the higher rates go into effect. Furthermore, they don't have to tell you when you will be late or over your limit. You may not even learn that your rate has increased until you get a bill that includes the new rate.

Self-defense: Call the issuer to ask about possible penalties before signing up.

5. A "TWO-CYCLE AVERAGE DAILY BALANCE"

If this phrase appears in the disclosure box, throw away the application. The two-cycle method is the sum of the average daily balances for two billing cycles.

Solution: More than 85% of the industry uses a method that calculates the balance by adding all new purchases to the outstanding debt and then dividing by the number of days in the billing cycle. This is much better than the two-cycle method.

6. BALANCE-TRANSFER RESTRICTIONS

Some cards limit the amount you can transfer from another card, while others cap the number of transfers you can make in a particular period.

Other issuers treat balance transfers as cash advances, hitting you with a ridiculously high interest rate and charging you interest immediately rather than waiting until after your first bill arrives.

The information provided in the disclosure box is often vague. Sometimes an issuer will say that balance transfers are just like cash advances, but they won't mention the cash-advance rate.

7. BAD CASH-ADVANCE TERMS

Issuers must tell you what they charge if you use your card to borrow cash. The fee is usually 2% of the total borrowed.

Trap: They don't have to disclose the interest rate for borrowing the cash. It is often much higher than the interest rate on your card's regular balance.

COMPUTING FINANCE CHARGES

It's not just the finance charge that determines the amount of interest you owe on your credit card balance. There are three different methods card issuers can use to determine the monthly balance itself, which has a major influence on what you are charged.

Assume an 18% annual finance charge.

METHOD	May 1 Billed amount	May 15 You pay on time	June 1 Interest you'll owe
Adjusted balance	$2,000	$1,000	$15.00
Average daily balance	$2,000	$1,000	$22.50
Previous balance	$2,000	$1,000	$30.00

Example: It's not unusual for a card with a 15% interest rate to raise that rate up to 21.9% for a cash advance.

Solution: Call the issuer's 800 number and ask about its cash-advance terms before you borrow money with your card.

Here are some good credit card deals. These have low rates and none of the problems cited in the example above.

- **AFBA Industrial Bank** (800-776-2265). Introductory rate for the first six months is 8.5%. After that it increases to 11.4%. Annual fee: None.

- **People's Bank** (800-426-1114). This has a fixed rate of 13.9%. It will be this rate for as long as you own the card. Annual fee: None.
- **PNC Bank Prime Value** (800-762-9901). Six-month introductory rate is 7.9%, thereafter, prime plus 3.75%. Annual fee: $18 for standard, $28 for gold.
- **USAA Federal Savings** (800-922-9092). The 12.5% rate is variable. It changes every quarter and is tied to the prime rate. Annual fee: None.
- **Wachovia First Year Prime** (800-842-3262). Current introductory rate is the prime rate for the first year. Then it moves to prime plus 3.9%. Annual fees: $18 for standard, $28 for gold.

Gas Station Trap

Gas Tip
If you pay by credit card, have the attendant ring up the purchase. Don't pay through the automated pump.

Paying for gas at an automated gas pump could tie up dollars on your credit line. Stations may block off amounts up to $50 (even though the actual purchase price may be less than half that) on your card to protect themselves against fraud. The authorization or credit hold stays on your account for two to eight days—or as long as three weeks—before that part of your credit line is unfrozen.

Credit Card Billing Errors Alert

Report credit card billing errors in writing within 60 days of the postmark on your statement. Write to the address listed on the statement for billing errors—it may not be the one where you pay bills. Send the letter by certified mail, return receipt requested, for proof that you responded properly. The card issuer must investigate your claim and tell you in writing within 30 days that it is investigating. It must resolve the problem within 90 days or two billing cycles.

Big Credit Card Mistake

Increasing numbers of credit card owners are not signing their credit cards in the mistaken belief that this helps fight credit fraud.

Why: They fear that if a signed card is stolen, the thief will be able to practice forging their signature before using it, and that the card issuer will then refuse to provide a refund for a charge made with a genuine-looking signature.

Reality: It's much more dangerous to have an unsigned card—the thief can sign it him or herself and use it as identification for all kinds of purposes, as well as making charges, since the signatures will obviously match. Forcing a thief to work to copy your signature is a deterrent to crime.

Fine-Print Secret

Misleading retail ads might read "no interest is due for a set period," such as 90 days or one year. But if the bill is not paid when due, interest may be charged dating back to the date of purchase. And rates for this type of offer—typically made by stores or store-brand charge cards—can be substantially higher than already high bank card rates.

Self-defense: Read the fine print very carefully before accepting a supposed no-interest offer.

You Can't Borrow Your Way out of Debt

Don't enter a loan-consolidation agreement that stretches out the term of your borrowing, no matter how attractive its advertising sounds. Even if you obtain lower monthly payments, you'll pay much more interest over the long run.

Exception: If you can obtain a reduction in the interest rate you're paying on your total borrowing, loan consolidation may make sense. This might be possible if you pay off high-rate, nondeductible credit card interest with funds obtained through a home equity loan carrying a lower rate of interest that is deductible.

FREE VISA-M/C INFORMATION For people with credit problems!!

FIGHT BACK!!

ERASE BAD CREDIT

FROM YOUR CREDIT PROFILE
— LATE PAYMENTS
— REPOSSESSIONS
— CHARGE-OFFS
— BANKRUPTCY, ETC.

GUARANTEED RESULTS!!

Possible Bankruptcy Indicator
Baby boomers go bankrupt more often than any other group. Boomers make up 42% of the adult population—but 58% of personal bankruptcies. Most common reason for bankruptcy: high credit card debt.

Baby Boomers

42% of population

58% of bankrupcies

Before Applying For Credit

Obtain a copy of your credit file from Equifax, Trans-Union Credit Info., TRW or your local credit bureau. Review the contents. If the credit file contains incorrect negative information, have it corrected. If the negative information is correct, add an explanation to the file and prepare personal financial statements that show your net worth, income and expenses.

Lenders will want this information, so drawing it up in advance will impress them and give you a chance to show debts and obligations in a more favorable light. Drawing up these statements also will provide you with a better picture of your current financial condition.

Name Confusion in Credit Reports

If you are a "Junior" or "Senior," or have a common last name, someone else's credit information may be put in your file. Even if the other person has a perfect credit record, your loan application may be rejected if his or her borrowing added to your own puts you over your limit.

Self-defense: When applying for credit, use your full middle or maiden name, or both, to be sure your file isn't confused with another's.

Certificates of Deposit

When interest rates are high, it may be worthwhile to pay an early withdrawal penalty on older CDs bought at a lower rate. The penalty for early withdrawal is six months' interest on CDs with maturities of more than one year, and three months' interest on CDs with maturities of less than one year.

Example: 12 months ago you invested $1,000 in a five-year CD yielding 5%. If you withdraw the money now, you'll lose six months' interest: 2.5%, or about $25. The new CD yields 7.4%. That's 2.4% a year more than the old CD, or $24 a year for a total of $96 by the time your old CD would have matured.

The same strategy applies in the future. If you buy a five-year CD tomorrow and rates jump quickly to 9%, close out that CD and buy a new one.

Here's how: To determine if it's worth absorbing a withdrawal penalty on a CD, subtract your current interest rate from the rate you could get on a new CD. Multiply the result by the number of years remaining on your existing CD. This number must offset the withdrawal penalty.

Long-term strategy: You can avoid anxiety about early withdrawal penalties and rising rates if you buy CDs with different maturities: six months, one year, three years and five years. Then, as rates rise and your CDs mature, you can reinvest the amount at higher rates.

When to Reinvest in a New CD

  7.4%   New interest rate
−5.0%   Current interest rate
= 2.4%

2.4% x 4 (years remaining in current CD) = 9.6%

9.6% x $1,000 (amount of CD) = $96

$96 is greater than $25 (withdrawal penalty) by $71.

Therefore you should reinvest in the new CD.

Get Higher Returns

Put your excess savings into higher-paying six-month or one-year CDs or in money market funds. If interest rates are going down, buy CDs; if they are going up, buy money market funds. Consider out-of-state banks, which may pay higher rates.

CD-Buying Strategy

Before buying a bank CD, ask yourself the following questions.

1. **Regardless of the interest rate, what will its dollar value be on maturity?**
2. **Is there an early withdrawal penalty, and how does it apply?**
3. **Am I entitled to a higher rate as a current customer of the bank?**
4. **Are higher rates offered for larger deposits, and are such deposits federally insured?**

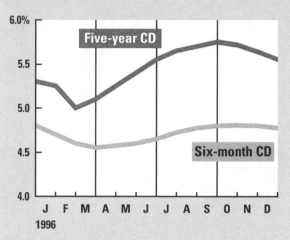

CD Rates Remain Steady
Average yields on new six-month and five-year certificates of deposit haven't fluctuated too much recently.

Copyright: Bank Rate Monitor

Get a Better Rate On CDs

Before investing in a certificate of deposit, check the yields at out-of-state banks. They may be higher than at your local banks. The difference in rates from one bank to another can be several percentage points.

Major financial magazines and newspapers, like *Barron's*, often list banks with the best nationwide rates. Their 800 numbers usually appear next to the interest rates.

Opportunity: Look for special CDs with unusual features, such as ten-month terms or the right to withdraw and reinvest at a higher rate if interest rates go up. Or consider buying CDs through a stockbroker. Some brokerage firms negotiate higher interest rates with banks and pass them along to their customers.

Important: Make sure that the institution you choose is federally insured. That way you have FDIC protection of up to $100,000.

SOURCES

Sources are listed in the order in which their contributions appear. A source may have contributed part or all of an article, or a series of articles.

David Barr, FDIC

Edward F. Mrkvicka, Jr., Reliance Enterprises, Inc.

Cindy Fuller, American Bankers Association

Edward F. Mrkvicka, Jr., Reliance Enterprises, Inc.

Edgar Dworsky, Massachusetts Executive Office of Consumer Affairs and Business Regulation

Mary Hunt, publisher of *Cheapskate Monthly*

Edward F. Mrkvicka, Jr., Reliance Enterprises, Inc.

Jens Jurgen, Travel Companions

Lisa Harris, Federal Trade Commission

Robert McKinley, RAM Research

Gerri Detweiler, author of *The Ultimate Credit Handbook: How to Double Your Credit*

Robert McKinley, RAM Research

Gerri Detweiler, author of *The Ultimate Credit Handbook: How to Double Your Credit*

Ruth Susswein, Bankcard Holders of America

Edgar Dworsky, Massachusetts Executive Office of Consumer Affairs and Business Regulation

Bob Hammond, author of *Life After Debt: How to Repair Your Credit and Get Out of Debt Once and For All*

Elizabeth Warren, JD, professor at University of Pennsylvania Law School

David L. Scott, PhD, professor of accounting and finance at Valdosta State University

Julie Garton-Good, author of *All About Mortgages*

Lewis J. Altfest, CFP, L.J. Altfest & Co.

Joel Lerner, professor of business at Sullivan County Community College

Alexandra Armstrong, CFP, Armstrong, Welch & McIntyre, Inc.

Investing in Your Future
Make Your Money Grow

How to Set Your Financial Priorities

People are constantly trying to set their financial priorities. Today there is so much information rushing at you that it is often hard to know what issues to address and when. Though a great deal of what you do depends on your income, age is also a major factor in determining financial priorities.

To help you sort it all out, here are the biggest financial issues you should think about during each stage of your life.

IF YOU'RE IN YOUR 30s
Work on your savings

Develop good financial habits, especially focusing on a disciplined approach to saving regularly. This includes maximizing your participation in your company's retirement plan. If you work on establishing good habits now, these patterns will stay with you for the rest of your life.

Rule of thumb: If you can save 15% of your gross annual income, which includes contributions to your 401(k) or 403(b) plan, you'll be in good financial shape by the time you retire. If you have children, you'll need to save even more to provide for their college tuition costs.

Take on investment risk

At this stage of your life, you've got to take prudent risk with your investments in order to outpace inflation, which is now about 3% per year.

The best way to do that is to own a diversified portfolio of stocks and stock funds. Some younger people shy away from stocks because

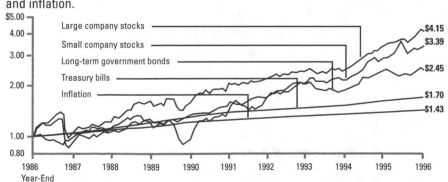

Growth During the Past Decade
Wealth indices of investments in small and large U.S. company stocks, bonds, bills and inflation.

Large company stocks — $4.15
Small company stocks — $3.39
Long-term government bonds — $2.45
Treasury bills — $1.70
Inflation — $1.43

Year-End: 1986, 1987, 1988, 1989, 1990, 1991, 1992, 1993, 1994, 1995, 1996

IN YOUR 30s:
Long-Term Goals

- ● **Choose moderately high-risk investments.**
- ● **Begin aggressive retirement savings.**
- ● **Buy adequate life insurance.**
- ● **Buy adequate disability insurance.**
- ● **Establish an estate plan.**
- ● **Plan for your children's college education.**
- ● **Beware of amassing debt.**

they think investing is too complicated, but stocks are the only investments that will grow considerably over ten to 20 years.

Determine your insurance needs

Be sure you have adequate life and long-term disability insurance. Determine whether your policies cover your needs. If you own your home, make sure you have replacement-cost coverage on the structure and its contents. If you rent, make sure you have renters' insurance to cover your possessions.

Watch your debt

Be judicious about credit card debt, car loans and car-lease payments. Some people in their 30s amass so much debt they spend much of their 40s and 50s repaying it. Mortgage debt can also hurt, so think twice before selling a home to buy a more expensive one. If you trade up, you will accumulate even more mortgage debt. Higher mortgage debt could lead to trouble if the real estate market turns sour and you need to sell, or if you leave your job and can't make the payments.

Work on your career

Arguably, in your 30s, your biggest asset is your future earnings potential. Don't change jobs unnecessarily. It will show on your resume and could hurt your career.

Come to work a little early, stay a little late and do your professional reading each week. The extra effort during your most energetic years will help you stand out throughout your career.

It will also help your income. The sooner you get to a high compensation level, the sooner you will benefit from a variety of pay-offs. These benefits include more dollars in your paycheck with every cost-of-living increase, higher company contributions to your pension plan and lucrative fringe benefits, such as company-paid life insurance.

Plan your estate

Set up an estate plan shortly after you marry, and update it as soon as you have children. Make sure you have a will, a living will and a durable power of attorney. Review these documents with your estate attorney every three years.

IF YOU'RE IN YOUR 40s
Size up your retirement needs

Even though you're still many years away from leav-

IN YOUR 40s:
Mid-Term Goals

- ● **Lower your investment risk to moderate.**
- ● **Project your annual retirement income and expenses.**
- ● **Keep retirement funds growing.**
- ● **Teach your children about money.**
- ● **Monitor your parents' finances.**
- ● **Beware of high-risk speculation.**

ing the workforce, this is the time to project your annual retirement income and expenses. This calculation will help you determine exactly how much you need to save. This step is particularly important if you hope to retire early, which generally takes years of careful financial planning and heavy-duty saving.

Reduce your investment risk

In your 40s, when you're starting to accumulate some wealth, you may be tempted to speculate with it.

Before you do that, sit back and think about your hard-earned money. Speculation offers the promise of great riches, but more often than not, it is money down the drain. If you plan to leave work and start your own business, don't risk all of your money. It's better to bring in partners who are extremely experienced in such ventures.

Teach your children about money

Make sure your children understand the importance of saving, how to invest and the dangers of debt. If they are financially responsible, you're less likely to end up supporting them in your old age.

Also, don't let your children's college costs interrupt your retirement-savings plan. If you stop saving for retirement, it could put a big dent in your ability to retire. If necessary, it's better to take out some loans for college.

Check in on your parents

Keep a dialogue going with your parents so you can help them steer clear of the financial problems that are commonly faced by seniors. Talk to them about the state of their housing, investments, health care and insurance.

IF YOU'RE IN YOUR 50s
Take a hard look at your estate plan

Your estate may have grown to the point that you can benefit from advanced estate-planning techniques, such as marital and life insurance trusts.

Both types of trusts can make sense, even for estates that are worth less than $1 million, and they can save your heirs a whopping amount in estate taxes.

Think about your retirement lifestyle

You're now at the stage when you can accurately estimate what your retirement income will be, depen-

ding on when you choose to retire. Use this information to make important retirement lifestyle decisions, such as where you're going to live and how often you will be able to travel.

Evaluate the importance of your job

Be leery if your company offers you an early retirement package. There's almost always less to these packages than meets the eye. Many people accept offers with no idea of how financially ill-prepared

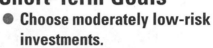

IN YOUR 50s:
Short-Term Goals
- **Choose moderately low-risk investments.**
- **Estimate retirement income.**
- **Plan the specifics of your retirement.**
- **Fine-tune your estate plan.**
- **Consider establishing trusts.**
- **Evaluate the future of your career.**
- **Be wary of early retirement.**
- **Beware of scams.**

they are for retirement. If the alternative is losing your job, however, you may have no choice.

Be realistic about your job prospects if you decide to leave your company before you reach age 65. It's safest to assume that you'll never earn another cent after you retire. If you do, great, but don't count on it. You may think you can live comfortably on your current savings. But how much will be left after 30 years, when your cost of living has doubled? Before you retire early, be sure you will be well-funded throughout your retirement years.

Beware of too much advice

Carefully evaluate major financial commitments that are marketed to people in their 50s. Be wary of living trusts, pension-maximization insurance, nursing home insurance and investments that offer extravagant yields. While these financial products may make sense for some people some of the time, many people should stay far away from them.

Jonathan Pond Answers the Top Investment Questions

During the many speeches that I give around the country each year, I'm asked hundreds of questions about money and investing. Here are the answers to the questions people ask most frequently.

SHOULD I TAKE MY RETIREMENT MONEY AS A LUMP SUM OR ANNUITY?

Many pensions offer retirees a choice of two forms of payment: a little at a time through an annuity or a lump sum. This decision could be the most important financial decision of your life, but it is very hard to get an objective opinion.

Reason: The annuity is an insurance-industry product, so people in the insurance business are likely to tell you to take your pension as an annuity. People in the investment management business will tell you to take it as a lump sum and roll the money over into an investment account.

The answer to this question draws attention to an important lesson. There are few all-or-nothing decisions in personal finance. People who are willing to sacrifice some potential income for the assurance that they will receive steady payments are best served by taking part of the money as a lump sum and part as an annuity.

Strategy: If you retire at or before the normal retirement age, you generally should take the lump sum. Then, when you are older, there is nothing to prevent you from investing in an annuity.

There are, however, some very innovative annuity products being developed, such as immediate payment variable annuities. These invest your money in mutual funds, and you begin receiving investment payments immediately.

In a few years, you probably will have a better choice of annuity products. If you can't wait, shop around. Don't just take the annuity your employer or broker offers.

Caution: If you or your spouse goes into a nursing home, your lump sum distribution will be used to help pay nursing home costs. A lot of people in that situation wish they had chosen an annuity for part of their savings because nursing-home care has wiped out their long-term savings. An annuity at least assures a continuing income for your spouse, and for you if you leave the nursing home.

IF I MAKE JUST ONE INVESTMENT, WHAT SHOULD IT BE?

Here are two possible candidates.

1. 20-year zero-coupon Treasury bond. These bonds sell at discounts to their face values, so you receive the full amount when they reach maturity. If you buy a 20-year zero-coupon bond now, your money will grow at an annual rate of around 8%. In 20 years, it will almost quintuple with no risk. But you should buy zero-coupon bonds only for your tax-deferred retirement account. Otherwise, you will have to pay income taxes on imputed interest, interest you don't receive in cash until the bond matures but that the IRS requires you to pay taxes on each year you own the bond.

2. A fund that invests in science and technology stocks. Our economy is in a fundamental period of transition. The old blue-chip manufacturers have had their day. A new generation of blue-chip stocks is emerging, and, of course, many of them will be science and technology companies.

How Hard is Your Money Working?

Annual rates of return of different types of investments.

Small stocks	12.5%
Real estate	11.1%
Dow Jones Industrials	10.1%
Bonds	5.2%
Treasury bills	3.7%
Inflation	3.1%

Source: © Computed using data from *Stocks, Bonds, Bills & Inflation 1997 Yearbook™*, Ibbotson Associates, Chicago (annually updates work by Roger G. Ibbotson and Rex Sinquefield). Used with permission. All rights reserved.

Treasurys Are Not Fully Tax-Exempt

U.S. Treasury securities are exempt from state and local taxes, but not from federal income tax. They are therefore especially attractive in high-tax states such as New York, California and Massachusetts.

Bonus: Treasurys are considered the safest investments available.

Types:

- **Bills** mature in one year or less.
- **Notes** mature in one to ten years.
- **Bonds** mature in ten to 30 years.

HOW MUCH SHOULD I INVEST IN STOCKS VS. BONDS?

Rule of thumb: Multiply your age by 80% (0.8). The result will give you the maximum percentage that you should invest in bonds for the long term.

Example: At age 50, you should have at most 40% of your portfolio in bonds (0.8 times 50). I would put 50% of that money in highly rated municipal bonds, 25% in corporate bonds and 25% in Treasury bonds of different maturities, or in mutual funds that invest in those bonds.

Municipal bonds, particularly those in your home state, may provide a significant yield advantage over Treasurys for investors in the 28% or higher tax bracket.

Example: A ten-year Treasury bond might yield 8%, while a ten-year municipal bond yields about 6.6%. But once you take federal income tax out of the Treasury bond interest, its yield drops to 5.52%. If you were in the 31% or higher federal tax bracket, the municipal advantage would be even greater.

The rest of a sound long-term portfolio should go into growth investments, particularly stocks. That strategy may strike some investors as dangerous, but you can reduce your risk by spreading your equity holdings among different sectors of the stock market. When one or more sectors decline temporarily, your other sectors will rise.

Try putting 40% of your portfolio into income-producing stocks or funds that hold these stocks. Divide the rest of your portfolio evenly among growth funds, foreign stock funds and small-cap funds.

WHAT KIND OF ESTATE PLANNING DO I NEED?

At the very least, you should have three documents.

1. Will. Make sure that it is valid and up-to-date.

2. Living will. This tells doctors whether or not you want to be kept alive on a life-support system if you're terminally ill.

3. Durable power of attorney. This appoints someone to run your finances if you become incapacitated. If you neglect to draw up one, the court will decide who will look after your finances, and the court's choice is not always best.

Important: If you or your spouse has an estate that is valued at more than the exemption amount ($625,000 in 1998, increasing to $1 million by 2006), you will need a credit shelter trust. It allows each spouse to take advantage of the exemption amount from estate taxes. By creating such a credit shelter trust, if you both live to 2006, you can ensure that your estate of $2 million or more will avoid paying more than $225,000 in taxes when the surviving spouse dies.

SHOULD I PAY DOWN MY MORTGAGE EARLY?

Many people argue against doing this. They believe that the money you use to pay down your mortgage at a faster rate could be invested elsewhere for a higher return.

How Much Life Insurance Do I Need?

Start out by considering two numbers.

1. Minimum amount of coverage: five times your annual spending, including taxes.

Example:

$50,000	**Annual earnings**	
− 5,000	**Annual savings**	
= 45,000	**Annual spending**	
x 5		
= **$225,000**	**Minimum insurance coverage you need**	

That amount will provide your family with time to get on a firmer financial footing if something happens to you.

2. Maximum amount of coverage: Ask an insurance agent to provide an estimate. Believe me, the agent won't leave much out.

For most people, the best amount lies between the minimum and the maximum.

Example: If you have children who are not in college yet, you might insure your life for five times your annual spending, plus a sufficient amount to pay off your mortgage and fund the children's college educations.

They also point out that mortgage payments are tax deductible. Even so, it's a good idea to reduce the time it takes to pay off a home loan.

Reasons: Your return on other investments will rarely be much higher than the interest payments you'll save by paying down the mortgage. Also, one of the most important things for investors is the ability to sleep well at night. I think there is a major psychological benefit to knowing that you are paying down your mortgage at a rapid rate.

It is great to enter your retirement mortgage-free. Even an extra $100 a month can make a big difference in your lifestyle.

WHEN SHOULD I SELL A MUTUAL FUND?

Let's assume that you bought a mutual fund because it had a solid long-term record, and nothing has changed about the management of the fund.

A fund has to perform below the average for funds in its category for two consecutive years before you should consider selling it. For instance, a growth fund must trail other growth funds, and a small-company fund must trail other small-company funds.

You can find the category averages in *Barron's* every week under Lipper Mutual Fund Performance Reports.

This approach means being patient, but it will probably be rewarding. When a good fund underperforms for a year, it often snaps back and does very well afterward.

How to Build a Little Cash into Big Bucks

Don't be embarrassed about investing small amounts. Whether you start with $500 or $5,000, you can build a meaningful portfolio faster than you think possible.

Example: If you invest $500 a year at 8% compounded annually, it becomes $2,933 in five years. You'll have $7,243 at the end of ten years. At the same rate, $5,000 a year becomes $72,430 in ten years.

Don't Be a Clock-Watcher
Don't follow your stocks and mutual funds daily. Short-term profits and losses may color your views of an investment.
More important: The long-term trend. Monitor progress monthly. You'll stay on top of the trends without being sucked into making an emotional decision based on short-term volatility.

Note: Investors seeking high returns are obliged to use investments like stocks and bonds, securities that carry substantial risks.

Before you invest for relatively high returns, prepare for emergencies: stash six month's worth of take-home pay in a money-market mutual fund or an interest-bearing checking account. Use any cash in savings accounts to fund your emergency stash, as savings accounts pay the lowest interest rates. Service charges on multiple accounts add up.

You can move into the stock market modestly with $500. There are even a pair of mini-investor programs that will let you avoid the additional cost of brokerage commissions.

At least 30 solid public companies sell shares directly to the public. Some of these are Exxon, Johnson Controls, Procter & Gamble and Texaco. Call the shareholder relations department of big companies that interest you and inquire if you can invest directly. In addition, more than 20 public utilities allow direct stock purchases if you live in their service areas.

IT PAYS TO BE A DRIP

No one likes to pay commissions, not even to a friendly broker. Besides, many brokers won't take $500 accounts. More than 1,000 companies maintain Dividend Reinvestment Programs (DRIPs), however. Their shareholders can buy more stock by automatically reinvesting dividends. Most DRIP companies

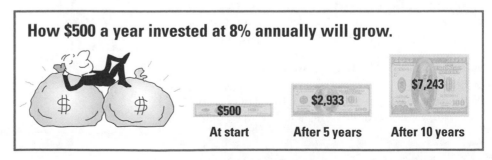

How $500 a year invested at 8% annually will grow.

$500	$2,933	$7,243
At start	**After 5 years**	**After 10 years**

are solid companies like AT&T, Clorox, DuPont, Heinz, Kellogg, Texaco and Procter & Gamble.

Some DRIPs entail a fee, but the fees are nominal, far less than a broker would charge. Many DRIPs also offer 3% to 5% off the market price of new shares, something no broker will do. Some companies will enroll you with a single share, while others require 15 to 100 shares.

DRIP companies sometimes let shareholders make cash payments into their accounts to buy more shares. AT&T has an optional cash plan starting at $25. For a list of 900 companies offering DRIPS, obtain *Standard & Poor's Directory of Dividend Reinvestment Plans* ($39.95), 800-221-5277. The directory should also be available at your public library.

ORGANIZE AN INVESTMENT CLUB

Learn about stocks, the economy and interest rates. Join the National Association of Investors Corporation (NAIC), 711 W. 13 Mile Rd., Madison Heights, Michigan 48071. Monthly dues to buy stocks range from a minimum of $20 to whatever you can afford.

NAIC's Low Cost Investment Plan lets members buy shares directly from the more than 150 participating companies. There is a one-time charge of $7 per company. Most participating companies do not charge commissions.

KEEP ON SAVING

Have your employer deduct a set sum from each paycheck, say $50, and transfer it to the money-market fund of your choice.

Be sure to set aside the maximum $2,000 a year in a tax-sheltered IRA. Use a Keogh plan to shelter up to 20% of any self-employment earnings.

You can fund these plans by making small contributions several times a year. If, at age 45, you and your spouse both set aside $2,000 a year on a tax-deferred basis and earn 10% returns compounded, you'll share $115,000 at age 65.

Don't ignore investment plans at work. Tax-deferred plans such as 401(k)s or stock purchase plans are usually good deals, especially if the company matches your contribution. Consult your benefits officer for details.

DIVERSIFY

When you raise the next $2,000, diversify. It is risky to put all your money in one place. Your $2,000 isn't enough to make several individual investments, how-ever, so buy shares in a mutual fund to resolve this issue neatly.

Mutual funds buy securities issued by scores of companies using a pool of dollars paid by hundreds of fund shareholders. The combined monies are invested and managed by professionals in diversified portfolios of stocks, bonds, various money-market papers or a mix of these securities. Unless you need a broker's guidance, buy no-load funds. Studies offer no evidence that load funds outperform no-load funds. No-load funds are sold by the fund companies themselves.

Caution: A few of the no-load funds may include redemption fees which can amount to up to 1% to 2% of market value.

CLARIFY YOUR GOALS

Do you want a fund for income or growth? Do you want a fund that consists primarily of stocks, bonds or some of each? Do you want a high-risk speculative fund or a more conservative one?

Each fund has different objectives stated at the beginning of the fund's official description on file with the Securities & Exchange Commission. You can also call the individual fund's 800 number to get its prospectus. The largest category of common stock mutual funds is growth funds. They tend to outperform other types of stock funds over the long term. They are best for those willing to assume moderate risk, who can also hold shares for two years or longer.

Steady Eddies

Out of all the stock funds, a few have had gains most years since 1978.
- Phoenix Growth (800-243-4361).
- Merrill Lynch Capital A (800-637-3863).
- Investment Co. of America Growth & Income (800-421-9900).
- John Hancock Sovereign Growth & Income (800-225-5291).
- CGM Mutual Balanced Fund (800-345-4048).

Ginnie Mae mutual funds

These funds aim for high income and low risk, and more often than not succeed. Ginnie Maes are bundles of Federal Housing Authority and Veterans Administration mortgages.

Ginnie Mae funds hold these Ginnie Mae certificates. The minimum required purchase is usually

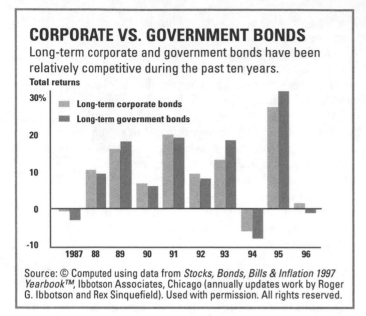

CORPORATE VS. GOVERNMENT BONDS

Long-term corporate and government bonds have been relatively competitive during the past ten years.

Total returns

■ Long-term corporate bonds
■ Long-term government bonds

Source: © Computed using data from *Stocks, Bonds, Bills & Inflation 1997 Yearbook™*, Ibbotson Associates, Chicago (annually updates work by Roger G. Ibbotson and Rex Sinquefield). Used with permission. All rights reserved.

$1,000 to $2,000. Buy them for the generous yields that they frequently offer.

U.S. Treasurys

Treasurys are a good investment when safety is paramount. The government guarantees it will pay you back. Treasurys are especially liquid and can be sold at any time. Interest earned is exempt from both state and local income taxes.

If you don't have the requisite $10,000 to buy a one-, three- or six-month T-bill directly, consider a Treasury-only money-market fund like the Benham Capital Preservation fund (800-345-2021). Minimum purchase: $2,500.

HEDGE YOUR BETS

Consider corporate bonds and tax-exempt municipals when you have $5,000 to invest. (All bonds, even Treasurys, are essentially IOUs—you are lending the issuer money.)

Bond ratings are important. The highest quality bonds are rated AAA. Medium-grade bonds are rated BBB, BB or B. Those rated CCC or lower are speculative. Inexperienced and conservative investors should stick to bonds rated A or better.

Corporate bonds are a good investment for those seeking high fixed income who can endure risks of changing interest rates. They're best, however, for those who can hold the bonds to maturity, at which point the bonds will be retired at full face value.

You can buy corporates or munis from a broker.

The minimum purchase is usually $5,000 to $10,000. But experts argue that a bond portfolio of less than $100,000 cannot be diversified well enough to protect the investor against bond defaults and calls. (Generally, calls are permitted after five years.) Issuers will call, or retire, bonds when new ones can be issued at lower cost during periods of declining interest rates.

Smaller investors are usually better off investing through a corporate bond mutual fund which offers professional management.

Tax-exempt municipal bonds pay lower interest rates than taxable bonds and are not appropriate for people in low tax brackets. They are also not prudent for use in already tax-deferred retirement accounts such as IRAs. Yet for those in high tax brackets, munis can really pay off. For instance, if you are married, file a joint return and earn $45,000 a year, you would need to receive a yield of 10.76% on a taxable investment, such as a corporate bond, to equal a 7.75% tax-exempt yield.

Have Your Portfolio Reviewed over the Phone

A new call-in service, Wealthy & Wise, examines investments and advises on how to save fees, reduce risk and better meet investment goals.

How it works: You fax or mail in a description of your investment holdings, and discuss your financial goals and priorities over the phone. You then receive by mail an analysis of your portfolio holdings with suggested changes, and get a follow-up call to discuss changes. Advice is directed to personal needs, so if you have little time to manage investments, a "low maintenance" portfolio will be recommended.

Fee: Around $125 per hour.
More information: 800-275-2272.

Financial Planners Are Not All Alike

Fee-based financial planners are not the same as fee-only planners. Fee-only planners take a flat fee or percentage of your assets but no commissions. They

How Investors Prefer to Pay Their Financial Advisers

Results of a survey of 4,103 consumers over age 30 with a household income of at least $40,000.

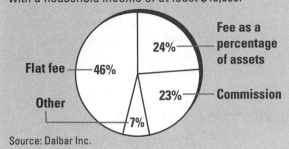

- Fee as a percentage of assets — 24%
- Commission — 23%
- Other — 7%
- Flat fee — 46%

Source: Dalbar Inc.

may have less incentive than commission-based planners to sell you additional products. Fee-based planners take up-front fees plus commissions on trades.

Self-defense: Get in writing exactly how a planner will be compensated before you sign an agreement. When in doubt, choose a fee-only planner.

When to Use a Bond Market Loss

Bond market losses can be used to produce tax gains, if you know how to perform a timely bond swap.

Approach: In a typical swap, you would sell older bonds at a loss, use that loss to offset capital gains and buy new bonds that are paying today's higher interest rates. If losses exceed capital gains, or if you have no capital gains, up to $3,000 in losses can be deducted from ordinary income. If losses exceed $3,000, they can be carried over and used against income in future years.

Warning: The new bonds can be similar to

the older bonds you sold, but they can't be "substantially identical" to the old bonds. That would violate the wash-sale rule and wipe out your loss deduction.

Important: Never trade securities solely for tax reasons. Only trade them if it makes sound investment sense for your portfolio.

Terry Savage Tells Investors What They Need to Know

Wise investing isn't as mysterious or complex as some people make it seem. It's actually quite simple, and you don't need a lot of money to achieve financial security. The stock market and interest rates are always volatile, so you must take a long-term perspective. Here's what you need to know.

START EARLY

Many people assume that you need a lot of money to make money. In reality, time can be your best asset. The earlier you start, the better.

The secret is compounding: money making money. The longer your money grows, the better off you will be.

It Pays to Start Early

Tom and Mary both start working at age 25. Mary puts away $200 a month in the company retirement plan until she reaches age 65. Her total investment is $96,000, and inside the plan her money grows at 9%, tax-deferred. When Mary reaches age 65, her account is worth about $850,000.

Meanwhile, Tom decides to wait awhile before setting aside money for retirement. He starts at age 45. Realizing that he's behind, Tom saves $400 a month, also growing at 9%. By age 65, Tom has invested the same total of $96,000. But at retirement, Tom's account is worth only $258,000.

Lesson: Start saving as early as possible.

Mary invests $200 a month starting at age 25

| $96,000 total investment | = $850,000 at age 65 |

Tom invests $400 a month starting at age 45

| $96,000 total investment | = $258,000 at age 65 |

SHELTER INVESTMENTS FROM TAXES

Not paying taxes as your investment earnings accumulate can make a big difference in your total savings over the long run.

Example: If you contribute $2,000 to an IRA each year and it grows at 10% (approximately the historical average of the stock market) your account will be worth more than $361,000 after 30 years. Outside this tax-sheltered account, the same amount would grow to only about $198,000 for someone in the 31% tax bracket.

Strategy I: Sign up for your company's 40l(k) retirement plan. Contribute the maximum amount allowed

Strategy II: If you are self-employed, consider a Keogh or SEP retirement plan.

Strategy III: You can contribute $2,000 a year to an IRA even if you are covered by a company plan. You just can't deduct the contribution unless your Adjusted Gross Income (AGI) is less than $30,000 for individuals or $50,000 for couples. But even non-deductible IRAs grow tax-deferred, a big plus.

Strategy IV: You can contribute $2,000 a year to a Roth IRA.

LEARN TO TAKE RISKS

Risk and reward are two sides of the same coin. In order to have larger rewards, you must take more risks. The trick is to act only when the risk/reward balance is in your favor. That means always asking questions about risks in an investment.

Example: If money-market funds are paying around 5% and someone suggests an investment in 30-year U.S. government bonds that pay about 8%, that would mean taking more risk. In this case, it's the risk of being locked into 8% for 30 years if interest rates move higher.

Your perception of risk may change, depending on your time horizon.

Example: The stock market can be very risky if you're talking about a one- or two-year investment period. But risk diminishes over time, and, going back to 1926, there has never been a 20-year period during which the stock market lost money.

Currently, the stock market is as highly valued as it has been at any time this century. When compared with dividend yields and earnings, stock prices are relatively high. That makes today a high-risk entry point. But if you're willing to stick with a regular investment plan, you should come out far ahead of "safe" money investments, such as bank CDs or Treasury

bills. Unfortunately, most people fail to take a long-term perspective. They stop investing when the market declines and sell when the market is at or near its low point. The key is to understand your risk tolerance and invest accordingly.

Strategy: If you want to invest in individual stocks but are afraid that your investment plans will be derailed by fear or greed, set stop-loss orders to sell your stocks when the prices drop 10% to 15% below current market prices.

DIVERSIFY YOUR PORTFOLIO

Don't gamble with your investment plan. While you can make a lot if you put all your money in a stock or industry that takes off, you can also lose a lot.

Strategy: Diversify your investments. One mutual fund, or several, will allow you to own a broad range of stocks and bonds with different growth characteristics. The funds you choose depend on your goals and when you need the money.

When you invest with a family of funds, you also can leave some investment dollars in a money-market fund and wait for buying opportunities. Or let the fund family diversify for you. For example, many well-known fund families offer funds that invest in their other mutual funds.

Face Your Feelings

Confront two basic emotions: fear and greed. Fear paralyzes you, and that can be expensive. Greed makes you take risks you can't afford. Remember the old market rule: Desperate money never makes money.

BEWARE OF BONDS

For decades, bonds and utility stocks provided steady income, offered little possibility of default and maintained value over time. That changed when interest rates and fears of growing inflation began to rise.

Key: When interest rates rise, bond prices fall. If you buy a 30-year bond, a 1% rise in interest rates will result in a 12% loss of market value for your bond if you need to sell it.

Inverse Relationship

When interest rates go up,

bond prices go down.

LIMIT YOUR INVESTMENT COSTS

Market risk is easy to understand: If the value of your investment goes down, you lose money. But there are hidden costs that have nothing to do with risk, like commissions and markups. These costs are not always so obvious. A salesperson may take as much as 8% off the top of your mutual fund investment in commission, money that's not working for you. Or, when you buy bonds, the dealer may mark up the price without showing it on your sales confirmation.

Strategy: Before buying, ask the broker how much he or she is making on the transaction. It is fine to pay for good advice, but check prices with several companies to make sure you are getting the best deal.

Smarter Long-Term Stock Investing

Money that is needed within three years shouldn't be invested in the stock market. The best way to invest in stocks is with a long-term view, under which you feel free to buy stocks as the market is falling, since that's when stocks are cheap. But because the market can always fall further, you can't do this with money you may need soon.

Strategy: Invest any money you are afraid to lose in Treasury notes. Invest only long-term funds in stocks or stock mutual funds.

Learn to Recognize Opportunities

The daily grind of negative news presents opportunities for investors. Effective investment is for the long term. If you allow frightening daily headlines to create indecision, you will not focus on a long-term investment strategy. The stock market often responds negatively to bad news for a time, but its long-term trend is up and successful investors always look at the long term.

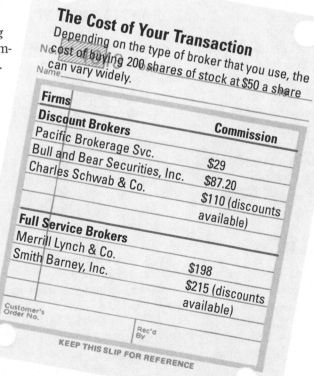

The Cost of Your Transaction

Depending on the type of broker that you use, the cost of buying 200 shares of stock at $50 a share can vary widely.

Name _____

Firms	Commission
Discount Brokers	
Pacific Brokerage Svc.	$29
Bull and Bear Securities, Inc.	$87.20
Charles Schwab & Co.	$110 (discounts available)
Full Service Brokers	
Merrill Lynch & Co.	$198
Smith Barney, Inc.	$215 (discounts available)

Customer's Order No.

Rec'd By

KEEP THIS SLIP FOR REFERENCE

Think Beyond Taxes

Never make any investment decision based solely on tax considerations. Taxes are only one factor in deciding where and how to invest.

Most important: whether or not it is a good investment.

Don't Rely on Investment Newsletters

Any investment adviser can find two dates between which his or her picks beat the market, and these are what get advertised when letters promote their "market beating" returns. A second way letters mislead is by publicizing a few picks they made that beat the market, while ignoring many others that didn't. In fact, around 80% of letter editors fail to even match the market over time.

Caution: Even the select few newsletters that actually do beat the market over time are prone to exaggerate their results in advertising.

Frugal Investing

Investing isn't as scary or as hard as it seems. It also does not have to be very expensive. Here are five rules for becoming a successful investor.

1. Reduce your risk by putting your investment dollars into at least four different asset categories that are likely to react in different ways to economic events.

2. Reduce your investment cost by dollar cost averaging, investing the same amount of money regularly, no matter what the financial markets and the economy are doing.

3. Hold on to investments for as long as you can.

4. Plan well in advance when to draw cash out of your investments to meet expected needs such as college tuition, a down payment on a house or supplemental retirement income. Otherwise you'll hurt the long-term return on your portfolio.

5. Pay little or nothing to acquire, hold or liquidate your holdings by buying no-load investments.

Sheldon Jacobs' Rules for Successful Investing Now

No matter what your circumstances, certain basics will significantly improve your performance as an investor, and provide you with a more comfortable and enjoyable retirement.

Here are the ten rules that should bring you considerable rewards in the 1990s and beyond.

1. INVEST EARLY AND OFTEN

The sooner you put your money to work, the more you get to take advantage of the power of compounding. Trying to play catch-up, on the other hand, doesn't work as well.

Added benefit: Investing frequently can help remove market timing anxiety. Since almost no one can really time the market, this helps save time and needless worry.

Furthermore, when you invest a set amount each month or each quarter, you automatically practice dollar cost averaging.

Strategy: Make IRA, SIMPLE, SEP or Keogh contributions as early in the year as you can. That allows the money to grow tax-free for longer. Don't wait until the last legally permissible moment. By disciplining yourself to move just a little faster, you'll end up with thousands of dollars more in your pocket over time.

2. FAVOR EQUITY MUTUAL FUNDS

People still don't realize how much more powerful stocks are than bonds. Over time, stocks outperform bonds by more than two to one. For the 70 years ending in December 1996, according to Ibbotson Associates in Chicago, stocks rose 10.7% per year. Long-term government bonds, by contrast, rose only 5.1% per year. That average annual differential adds up over time.

Dollar Cost Averaging

Dollar cost averaging uses the volatility of the securities markets to your advantage. The simple technique has two steps.

Step 1: Select a regular time period (monthly, or every other month) to contribute a fixed amount of new cash to your investment portfolio.

Here's how it works when you invest $100 each month.

Step 2: Stick to this plan for ten years or longer. You will buy **more** shares as the market falls, and **fewer** shares as the market rises.

Strategy: Depending on your time horizon, you could put up to 75% of your assets in stocks even if you're already in your 50s.

3. PREPARE FOR RETIREMENT

It's quite likely that you'll spend 20 years or more in retirement. By definition, that means you should think like a long-term investor.

Yes, once you're retired, you may have to choose some investments solely because you need the income. But don't seek more current yield than you need. This will hurt the long-term performance of your capital.

Strategy: When retirement is five years away, switch some money from more aggressive to less aggressive stock funds. Almost invariably, these funds will have somewhat higher yields.

4. KEEP COSTS LOW

Don't buy any funds with total expense ratios of more than 2%. True, some funds will overcome this disadvantage, but few do. Because bond funds show much less performance variance, you should pay particular attention to the expenses levied by competing bond funds. An extra 50 basis points (100 basis points = 1%) may be really significant here.

5. SWITCH RATHER THAN FIGHT

If a fund begins underperforming its peers, for instance, if one of your growth funds is badly beaten by other growth funds for two or more quarters, move to another fund with similar objectives.

In investing, blind loyalty is not rewarded.

6. AVOID THE ELEPHANTS

For the small capitalization portion of your portfolio, buy funds that have less than $300 million in assets. Once funds surpass that level, it's more difficult, although certainly not impossible, for them to be effective in the small-capitalization arena.

7. DIVERSIFY

Make sure you own enough different types of funds to smooth out

Stunting Our Own Growth?

Individual U.S. investors hold a relatively small percentage of their financial assets in the equity market (mutual funds and stocks), despite the market's proven record of long-term growth.

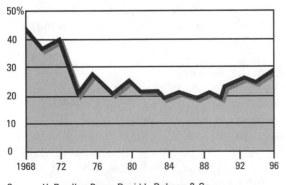

Source: H. Bradlee Perry, David L. Babson & Co.

your performance over time and to take advantage of shifting market trends.

A person with $400,000 or more should own about nine funds.

Strategy: Don't take needless risks by concentrating on one or two types of investments.

MARKET UPS AND DOWNS

	1980	1985	1990	1995
Large company stocks	↑ 32%	↑ 32%	↓ 3%	↑ 37%
Corporate bonds	↓ 3%	↑ 30%	↑ 7%	↑ 27%

Source: © Computed using data from *Stocks, Bonds, Bills & Inflation 1997 Yearbook™*, Ibbotson Associates, Chicago (annually updates work by Roger G. Ibbotson and Rex Sinquefield). Used with permission. All rights reserved.

8. INVEST ABROAD

International funds can enhance diversification and performance without adding to long-term risk. If retirement is more than ten years away, put 30% of your money in international funds. If it's five to ten years away, make it 25%, and then reduce it to 20% during your retirement.

9. AVOID INDIVIDUAL STOCKS

Almost all investors will do better over time if they let professionals manage their money.

Exception: Buy a stock when you know more about it than Wall Street does. This won't happen often, but it may happen sometimes.

10. KNOW YOUR GOALS

You should sit down and figure out what you'll need to retire in the style of your choice.

Strategy: If you're on course, relax, but stay on course. If not, make adjustments now in either your savings or investment strategy. Doing so sooner rather than later will pay enormous dividends and help you sleep better.

What Is Tax-Free Income Worth?

To find out, divide the yield from a tax-free investment by one minus your tax bracket. The result shows how much you would have to earn from a taxable investment to get the same after-tax return as from the tax-free one.

Example: A tax-free municipal bond pays 4% and you are in the 31% bracket. Divide 4% by 0.69 (which is 1 – 0.31). The result is 5.797%. So a taxable investment must pay more than 5.797% to give you more after-tax income than the tax-free bond.

Strategies for Getting Higher Yields

First, make sure the cash portion of your portfolio is really working for you. Avoid the banks if you can.

Short-term Certificates of Deposit (CDs), like bank money-market deposits, offer returns that are simply not competitive. In spring 1997
- The average three-month bank CD yielded around 4.10%.
- The average bank money-market account yielded around 2.60%.
- The average nonbank money-market fund yielded around 5.00%.
- The return offered by the average six-month CD was better than it had been, around 4.80%, but it was still far below all the other investments that follow below.

Strategy: If you're determined to put your money in paper that matures quickly because you think rates will spike up or you know you'll need to access the money soon, at least get paid a decent rate while pursuing this course: Buy Treasury instruments instead of CDs.

TREASURY NOTES

Treasury notes, which come in two-, three-, four-, five-, seven- and ten-year maturities, are a safe investment.

Strategy: Ladder your investments in notes of up to five years. Put the bulk of the money (perhaps 70%) in a five-year note and then invest 10% each in two-, three- and four-year notes.

How Treasury Bills Compare to Inflation

Annual total percent Treasury bill returns and inflation from 1987 through 1996.

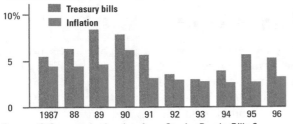

The minimum purchase for two- and three-year notes is $5,000. The minimum purchase for longer maturities is $1,000.

You can purchase them from a bank or broker (you'll pay a small commission), or directly from the Federal Reserve at no charge. The savings you'll get by going direct are worth the minutes of additional work. Contact the nearest Federal Reserve Bank either in person or in writing, fill out the required form and send a certified check for the amount you want.

TREASURY BILLS

If, for whatever reason, you don't want to commit to an extended holding period, consider T-bills. The yield differential between short-term CDs and T-bills is significant, an indication that banks haven't yet adjusted to the new interest rate climate.

Actually, the differential is even bigger than it seems because interest on T-bills is also exempt from state and local taxes. You buy T-bills the same way you buy Treasury notes.

CDs

If you're determined to own CDs because you like the convenience and the fact that you can buy them in person, here are some good approaches.

- Before you buy, shop aggressively for the best rates. It's unlikely that you'll find them at your local bank. Check *Barron's* or *Money* or the Wednesday edition of *The Wall Street Journal* for listings of the top rates. Keep in mind that the financial stability of the bank is not as important as it would be in other circumstances, since amounts under $100,000 per bank are generally insured by a federal agency.

- Get a better CD rate through a full-service broker. Brokers cut special deals with big banks to get higher CD rates than individuals.
- If you're stuck with a CD you bought when rates were lower, take out your money and pay the early withdrawal penalty.

Here's how: Assume that an old CD yields 5%, and when you break it you'll lose six months' interest (2.50%). The new CD, however, could yield 7.50%. That's 2.50% a year more for four years! To keep the old CD because you don't like to pay a penalty is penny-wise and pound-foolish.

The same strategy applies to the future. If you buy a five-year CD tomorrow and rates quickly jump to 9%, be prepared to break the CD and buy a new one.

MONEY-MARKET FUNDS

Most people with significant assets have too much of their money in money-market funds, which means they're sacrificing several percentage points of yield. Don't be intoxicated by the liquidity of such funds.

Strategy: Your amount of liquid assets (and this includes CDs and bonds that will soon be maturing) should not exceed a half year's worth of expenses.

Shop for a good money-market fund, but don't concentrate on getting the absolute highest yield. Yields change frequently and some of today's leaders may be using derivatives to pump up their returns.

GINNIE MAE FUNDS

Ginnie Mae funds are not risk-free, but they're considerably less volatile than many bond funds. That means they offer less downside risk but also less potential for capital appreciation.

Strategy: Buy mutual funds rather than individual Ginnie Mae issues. That gives you the diversity you need. This strategy will also prevent your accountant from being driven crazy by Ginnie Mae accounting rules.

MUNICIPAL BONDS

If your combined tax rate is 40%, the average five-year muni bond yielding 5.3% would have a tax-equivalent yield of 8.8%. That's almost 1.5% better than the best five-year CD.

Strategy: You should have at least $150,000 to invest in muni bonds before you begin buying individual issues rather than mutual funds. If you can hold issues until maturity, you eliminate the interest rate risk.

Your Taxable Equivalent Yields

Federal marginal tax rate	Municipal yield		
	4.00%	**5.00%**	**6.00%**
31.0 %	5.80%	7.25%	8.70%
36.0	6.25	7.81	9.38
39.6	6.62	8.28	9.93

How to Figure Your Own Returns

Work out returns on investments yourself. Don't rely on an investment adviser to tell you how your investments are performing.

Here's how: Take an investment's current value, subtract its value from one year ago and divide the result by the value from one year ago. The answer is the return for the year.

Example: If a stock was worth $1,000 one year ago and is worth $1,150 today, your return is 15% ($1,150 minus $1,000 divided by $1,000).

Goal: A professional adviser should obtain a return on your investments of 2% to 4% above the rate paid on five-year CDs.

Rate of Return Wake-Up Call

Here is an example of the actual returns you will see on your investments after factoring in a 36% tax rate and a 4% inflation rate.

Return	Return after taxes	Return after taxes + 4% inflation
5%	3.16%	-0.84%
8	5.06	1.06
11	6.96	2.96

Secrets of Donna Waldron's Successful Investment Club

When we started The Burlington Stockettes investment club in 1982, our plan was to disband after ten years and spend our profits.

By our tenth-anniversary meeting, however, we were having too much fun to quit.

While the club had provided us with an invaluable, hands-on course in investing and good returns on our money, it had also created a warm community of friends.

In fact, our very survival would not have been possible had we not taken steps in advance to ensure that problems and disagreements did not escalate. Here are our secrets for staying happily together.

LIMIT SOCIALIZING

Our 15-member club is a diverse group. While we are all women, our occupations vary and our ages range from 46 to 75. We all love to catch up with each other at these meetings, a spirit that has helped us stay together, but we also know where the fun ends and business begins.

Strategy: Allow for a chitchat period before or after each club meeting. Ours is before and usually lasts one hour. Once the meeting starts, we focus exclusively on the stock market and the investment decisions that need to be made.

ELECT OFFICERS WITH SPECIFIC DUTIES

Many clubs feel that a hierarchy works against the spirit of a club, but most freewheeling clubs do not last very long.

Our club has four officers: president, vice president, secretary and treasurer. All officers, except the treasurer, are rotated each year to give everyone the opportunity to hold each office.

1. President

She prepares an agenda and runs each monthly meeting.

Example: As president, when things start to unravel, I say, "We really

STUDY THE BALANCE SHEET

When reading a company's annual report, ignore the public relations material and typical corporate self-congratulation usually found up-front in the reports. Turn to the numbers at the end. Subtract current liabilities from current assets to find out if the firm has enough working capital to keep going even if business falls off. Then divide current assets by current liabilities to get the current ratio. A 2:1 ratio is acceptable for manufacturing firms, while a smaller ratio means the company could run into short-term cash-flow problems.

need to get back on track," "Let everybody listen," or "Excuse me, I can't hear."

2. Vice President

She presides over the meeting if the president is unable to do so.

3. Secretary

She takes down the minutes of each meeting and mails them to the members and our stockbroker about two weeks before the next meeting.

4. Treasurer

She keeps our books and financial records and collects the $20 monthly dues that are used to buy stocks and cover our costs. We try to have the treasurer stay in office for three to five years.

KEEP THE MEETINGS FORMAL

Disorganization leads to disunity, which can cause a club to disband.

Strategy: Once our meetings begin, we follow *Robert's Rules of Order*, a book of parliamentary procedure that is sold at most bookstores. This procedure is stiff, but there must be rules of conduct that everyone respects and by which everyone abides. Otherwise, it's simply too easy for important work not to be discussed and acted upon.

CHOOSE THE RIGHT STOCKBROKER

A broker whose style does not match that of the club can cause many problems. The broker should make stock recommendations that conform to the club's investment criteria, and the treasurer should be comfortable with him or her.

Example: One of our early brokers was a disaster. He was condescending and didn't take us seriously. After two years, we got rid of him. We should have done so after two months, but we were new to investing and afraid to make the change.

SPREAD THE HARD WORK AROUND

One of our rules is that every member must follow at least one or two stocks and report on them at our monthly meetings. These may be stocks that we already own, or stocks that we're thinking of buying. This allows all members to be actively involved.

CHOOSE NEW MEMBERS CAREFULLY

Many clubs give little thought to this process. Their only goal is to find and attract people who are more savvy than the current members are about investing, in the hope that the new members will boost the club's performance.

Before we accept a new member, we try to make sure that she is more interested in learning about the stock market and investing than in making a quick buck. We ask questions about her investing experience, what kinds of stocks she likes and what she considers to be a reasonable rate of return. We want members who are realistic, not those who expect huge portfolio growth overnight.

DON'T PERSONALIZE MISTAKES

It is inevitable that a club is going to pick some losing stocks. Resist the urge to blame the person who originally suggested the stock, even in private. The result will always be divisive and corrosive to the club's group spirit.

BE WILLING TO CHANGE

Our club almost fell apart in its first few years. Our portfolio was performing miserably in a rising market. We were losing between 7% and 10% a year.

Solution: Instead of letting failure get to us, we sat down and worked to identify the problem. We realized that we hadn't been investigating companies carefully enough, so we changed our procedures. From then on, no one could recommend buying or selling a stock unless she had very hard data to back up her opinion.

Investment Clubs: Partnerships or Corporations?

Investment club partnerships have more tax advantages than clubs set up as corporations. A partnership does not pay taxes; partners are responsible for reporting their shares of the club's income on their personal tax returns. In a corporation, the club itself must pay corporate taxes on earnings. Then its members must pay individual income tax on money paid to them as dividends. Consult your attorney and your accountant for more information.

The Buck Stops Here

Some experts say there is an inherent difference between men and women investors. When men lose money, they tend to blame the market or their broker, while women tend to blame themselves.

Crisis-Proof Your Investments

While dramatic rises in the markets result in profits and excitement, declines often follow, creating fear and anxiety.

Here are four easy steps that will help investors stay free from daily worry.

STEP 1: DETERMINE THE RIGHT MIX OF STOCKS AND BONDS.

If you are going to reach long-term goals, you must make a commitment to invest at least some of your money in stocks.

You also should hold some bonds so that you aren't totally at the mercy of the stock market's swings. As a rule, the younger you are, the greater the proportion you can commit to stocks because you can afford to ride out such fluctuations.

Strategies: If you are willing to accept moderate financial risks, your age can represent the approximate percentage of long-term savings that you should invest in bonds. Invest the entire remainder in stocks.

BEFORE YOU CHOOSE AN INVESTMENT FIRM

Check out an investment advisory firm before committing your money to any investment.

Dun & Bradstreet (800-362-2255) will report on a firm's credit history, background, liens, lawsuits and judgments filed against it. Cost: $79.

The National Association of Securities Dealers (800-289-9999) reports on the disciplinary history of persons in the brokerage industry. Cost: Free for individual investors and $30 per request for corporate inquiries.

Nexis Express (800-843-6476) will conduct a search of past and pending litigation against a firm. Cost: $25 per search plus $5 per document.

If you want to take on somewhat more risk, subtract your age from 110. The result is the minimum percentage of your long-term investment portfolio that should be allocated to stocks.

Example: At age 50, an investor who wants to take moderate risks should adopt a portfolio that includes a 50% stake in bonds and a 50% stake in stocks. If you want to be more aggressive, you could invest at least 60% of your portfolio in stocks and only 40% in bonds. It is best to rebalance investments within the IRA portion of your portfolio, which is tax-deferred. Also, use a discount broker to reduce your commissions on stock and bond sales.

Using Your Age to Allocate Your Money

Moderate risk

Your age	25
Equals your bond allocation	25%
(Stock allocation	75%)

High risk

110	110
Minus your age	-25
Equals your stock allocation	85%
(Bond allocation	15%)

Important: Short-term income investments, such as money-market funds or bank savings accounts, have no place in long-term investment portfolios. They simply don't provide the returns you need to beat inflation over time.

Some people insist on holding large sums, perhaps six months' worth of income, in an emergency reserve. But since most investments can be sold in a matter of days, it doesn't make sense to keep money languishing for years on end in such low-paying investments.

STEP 2: CHOOSE THE RIGHT TYPES OF STOCKS & BONDS

Studies have shown that long-term investment success is far more dependent upon allocating your money appropriately among the various investment categories than it is on trying to select the best-performing investments.

By far, the best strategy is to divide savings among a range of mutual funds. That way, some of your funds will be working for you even when others are not, and you won't feel left out when one sector is doing particularly well, since chances are you will own a piece of it.

Stocks

Investors who are willing to take moderate risks can divide their portfolio holdings as follows.

- Growth stocks: 20%.
- Growth and income stocks: 40%.
- Small-company stocks: 20%.
- International stocks: 20%.

If you're an aggressive investor, split your stock holdings equally among these four categories.

Trap: Many investors start out by committing too much money to a sector fund, which invests in stocks of companies in a single industry or related industries. That is a risky approach. If you invest in sector funds at all, limit those investments to 5% to 10% of your long-term portfolio.

Bonds

Divide your holdings equally between long- and either short- or intermediate-term funds that invest in corporate, municipal and U.S. government bonds.

Important: You will need approximately $25,000 to divide among the different stock and bond funds. If you have less, start by investing your stock money in growth-and-income funds and your bond money in government bond funds.

Beginning investors can start with a single balanced fund, which divides its money between stock and bond investments.

STEP 3: SELECT GREAT FUNDS

If you pick funds that are solid long-term performers, you won't have much to worry about.

STEP 4: PERIODICALLY REBALANCE YOUR INVESTMENT ALLOCATION

This strategy is very important to the success of your long-term investments. Changes in the financial markets can have a big impact on your portfolio and possibly leave you holding the wrong mix of investments in your portfolio.

Example: A sharp run-up in stock prices might increase the value of your stock funds. The result is that they will account for a greater percentage of your overall portfolio than before. After a few years, you may be holding a much riskier portfolio than you realize or intend.

Strategy: About every six months, return your investment allocation to the original percentages you established.

Example: Let's say you set up a 60% stock/40% bond split, but stock prices have climbed to the point that stock funds now account for 67% of your portfolio's total value. Sell shares in your stock funds so that your stock allocation is 60%, and use the resulting money to add more to bond funds.

Important: If you have to make a major change in your current investments right now to achieve an appropriate allocation of funds, do it gradually. Don't go from 0% in stocks to 50% overnight. You might wind up investing just before a major market decline that will cause you to suffer a heavy loss. Instead, sell and reinvest gradually.

Example: If you currently have 100% in cash investments and want to get to a 60% stock/40% bond allocation, here is a sensible schedule.

1. For the first six months, gradually build up to 20% stocks, 15% bonds and 65% money-market funds.

2. Then, for the next six to 12 months, go to 40% stocks, 25% bonds and 35% money-market funds.

3. After two years, you can redistribute your investments to your desired 60%/40% split.

Much Shrewder Investing

Frequent switches hurt investment returns.

Reasons: Switches incur fees that must be overcome with superior performance just to break even. People naturally tend to buy high, when the market is hot, and sell low, when things look bad, just the opposite of the desired investment strategy. Timing mistakes hurt returns more than correct timing decisions can help.

Don't Drop Out
Being out of the market during the ten worst of the last 50 years would have boosted your average returns only modestly, from 12.9% to 15.4% annually. But being out of the market during the ten best years would have cut your returns by more than half, to only 6.2% from 12.9%.

Muni Bond Opportunities

Investors who want municipal bonds should consider buying individual issues instead of purchasing bond mutual funds.

Studies have shown that the average municipal bond investor has $50,000 invested. Such an investor could put $10,000 in each of five different municipals, with different maturities ranging between seven and 12 years. Most bond funds have much longer maturities and are thus vulnerable to price declines as interest rates rise. Many funds contain risky derivatives.

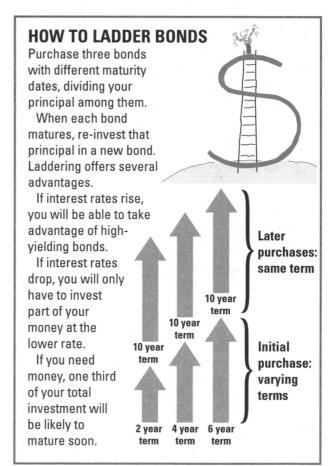

HOW TO LADDER BONDS
Purchase three bonds with different maturity dates, dividing your principal among them.

When each bond matures, re-invest that principal in a new bond. Laddering offers several advantages.

If interest rates rise, you will be able to take advantage of high-yielding bonds.

If interest rates drop, you will only have to invest part of your money at the lower rate.

If you need money, one third of your total investment will be likely to mature soon.

Later purchases: same term

Initial purchase: varying terms

10 year term

10 year term

10 year term

2 year term

4 year term

6 year term

Important: Buy AAA-rated insured municipals that have an ironclad no-call provision. Ladder the maturities so that each $10,000 bond comes due in a different year so that your interest rate risk is minimized.

Jonathan Pond Tells How to Avoid the Most Common Investing Mistakes

You can improve your investment returns and lower your taxes by making the right investment decisions. Unfortunately, many investors over 50 inadvertently shoot themselves in the foot. They make simple mistakes that could be easily avoided. Here are the most common errors investors make, and the appropriate action they should take instead.

SELLING TOO SOON

The inclination to sell a losing investment or an underper-former is greater for people over 50.

Reason: You think you can't afford any kind of loss or performance disap-pointment.

Example: I know many people who want to sell their international mutual funds because these invest-ments have dramatically lagged behind the U.S. market. Now, however, is precisely the wrong time to sell international holdings. I think they offer much better growth opportunities than U.S. stocks.

Strategy: Instead of bailing out, buy more.

Exception: If an individual stock has been a dog for a long time, dumping it may make a lot of sense.

Simply ask yourself: "Knowing what I now know, would I choose to buy this stock today?" If the answer is no, sell it.

CHANGING TOO MUCH AS YOU AGE

It's wrong to ditch a smart investment strategy just because someone says you should, or because you've reached a certain age at which you think you're supposed to turn your entire investment approach upside down.

Challenge: Most people in their 60s and 70s still need to be long-term investors.

Strategy: Even when it is time to make your port-folio more conservative, when you need income to live on, don't make drastic changes. Instead, invest for both growth and income.

NEGLECTING TO SAVE DURING RETIREMENT

Many retired people think they're doing well if they can live off the income from their principal without making outright withdrawals. But that's not good enough. This approach ignores inflation.

Strategy: Most retirees will have to keep saving into their mid-70s or beyond because of inflation. If you don't, eventually the income you receive won't be enough to sup-port you. Then you'll have to invade principal, your income will start to drop and the situation will continue to worsen.

BUYING ANNUITIES IMPROPERLY

Deciding what to do with a lump-sum distribution from an employer may be the most important financial decision you ever face.

Strategy: Don't buy an annuity imme-diately. Remember, there's no rush. Even waiting a few years is fine.

Reasons: You need time to shop for the right annu-ity. (You can add hundreds of dollars of annual annu-ity income by shopping around.) The older you are when you buy your annuity, the higher your annuity income will be.

FAILING TO INVESTIGATE THE NEW TYPES OF ANNUITIES

Variable immediate-pay annuities may be the right option for you, but you have to know about them be-fore you can buy them. With variable immediate-pay annuities, your investment is put into several mutual funds and your payout begins immediately. The

Is my estate plan solid?

Should I change my strategy?

Do I need to keep saving?

Am I selling too soon?

Should I abandon my tax-deferred investments?

Estate Plan

Portfolio

amount paid will rise if your funds rise, and fall if they fall. You have to be able to tolerate this risk, but the long-term history of the stock markets says that you'll be rewarded.

ABANDONING TAX-DEFERRED VEHICLES
When many people get close to retirement, they think they no longer need to participate in IRAs and similar savings vehicles.

Strategy: Realize that even if your contribution isn't tax-deductible, there is still great value in having money accumulate on a tax-deferred basis. But isn't this inconsequential if you're just a few years from retirement? Not at all. Every incremental increase in income helps.

TAPPING THE WRONG ACCOUNTS
Many people withdraw too much from their tax-deferred accounts.

Reason: They regard their taxable accounts as their life savings, and therefore untouchable. This thinking is counterproductive.

Strategy: Eat into the principal of your taxable accounts first. That way, you won't interrupt the tax-deferred asset growth you're enjoying. In addition, you will probably end up paying a much lower tax bill.

Reason: The bite on a tax-deferred account is likely to be higher when you do make a withdrawal because you haven't paid any taxes on this money since you opened the account.

THINKING GROWTH AND INCOME ARE IN CONFLICT
Actually, they can work beautifully together. Take a page from the playbook of rich folks. They often buy stocks in top-quality companies that have a history of raising their dividends.

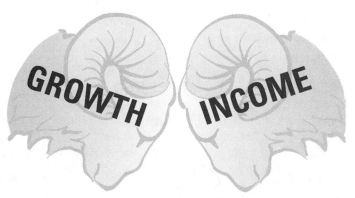

Reason: Over time, steady dividend increases sharply boost current income. The appreciation of the stock takes care of the growth portion of the equation.

Strategy: To increase your income, review *Value Line* at your library to find a list of companies that regularly raise their dividends.

Common Money Management Mistakes

Either because of bad habits, false assumptions or simple lack of knowledge, millions of people make avoidable financial errors. No matter what the cause is, the cost of such mistakes can be enormous.

Result: You, your spouse and your heirs may suffer needlessly. Here are some of the most common mistakes to avoid.

NOT ADJUSTING INSURANCE AS YOU AGE

Consider converting your term insurance to a whole-life policy or cutting the amount of your coverage. At the very least, reassess your insurance needs.

You probably began buying term insurance many years ago because it offered the biggest death benefit for your premium dollar. That benefit would have covered tuition costs and the mortgage, and provided for a surviving spouse. But the kids have graduated, the mortgage is paid and you now may have sufficient assets to handle the needs of a surviving spouse.

Do you need insurance at all? Quite possibly the answer is still yes.

Reason: To pay estate taxes. Yes, everything does pass tax-free to your surviving spouse. After that, however, assets of more than the exemption amount ($625,000 in 1998, increasing to $1 million by 2006) will be taxed upon your spouse's death at rates of up to 55%.

Strategy: Life insurance held outside your estate in an irrevocable insurance trust can be used to pay estate taxes.

Note: Be sure to set up the irrevocable trust before you buy a new permanent life insurance policy that continues coverage to at least age 85 or 90. Then, buy the policy in the name of the trust. Pay for the insurance by gifting money to the trust and having trustees pay the annual premiums. Consider the new types of flexible policies that let you alter both annual premiums and death benefits.

NOT UNDERSTANDING YOUR RETIREMENT BENEFITS

All the planning in the world won't work if that planning is based on false assumptions.

Strategy: Check on your retirement benefits at work. If you have a pension plan, be aware that some promises can change.

ACCEPTING BAD EARLY-RETIREMENT PACKAGES

Begin by asking your company to give you a statement of your retirement benefits based on your current earnings.

Strategy: If you're considering early retirement, be absolutely sure of how benefits will be lowered if you miss out on a few years of peak earnings. Many early retirement buyout packages offer to credit additional earning years. Some also bridge the health insurance gap until you qualify for Medicare. Be wary of packages that don't have these benefits.

MISHANDLING YOUR 401(k)

Be sure you're making your maximum contribution and reevaluate your investment choices regularly. Many people put too much of their retirement money in their company's own stock.

Strategy: Be sensibly aggressive. You should not have too much riding on any one stock or mutual fund. After all, once you've retired and you're no longer making contributions to your 401(k), it will take a long time to make up for a major loss.

Don't Count on It

Americans who expect to rely on Social Security payments during their retirement years should re-evaluate their plans. The funding projections for Social Security have dropped radically since the mid 1980s, indicating that retirees will have to rely more and more on their own savings.

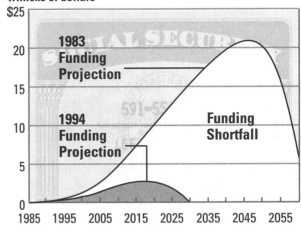

Trillions of dollars

Source: 1983 and 1994 Social Security Trustees Reports

COUNTING ON SOCIAL SECURITY

The standard advice is to check with Social Security to see how much you can expect to get. Those who are bearish on Social Security think you'll be better off if you assume that any benefits you get will be entirely supplemental income.

Strategy: Don't lose sleep over the worst-case Social Security scenario, but be prepared. Put as much money as possible in a 401(k) and even in a nondeductible IRA. When you've reached the maximum in contributions, consider buying tax-deferred annuities backed by a top-rated insurance company.

NOT CHECKING HEALTH INSURANCE ALTERNATIVES

If you are planning to retire early, it's important to price alternative health insurance plans. True, your retirement plan may offer an 18-month COBRA (Consolidated Omnibus Budget Reconciliation Act of 1986) extension of your coverage, but that's not going to cover you for long.

Ask yourself: "Can I really afford early retirement if I have to cover my own health insurance?"

Strategy: Contact AARP and local HMOs to get an idea of your choices.

OVERPAYING FOR LONG-TERM CARE INSURANCE

You probably only need a policy that will cover three years in a nursing home.

Strategy: A policy will be cheaper if you pay the first three or six months out-of-pocket. Inflation-adjustment riders increase the cost of coverage, but they may be worth it; nursing home costs are rising.

NOT HAVING A SOUND ESTATE PLAN

Find an experienced estate planning attorney. Have him or her review existing documents and create any new estate planning instruments you might need.

Best option: Set up a living trust. Name yourself and your spouse as cotrustees and a trusted younger relative or attorney as successor trustee. Make sure you transfer title to all your properties into your living trust.

Warning: If you don't, your estate will have to go through probate in every state in which you own property.

Never Invest with Phone Marketers

It is all right to deal with a broker or mutual fund by phone, but never deal with a stranger who calls you. Some calls may be legitimate, but few are. Just hang up.

Just say no.

Warning: Never invest when a seller tries to rush you or impose a time limit. Any legitimate investment should give you plenty of printed information to read, and adequate time to digest it and ask questions.

On-Line Investment Advice Alert

On-line investment advice varies greatly in quality. A lot of excellent information is available, but scam artists also operate in this unregulated environment.

Rule of Thumb: Use computer networks to collect data that help you form your own opinion. Beware of hype and promises delivered over a network.

- Don't assume that bulletin boards police those who make claims through them.
- Don't rely on advice received from any person who hides his or her identity.
- Don't believe any claims about "inside information" or "pending news releases."
- Don't overlook the conflict of interest that exists when a person who touts an investment is also selling it.

What Every Married Woman Should Know About Money

Any married woman today is likely to fall victim to one of the Three Ds: Death, Divorce or other Disasters. Consider these stunning statistics.

- About one-half of all marriages end in divorce.
- Nearly 80% of married women become widows and remain widows for an average of 15 years.
- If your husband is 40 or younger, he is three times more likely to be disabled than to die, and after

age 55 the chances are he will be disabled for a year or more.

Yet few wives know much about family finances beyond routine, day-to-day matters. Even many high-powered career women tend to abdicate a role in family investment decisions and planning. But if a woman heard about a vaccine for a disease that was bound to strike one out of two people, she would probably dash to the doctor to get it.

No woman should be ignorant about money. She should know how it is spent, where it is kept, how it is invested and how it is owned. Ignorance will leave a woman vulnerable while she is married and in serious trouble when she is no longer married.

The more a woman knows the better off she is. It is vital to know the law in your state as it applies to marriage. Women should know their rights and what will happen to them in case of divorce or death.

COMMUNITY-PROPERTY STATES

There are some variations, but basically each spouse owns half of all the property amassed during the marriage, no matter who earns the money or what name is on the title.

Exceptions: inherited property and gifts.

Debts are also community property. If a husband borrows money that he then blows at a casino in Las Vegas, half the debt is his wife's.

The more a woman knows, the better off she is financially.

COMMON-LAW STATES

A spouse doesn't automatically own half the property. Joint ownership has to be specified when property is acquired. Otherwise, ownership rests with the title holder, who has the right to sell or mortgage the property, even if it is the family home. If a spouse dies without property in her name, she has nothing to leave for the support of aged, dependent parents or other heirs.

In the case of divorce, however, the assets a couple acquired during the marriage become marital property to be divided.

Note: The split is rarely 50/50.

THE BOTTOM LINE

Knowing a wife has some legal rights to her husband's money, as he does to hers, can and should spur her to take an active role in family finances. Here are six things women usually don't know about their husband's money, but should.

● How much he spends.
● How much he has.
● How much he owes.
● How much insurance he has and what kind.
● How the assets (savings accounts, property and stock) are held.
● How he is leaving the assets (his will).

One way a wife can begin learning about her husband's money (and

WOMEN ON THEIR OWN

Women have a 90% chance of being on their own at some point during their lives, either because they never marry or because they are divorced or widowed. That means all women need to be prepared to handle their own finances.

Women's marital status	Age group					
	30s	40-54	55-64	65-74	75-84	85 and over
Percent never married	12.8	5.9	4.1	3.8	4.0	8.0
Percent married	66.7	68.3	66.1	52.4	30.3	13.3
Percent divorced	14.1	16.6	12.6	7.7	4.1	2.9
Percent widowed	1.2	4.7	13.9	34.2	59.9	73.7

Source: U.S. Bureau of the Census, 1994   Table does not include married women living apart from their husbands.

her own), is to think of the family as a company. Make up the same kind of corporate reports that a business would. Start with what the family has.

ASSETS

Make a list of all the family assets, including the following.
- Personal property (house, furniture or car).
- Financial assets (stocks, bonds and savings accounts).
- Real estate, business partnerships and hidden assets, such as stock options, pension funds and insurance (cash and benefit value).

Indicate how each asset is owned.

DEBTS

Look at what the family owes: its liabilities.
- Outstanding taxes.
- Mortgages.
- Loans (business, personal, car and home equity).
- Credit card debt, installment debt and margin debt on brokerage accounts.

The family's net worth is the difference between assets and liabilities.

UNDERSTAND THE CASH FLOW
The other important corporate report is a cash-flow statement: how much money is coming in and how much is going out.

Make a list of total income, from salary and bonuses to dividends and interest. Then track expenditures, including every item right down to newspapers and magazines. The two should be equal. If outgoing is larger, then your family is spending too much.

Having a firm grasp of the facts and figures enables a woman to know how she would manage on her own if something happened to her husband or the marriage. If she doesn't know now, she'll really have problems later on.

A woman who doesn't understand her family's finances can't play an equal role in making financial decisions. Ignorance can leave her feeling dependent and vulnerable. Knowing about the assets, helping to keep the records and taking part in decision-making are all part of the economic partnership that modern marriage is supposed to be.

CREATE A WILL
If a couple makes financial decisions together, they will probably discuss wills. The contents of a husband's will shouldn't come as a surprise to his wife.

Some couples think that if one spouse dies without a will (intestate) the surviving spouse will inherit everything. Not true. Except for jointly-held assets, state law dictates how the money will be disbursed.

Examples:
- In Oklahoma, a surviving spouse receives one-half the estate. Children get the other half. If there are no children but a parent or sibling survives the husband, the widow gets all the marital property plus a one-third interest in the remaining estate.
- In California, a community-property state, each spouse already owns half the marital property. The surviving spouse inherits half of her husband's community property and a portion (from one-third to one-half, depending on surviving children, parents or siblings) of his separate property.

TALK TO YOUR HUSBAND
It is hard to admit vulnerability, especially in money matters. Whether based on a tradition of dependence or the reality of lower wages, a lot of women, even those with substantial earning power, fear they will wind up destitute.

Women have taken care of home, husband, children and parents. It is time they started taking care of their finances. The keys to financial freedom are knowledge and participation.

Alexandra Armstrong's Investment Strategies For People Over 50

Some financial professionals use strict rules to manage money for people over age 50. Those rules are often wrong, and, even when valid, they certainly don't apply to everyone. Far more important than so-called rules are guidelines with built-in flexibility.

PRERETIREMENT TACTICS

● **Begin with a solid asset-allocation model.** Forget those rigid rules, like "subtract your age from 100 to determine the equity percentage of your portfolio." These equations are glib answers that cause many people to put too much money in bonds. Furthermore, they say nothing about what kind of equities you should own during the different stages of your life.

Here's a good asset-allocation model that works for most people over age 50 who haven't retired:
1. Stocks: 65%.
2. Bonds: 25%.
3. Cash: 5%.
4. Other (Real Estate Investment Trusts, partnerships or leasing): 5%.

Don't blindly accept this model, however. If the equity percentage feels high, adjust downward. Just don't add too much to the cash category.

● **Change asset allocations within categories.** Not enough investors do. Become more or less aggressive by maneuvering within an asset class.

● **Have a strategic equities mix.** The same logic applies to stocks. Here's a good stock allocation model:
1. U.S. stocks: 67%.
2. International stocks: 33%.

If international stocks scare you, that's understandable. After all, some emerging markets have imploded in the past few years, and international

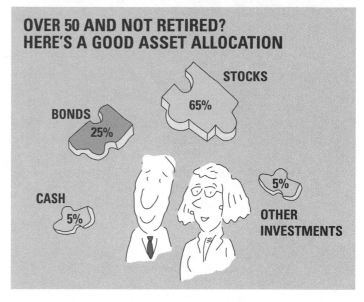

OVER 50 AND NOT RETIRED? HERE'S A GOOD ASSET ALLOCATION

STOCKS 65%

BONDS 25%

CASH 5%

OTHER INVESTMENTS 5%

equities in general have dramatically underperformed the American market recently.

Nonetheless, the long-term outlook remains excellent. In spite of poor recent returns, Morgan Stanley's EAFE Index of foreign markets has beaten the S&P 500 in 16 of the past 25 years.

Solution: Have half of your international holdings in emerging markets and the other half in blue-chip stocks. Or take a more conservative approach by concentrating on blue chips.

If you're nervous about international stocks, invest slowly. Put in a modest amount each month to dollar cost average. That way, the added volatility of international markets can work in your favor.

● **Avoid single-country funds.** They're a real gamble, and you're more vulnerable to currency swings because the fund's assets are in only one country's currency.

● **With U.S. stocks, a good allocation is**
1. Blue chips: 50%.
2. Small- & mid-cap: 40%.
3. Aggressive growth: 10%.

Small- and mid-cap stocks are attractive because they have more earnings growth potential than large-cap stocks and because they haven't had as good a run as other market sectors.

A strategic equities mix for working people over 50 should include blue-chip, small and mid-cap, aggressive growth and international stocks.

AGGRESSIVE GROWTH

Consider technology sector funds that have good long-term prospects. These less traditional vehicles include the following.

- **Real Estate Investment Trusts (REITs).** REITs are publicly traded stocks with yields much higher than the average equity.

  Note: Their price movement is tied more to fluctuations in the interest rate than to stock market swings.

- **Real estate partnerships.** The reputation of partnerships has been sullied, but good ones still exist.

  Warning: Don't buy unless you're being guided by someone you trust.

- **Bonds.** If your tax bracket is 28% or more, A-rated (or better) municipal bonds still make sense on an after-tax basis. Bonds with maturities of ten to 15 years are a good choice, no matter what your age. (If you die before the bonds mature, the bonds pass intact to your heirs.)

SAVE, SAVE, SAVE

Don't make the mistake of depositing interest payments, dividends and distributions into your checking account. This is money to invest, not spend! You may need the money later on. Besides, if you keep the money invested, compounding will work in your favor.

RETIREMENT TACTICS

Meet your income needs. Shift some money into utilities, REITs and bonds to generate income, but remember, some blue chips still provide healthy yields as well. Don't dump them without careful thought. International stocks pay notoriously low dividends. If you need income, these aren't for you.

Gradually become more conservative. Change the mix within asset categories. You could eliminate aggressive growth and emerging-market funds. Switch some, or all, of small- and mid-cap holdings into blue chips.

Always Be Prepared

Unpleasant financial shocks are easier if you're always living on no more than 90% of your salary. Then most financial surprises won't be a huge blow to your lifestyle.

How to Live Fee-Free

It's easy to save money by reducing or eliminating annual financial fees.

UP TO 40% OFF COMMISSIONS

If you're an active investor and you make your own investment decisions, consider using a discount broker. It can drastically reduce your commissions.

Discounters aren't all the same. Traditional discounters such as Charles Schwab (800-435-4000) and Fidelity (800-544-8888) offer some services such as free investment research. They will also save you as much as 40% on commissions. Deep-discount brokers such as Wall Street Discount (800-221-4034) and Arnold Securities (800-328-4076) take a more bare-bones approach but offer even bigger commission cuts.

Potential annual savings: What you save depends on how many trades you make each year. The greater the number, the greater the savings.

NO-LOAD MUTUAL FUNDS

Many mutual funds sold by brokers carry sales charges, or loads, of 2% to 5%, which are used to compensate the brokers who sell them to individual investors.

Strategy: Choose no-load funds, such as those sold by Vanguard, T. Rowe Price and Fidelity. On a $1,000 investment, you could save as much as $50.

Also avoid the high annual fees that some funds charge. Choose stock funds with annual fees of less than 1.25% and bond funds with annual fees of less than 1%.

Potential savings: roughly $150 on an investment of $10,000 annually.

How Big Winner Doug Raborn Picks Winning Stocks

Well-run, well-positioned companies with attractive stock prices are getting harder to find. This trend does not mean that you should avoid the stock market completely. Over the long term, stock market surges tend to occur in short, unpredictable bursts. You won't benefit if most of your assets are in cash.

The key is smart stock picking. If you choose well, you won't need dozens of different companies to maximize your portfolio's potential for profits. In my typical client's portfolio, for example, there are only about 12 stocks. Here are my stock-picking secrets that anyone can use.

BUY STOCK IN COMPANIES YOU UNDERSTAND

If you like a company's product, you'll probably like its stock.

Of course, a preference for a company's product is not the only reason to buy a stock, but it is an essential first step. If I understand what the company makes and I use its products at work or at home, I will have a pretty good idea of whether the company is on the right track.

Example: A few years ago, we purchased Dell Computer equipment for the office and were very pleased with it. I knew that if Dell products met our needs, they probably were meeting the needs of many other companies. So I bought Dell stock in May 1991 at an average price of $16. I sold it in February 1993 at $37, more than doubling my clients' money in less than two years.

BUY STOCK NOT FOLLOWED BY ANALYSTS

Wall Street analysts tend to move in packs, praising or panning the same companies at the same time. As a result, some of the market's best values are overlooked, mostly because these companies are too small for big analysts to cover.

Many of the stocks in our clients' portfolios fall into this category. They are tracked by only three or four analysts. Just because these companies are small, however, doesn't mean they don't have great upside potential.

Investors must keep their eyes and ears open to find good stocks that analysts don't follow closely. Even if you don't personally own or use a product, your friends and relatives may. Their reactions can steer you toward some good companies.

Examples: You can ride in their new cars or listen to them talk about their new computers or sports equipment.

Another way to discover top-quality products is to read *Consumer Reports*. It is an excellent source of information on a wide variety of high-quality products.

Once you've decided on some good companies, call their public

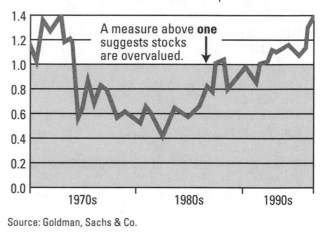

Do You Get What You Pay For?

Stocks have been increasingly overvalued during the 1990s, according to the cost of replacing their underlying assets. This graph shows the ratio of stock prices in the Standard & Poor's industrials to their replacement values.

A measure above **one** suggests stocks are overvalued.

Source: Goldman, Sachs & Co.

Small Companies, Big Growth

How one dollar invested in small company stocks at year-end 1925 would have grown through year-end 1996.

Index

$5,000
$1,000
$100
$10
$0.1

$4,495.99

Total Return Index

1925 1935 1945 1955 1965 1975 1985 1996

relations departments for a list of analysts who follow their stocks. If a company has a long list of analysts from big-name investment firms such as Merrill Lynch, Paine Webber and Smith Barney, forget about it. A much better sign is if only a handful of regional firms follow the company.

DON'T BE AFRAID OF CONTROVERSY

Consider buying into companies that are controversial, at least from the viewpoint of Wall Street analysts. Sometimes I'll buy stock in an undervalued company that is shunned by Wall Street. Many times analysts ignore a company's stock because they have a fundamental misconception about the company's product or future potential.

Example: Callaway Golf is a small maker of expensive golf clubs. Its share price declined by 30% in October 1993, when it was reported that much of its action came from investors who were short-sellers, investors who borrow money to buy a stock that they expect will decline.

In the case of Callaway, the short-sellers were wrong. Sales continued at their torrid pace. The short-sellers didn't realize that Callaway's patented golf club design was a breakthrough and that avid golfers will pay almost any price for equipment that delivers improved performance.

MEET THE PRESS

One of the best ways to find stocks that Wall Street believes are controversial is to follow the financial print and TV media. They often focus on which companies are unpopular with the investment community.

LOOK FOR LOW PRICE/EARNINGS RATIOS

I'm all for purchasing growth stocks, which sell at high prices and are expected to move even higher as the company grows. But I don't want the stock's price to be so high that the downside risk is perilous. A portfolio could be hurt badly if the stock drops dramatically.

The average price/earnings ratio of the stocks in my clients' portfolios is 12. That is below the market average. However, the average growth rate of my clients' stocks is 25%, vs. 14% for the S&P 500 Index.

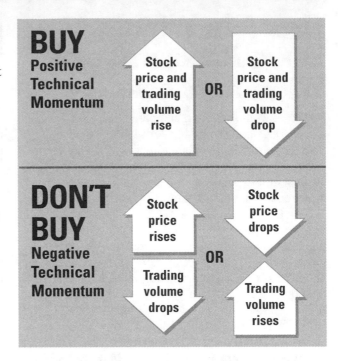

BUY Positive Technical Momentum — Stock price and trading volume rise OR Stock price and trading volume drop

DON'T BUY Negative Technical Momentum — Stock price rises / Trading volume drops OR Stock price drops / Trading volume rises

BUY POSITIVE TECHNICAL MOMENTUM

This means keeping an eye on a company's volume, or the number of shares it trades in a single day. A company's volume is listed in the stock tables next to its stock price.

It's best to buy when a company's price and volume rise, or when its price declines along with its volume.

Example: You've been following a stock and notice its daily volume is around 50,000 shares. After a few weeks, the price begins to climb and its daily volume is up around 150,000 shares. This would be a very positive sign indicating a buying opportunity.

KNOW WHEN TO SELL

My company has a rule for selling stocks. Generally, once a stock's price drops 20% from its high during the time we own it, we sell.

The 20% figure is arbitrary, but if the stock price drops by that much, it could be a sign of trouble. This automatic-sell strategy limits losses and removes the emotion from a difficult decision.

It's also important to sell when your stock produces a solid profit. On the upside, I sell when I've reached a target price. This target price is established by multiplying the company's expected growth rate by its earnings-per-share estimate for the following year. These numbers can be found in any company's analyst's report, which you can get through your broker.

Do Not Ride a Stock Down

Don't hold onto a declining stock, assuming that you've lost nothing until you sell those shares. In fact, in some cases, it is better to take a small loss by selling than to hold on to a declining stock for a long period.

Exercise: Say you now own stock shares worth $8,000 that you initially bought at a much higher price. Picture yourself as having $8,000 in cash. Ask yourself if you would invest the cash in the same stock today. If the answer is no, sell the stock and invest the proceeds as you would invest the cash.

Earnings vs. Cash Flow

Earnings are more important than cash flow for long-term investors. If a company's earnings rise over a period of years, the value of its stock cannot help but rise. If the trend for corporate profits is up, the stock market is sure to do well over a five-to-ten-year period, in spite of sell-offs that can occur in any given year.

Bill Staton Tells How To Become a Millionaire on $50 A Month

Mutual funds are giving individual stocks a good name. During the past few years, a growing number of investors have become less fearful of the stock market as they grow more comfortable with stock mutual funds.

Now many fund investors are thinking about taking the next step: investing in individual stocks. While this strategy may seem more risky than investing in funds, whose portfolios are managed by pros, it is not as complicated as it appears. You also don't need a lot of money to get started. You can invest as little as $50 a month and become a millionaire in about 40 years.

THE BIG SECRET

I came up with the figure of $50 after recently polling high school juniors and seniors. They told me that they waste at least $15 to $20 a week on things they

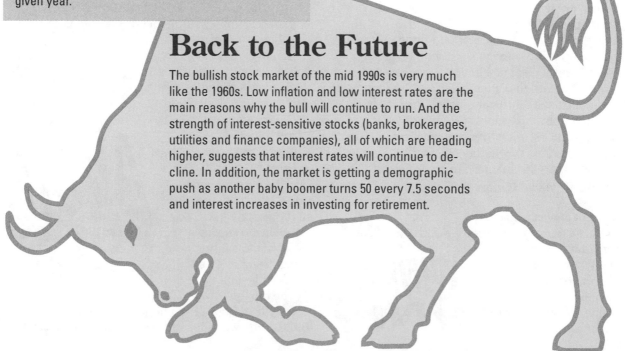

Back to the Future

The bullish stock market of the mid 1990s is very much like the 1960s. Low inflation and low interest rates are the main reasons why the bull will continue to run. And the strength of interest-sensitive stocks (banks, brokerages, utilities and finance companies), all of which are heading higher, suggests that interest rates will continue to decline. In addition, the market is getting a demographic push as another baby boomer turns 50 every 7.5 seconds and interest increases in investing for retirement.

don't really need, like snacks, candy and video games. That totals $60 to $80 a month, or $720 to $960 a year.

If that's how much passes through kids' hands each month, think about how much you must waste. Many adults tell me they waste much more.

If you could harness all that money, or even just $50 a month, and use it to start a regular investing program, you would be well on your way to becoming a millionaire, or maybe even a multimillionaire.

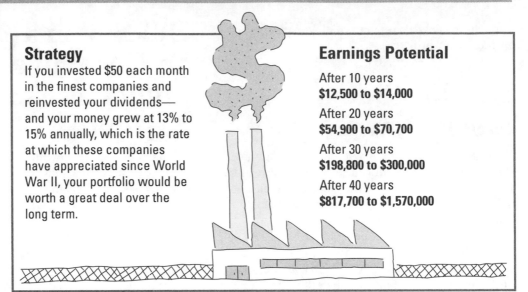

Strategy

If you invested $50 each month in the finest companies and reinvested your dividends— and your money grew at 13% to 15% annually, which is the rate at which these companies have appreciated since World War II, your portfolio would be worth a great deal over the long term.

Earnings Potential

After 10 years
$12,500 to $14,000

After 20 years
$54,900 to $70,700

After 30 years
$198,800 to $300,000

After 40 years
$817,700 to $1,570,000

THE EASY WAY TO INVEST

The key is to select the stocks of a few major companies that have had long histories of rising earnings and dividends. I call these stocks America's finest companies.

These make up my superior universe of stocks, which has consistently outperformed such broad market averages as the Dow Jones Industrial Average (DJIA) and the S&P 500 Index.

Important: Forget about market timing, a strategy that is followed by some experts who try to buy stocks when they are just about to rise and sell stocks just before they go into a slump. It's impossible to predict the future, and nobody can consistently time individual stocks or the market.

Strategy: Invest whenever you have some extra money, regardless of whether the market is up or down. Investing doesn't have to be difficult if you follow my five-point program.

1. Invest in proven winners

These are companies that have paid higher than average dividends per share annually for at least ten consecutive years. These companies consistently outdistance the stock market. You can pick proven win-

ners by using *Value Line* or *Standard & Poor's*, which are available in most libraries.

Make sure each company has a Dividend Reinvestment Plan (DRIP) that does not charge a commission. A DRIP uses stockholder's quarterly dividends to buy additional shares rather than sending the dividends to the stockholder in the form of cash payments.

Also, make sure each company has an optional cash payment plan, which allows stockholders to buy additional shares directly through the company without paying brokers. Call the investment relations departments of your target companies to determine if they have such plans.

Try to own between five and eight stocks, each in a different industry. This range will help your portfolio deliver outstanding results, and the diversity will cushion you during a downturn in one or two sectors of the economy.

2. Open a brokerage account

Use the account to purchase your initial stocks in these companies. To enroll in a company's DRIP, you must first own a single share of its stock.

Don't be intimidated by the thought of opening a brokerage account. It usually takes just a few minutes on the phone with a broker who will ask you for some basic information.

Then you'll need to complete some documents—and that's all.

Consider using a discount broker. Their commissions are typically 50% below those charged by full-service brokers. Though most don't provide investment advice or analysts' reports, you won't need their advice if you follow my five-point program.

On the other hand, don't worry too much about commissions, since you're only buying your first share of each company through the broker. You will be making future purchases directly through the companies.

3. Sign up for each company's DRIP

After you've enrolled in a DRIP, your next quarterly dividend will be used to buy a fractional share of stock.

Newly purchased shares must be registered in your name and held by the company or sent directly to you; they are not kept by your broker. Each quarter, the company will mail you a statement showing exactly how much stock you own.

4. Buy more shares commission-free

The company's optional cash-payment plan allows you to buy additional shares of stock by mailing the purchase price directly to the company without paying a commission for the new shares.

Typically, the minimum purchase price is $25 and the maximum ranges from $3,000 to $5,000.

I suggest investing in a different company each quarter, rotating among all of the companies you have chosen. At the end of the year, rebalance to concentrate future purchases in the underinvested companies.

5. Don't sell your stock

I don't advocate unloading your purchases unless you need the money, or unless a company is no longer paying higher dividends per share over ten consecutive years. If you need to sell stock, it can be done through the company.

The DJIA Bias

The Dow Jones Industrial Average (DJIA) has an upward bias that inflates it in comparison to other market averages.

Reason: The DJIA is price-weighted, so high-priced stocks have a greater impact on it than low-priced stocks. Thus, if a stock at $120 doubles in value, the DJIA goes up 270 points. But if a stock at $13 doubles, the DJIA goes up only 29 points. When stocks reach high levels, companies split them to reduce their value. Later price decreases carry less weight than earlier increases.

The Timing Pitfall

Don't try to time the stock market. In actual practice, timing usually means following the market: getting in after it rises and getting out after it falls.

Trap: No one yet has figured out how to consistently determine when big market moves will begin.

Dramatic market moves take place over short periods. For example, 50% of the stock market's rise during the past decade took place in only four of the 120 months. If you buy while following the market, you are likely to miss much of a market rise, buy high and have to sell low when the market falls. And no one is going to tell you when to buy again.

Dividend Payout Dates Vary

If you need income, invest so you receive dividend checks as often as twice a month, not simply once a quarter. Be sure you analyze the stocks, not focusing only on those that fit in with your payment schedule.

John Train Tells How To Piggyback Investment Masters' Winning Ways

One easy way for individuals to achieve above-average stock performance is to follow the advice of master investors. The trick, of course, is to find professionals who are a cut above the rest.

CHOOSING THE RIGHT MASTERS

In my opinion, a true master is someone who has consistently beaten the market averages for more than a decade.

The masters whom I follow include private investors Jim Rogers and Warren Buffett, as well as mutual fund managers Ralph Wanger, George Michaelis, Peter Lynch and John Neff.

HOW TO PROFIT FROM THEIR WISDOM

Investment gurus are featured in a wide variety of publications. The key is to fish in the right places, where they first discuss their ideas. Gurus often turn up in articles and on TV repeating their theories.

Don't blindly buy the stocks the masters recommend, but do use their ideas to help you decide which companies to research. Unless you study a company, you'll have no idea when to buy, or sell, its stock.

Pay attention to a master's discussion of emerging themes. Besides being outstanding stock pickers, some investment masters are brilliant economic thinkers. If two masters agree on a new trend, that could lead you to some interesting investment ideas. Here are my favorite information sources, many of which can be found at the library or obtained through your broker.

● *Barron's* (Weekly, $145/yr., 800-277-4136) often features the analysis and stock picks of these masters. Each year, *Barron's* publishes its Roundtable, in which ten masters discuss major trends. It appears in three consecutive issues in January and February. The participants all have great track records and take the discussion very seriously.

● *Investor's Business Daily* (252 issues for $189, 800-306-9744) highlights recent transactions of six top performing mutual fund managers. The information reflects activity through the end of the previous quarter, so there is usually a lag of several months. If two great fund managers are accumulating a stock, it's probably worth a look. *Investor's Business Daily* always lists a fund manager's performance for the current year and the preceding three years, so you can get a sense of how he or she has performed in different types of markets.

● *Portfolio Reports* (Monthly, $575/yr., 212-777-3330) tells you what 100 or so superior money managers are doing with their portfolios. Most people won't have time to follow all 100 money managers, so focus on ten or 12 whose styles you know best. See if they are systematically adding to their positions in a stock or have recently sold their shares. *Portfolio Reports* gives details on what managers have recently bought, but not on overall holdings. Information usually appears three to six months after a transaction has taken place.

- *Morningstar Mutual Funds* (26 issues for $425, 312-424-4288) updates its funds every two weeks on a ten-issue cycle.
- *Value Line Mutual Fund Survey* (26 issues for $295, 800-284-7607) tracks mutual fund managers three times a year. Funds are updated in a full-page analysis. Both *Value Line* and *Morningstar* list the largest holdings of each fund.

The Beardstown Ladies Investment Club's Secrets of Success in the Stock Market

Our experience has taught us that investors willing to do a little work will achieve outstanding results—under virtually any market conditions.

First of all, join the National Association of Investors Corporation (NAIC, 810-583-6242) and learn how to use its *Stock Selection Guides* to determine if the fundamentals and the current stock price are favorable when you are searching for a stock to buy.

Here's what to do next:

BUY STOCKS WITH STEADY, PREDICTABLE GROWTH

We seek companies whose sales and earnings have grown 15% a year over the past five- or ten-year period. We want to make sure that sales and earnings growth are projected to continue for another five years.

A small company should be projected to grow 12% to 15% or more. A medium-size company should grow at least 10% to 12% and a large established company should grow approximately 7% to 10%.

Strategy: We use *Value Line Investment Survey* for growth projections to compliment NAIC's *Stock Selection Guides*. *Value Line* ranks 1,700 stocks from 1 to 5, with 1 being the highest, for expected performance over the next year. We buy only those stocks ranked 1 or 2.

Caution: Earnings growth doesn't really impress us unless accompanied by robust sales growth. Otherwise, what you have is not a real growth stock.

If a stock doesn't have at least a three- to five-year history of earnings to analyze, avoid it as well.

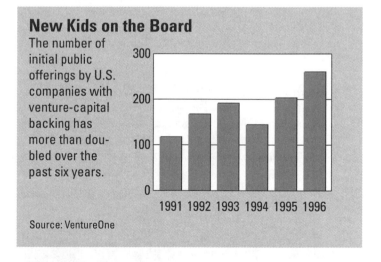

New Kids on the Board

The number of initial public offerings by U.S. companies with venture-capital backing has more than doubled over the past six years.

1991 1992 1993 1994 1995 1996

Source: VentureOne

DON'T OVERPAY

Before buying a stock, find out its earnings and high and low prices for the past five years. Divide each year's high and low price by the earnings for the year to get a set of five annual high and low price/earnings (P/E) ratios. Add them up and divide by ten to get the stock's five-year average P/E.

Strategy: Buy only if the current P/E is no higher than the five-year average P/E has been.

Note: Besides preventing us from overpaying, this technique also reinforces the virtue of patience. We've found that we do much better when we study a stock over time and wait for the P/E figures to be within our acceptable limits before we buy.

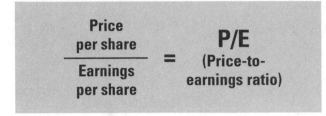

$$\frac{\text{Price per share}}{\text{Earnings per share}} = \frac{\text{P/E}}{\text{(Price-to-earnings ratio)}}$$

RELY ONLY ON RESEARCH WITH PROVEN VALUE

Experience has taught us to swear by *Value Line* and by our own common sense—and little else. We don't try to time the market.

Strategy: In addition to trusting *Value Line's* timeliness rankings, we rely on their safety rankings as well. We like to buy only those stocks that have a safety ranking of 1 or 2. We also restrict ourselves to stocks that are in industries that are ranked in the top one-third by *Value Line.* (In each issue, the survey ranks 97 different industry groups.) We prefer to buy companies that are ranked in the top 25 of all industries.

AVOID COMPANIES WITH SUBSTANTIAL DEBT OR UNRESOLVED PROBLEMS

Everyone makes mistakes, but it's hard to beat the market if your mistakes turn into disasters.

Strategy: One way to guard against this is to buy only stocks whose debts account for no more than one-third of capitalization. (This information is available from *Value Line,* Standard & Poor's directories or a company's annual report.) If the debt is greater than this, it is very important to find out how the company is using its debt, and whether the potential is there to benefit the shareholder. Similarly, we don't want to walk through a minefield if we don't have to. If a company

is facing a serious class action or patent infringement suit that could threaten its future, we'll wait for a favorable court ruling before buying its stock.

TAKE ONLY PRUDENT RISKS

Growth stock investors get hurt if their selections don't prosper, so make sure you choose companies with high potential. You want to have an upside/downside ratio of at least 3 to 1.

Technique: Use the NAIC's *Stock Selection Guides* to find a company's projected high and low prices five years from now.

Example: Subtract the current price ($25) from the high ($75). That leaves you with $50. Subtract the projected low ($15) from the current price ($25). That leaves you with $10. This gives you a ratio of 5 to 1 ($50 to $10), which means it's a good buy.

CONCENTRATE ON RELATIVELY STABLE STOCKS

Volatile stocks, stocks that move up and down much more sharply than the general market, have betas significantly greater than 1. (The term "beta" refers to a stock's relative volatility. The overall market has a beta of 1. A stock with a beta of 1 is neither more nor less volatile than the overall market.) We concentrate on stocks with betas between 0.9 and 1.1, which means, essentially, that they fluctuate about as much as the overall market.

SEEK GOOD MANAGEMENT

Look for managers with track records of success, and read the most recent annual reports to assess management's candor. If a company had some serious problems last year but the annual report reads like a whitewash, avoid investing in that company.

SELECT COMPANIES THAT ARE GETTING BETTER

How can you tell? The best way is to look for companies with rising profit margins. That's a powerful indication that a company has a strong competitive position.

SELL INTELLIGENTLY

When we buy a stock, we expect its price to double in five years. If it does, we reevaluate its prospects. Would we buy it again today? Does it still look strong? If it doesn't, we sell.

Projected Earnings Trap

Projected earnings are some of the least reliable statistics on Wall Street.

Example: Year-ahead earnings forecasts made by professional stock analysts for 399 companies over 11 years were found to be an amazing 57% too high on average. This creates both a trap and an opportunity.

Trap: buying a high-priced stock on the basis of inflated earnings forecasts.

Self-defense: Reduce forecasts by at least 10% to 15%, and then see if the investment still looks attractive.

Opportunity: exploiting analysts' errors. Stocks often move sharply up or down when reported earnings differ from forecasts. Look out for possible earnings surprises, and act quickly when they arise.

Best Way to Beat The Market

The simplest way to beat the market is by using the Dow Dividend Strategy.

Here's how: Each year, invest equal dollar amounts in the ten stocks out of the 30 Dow Jones Industrials that pay the highest current dividend yield. Over the last 20 years, this strategy has produced a 16.06% average annual return, 47% more than the 10.91% earned by the Dow Jones Industrial Average.

Here's why: The stocks typically have high yields because their prices fell during the prior year on bad news. But the high dividends cushion any further drop, and these are major companies that tend to recover from problems. In other words, you are buying temporarily depressed stocks at bargain prices.

Important Questions To Ask Your Stockbroker

When your stockbroker recommends a stock, bond, mutual fund or other investment, don't invest without first getting answers to these questions.

- How will this investment help me meet my investment goals?
- Is this the best course of action, or merely a suitable one?
- What are the worst, best and most-likely outcomes if I invest?
- Is the price negotiable?
- What is your commission on this sale? Will you receive any additional compensation from a third party?
- Can I buy this product on the open market, or can I purchase it only through your firm?
- Are you participating in a contest that will reward you for selling this product?

HOW TO FIGURE YOUR DIVIDEND YIELD

A stock's dividend yield is the percentage of the purchase price you get back through an investment's dividends each year. If you receive $6 a share in dividends on stock you buy for $100 a share, the stock has a yield of 6% (6 is 6% of 100). If you pay only $50 a share, however, your yield is 12% (6 is 12% of 50).

Purchase price	$100	$50
Annual dividend	$6	$6
YIELD	6%	12%

Stockbrokers and Their Fees
Most stockbrokers keep 30% to 45% of the commissions they generate. The more brokers sell in gross commissions, the bigger their cut. An average broker at one brokerage keeps 32% of commissions: On a sale of $10,000 of shares in a 4.5% load fund, the broker would earn $144.

Robert Hagstrom Reveals Warren Buffett's Secrets of Successful Investing

When Warren Buffett bought shares of American Express and PNC Bank Corp. in February 1995, the prices of both stocks quickly jumped as other investors rushed to buy them too.

Reason: During the past several decades, Buffett has built a $29 billion empire, largely through his extraordinary ability to pick winning stocks.

For the past ten years, I have studied Buffett's investment strategy and the candid letters he writes for the annual reports of his own company, Berkshire Hathaway.

Here are some of Buffett's golden investing rules.

INVEST IN WHAT YOU UNDERSTAND
Buffett believes that you cannot make an intelligent investment decision about a company and its future unless you have some sense of how the company makes its money. That is why he does not own shares in some promising sectors, such as high technology or pharmaceuticals.

HUH?

If you don't understand it, don't invest in it.

Example: Buffett says Bill Gates, Microsoft's founder and chairman, is the smartest man he has ever met. He also says Microsoft is a very dynamic company. But Buffett doesn't own shares of Microsoft because he doesn't understand the software business or how the company will make money over time.

LOOK FOR CONSISTENT OPERATING HISTORIES
Buffett prefers to invest in companies that have stood the test of time, surviving and flourishing through different economic cycles and competitive environments. These companies include Coca-Cola, The Washington Post Co. and Wells Fargo, but not General Motors or IBM.

He isn't interested in new companies because they do not have proven track records and the risk of new companies failing is so high.

Buffett shuns companies that are emerging from hard times as well. He believes it's a mistake to waste time trying to find struggling companies that are hoping to turn around their fortunes.

Strategy: Identify successful companies that have been producing great products or services for a decade or longer. Look for those companies that have generated steadily-increasing earnings.

INVEST IN THE BEST
Companies that make strong brand-name products dominate their categories. These products have great value because they are so well-known that consumers are not likely to accept substitutes. Many of these companies are also appealing investments because their products' prices aren't regulated.

Example: Coca-Cola has a strong position in the U.S. because its brand name and level of quality are so high. Customers will always be willing to pay more for that. Coca-Cola is also strong overseas, where it has much less competition. Pepsi-Cola, on the other hand, is number two in the soft-drink category in the U.S., and its presence overseas is not as strong as that of Coca-Cola.

Important: Avoid companies that make commodity-like products. These are products that consumers view as having plenty of substitutes, such as computers. Other commodity businesses include the automobile and airline industries.

Problem: Companies that make commodity products have to charge increasingly lower prices or else customers will buy from their competitors. As a result, the only way to succeed in a commodity business is to have low costs and keep prices low. This rarely does much for a stock's earnings or price.

INVEST IN COMPANIES WITH RATIONAL MANAGERS

A rational CEO invests surplus cash in projects that generate high rates of return, or turns the money back to shareholders by increasing the company's dividend or buying back shares on the stock market.

Example: When The Washington Post Co., one of Buffett's largest holdings, had excess cash in 1990, the company increased its dividend rather than using the money to increase the size of its business in ways that might not be economical.

Strategy: If you have invested in a company that generates extra cash, keep a close eye on how the managers spend that money. Read articles in the business press on what the company is doing.

LOOK FOR CANDID MANAGERS

Each year, Buffett writes a letter to the shareholders of Berkshire Hathaway. The letter is included in the annual report and is brutally honest about the company's financial position.

Example: In one report, Buffett acknowledged missing a $1.4 billion opportunity to buy shares of the Federal National Mortgage Association. He blamed the error on his own "amateurish behavior."

He believes this honesty helps him as a manager. If he can admit his failures in public, it makes him less likely to deceive himself in private. That's why he looks for this trait in the top managers of the companies in which he invests.

Strategy: When you read annual reports and press accounts, look for candid admissions of failure or difficulties.

Example: If a company's earnings did not grow as rapidly as analysts predicted, the annual report should include a full discussion of the problem and the reasons for it. Management's plan for solving the problem should also appear. Buffett's large stake in American Express may be due to the fact that its chairman has a reputation for such a candid approach.

LOOK BEYOND REPORTED EARNINGS

Most analysts look at a company's earnings per share to judge how well it is performing. Buffett points out

that since companies typically reinvest a large percentage of earnings in their firms, it should not be a surprise when a company's profits continue to grow. What is more important is the company's return on its resources, the return on the money that shareholders and others have invested. That is measured by dividing a company's operating earnings by its shareholders' equity.

You can find a company's historical return in the *Value Line Investment Survey*. Look under "Percent Earned Net Worth," which is a slightly more conservative figure than the correct return. Compare it with

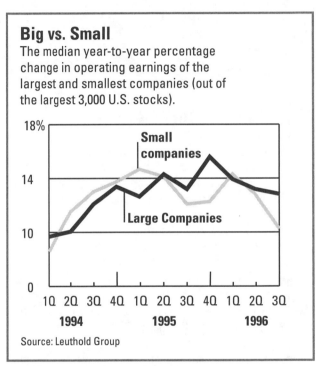

Big vs. Small

The median year-to-year percentage change in operating earnings of the largest and smallest companies (out of the largest 3,000 U.S. stocks).

Source: Leuthold Group

the figures for other companies in the same industry. If it's higher than the average of those companies listed in *Value Line*, that is a very good sign.

FIND COMPANIES WITH HIGH PROFIT MARGINS

Find a company's profit margin by dividing its earnings by its revenues. A high profit margin usually means that a company is keeping its costs down, a sign of an excellent investment.

Many companies don't start working to reduce costs until after their profits begin to slip. Buffett likes companies that keep costs down before things turn bad.

Example: Buffett constantly invests in Wells Fargo because it doesn't waste money on projects or expenses that don't add to the company's value.

Strategy: Check a company's net profit margin in *Value Line*, where it is listed along with earnings and sales. Then compare it with profit margins for other companies in the same industry. If it is higher than the average, that is another good sign.

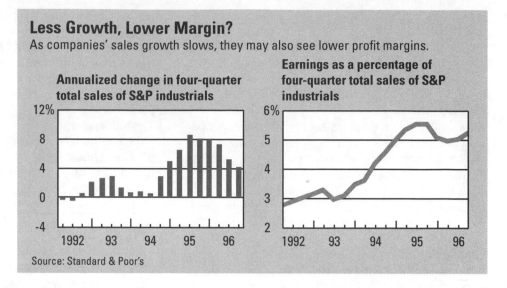

Less Growth, Lower Margin?
As companies' sales growth slows, they may also see lower profit margins.

Annualized change in four-quarter total sales of S&P industrials

Earnings as a percentage of four-quarter total sales of S&P industrials

Source: Standard & Poor's

LOOK FOR A MARGIN OF SAFETY

Buffett's role model was the famous investment theorist Benjamin Graham, who, nearly 60 years ago, preached the importance of buying a company's stock for considerably less than its real value, and thus building a margin of safety into your investment.

Buffett uses sophisticated financial formulas to determine when a stock is undervalued, based on projections about its future growth rate.

If you identify good businesses and then avoid paying outrageous prices for their stocks, you will at least steer clear of most disasters. That generally means buying a stock when its price is down, rather than when it is at an all-time or 52-week high.

Buffett puts it this way, "I am more greedy when people are scared, and more scared when people are greedy."

Another Stock Opportunity

A spun-off company often does well, even when it performed poorly as part of a larger firm.

Reason: Managers no longer take orders from higher executives who do not understand their business. This lets them cut costs, improve production and become more entrepreneurial.

Opportunity: 14% of recent spinoffs became takeover targets. In a takeover, the stock price of a company is sure to rise. In general, the odds of a takeover of a company are only 3% to 4%.

Stock Buybacks Are Rarely Completed

Companies announce buybacks with great fanfare, hoping investors believe the announcements to be a vote of self-confidence from the company.

Reality: In most cases no more than 20% to 30% of announced buybacks are actually completed. In some cases, if the buyback announcement is effective at boosting the stock price, very few shares are actually repurchased.

Happy **3**RD Anniversary, Mr. President

Boom Years in the Stock Market

The third year of a President's term is historically a boom year for the stock market. The S&P 500 has risen in the third year of every presidential term since 1943 by an average of 18.6%. And the market has risen more during the third year of Democratic presidential terms than Republican ones: 21% vs. 16.4%.

What to Expect to Earn from Stocks

Since 1802, common stocks have given investors an average return of 6.7% over inflation. And while sharp short-term swings in the market are common, over the long run this rate of return has been remarkably consistent. Remember to think about the big picture.

- Don't expect recent double-digit annual market gains to continue forever.
- Save for retirement expecting to earn no more than 6% or 7% from stocks annually.
- Don't worry about how short-term market swings affect your long-term stock investments.
- Be cautious about investing in the market money you will need within the next few years. In the short term, the market is unpredictable.

Bear-Proofing Your Portfolio Strategies With Douglas Raborn

If you're like most investors, you're probably nervous about where the stock market is headed over the next 12 months and whether the Dow Jones Industrial Average can climb much further.

Here are a few strategies to consider for preserving the value of your portfolio no matter what happens to the market. If you take action now, you will be able to relax in the future.

LOCK IN YOUR GAINS

Sell half of your position in stocks that have had big gains this year. This is one way to have your cake and eat it, too.

Example: Last year, you bought 1,000 shares of a company at $10 a share. Now the stock's price is $50. Even if you believe, for sound reasons, that the stock will go higher, you could protect your profits by selling 500 shares. That way, you would pocket $20,000 in gains (before commission and taxes) and still profit from the company's future growth.

SET STOP-LOSS ORDERS

Stop-loss orders authorize your stockbroker to automatically sell a stock once it reaches a price predetermined by you. This does not mean it will be sold at your price, however, but at the nearest available market price.

Example: Let's say you buy 1,000 shares of a company at $10 a share on the expectation that its earnings will grow at 20% a year. Then the company suddenly encounters supply problems and those expectations are dashed. Subsequently, the stock drops to $7 a share while you're away on a fishing trip.

Had you placed a stop-loss order to sell your stake at $9 a share, your position might have been liquidated before the stock lost another two points.

A good rule of thumb is to sell automatically when a stock drops 20% below its highest price since you've owned it.

DON'T BE TOO RISKY

When buying stocks, only invest if there is little downside risk. Don't be dazzled by the prospect of big gains without also considering the possibility of big losses.

I hold on to a stock if it has the potential to increase its value by at least one-third over the next 12 months. But I won't buy a promising stock unless I also think its downside potential, its negative risk for investors, is half that amount. To put it another way, I look for a reward/risk ratio of at least two to one.

Example: If we think a stock is likely to go up by 40% over the next year, it might be a potential purchase as long as we also think that it is unlikely to lose more than 20% of its value over the same period.

WHEN IN DOUBT, HOLD ONTO THE STOCK

The best approach to investing in stocks is to take a long-term view and to measure the success of your portfolio's performance over the next five to ten years, not the next quarter.

This strategy allows you to filter out the temporary surges and dips in stock prices and focus instead on what hopefully will be the steady increase in their market value.

There's something to be said for the advice of some successful older investors who say their secret was to buy stocks decades ago and stick them in a box. This strategy prevented the investors from selling when things got shaky or overheated. And because their stocks were generating dividends, these investors reaped the rewards of compounding: earnings producing more earnings.

DIVERSIFY BY BUYING BONDS

Bonds generate a flow of income which can be reinvested in stocks when a buying opportunity arises. There's no magic number for allocating a percentage of your portfolio to bonds or bond funds, so buy as many as you need to feel comfortable.

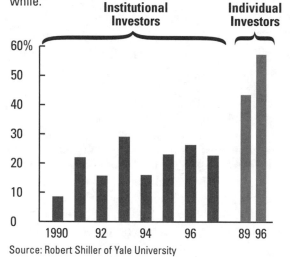

Speculators' Confidence

The percentage of institutional and individual investors who agree with the following statement: "Although I expect a substantial drop in stock prices in the U.S. ultimately, I advise being relatively heavily invested in stocks for the time being because I think that prices are likely to rise for a while."

Institutional Investors   Individual Investors

Source: Robert Shiller of Yale University

Stop-Loss Order Danger

A stop-loss order, which instructs a broker to sell a stock if it falls to a specific price, does not guarantee that you will get that price for your shares when they reach the stop-loss price. If there are no buyers at that price, the stock will continue to fall until it reaches a price at which buyers appear, leaving you with a larger loss than you thought possible. This is a real danger for thinly-traded issues in falling markets, so beware.

Better than Stop-Loss Orders

Better than stop-loss orders for knowledgeable investors are protective options.

Example: If a stock's share price has risen from $30 to $50, buy a put option exercisable at $45. This gives you the right to sell the stock at $45 anytime until the option expires. If the stock keeps going up, you still own it and are still making profits—minus the price you paid for the put. If it drops, no matter how far, your price of $45 is protected.

Alternative: Sell the stock at $50 and buy a long-term call option (one-year) exercisable at $50. This guarantees you can buy the stock for $50 plus the price paid for the call option. If the price drops, you need not exercise the option.

Shrewder Stock Picking

Buy stocks with annual earnings growth of at least 15%. There's no point in being part owner of a business that shows no growth.

   Also important is the stability of earnings growth. The stock of a company that shows steady growth at a given rate generally is a better buy than that of a company that achieves the same average growth rate with earnings that fluctuate sharply up and down from year to year.

William E. Donoghue's International Investing Strategies

The pundits, including myself, have been touting international investing as the wave of the future for most of the 1990s. Global diversification made sense in a global economy. The potential for growth of China is almost unlimited, tempting many investors to be extra-patient. Until low-cost Japanese credit dried up in 1998, low-interest loans to finance China's growth were relatively easy to come by. I had even visited Beijing, Manila, Taipei, Okinawa, and Hong Kong to witness this amazing economic growth and reported extensively on it. It was intoxicating. However, the party ended long before its potential was realized.

AVOID TEMPTATION TO BUY-AND-HOLD INTERNATIONAL STOCK FUNDS

The problem for investors is that the 1990s has been a time of boom and bust in international markets, which make up over half of the world's market capitalization. First, emerging market funds soared and then corrected severely and then the cycle repeated itself. If you invested over the full cycle from boom to bust to boom to bust, you might have broken even. If you were not too greedy and were willing to buy when there was "blood in the streets" and sell when others were just beginning to buy, you could have earned some excellent returns. But—saying that and doing it are, often, two different things.

International fund investing was, therefore, at best an intermediate term trading opportunity and not the prudent option for long-term buy-and-hold investments as we all wished it would be. In anticipation of a time when international investing again becomes favorable, allow me to give you some hints.

STICK WITH EXPERIENCED OPEN-ENDED MUTUAL FUNDS

When investing in international equity investments, it is wise to invest through open-ended mutual funds, which are much more liquid at net asset value than closed-end funds, which usually sell at discounts or premiums to asset value. Open-ended funds are always priced at net asset value per share and stand ready to redeem or issue shares at any time. Closed-end funds issue a fixed number of shares at one time and, if you want to invest after that time, you must buy from an existing shareholder. This allows the fund's managers to invest more boldly without fear of redemptions, but it means that the price of a closed-end fund can fluctuate widely, based on its portfolio fluctuation and its popularity with investors.

The bid-to-ask spreads between buy and sell prices of individual international stocks available to individuals can often be quite wide. Part of the problem with such stocks is that the information provided by the companies is often nowhere near the accuracy that domestic stock investors are used to, and the speculative nature of many stocks can harbor unpleasant surprises. These factors all argue for the diversification and professional management available from international mutual funds registered in the United States.

Best: Fund families such as T. Rowe Price, Scudder, Fidelity and others who have portfolio managers "on the ground" in the countries in which they invest. These fund families also have the experience of a long-term commitment to international stock investing, an essential element in these volatile markets.

EMERGING OR ESTABLISHED MARKETS?

International stock investing involves two basic types of funds: Emerging market funds and funds in established markets like Western Europe and Japan.

Emerging markets are often small economies, such as those in Southeast Asia, or larger economies just maturing and entering the world markets, such as Brazil and other Latin American markets. Wide diversification and experienced portfolio managers are good reasons to recommend investing in emerging markets through a mutual fund.

Established markets come in two categories: Stable and growing financial markets like Europe and unstable and shrinking financial markets like Japan. Europe is about five years behind the U.S. in downsizing and repositioning their economies as competitors on the global stage. That will hurt them in a recession and be a strong positive sign in an expansion period.

The Japanese market, however, is tempting for equity investors, since it is at record lows. Japanese shares are low-priced, not because they are cheap, but because they have low values. Japan has chronic economic problems, which will take a long time to work out. Avoid this market until they have made substantial progress in rebuilding their economy. Periodic rebounds in their stock market usually result in significant profit-taking and frustrating subsequent declines.

WATCH THE MARKETS AND THE CURRENCY

Investing in established markets should include assessing both the prospects for the financial markets in each country and the trend in the value of their currency vs. the U.S. dollar. Both factors are important. For example, even a falling stock market in a foreign country can still make money for U.S. investors if the U.S. dollar's value is falling versus that country's currency. When the stocks denominated in foreign currencies are valued in dollars, the decline in the value of the dollar can allow those investors to buy more dollars, and, hence, make a profit.

INTERNATIONAL FUNDS WORTH WATCHING

The only three major no-load funds with 15-year long-term track records through August 31, 1998 are the following.

- Scudder International Fund, 800-225-2470, 15-year average return: 13.96%
- T. Rowe Price International Fund, 800-638-5660, 15-year average return: 14.25%
- Vanguard International Growth 800-662-7447, 15-year average return: 14.09%

These are well-managed international stock market funds with long-term experience in the international markets. I recommended the Scudder and T. Rowe Price funds as early as 1983 (that's no misprint, I meant 1983). I would recommend them again after the current international financial crisis passes. When that time comes, these funds will likely be wise choices for 10%-30% of your long-term investment portfolio. Even then, you will want to monitor them closely and when you earn greater than domestic stock fund returns, prepare to sell these funds in good times and wait for the next market bottom before reinvesting. Overstaying your welcome and getting too greedy are unsuccessful strategies for international stock investors.

Be Willing to Invest Abroad

In 1969, U.S. stocks accounted for 85% of the value of all the stocks in the world. Today, the figure is only 40%, and the downtrend will continue. People who are not willing to invest outside the U.S. cut themselves off from a broad range of opportunities in many fast-growing markets.

Blue-Chip International Investments

Many of the 30 stocks in the Dow Jones Industrial Index now earn 50% or more of their revenues from international sales.

Examples: Exxon (79% of sales comes from abroad), Coca-Cola (68%) and IBM (59%).

Strategy: Ask your broker for a list of the stocks in the index. Then call companies in which you are interested and ask for their percentage of foreign sales for each of the past five years.

Good signs: Look for a blue-chip company whose foreign-sales percentage has grown faster than its domestic business during this period, and whose business is diversified among many different countries.

Sheldon Jacobs Answers Your Big Questions about Mutual Funds

Investors are pouring big money into mutual funds. Yet, I'm always surprised at how little most people know about the funds in which they invest.

Here are answers to the most common questions I'm asked by fund investors.

DO YOU HAVE TO READ A FUND'S PROSPECTUS?

Yes. Though a common prospectus can be complex, the good news is that you don't have to read all of it.

There are only two sections that are vital for making investment decisions. The rest is often information the fund has to mention in order to fulfill its legal obligations.

1. Statement of objectives

This outlines the types of investments the fund makes, such as in large- or small-capitalization companies, bonds or international stocks. It also discusses the strategy the fund's manager uses, such as investing for capital appreciation or for income. The statement is usually found in the first few pages of the document.

Statement of Objectives

While this section of the prospectus is usually in plain English, some fund families group all or many of their funds together in the same document. Be sure to look for the statements that relate to the specific funds in which you are interested.

2. Fee table

This discloses all the costs you'll pay to buy and own

IS YOUR FUND ON TARGET?

FUND OBJECTIVE

Funds have been known to stray from their stated objectives and invest in securities other than the ones described in their prospectuses.

Strategy: Make sure a fund is buying the types of securities you expect. You can do this either by monitoring its annual, semiannual or quarterly reports, or by calling the fund company and asking for the most recent top-ten holdings.

Although incomplete, a fund's stated objectives will at least give you an idea of what you may be getting into.

mutual fund shares. If it's a load fund, the table will tell you what the charges are to buy and sell shares.

It will also tell you if there are any management and 12b-1 fees, which are deducted from your account annually and used to pay for

Fee Table

marketing, distributing and advertising. The fee table is usually on page two or three of the prospectus.

Caution: Avoid funds that have total operating expenses of 2% or more for a domestic equity fund (slightly higher for an international fund) or 1% or more for a bond fund. This information can be found in the fee table or by calling the fund company.

HOW MANY FUNDS SHOULD YOU OWN?

That depends on how much money you have to invest in mutual funds.

If you only have a few thousand dollars to invest, buy one or two asset-allocation funds. They invest in a combination of stocks, fixed-income securities and cash, depending on the state of the markets.

If you have a much larger sum and you want to be well diversified, investing in ten funds is not out of line—provided there is little or no duplication in the investment style and portfolios of the funds.

WHAT RED FLAGS SHOULD YOU LOOK FOR?

The most important reason to avoid a fund is poor performance. However, one year's performance doesn't tell you enough about a fund. Three to five years is a much better indicator.

You've heard the adage that past performance is no guarantee of future results, and that's certainly true. But, for the most part, it's the only gauge investors have to rely on.

Strategy: Always compare a fund's performance with its peer-group average. You can check rankings in an independent fund research service such as *The No-Load Fund Investor*, or in newspapers and magazines. Avoid a fund if it has underperformed or performed wildly throughout its history.

WHEN DO BOND FUNDS MAKE SENSE?

Bond funds make the most sense for conservative investors when they want to diversify their bond holdings or to own a lot more types of bonds than just Treasurys.

It's a good idea to purchase riskier types of bonds, such as corporate bonds or high-yield bonds, through a mutual fund. The fund can buy far more types of issues than you can hold as an individual. In addition, it is often difficult for individuals to buy small amounts of these types of bonds through their brokers.

Beware: Bond funds aren't actually bonds. And bond-fund managers don't necessarily buy and hold each issue the way individuals would, collecting interest and getting back the principal. Instead, bond-fund managers are constantly trading, and their

Dubious Dealings

A mystery-shopping survey discovered an increase in bank broker transgressions.

	Aug. 1994	Jan. 1996
Did not disclose lack of FDIC insurance (orally)	20%	27%
Did not complete a customer profile (before pitch)	12%	23%
Did not describe sales charges	17%	23%
Did not discuss mutual fund risk/principal fluctuation	6%	11%

Source: Prophet Consulting

funds, therefore, are subject to the daily price fluctuations that typically occur in the bond market.

Though bond funds provide more stability than stock funds, there are many different types of bond funds with different levels of risk.

Example: A Treasury bond fund has no credit risk, but it has high interest rate risk. Other funds, such as high-yield bond funds, have less interest rate risk but more default risk.

Municipal bonds are best for those people looking for tax-advantaged investments. Funds are often a great way to invest in municipal bonds because they diversify your credit risk, and because municipal bonds are often hard for individuals to obtain.

What the Wealthy Do with Their Money

The wealthy today invest in mutual funds far more frequently than they did a few years ago. Mutual funds used to be considered crass, and the wealthy preferred private money managers. But as fund performance has improved, people with $100 million or more in assets are increasingly putting their money into the same well-performing funds favored by smaller investors.

---

will create problems when computing taxable capital gains on sales of shares. Instead, take dividends in cash and then, if you wish, use the cash to buy extra shares. Your price records will be much simpler.

Note: When fund shares are held in a retirement account, capital gains are not an issue, so dividend reinvestments aren't a problem.

Sensible Mutual Fund Investing

Invest automatically. Your broker or fund manager can transfer a set amount of money periodically from your checking to your investment account. It's both more disciplined and easier than making investments by hand. But, some experts say not to automatically reinvest dividends in taxable mutual funds because it

Smart Investing

Remember that around 80% of fund managers fail to beat the market, so it's unlikely that the average amateur can do so.

Better plan: Diversify investments to minimize risk and manage them so as to avoid losing money while earning a fair return. Then, over time, look for situations where your own business knowledge gives you an advantage over the experts.

Example: Speculating in pork bellies is risky, even for professional traders. But if you're in the pork business, the day will come when you know the price is about to go up or down. By taking advantage of just a few such opportunities during your life, and investing for safe returns otherwise, you may become wealthy.

Who Owns Mutual Funds?

Overall, 37% of U.S. households were invested in funds in 1996. Here is the percentage holding funds in different income groups.

18% of households earning less than $35,000 invest in mutual funds.

41% of households earning $35,000 to $49,999 invest in mutual funds.

58% of households earning $50,000 to $74,999 invest in mutual funds.

73% of households earning over $75,000 invest in mutual funds.

Source: December 1996 Fundamentals, Investment Company Institute, Washington, DC

Don Phillips' Mutual Fund Strategies

Americans do not save enough. They also do not invest enough. Even people who put away money for long-term goals, such as college, a home down payment or retirement, do so in the least risky ways: in certificates of deposit and accounts paying fixed rates of interest, or in government bonds.

Problem: Investments like these produce returns roughly equal to the combined rate of taxes and inflation. The only way to beat taxes and inflation over the long haul, to actually increase your wealth rather than just preserve it, is to invest in common stocks.

The problem, of course, is that stocks are risky. So, for small investors, I believe mutual funds are the perfect way to invest in stocks. I invest in them because I don't have the time or the inclination to do the research necessary for individual stock investing.

Funds offer the following advantages to the small investor who wants to invest in common stocks.

CONVENIENCE

Scores of excellent mutual fund companies offer a broad range of funds. You can open an account with a single fund family that offers funds that invest internationally as well as domestically, in big companies and small ones, and in various styles, such as growth or value.

Bonus: If you choose to invest in one of their other funds in the future, all your paperwork will arrive on a single statement in one envelope.

PROFESSIONAL MANAGEMENT

The fund industry tends to attract some of the best professional stock pickers in the business.

It is no coincidence that three of the most successful money managers of our time, John Templeton, Peter Lynch and John Neff, each made his mark in funds rather than private money management.

Mutual funds provide the best-lit playing field in the investment industry today.

INSTANT DIVERSIFICATION

The typical equity mutual fund today has positions in literally hundreds of individual stocks.

This significantly reduces your risk of stock investing. You are less vulnerable to the kind of unforeseen events that can batter an individual company's shares.

A well-diversified portfolio is less volatile and less prone to wild price swings than one made up of only a few stocks.

AFFORDABILITY

It is possible to begin an investment program with any of more than two dozen no-load mutual fund families that require an initial investment of $50 and a minimum monthly contribution of just $50. That entire sum goes to work at once. The only fees you pay are the annual expenses the fund incurs, which average less than $1.50 for every $100 invested.

By contrast, if you were to buy $50 worth of common stock every month, you might pay commissions equal to, or even greater than, that amount.

DISCIPLINE

Although investing $50 a month doesn't sound like a lot of money, over time it can grow into a sizable nest egg: more than $3,500 in just five years. Given the stock market's historic rate of return, it can grow enough to pay for a few years of college 18 years down the road. And, based on a 10% compounded return, it adds up to more than $280,000 in the 40 years it would take a 25-year-old to reach retirement age.

RISK REDUCTION

Stock prices and the value of shares of mutual funds that invest in them fluctuate from day to day and month to month. If you invest systematically, putting in $50 a month, you tend to even out these price swings over time.

LESSONS IN INVESTING

As you invest regularly and follow the progress of your investments, you will learn more and more about financial markets.

The most basic lesson you'll learn is that it's easy to say, "Buy low, sell high," but it's hard to do. The natural inclination of people whose investments go up in value is to put in more money, and when they go down, to sell them. By investing the same amount every month, regardless of whether the market is up or down, you take advantage of the fact that stock prices have risen an average of two out of every three years since the 1920s.

To begin a regimen of investing $50 a month in a stock mutual fund, you first need to choose one fund. If I could only pick one fund in which to invest, my choice would be an all-weather fund from a long-established company that has a consistently strong, five-year record of excellent returns in good years and a history of not losing too much in bad years.

YOUR SECOND FUND

After you have been investing for at least one year and you have more money available, begin putting an additional $50 a month into a second fund within the same fund family. I favor international diversification for this second fund. Foreign markets tend to zig when the U.S. zags.

If you are investing for ten years or longer, new research shows that there isn't much difference between load and no-load funds.
Reason: While load funds take a bite out of three- to five-year returns, the expense is absorbed over the longer term, making the two types of funds competitive.

YOUR THIRD FUND

When the time comes to add a third mutual fund, I favor a small-company fund. Most mainstream funds, as well as international funds, are heavily weighted with big companies. A small-company fund can add the most distinctive voice to the choir. By the time you're ready to add this fund, you'll have the real-life market experience to make a choice based on your investment focus and tolerance for risk.

A WINNING INVESTMENT STRATEGY

By investing systematically and not trying to time the market, you will probably have made a lot more money than you would have investing at a fixed rate of interest, and will not have taken on undue risk.

The rules for investing this way are the same for each of the fund companies that offer this systematic investment service.

● You send a voided check so the company can verify your checking account number. From then on, $50 is deducted automatically from your checking account once a month.

● If you have to stop making contributions before you reach the company's minimum, usually $2,500 to $3,000, your account will probably be closed and all moneys in it returned to you.

Caution: Don't send any money until you've received prospectuses and enrollment materials from the fund family. You can get these by calling its 800 number.

Then, jump in. The only other investment alternative is to tread water.

Portfolio Managers And Performance

The portfolio manager of a mutual fund may not be the key individual that he or she is made out to be, especially when the fund is a member of a large fund family that has a big research staff. In fact, high turnover among fund managers is a good sign when a fund family is promoting new talent and eliminating bad performers.

Example: Fidelity's fund managers have an average tenure of only 15 months on their current jobs, and there is little difference in the performance records of senior and junior managers.

How to Make Your Money Work Faster

Use automatic payroll deductions to invest in mutual funds instead of automatic deductions from your bank account. This strategy puts your money to work for you even faster. Leading fund families such as Fidelity, Dreyfus, Invesco, T. Rowe Price and Vanguard will arrange to have periodic investments in an amount you determine made by automatic transfer directly out of your paycheck. The Charles Schwab & Co. discount brokerage will also arrange payroll transfers for customers using its OneSource account.

Alan Lavine and Gail Liberman's Mutual Fund Opportunities

Every day, investors see ads and articles touting funds with recent returns of 30%, 40% or 50%. These numbers don't mean what they seem to mean. Don't get greedy, and don't chase after funds with hot recent returns.

Reason: These stellar returns are at least partly due to the recent runaway bull market, the surge in specific sectors and luck.

Rule of thumb: Never buy a fund based only on its performance for the past year or three years.

DECIDE WHAT KIND OF INVESTOR YOU ARE

These days, a lot of investors who really aren't very aggressive say they seek annual returns of 15% or more. That's 5% above the historic return of stocks. It sounds pretty aggressive to us.

The funds with the best chance of giving you such returns are pretty risky. Are you the kind of investor who can tolerate that much risk?

To find out, take a risk-assessment test offered by some brokers, financial planners and authors. Basically, if you're unwilling to accept a double-digit loss in a single year, want regular income and feel comfortable building your wealth gradually, then you are a conservative investor.

If your risk-tolerance is higher, you're either a moderate or aggressive investor. You can't possibly choose the right mix of funds until you complete such a self-assessment.

KNOW THE RISKS OF SPECIFIC INVESTMENTS

Many people don't know that bond funds are risky, and relatively few people know precisely how risky they are. If interest rates rise 1%, the value of your government securities bond fund could decline up to 10%, depending on the average maturity of the bonds in the portfolio.

Example: In 1994, when interest rates shot up more than 1%, aggressive, long-term government securities bond funds, such as Heartland U.S. Government Securities Fund, lost nearly 10%. Even less risky intermediate-term bond funds, like Fidelity Government Securities, lost 5%.

START WITH A CORE INVESTMENT

Almost any mutual fund investor over age 40 who wants some exposure to stocks should own a solid blue-chip or growth-and-income fund.

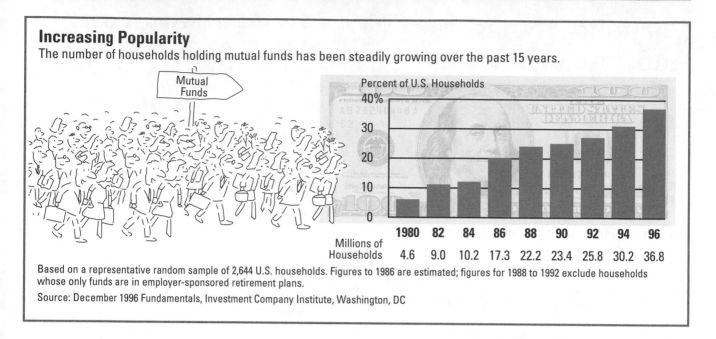

Increasing Popularity

The number of households holding mutual funds has been steadily growing over the past 15 years.

Percent of U.S. Households

	1980	82	84	86	88	90	92	94	96
Millions of Households	4.6	9.0	10.2	17.3	22.2	23.4	25.8	30.2	36.8

Based on a representative random sample of 2,644 U.S. households. Figures to 1986 are estimated; figures for 1988 to 1992 exclude households whose only funds are in employer-sponsored retirement plans.

Source: December 1996 Fundamentals, Investment Company Institute, Washington, DC

DIVERSIFY

Only after this core holding is in place should you think of diversifying. Diversification lowers your overall risk and smoothes out the performance of your portfolio.

START SLOWLY WITH RISKY INVESTMENTS

Don't make your entire commitment when you write your first check.

Strategy: Invest the minimum and then slowly build your position to the desired level on a monthly basis over six, 12 or 36 months. Not only will you benefit from dollar cost averaging, but you'll sleep much better if your new investment goes into a tail-spin soon after your first purchase.

LEARN FROM TRACK RECORDS

We think many mutual fund investors look at track records the wrong way. They tend to look for high performers that may be flashes in the pan or simply improper investments for them.

Strategy: Seek funds with long-term records of consistency that either come close to matching index funds or slightly outperform them. Why? Because these records, achieved over ten, 20 or 30 years, tell you a lot about the organizations behind the funds. You learn that each fund family has a certain style of investing, and can choose one that is right for your needs.

Note: If the fund manager leaves, it's unlikely that he or she will be replaced by someone with a very different philosophy.

Strategy: One of the best ways to use a fund-rating service is to see how well different funds perform in a down market. This performance tells you a lot about a manager's ability and helps prepare you for a worst-case scenario.

Warning: Don't be impressed by a fund that has two great years and then a string of mediocre ones. Its long-term record may still be impressive, but this history is nonetheless a bad sign. It suggests that the manager was lucky for two years and probably won't be so again any time soon.

REBALANCE YOUR PORTFOLIO EVERY YEAR

If you've found a mix of domestic, international, bond and money funds that is appropriate, your work isn't done yet. On the same date every year, make adjust-

DOMESTIC FUNDS
BOND FUNDS

INTERNATIONAL FUNDS
MONEY FUNDS

ments so that your asset mix always matches your original allocation targets. This encourages buy low/sell high discipline. After all, you'll only be over-weighed in an asset class that has outperformed the others. And it helps reduce risk. If you never make adjustments, a long bull market might cause stocks to jump from 50% of your portfolio up to 75%. That's fine for some people, but is it fine for you?

THE RIGHT BOND FUNDS
To reduce your risk, stick with short-term and intermediate-term funds.

Strategy: Buy the safest bond funds you can, which means funds that buy only U.S. government securities.

Educated Success
Minimize risk by under-standing the businesses you invest in, knowing how they can lose money and taking on only those risks you are comfortable with.

How to Beat the Market

Buy low and sell high is the golden rule of investing.

Here's how: Dollar cost average, or invest the same amount of dollars each month. When stock prices drop, you buy more shares, reducing the average cost at which you buy.

Aggressive alternative: Value average by investing to increase your portfolio's value by a set dollar amount each month.

How to Value Average
Goal: Increase portfolio by $500 a month.

IF Portfolio's value rises by	$200
THEN Invest that month	$300
IF Portfolio's value drops by	$200
THEN Invest that month	$700

Example: You want your portfolio to go up $500 each month. If it rises $200 due to stock price moves, you invest only $300. But if it drops $200 due to price moves, you invest $700. The result is that the buy-low effect is magnified. Studies show that value averaging beats dollar cost averaging 90% of the time.

What Mutual Fund Managers Don't Want You to Know

When markets perform poorly and business drops off at mutual funds, some fund managers take bigger risks, while marketers look for ways to polish their funds' images. There's nothing illegal about either procedure, but the results can confuse the average investor.

Here's how some funds bend the rules and how you can stay informed and protect your money.

DON'T TRUST THE NAME
In an effort to offset lackluster performance, some funds have gone beyond their original mandates, expanding into other types of investments.

Unfortunately, a fund can legally call itself almost anything it wants. The Securities and Exchange Commission (SEC) requires that only 65% of a fund's assets be invested according to the strategy outlined in its prospectus. As a result, a fund's name can mislead average investors who may not understand this subtlety or know the SEC rules.

Example I: Last year, one growth and income fund didn't provide much income—yielding only 0.5%, which is about the lowest yield of any mutual fund with the word "income" in its name.

Example II: At times, one insured municipal bond fund had 30% of its assets in municipal bonds that were not insured.

Important: Before you invest, call the fund and ask about its holdings. Are they the kinds of securities you want to own? Do they accurately represent the impression you had from the fund's name? If you already own the fund, is it still investing the way you want it to?

HIDDEN EXPOSURE TO FOREIGN SECURITIES

Although many funds state in their prospectuses that their stakes in foreign securities are limited to 10% of their portfolios, this self-imposed cap is often circumvented by buying American Depositary Receipts (ADRs).

ADRs are listings by foreign companies on U.S. stock exchanges, and they are purchased through brokers just as you would purchase stocks.

While ADRs can be great investments, having them in your portfolio means you have more foreign risk.

Example: One growth fund whose prospectus states that it has a 10% cap on foreign securities has nearly 25% of its assets in foreign stocks and ADRs.

Strategy: Give your mutual fund portfolio a checkup. Analyze all the holdings in your fund to determine the real percentage of your investments tied to foreign markets. While the fund will provide you with the percentage over the phone, make sure that any ADRs are part of the total percentage.

YOU MAY OWE TAXES ON LOSING FUNDS

In their struggle to outpace a gloomy market, many mutual fund managers buy and sell stocks more frequently. When these buy-and-sell transactions occur, there frequently are capital gains, which means that there are taxes to pay on those gains.

In many cases, the funds take those gains for legitimate strategic reasons. But the effect is that shareholders owe taxes on those gains, even though other holdings may have lost more money and overall the fund may have performed poorly for the year.

Example: One growth stock fund, with a return of negative 6.7%, paid out $1.08 per share in capital gains at the end of the year. That was 10.2% of its price per share.

Funds that do a lot of trading have annual turnover ratios that are greater than 100%. This information can be obtained through the fund. Funds that do a lot of trading, such as growth or aggressive growth funds, are best bought for your Individual Retirement Account (IRA), since the capital gains are tax-deferred.

Index funds are better for taxable holdings, since they buy and sell stocks less frequently.

WHO'S IN CONTROL

More and more funds are using teams to manage their assets. From the fund's perspective, a team keeps one manager from making too much of a name for him or herself. It also deters investors from pulling out their money when a star manager leaves for another fund.

Problem: With a team, you never know who is the brains of the operation, or whether you should pull out your money because the person behind the fund's success has left.

Self-defense: Call the fund annually, and ask for the names of the managers. Then ask who is responsible for investing the money. If the response is "the entire team," ask for the name of the team leader and about his or her experience. Also ask how long each team member has been with the fund.

PERFORMANCE NUMBERS ARE BECOMING CLEARER

Ads that promote funds often cast them in the best light by comparing their performances with benchmarks that make them look good, or by ignoring

FUND MANAGERS DON'T WANT YOU TO KNOW ABOUT

- Investing styles that conflict with the fund's mandate.
- Overexposure to foreign markets.
- Capital gains from frequent transactions.
- Who's really managing the fund.
- Deceptive performance figures.

benchmarks that make them look bad.

Example: In the 1980s, one group of funds regularly compared itself with the S&P 500 Index in a prominent box in the shareholders' report. In 1989, when the funds didn't do well, the box disappeared.

This trend is changing. The SEC now requires that returns be calculated uniformly on shareholders' reports. Now that funds must be consistent, be vigilant in monitoring their performance. Take a look at last year's performance to see how a fund did in that market. And compare the funds' three- and five-year returns.

When Not to Buy Closed-End Funds

Closed-end funds are never good buys when they first offer shares. The funds sell a predetermined number of shares, then close. Thereafter, they are traded like stocks on a stock exchange. But the initial share price includes an underwriting fee, usually around 7%.

Result: Most closed-end funds quickly trade at a discount to their underlying assets. If you like a fund, wait until it begins trading and then buy it.

Useful: Find out the fund's Net Asset Value (NAV) and the actual worth of its investments, and try to buy when it is trading at a discount to its NAV.

Mutual Fund Churning Alert

Churning of mutual funds in brokerage accounts is becoming a more common abuse than churning of stocks. Churning occurs when a broker repeatedly places buy and sell orders in an account to generate commissions.

Key: Computer monitoring of customer accounts to detect excessive commissions is

making it harder for dishonest brokers to get away with churning stocks. But mutual fund churning is more difficult to detect because commissions on the sale of fund shares usually aren't spelled out. Thus, unsuspecting mutual fund investors end up paying more in capital gains taxes and fees.

Defense: Monitor your account statements carefully to detect excessive trading, and communicate any concerns you have by writing a letter to the brokerage firm.

Mutual Fund Trap

While banks may pressure you to buy mutual funds, they're not the best place to buy them.

Reasons: Banks collect fees from mutual fund companies to sell their products. The bank may be more influenced by the prospect of this fee than the fund's performance. That fee (load) comes out of your pocket in the form of higher costs, lower returns or both. Usually, you will do better buying no-load funds.

Caution: Mutual funds purchased from banks are not federally insured like other bank deposits. So don't think you are buying safety when you purchase mutual funds from a bank.

Review Your Mutual Fund Portfolio with Michael Stolper

Financial experts typically urge investors to review their mutual fund portfolios annually. Unfortunately, many investors are not sure exactly what questions to ask themselves about their funds or how to evaluate the answers.

Here's a checklist for reviewing funds. Use these six points to determine if the fund choices you have made in the past still make sense for you now.

1. CONSIDER THE RISK PROFILE OF EACH FUND YOU OWN

Don't pay much attention to a fund's current beta or standard deviation. These terms are academic rather than real-world definitions of risk.

Instead, evaluate how much a fund lost during recent bear markets: the periods from August 1987 through October 1987, and from January 1973 through December 1974. For funds that originated after these dates, check smaller market corrections: the periods from July 1990 through October 1990, and from February 1994 through April 1994. That way, you'll learn how much money your funds might lose in a bad situation.

Strategy: Call your fund or check with *Morningstar Mutual Funds* to find out how a fund fared during these periods. If the information leaves you feeling overexposed to potential losses, sell at least some of your shares.

Example: Let's say you invested 25% of your portfolio in one fund in early 1996 because of its impressive 31%, three-year annual average return. When you look at the fund's historic performance now, you find that it lost 31% in 1987. This year, it has lost 2.5% while the average equity fund has lost only 0.1%. Cut your holdings in a fund like this by half, and you will sharply reduce your potential loss in a worst-case scenario.

2. REVIEW PERFORMANCE AT LEAST ONCE A YEAR

A fund's performance for the past year should not drastically lag behind the performance of its category as a whole.

Don't give that performance more weight than it deserves, however. You don't want to sell every fund that doesn't meet your performance expectations. Instead, review your fundamental reasons for owning each fund.

Even great fund managers have periods when their funds trail the Dow Jones Industrial Average (DJIA) or the S&P 500 Index. But when a manager has been doing a good job for 15 years, you can usually assume that he or she will continue to be successful.

Strategy: Call each fund in your portfolio to check its performance since the date you first purchased shares. When a fund has delivered a disappointing return during the period in which you have owned it, or during the past 12 months, find out what has changed. If your reasons for buying the fund in the first place were valid and remain valid, for example, you bought the fund because its manager has a solid long-term record, then keep it.

But if you originally bought a now-disappointing fund because you saw it on a list of seven top performers last year, dump it. The fund probably won't even come close to repeating its performance, and it will take too many years to make up a dramatic loss.

3. FIND OUT WHO IS RUNNING YOUR FUND NOW

When you buy a fund, you are hiring its manager for his or her record. If the manager has changed, it's as if someone replaced your lawyer or accountant without asking your permission. Presumably, the old manager was responsible for the record that attracted you to the fund in the first place.

Strategy: Call each fund, and ask if the manager has changed since you purchased your original shares.

If there is a different man-ager, ask about his or her record. If the new manager has an unimpressive or nonexistent record, no matter which fund he or she managed, sell all your shares and invest your money elsewhere, even if the fund is doing well at the time. The fund's sponsor may try to impress you with a spiced-up biography of the new manager, but don't be swayed by anything short of a

---

Gains by Market

Below are the cumulative gains for six major market indexes through April, 1996.

Index	Year Started	Price Gains		
		1 Year	5 Years	10 Years
DJIA	1896	29.0%	90.1%	213.3%
Nasdaq Composite	1971	42.0	147.5	213.0
NYSE Composite	1966	26.7	71.0	158.7
Russell 2000	1984	31.0	105.3	135.4
S&P 500	1957	27.2	74.3	117.8
Wilshire 5000	1974	29.4	81.6	167.6

bona fide track record.

Exception: If the new manager was trained by his or her predecessor, consider retaining your shares for at least a trial period.

Example: Fidelity Magellan is one of the most difficult funds to run because it is huge. But there was an effective management succession, from Peter Lynch to Morris Smith to Jeff Vinik. Each studied at the knee of his predecessor.

4. ELIMINATE UNNECESSARY FUNDS

There is no reason for you to own six, eight or ten funds in each portfolio set up for different goals, such as retirement or college savings. When you invest in too many funds, it is difficult to keep track of what's going on.

Strategy: Prune your portfolios. In general, it's not necessary to have more than four funds. These funds should include

1. A quality growth fund that invests in shares of well-established growth companies.

2. A small-company growth fund that invests in shares of small firms.

3. A value fund that invests in undervalued stocks of neglected companies.

4. An international fund that invests in firms overseas.

5. ELIMINATE REDUNDANCIES IN YOUR PORTFOLIO

Most investors don't realize that when a particular fund is doing better than the DJIA or the S&P 500 Index, it is often because that fund's overall investment category is hot at that particular time.

Example: When small-company stocks or foreign stocks are doing well as a group, most funds that buy them as a matter of policy look like winners. As a result, if you go out and buy several top-performing funds at the same time, you will likely end up

with several funds that own the same types of securities. When those types of securities lose ground, your portfolio will suffer a serious blow.

Action: Ask representatives from your funds to send you their most recent quarterly reports. Compare the funds' top-ten holdings lists. If there are more than three or four duplicate holdings, call the funds to verify that they still own the stocks. If they do, keep only the fund with the best five-year performance record.

6. REVIEW YOUR EXPOSURE TO EMERGING MARKETS

In addition to the basic funds that I have mentioned above, I would also consider adding an emerging-markets fund if you don't already own one. Such funds invest in shares of companies in developing countries in Asia, Latin America and elsewhere.

Action: Consider investing as much as 20% of your portfolio in an emerging-markets fund, depending on your age and investment goals.

Caution: Emerging-markets funds are risky and can experience great years and terrible years. Only invest money that you can leave in place for five to ten years. The rule about selling funds with big declines does not apply here since annual swings of as much as 20% up or down are common in the emerging-markets category.

Strategy: If you have money in a retirement savings account and at least 25 years before you retire, stake as much as 20% in emerging markets. If you're already retired, reduce your exposure to 10% or less.

Two-thirds of the world's population is in the early stages of creating Western-style market economies. It's going to be a 30- to 40-year phenomenon.

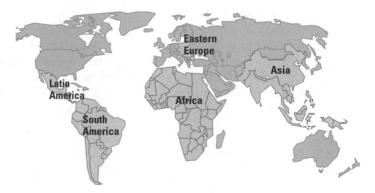

Sheldon Jacobs' Secrets of Personal Investing

It's an old story, but one that still rings true. Talented businesspeople build fabulously successful careers, advancing to the point at which it seems that financial worries will never again be a problem, and then wake up one day to the unpleasant fact that their personal wealth is growing far less rapidly than their success.

The explanation is simple. Many people who do extremely well in business fall down on the job when it comes to managing their personal finances.

SHIFTING GEARS

Getting your personal finances into healthy shape isn't that difficult these days, thanks to the availability of more than 5,000 mutual funds investing in everything from growth stocks to foreign securities to U.S. Treasury bonds.

By picking the right mix of funds, you can match the return you want to get with the degree of risk you are willing to take. Mutual funds are managed by investment professionals.

Important: The right mix of mutual funds can be used for your own personal investment portfolio. It also can be used in your business's pension plan or your 401(k) defined contribution employee retirement plan.

ASSET ALLOCATION

Having the right mix of stocks, bonds and cash in your portfolio is the greatest single determinant of investment success.

As a starting point, I suggest a mix of 75% stock funds and 25% bond funds for the average person.

Strategy: If you're younger than 45, then you have longer time horizons and can take more risks with your money. In this case I would raise the stock portion to 90% and cut the bond portion of your portfolio to 10%, or even put 100% in equities. If you are older, increase the bond portion to between 35% and 65%.

Important: If your business or profession is cyclical and a bad season could put you in a financial bind, consider opting for conservative short-term bond funds, especially ones that invest in U.S. Treasury securities. These funds produce returns that outrun inflation, and offer a

---

Reality Check

My experience is that successful business people often make one of the following three investment mistakes.

Mistake	How it hurts you
Being too busy Business takes up so much time and energy for some people that personal investing gets shunted aside.	If you're always too busy or preoccupied, you'll never get to first base with your investing.
Being too daring With little time to think through a prudent investment strategy, many busy business people invest on hunches or on tips heard at the office.	If you only play for the big win, responding to every tip and rumor that comes along, you probably won't have any wins at all.
Being too cautious Some successful people are so afraid of losing their hard-earned wealth that they cheat themselves out of investment earnings by sticking to the safety of insured bank accounts and government securities, despite miniscule returns.	If you are overly cautious, seeking safety in bank accounts, you risk losing everything. The low return that bank accounts pay will be more than consumed by inflation and taxes, and you'll end up with far less money than you started with.

Each of the mistakes above is potentially very damaging over time.

considerable degree of safety as well.

Note: The investment mix of your company's 401(k) plan should have a broad enough mix of both stock and bond funds to satisfy the asset allocation needs of both younger and older workers.

Beware Hidden Loads

Many mutual funds that advertise themselves as having no load in fact charge a hidden load in the form of 12b-1 fees. These fees are imposed continuously to cover marketing expenses and can cost more than a sales load. While an up-front sales load is charged only once, 12b-1 fees are charged every year. Fund 12b-1 fees can be as large as 1% annually. These fees significantly reduce returns over time.

Strategy: A 12b-1 fee of 0.1% or less is small enough to be ignored when choosing a fund. Fees of up to 0.3% correspond with management charges on other investments, and are acceptable. Fees much above 0.3% should be avoided.

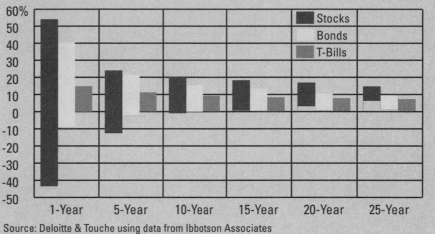

Nominal Returns for Period 1926-1996
The returns on stocks, bonds and Treasury bills fluctuate considerably within a single year, but become more stable the longer you hold on to them.

Source: Deloitte & Touche using data from Ibbotson Associates

No-Load Fund Performance
No-load mutual funds perform as well as funds that charge sales loads.

Most recent study: No-load funds performed slightly better than load funds over the last 23 years, without even considering the additional cost of the sales load.

How Don Phillips Fine-Tunes His Mutual Fund Portfolio

On New Year's Day, my wife and I will do what we have done for the past ten years. After taking the kids sledding, we'll come home, light a fire in the fireplace and spend three hours reviewing all our mutual fund investments.

The first of the year is an ideal time to examine how your funds have performed over the past year and determine if you need to rearrange your portfolio.

Here's what to do on New Year's Day.

PRICE YOUR PORTFOLIO
The first thing I do is turn to the financial pages of the December 29 newspaper and get the closing prices for all the stocks and mutual funds my wife and I own, including those in our retirement accounts. This will give me the market value of our financial assets and help me compare our position with that of the previous year.

It will also help me to assess our family's overall asset allocation and review how our resources are divided among stocks, bonds, cash and real estate.

Then I focus on our net worth: our assets minus

our debt. Even though there are computer programs to do this, I calculate our net worth using pencil and paper. I enjoy it. It's sort of a personal activity, and since I don't do it that often, it's not that onerous.

I also enjoy filling in the boxes at the bottom of the page that give our family's current net worth and asset allocation.

ESTABLISH FINANCIAL GOALS

I try to imagine what I want this page to look like one year from now. Given the market's great performance in the past three years, there's a good chance that the equity portion of my portfolio will be way up once I do my calculations.

And since I think the stock market is overvalued right now, my goals for 1998 are to build up our cash position and use some of it to pay down our mortgage. Currently, our family has about 5% of our assets in cash. I would like to double that by December 1998 by saving more of our income.

Strategy: In order to reach our annual goal of saving a large chunk of our income, my wife and I both invest systematically by participating in automatic investment plans offered by different mutual funds. At the start of the year, we decide how much money we want to allocate to each fund.

We also increase the annual amount we invest to keep pace with our rising incomes. When we prepare our financial plan for the coming year, we aim to contribute an additional percentage to the funds in our portfolio each month.

I prefer to stagger the funds' automatic investment dates throughout the month so that we don't have a huge outflow from our bank account at one time.

Then I write two $2,000 checks for our contribu-

Happy New Year

Now that you've celebrated,
★ Assess your net worth.
★ Update your financial goals.
★ Reevaluate your holdings.
★ Check your risk level.
★ Decide what funds to add.

tions to nondeductible IRAs (we don't qualify for the deductible in Roth IRAs). It gives me a lot of satisfaction to know that we've set aside this retirement money so that it can begin earning interest early in the year.

REEVALUATE CURRENT HOLDINGS

When I judge a fund, I look at who's managing it and his or her investing philosophy. If I'm satisfied with the original reason I bought the fund, I hold on to it. If the portfolio manager responsible for its performance is no longer with the fund, I consider a switch. In terms of philosophy, I see if the fund's portfolio looks different than it did one year ago.

Strategy: I gather the most recent performance figures before New Year's Day. I compare each fund's performance with the appropriate benchmark, such as the S&P 500 Index for a blue-chip stock fund. If a fund is doing poorly, I ask myself if I can explain it away—Is every fund with the same objective doing just as badly, or is there some reason that the fund is lagging behind its peers? If I can't explain away the lackluster showing, I consider selling.

CHECK YOUR RISK LEVEL

My goal is for us to have a portfolio diversified among large- and small-cap funds, and domestic and international funds. I like value managers, who look for bargain-priced stocks with low price/earnings multiples, rather than growth managers, who seek companies with the prospect of future earnings gains regardless of how expensive they may be.

Caution: Mutual fund names can be misleading. People who think their portfolios are diversified may find their holdings are in fact very lopsided.

DECIDE WHAT FUNDS TO ADD

Each year, I expand my portfolio by one mutual fund to create diversity.

Strategy: To determine if our portfolio will be diversified once we add a fund, I rely on *Morningstar Mutual Funds*. I check the style boxes that indicate whether the fund manager is using a growth or value approach to investing, and whether the manager favors large-, mid- or small-cap stocks.

I also check the fund's major holdings and the weightings of different sectors such as services, consumer durables and financials. I don't bother examining individual holdings and comparing them among funds; it is too difficult.

I also check to see how much cash a fund is holding. Some portfolio managers may hold as much as 20% in cash as a defensive move, which may not fit with my own goals if I buy a fund expecting it to be fully invested in the stock market.

Mutual Fund Explosion

The 1990s have seen incredible growth in the net new cash inflow into stock mutual funds.

Source: Investment Company Institute, Washington, D.C.

attract new investors. In some cases, this strategy works. But it also can backfire, making this type of fund extremely risky.

Self-defense: Stick with larger funds. Their managers are more conservative because they don't want to scare away shareholders who have entrusted them with billions of dollars.

PAY CLOSE ATTENTION TO BOND-FUND MATURITIES

Bond-fund investors can cut risk by buying funds with shorter maturities. Long-term bonds are hit much harder than short-term bonds when interest rates rise.

If rates rise from 6% to 8%, investors no longer want the old 6% bonds; they would rather buy new 8% ones. Since fewer people would want to hold the 6% bonds over many years given the new interest rate climate, the longer bonds drop further in price.

Solution: Seek a comfortable risk/reward balance by buying a bond fund with a variety of maturities.

AVOID FUNDS WITH HIGH EXPENSE RATIOS

High expenses (greater than 1.5% for a stock fund and 1% for a bond fund) reduce your profits. In some cases, they also mean more risk. Managers of funds that charge shareholders high expenses are more likely to invest in higher-risk securities to produce higher returns and justify expenses. This is especially true for bond funds. Call each of your funds to find out its expense rate.

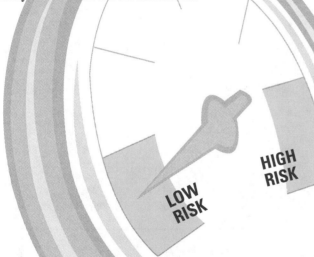

HIGH RISK

LOW RISK

How to Reduce Mutual Fund Risk

Mutual funds are terrific investments, but many people are confused by the growing number of choices and are troubled by the stock market's volatility. Here are some strategies for reducing mutual fund risk.

AVOID SMALLER FUNDS

Funds that have assets of less than $200 million tend either to perform extremely well or to be major disappointments. That's because their managers take big chances, hoping that a heroic performance will

DIVERSIFY INTELLIGENTLY

Don't simply seek safety by investing in more funds; choose your mix carefully. Six funds can be as risky as one if they all have the same investment style.

Common Mistake

Don't rush out and buy last year's top-performing mutual funds. The odds are good that their high rankings were due to similar investment styles and objectives.

Solution: When diversifying, buy stock funds that have different investment philosophies, such as value, growth or equity income. Also, buy funds that invest in different sized companies: small-, mid- and large-cap stocks. A phone representative from each fund should be able to tell you in which types it invests.

MAINTAIN SIGNIFICANT INTERNATIONAL EXPOSURE

The world's stock markets do not always move in the same direction at the same time. By being invested in a fund that invests abroad, you are limiting your risk if the U.S. market falls.

Although there are many excellent mutual funds that invest abroad, many domestic funds also have sizable international holdings. Some have as much as 20% in foreign stocks.

Long-Term Funds Make Sense

Sticking with a good stock mutual fund with a long-term focus will probably make you more money than jumping from hot idea to hot idea. Consider investing in an index fund whose performance closely matches that of a major market index, like the S&P 500 Index.

Caution: About 80% of money managers fail to out-perform the S&P 500 Index consistently.

The Index Trend

The total assets (in billions) and number of stock funds indexed to the S&P 500 soared in the first part of the 1990s.

Assets in Index Funds

Number of Index Funds

Source: Morningstar Inc.

Easy Way to Pick a Stock Fund

The best way to pick a stock fund is to first reduce the number of funds from which you have to choose. Following these guidelines, you can easily exclude most of the approximately 4,200 existing stock funds from your list of suitable investments. That leaves fewer than 200 funds from which to pick.

Eliminate those funds that specialize in specific market segments.

Eliminate the funds which charge loads (sales commissions) that eat into your investment.

Eliminate any fund that charges more than 1.5% per year for expenses.

Eliminate all the funds that have investment minimums above $5,000

Eliminate the funds whose managers have run them for less than three years.

Eliminate the consistent losers.

Biggest Mutual Fund Mistakes

The biggest mistake mutual fund investors make is buying funds without a coherent overall investment plan. People read about a fund or sector that is hot. Then they decide to buy those new funds without considering how it will affect the diversification of their portfolio and their investment objectives. Everyone should have a predetermined risk level for his or her portfolio against which new investments must be weighed. But it's a mistake to have only conservative investments like Certificates of Deposit (CDs). CDs can't provide the growth and inflation protection necessary for retirees who are increasingly living 30 years or more after they stop working.

Mutual Fund Tax Traps

Mutual fund shares are easy to buy, but calculating the capital gains tax on shares that you sell can give you headaches at tax time. Here are the biggest mutual fund tax traps and how to avoid them.

BUYING MUTUAL FUND SHARES LATE IN THE YEAR

A mutual fund's share price is based on the Net Asset Value (NAV) of the fund's portfolio. Under federal law, a mutual fund must distribute to shareholders any capital gains it has realized through the selling of stock during the year, and any dividends it has received from the securities in its portfolio.

Immediately after these capital gains and dividends are distributed, the NAV of the fund's shares drops and the gains and dividends are taxable to the shareholder.

Example: An investor buys a mutual fund at $20 per

share on December 10. On December 15, the fund distributes capital gains of $1.50 per share and dividends of 50¢ per share. Even if the capital gains and dividends are reinvested in additional fund shares, they are considered distributed for tax purposes. The NAV has dropped to $18 per share now, and the new investor has to pay income tax on what is really a return of capital.

Solution: Before investing in a new mutual fund or buying additional shares in a fund you already own, call the fund company and ask for the appropriate amount of taxable gains that might be distributed to you relative to your investment. Wait until after the distribution date to buy shares. You can also limit taxable capital gains by investing in index funds, whose managers do not buy and sell stocks as often as other fund managers.

Information about fund turnover is published in *Morningstar Reports*, which is available at many public libraries.

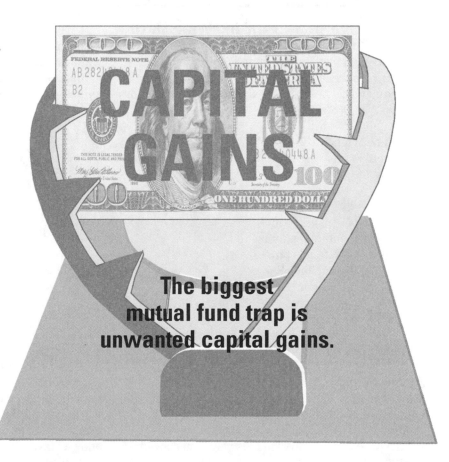

The biggest mutual fund trap is unwanted capital gains.

MUTUAL FUND TRICKS

Poor mutual fund performance may be disguised by the general stock market run-up of recent years. Funds with high expenses and poor returns relative to their competitors may still have turned in positive results that satisfy non-analytical investors.

Self-defense: Don't be happy with a fund just because it made money during the bull market. Compare your fund's performance and expense level with those of other funds that have similar objectives. If your fund doesn't measure up, consider switching.

NOT UNDERSTANDING THE DRAWBACKS TO MUNICIPAL BOND FUNDS

Many people have been attracted to municipal bond funds by advertisements touting tax-free income. Unfortunately, some of these ads imply that investors can avoid all taxes on such funds.

Reality: Municipal bond funds actually have several tax traps.

1. Capital gains trap

The tax-free claim made in ads applies to interest paid on the bonds in the fund's port-folio, not to the capital gains that may result when the fund manager trades bonds.

Strategy: Be prepared for some capital gains, or look for a fund with low turnover before buying.

2. State tax trap

Municipal bond funds avoid federal taxes but bond holders may be liable for state taxes.

Strategy: Buy shares in a fund that invests in bonds issued by your state. This way, you'll avoid federal and state taxes.

3. AMT trap

Though certain municipal bonds are exempt from regular income taxes, they are taxable to people who are liable for the Alternative Minimum Tax (AMT).

Strategy: Check with your tax adviser. If you are liable for the AMT, check fund prospectuses to find a bond fund that holds no AMT preference bonds, or reconsider whether higher-yielding taxable invest-ments would result in higher after-tax returns.

4. Social Security trap

Although municipal bond interest is tax-exempt, it is included in the income base for determining whether Social Security payments are taxable.

Strategy: If you are a middle-class Social Security recipient, check with your tax adviser to see whether you would be better off investing in Treasury or cor-porate bonds.

NOT REALIZING CERTAIN FUND PRIVILEGES ARE TAXABLE

Two convenient services of mutual funds are

1. The ability to write checks on fund holdings.
2. The ability to switch from one fund to another within a fund family.

Trap: Both services are considered sales of fund shares. Therefore, they are taxable events. That's because shareholders who exercise these privileges may incur capital gains.

Strategy: Put money you are going to spend within a few months, for tuition, insurance or vacation, in a money-market fund. In these funds, the NAV always stays at $1 per share, so check-writing has no tax consequence. Also, be mindful of possible tax consequences before switching funds.

PAYING TAXES TWICE

This is quite common. Say you invested $3,000 in a fund ten years ago and had the capital gains and divi-dends reinvested, as most people do. Now you need to put a new roof on your house, so you sell $10,000 worth of fund shares. Many people who prepare their own tax returns assume that they have a $7,000 gain and pay taxes on it.

Reality: Much of that $7,000 represents the reinvested capital gains and dividends on which you have paid taxes year after year.

Strategy: Keep a permanent file folder for each fund you hold. Keep a copy of the quarterly and annual statements that you receive.

Copy the amounts of reinvested dividends and capital gains onto a pad or a spreadsheet, and keep an up-to-date copy. This will help you see what you have invested in the fund initially and through reinvestment, so you can calculate your real gain or loss.

PAYING TOO MUCH TAX WHEN SELLING FUND SHARES

The two most common methods for calculating tax liability are

1. First shares in, first shares out.
2. Average cost of all shares purchased.

Both strategies are easy to use if you keep an up-to-date list or spreadsheet with the number of shares added each year through distributions, as well as any sold or bought over the years.

Strategy: Calculate your taxes using both methods. Use the one that benefits you. The IRS accepts either calculation.

Important: You must stick with whichever method you initially choose when calculating taxes for as long as you own shares in the fund. You can use different methods for different funds, however.

First in, First out Trap

If you can't specifically identify the shares you're selling by referring to your records, the IRS requires you to use FIFO (first in, first out) in calculating your gain on the sale. This assumes that the shares you sold were the first ones you bought, usually the ones with the lowest cost and highest built-in gains.

Strategy: Keep detailed records of each fund purchase: date of purchase, total amount paid, price per share and number of shares. Then, when you go to sell shares, you can sell those that will produce the lowest taxable gain, generally the shares you purchased last. When you can identify the shares you're selling, you can pick which ones to sell and control the amount of tax you pay.

How Safe Are Money Market Mutual Funds?

No investor has ever lost money investing in a modern money-market mutual fund, and it is highly unlikely that anyone ever will.

While some money-fund managers have bailed out or injected extra capital into their funds to cover losses caused by derivatives, no investor has lost any money to date. Very simply, the choice the fund managers are given by either their independent directors or the Securities and Exchange Commission is likely to be, "Make the investors whole or we will replace you with managers who will!"

A money-fund investment management contract is a highly profitable business asset.

Example: BankAmerica Corp., parent of investment adviser Bank of America, bailed out two institutional money funds managed by Bank of America to the tune of $67.9 million.

Safety: All money funds are reasonably safe.

Ironically, the money funds with the highest yields are often the safest. These funds are not those

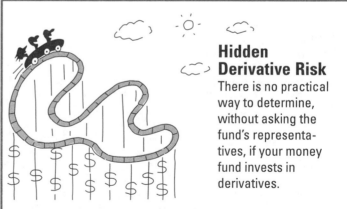

Hidden Derivative Risk
There is no practical way to determine, without asking the fund's representatives, if your money fund invests in derivatives.

taking extra risks, but funds that are subsidizing the funds' expenses for marketing reasons.

The funds that took unnecessary risks were the funds that wanted to charge their full management fee and provide extra returns as well. That strategy backfired on the managers, but, thankfully, not on the investors.

Best Reason to Pick Money-Market Funds

Money-market mutual funds on average become a better deal than bank money-market deposit accounts when interest rates rise, since the interest rates offered by money funds rise faster than those offered by bank funds.

Reason: Money funds invest in shorter-term instruments to take advantage of higher rates sooner. They pass on those rates immediately to their owners, shareholders like you. Banks pay you what they choose, not what they earn. So banks try to keep rates down to maximize the profit they earn from the difference between the rates they pay on deposits and the rates they charge on loans.

Note: Recently, the average rate paid by money-market mutual funds has gone up, while the average rate paid by banks has remained flat.

SOURCES

Sources are listed in the order in which their contributions appear. A source may have contributed part or all of an article, or a series of articles.

Jonathan Pond, Financial Planning Information, Inc.

Nancy Dunnan, author of *How to Invest $50–$5,000*

Stephanie Gallagher, author of *Money Secrets the Pros Don't Want You to Know*

Darryl Reed, Money Minds

Harold Evensky, investment adviser

Robert Garner, Ernst & Young, LLP

Terry Savage, author of *Terry Savage's New Money Strategies for the '90s*

The Beardstown Ladies Investment Club

Tod Barnhart, author of *The Five Rituals of Wealth: Proven Strategies for Turning the Little You Have into More than Enough*

Joel Lerner, professor of business, Sullivan County Community College

Mark Hulbert, editor of *Hulbert's Financial Digest*

Scott Spiering, Spiering & Co.

Sheldon Jacobs, editor and publisher of *The No-Load Fund Investor*

Jay Schabacker, Schabacker Investment Management

Lewis J. Altfest, CFP, L.J. Altfest & Co.

Donna Waldron, The Burlington Stockettes

The Beardstown Ladies Investment Club

Jonathan Pond, Financial Planning Information, Inc.

John Markese, American Association of Individual Investors

Marilyn Cohen, L&S Advisers

Jonathan Pond, Financial Planning Information, Inc.

Terry Savage, author of *Terry Savage's New Money Strategies for the 90s*

Robert Carlson, editor of Bob Carlson's Retirement Watch

North American Securities Administrators Association

Shelby White, author of *What Every Woman Should Know About Her Husband's Money*

Alexandra Armstrong, Armstrong, Welch & MacIntyre

Kathryn Marion, editor of *Reality Check Gazette*

Jonathan Pond, Financial Planning Information, Inc.

Douglas Raborn, Raborn & Co.

Gary Pilgrim, PBHG Growth Fund

Peter Lynch, former manager of the Fidelity Magellan Mutual Fund

Bill Staton, CFA, The Financial Training Group

Ralph J. Acampora, Prudential Securities, Inc.

John C. Bogle, The Vanguard Group

John Train, Montrose Advisors

Betty Sinnock, The Beardstown Ladies Investment Club

Michelle Clayman, New Amsterdam Partners

Dale Domain and **David Louton**, University of Regina and Bryant College

John Markese, American Association of Individual Investors

Dan Jamieson, editor of *Registered Representative*

Robert Hagstrom, Lloyd, Leith & Sawin

Peter Lynch, former manager of the Fidelity Magellan Mutual Fund

Charles Biderman, editor of *Liquidity Trim Tabs*

Kenneth L. Fisher, money manager

Jeremy Siegel, The Wharton School

Douglas Raborn, Raborn & Co.

Louis Rukeyser, editor of *Louis Rukeyser's Wall Street*

Gary Lahey, Chicago Board Options Exchange

William J. O'Neil, publisher of *Investor's Business Daily*

William E. Donoghue, editor of *Donoghue's Wealth Letter*

James B. Rogers, Jr., author of *Investment Biker: On the Road with Jim Rogers*

Steven Camp, author of *Money: 127 Answers to Your Most-Asked Financial Questions*

Sheldon Jacobs, editor and publisher of *The No-Load Fund Investor*

Robert Carlson, editor of Bob Carlson's Retirement Watch

Charlotte Beyer, Institute for Private Investors

James B. Rogers, Jr., author of *Investment Biker: On the Road with Jim Rogers*

Don Phillips, publisher of *Morningstar Mutual Funds*

Sheldon Jacobs, editor and publisher of *The No-Load Fund Investor*

Don Phillips, publisher of *Morningstar Mutual Funds*

Alan Lavine and **Gail Liberman**, writers for *The Boston Herald*

Charles B. Carlson, CFA, editor of *Dow Theory Forecasts*

Don Phillips, publisher of *Morningstar Mutual Funds*

Mark Hulbert, editor of *Hulbert Financial Digest*

Dan Brecher, Fischbein, Badillo, Wagner, Itzler

Martin Weiss, Weiss Research, Inc.

Michael Stolper, Stolper & Co.

Sheldon Jacobs, editor and publisher of *The No-Load Fund Investor*

Norman G. Fosback, Institute for Econometric Research

Don Phillips, publisher of *Morningstar Mutual Funds*

Tod Barnhart, author of *The Five Rituals of Wealth: Proven Strategies for Turning the Little You Have into More than Enough*

Sheldon Jacobs, editor and publisher of *The No-Load Fund Investor*

Ross W. Nager, Arthur Andersen & Co.

Sheldon Jacobs, editor and publisher of *The No-Load Fund Investor*

Carole Gould, Esq., author of *The New York Times Guide to Mutual Funds*

William E. Donoghue, editor of *Donoghue's Wealth Letter*

Mastering Health Care

Hold on to Your Family's Health and Your Savings

Cut Your Family's Medical Bills Now

Here are some surefire ways to reduce out-of-pocket medical expenses right now.

HOSPITALS

Make sure your hospital stay is necessary

Studies show that only one of every eight hospital admissions is medically necessary and only one of every five operations really makes sense. So when you're told you should have a certain procedure or test, be appropriately skeptical.

Ask the right questions

The right questions concern both health and money. Often the answer that is best for your health is also best for your wallet. Ask your doctor the following questions about any recommended procedure.

- What are the risks of the procedure?
- Which hospital do you suggest and why?
  Reason: Some hospitals are safer than others, some are cheaper and some are both.
- Can I have this procedure done as an outpatient?
- Are there any less invasive alternatives to this type of surgery?
  Examples: You may be able to try clot-dissolving

drugs instead of heart bypass surgery, or a lumpectomy instead of total breast removal for a breast tumor.

Always get a second opinion

An eight-year study by the Cornell Medical Center found that one out of four second opinions recommends against an operation. The long-term survival rate of people who take such advice is excellent. So, even if your insurance company doesn't require a second opinion, get one. And always be sure to ask a lot of questions of your doctors, since you are the one who makes the final decision regarding your treatment options.

Pick your hospital

Don't let it pick you. Years ago, no one shopped for a hospital. Today, 35% of patients do. Clearly, this is the best option only if you have time to shop around before your surgery is necessary.

Opportunity: Community hospitals may be up to 25% cheaper than

Operations Most Often Considered Unnecessary

Be particularly diligent about getting a second opinion in these cases.

- Tonsillectomies.
- Coronary bypasses.
- Gall bladder removals.
- Cesarean sections.
- Pacemaker surgeries.
- Joint surgeries.

When You Can't Afford Care

Hospital Care
Hill-Birton Uncompensated Services Toll-Free Hotline: 800-638-0742. This hotline provides information on hospitals required to serve those who can't afford hospitalization. Call Monday through Friday, 1:30-3:30pm. Eligibility is determined by family size and income.

Prescription Medication
Pharmaceutical Manufacturers Association (PMA): 800-PMA-INFO. PMA will send you a *Patient Assistance Directory* with information on free drug programs.

Children's Immunizations
The American Social Health Association: 800-232-2522. Call for information on recommended children's immunizations and referrals to local health departments in your area.

Clinical Studies
Patient Recruitment & Referral Center at the Clinical Center of the National Institute of Health (NIH): 301-496-4891. The Center offers information on whether you might qualify for clinical trials the NIH performs around the country.

Save on incidentals
Check to see what the hospital charges for various services before you check in. The most frequently hidden hospital costs are the $50-$100 fees for providing routine information when filling out forms. These charges are levied by 25% to 30% of hospitals. If yours is one of them, ask to fill out the papers yourself—assuming, of course, that you are well enough to do so.
Example: Hospitals charge a bundle for health and beauty aids.

for-profit hospitals, which order more tests and have bigger markups on procedures and services.

Most doctors are affiliated with more than one hospital, so discuss your options, balancing cost against the success rate for your type of surgery.

Look for the least-expensive option
Many procedures that used to require overnight hospital stays can now be done on an outpatient basis, which can be up to 50% cheaper than a regular hospital procedure. When you discuss outpatient alternatives with your doctor, ask about new, minimally invasive surgical techniques, which can be considerably less expensive and less traumatic.

Caution: Never assume that your doctor or surgeon will automatically recommend the cheapest way of treating your medical problem. Ideally, you should go to an office visit prepared to ask about a variety of options you have already researched.

Resist unnecessary tests
Always ask your doctor why a hospital test must be done. The tests most frequently over-ordered are urinalyses, chest X-rays and two types of blood tests: one that measures white blood cell count and another that measures the amount of time it takes blood to clot. Once in the hospital, insist on advance approval of tests and procedures.

In some cases, you can save more than $100 by bringing your own toiletries and pills (if you are already on the appropriate medications before being admitted). It may also be cheaper to fill new prescriptions outside the hospital while you are a patient.

HOSPITAL BILL
Are You Paying Too Much?
A General Accounting Office study found overcharges in 99% of all hospital bills. Why does this matter to someone who has health insurance? Because more and more plans are requiring patients to share hospital costs.

Strategy: Request a fully itemized bill and review it carefully. Here's what to look for.
● Duplicate billings (often for tests).
● Shoddy testing (don't pay for unreadable X-rays).
● Unauthorized tests (if you previously specified that you wanted advance approval).
● Phantom charges (often for sedatives and other medications that may never have been administered to you).
● Bulk charges (If you see a broad heading such as "radiology" or "pharmacy," you can't possibly know if the total is accurate. Ask for a more detailed breakdown of the charges incurred.)

KEEP THIS SLIP FOR REFERENCE

DOCTORS

Get your money's worth

Show up as prepared for each doctor's visit as you would for an important business meeting. Bring notes about your medical history, symptoms, medications and questions that you want the doctor to answer. Have your doctor explain what she or he is writing in your file.

Once you pay the bill, you're entitled to a free copy of the lab report. Ask your doctor to explain it to you.

The more you know, the better able you will be to gauge what treatments are appropriate and which expenses are worth questioning.

Let your fingers do the walking

Take advantage of a doctor's phone hours, which will save you time and money. A Dartmouth Medical School study found that this saved each patient an average of $1,656 over a two-year period.

Warning: There's a difference between avoiding unnecessary visits to specialists and forgoing important preventive measures. People who save money by avoiding flu shots or treatment for high blood pressure are making serious mistakes.

Avoid the annual physical

Symptom-free adults under age 65 can save $200 to $500 a year by reconsidering whether they really need an annual physical. The American Medical Association's guidelines suggest a full checkup every five years for adults ages 21 to 40, and every few years thereafter, depending on their health. Doctors themselves get physicals less often than do other professionals of the same age.

INSURANCE

Increase your deductible

Talk with your insurance agent or with the benefits person at your company. The amount you could save each year may be substantial, particularly if you are a healthy adult.

Avoid being overinsured

Be prepared to absorb some occasional minor expenses rather than seek a policy that covers every penny of your expenses all the time. This kind of insurance policy is never a bargain.

Fight back if your benefits are denied

Surveys show that policyholders who contest denials get partial or complete satisfaction 50% of the time.

DRUGS

- Ask your doctor to prescribe generic drugs when appropriate.
- Ask your doctor for free samples of prescribed medicines.
- Cut back on over-the-counter (OTC) medicines. Most OTC remedies for colds, pains and minor problems don't really do any good. In fact, only 30% of all OTC medications can prove their claims.

Quit Smoking And Save on Insurance

Smokers pay double for term insurance at most life insurance firms. Cash-value policies might be about 50% higher depending on age and gender. So quitting smoking can cut premiums in half. Ask your insurance company or agent for more information.

Test Your Hearing over the Phone

A free hearing test by phone can reassure you about a feared loss of hearing, or warn you of the need for medical attention. The call involves listening to four tones in each ear. Failure to hear a tone warns of a problem. Call 800-222-EARS between 9am and 5pm Eastern time to obtain the phone number of a local hearing clinic through which the test will be administered automatically.

It Pays to Speak Up

Nearly all doctors are cutting their fees for patients, but you have to ask.

Important: Negotiate directly with the doctor.

Also: Think of your visit as a business transaction—you are paying for a service. Doctors can't afford to lose customers.

Helpful: Call around to find out what other doctors charge their patients.

Negotiating examples: Ask for a flat price to remove several moles (instead of paying per mole), a lower cost for a flu shot or quantity discounts for regular treatment of a chronic condition (such as allergies).

Smart Ways to Cut Your Medical Bills

In the ten years between 1980 and 1990, U.S. expenditures on health care more than doubled.

In 1990, each citizen's share of the bill was $2,566. By the year 2000, the Health Care Financing Administration predicts that each share will soar to $5,712. That's $22,848 for a family of four.

Here's how to stretch your health care dollar without sacrificing top-quality care.

1. STAY WELL

The cheapest illness to treat is the one you never get. Adjust your lifestyle to reduce your risk of serious (and expensive) ailments, particularly cancer and heart disease.

What to do: Exercise for at least 30 minutes three times a week (see a doctor first if you're older than 35 or have a medical condition), eat a low-fat, high-fiber diet, have no more than two drinks a day and don't smoke.

2. CHECK OUT FREE HEALTH CARE

In many parts of the country, shopping malls and drugstores offer everything from eye exams and flu shots to screenings for high blood pressure, diabetes and cancer. These services are not scams. Yes, they publicize the store or hospital offering them, but they also provide free valuable care. The same tests can cost upward of $200 in a doctor's office.

3. READ YOUR INSURANCE POLICY

Find out exactly what's covered, and be sure to submit claims for everything for which you can expect reimbursement. People often assume they can't get reimbursed for incidental items, such as the small lancets diabetics use to obtain blood samples. Many policies do cover such items, but you have to submit a claim for them be reimbursed.

4. ASK ABOUT ASSIGNMENT

That means doctors accept the portion that the health insurance company pays as full payment for your bill. More doctors take assignment than you might think, because collecting from nonpaying patients is such a hassle.

5. SCRUTINIZE YOUR HOSPITAL BILLS

Hospital bills are notoriously inaccurate, and in cases where inaccuracies occur, they favor the hospital at least 80% of the time.

Example: Before surgery, many items are placed in the operating room just in case the doctor needs them. Patients are mistakenly billed for them even if the doctor never uses them.

Self-defense: Check with the surgeon after surgery. Did they use all the equipment and supplies you were billed for? Was medication ordered that you never needed? If you find discrepancies, call the hospital billing department and ask that your bill be reduced.

6. AVOID EMERGENCY ROOMS

In a true emergency, of course, a visit to the ER can save your life. But using the ER for nonemergency care is very expensive. You'll pay up to ten times more than you would for the same treatment in your doctor's office.

If your child has an earache Saturday night, phone your doctor. He or she should be able to give you an idea of how serious the problem is, and may be able to treat the illness swiftly and cheaply by writing a prescription or recommending simple, at-home care.

7. TALK TO YOUR PHARMACIST

Pharmacists are often knowledgeable about simple but effective ways to cut prescription costs.

Example: Buy a 90-day supply of drugs rather than three 30-day supplies. That way, you might be able to pay only one co-payment instead of three.

Some insurance companies have special arrangements with mail-order pharmacies. Making use of such an arrangement can lower your drug bills even more. If not, a discount pharmacy in your community is likely to have lower prices than most mail-order pharmacies.

Biggest Health Care Mistake

Not adequately understanding what types of emergency room visits are covered by your HMO is a big mistake.

Problem: More HMOs are refusing to pay bills for visits that aren't life threatening.

Solution: Find out now what your HMO considers to be life threatening. Ask the HMO "what if" questions to see if it covers the situations you describe.

Mail-Order Prescriptions Can Save Money

It usually takes two weeks to have a prescription processed. Many mail-order firms deal only with patients belonging to specific insurance plans. But some sell directly to the general public, like Medi-Mail (800-331-1458) and the American Association of Retired Persons (800-456-2277).

Shop Around for Medications

Some pharmacies charge as much as they can. Others sell some medications below cost to get customers into their stores, so that they can sell them other profitable products. Most are somewhere in the middle. Do not hesitate to call several pharmacies, and take your business wherever the prices are consistently lowest.

Better Way to Buy Cough Remedies

Get single-ingredient products (suppressant, expectorant or decongestant) depending on what type of cough you have. Generics are as effective as name brands and much less expensive. Follow warning labels; some remedies can cause drowsiness.

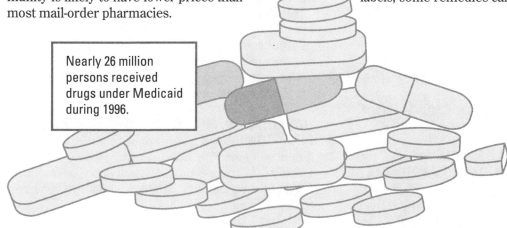

Nearly 26 million persons received drugs under Medicaid during 1996.

Save on Medicines

Buy double-strength pills (if your doctor will prescribe this way) and cut them in half with a pill cutter. Pill cutters cost about $5.

Alternative: Home remedies like drinking plenty of fluids, gargling with a mild saline solution or rubbing your chest with camphor ointments, menthol salves or pure peppermint oil can be helpful. If a cough lasts more than a week without any improvement, call your doctor.

How to Buy the Right Health Coverage

If you are among the 37 million Americans who do not receive health coverage at work, it is still possible

to find a great health insurance policy.

There are even options for people who are dissatisfied with the coverage they receive from their employers.

Here are the most important health-coverage questions people are asking now.

WHAT ARE THE LEAST-EXPENSIVE HEALTH-COVERAGE OPTIONS AVAILABLE?

For individuals and their families, there are two: Health Maintenance Organizations (HMOs) and Preferred Provider Organizations (PPOs).

> **TIP**
>
> ### Steer Clear of Vitamins With Herbs
>
> Don't pay extra for vitamin supplements with herbal ingredients. Herbal substances are of questionable value, and may interfere with vitamins in a manner that blocks your body from absorbing them. So you may wind up paying more for less.

HMOs

HMO plans are usually the most affordable for individuals or families, and they provide medical care through networks of physicians.

Benefits: With an HMO, you won't have to fill out forms after each doctor's visit as you would with a traditional insurer. You will probably pay $5-$10 per doctor visit and have no deductible.

How HMO coverage works: When you are ill, you first consult your primary care physician, who is also known as the gatekeeper. Your primary care physician can then treat your illness, or refer you to a specialist if he or she deems it necessary.

Exception: Most plans permit women to visit a gynecologist without a gatekeeper referral.

If you choose an out-of-network doctor or hospital, you are generally not covered. You also must first obtain permission from your primary care physician to see an in-network specialist. Out-of-network specialists are not covered at all.

PPOs

PPO plans are slightly more expensive than HMOs. They too provide medical care through a network of doctors.

Big difference: There are no gatekeepers, so you can consult a specialist without first getting a referral from your primary care physician. Your copayment, or fee, for each doctor's visit is comparable to HMO rates. Remember, out-of-network doctors and hospitals are not covered.

HOW DO MONTHLY COSTS OF HMOs AND PPOs COMPARE?

A family of four with HMO coverage in any major U.S. city could expect to pay about $500 per month. For PPO coverage, that would be about 5% higher, or $525 per month.

WHAT IF YOU DON'T LIKE THE IDEA OF NETWORK CARE?

Many insurance carriers have stopped selling traditional or indemnity plans to individuals. Insurers that still sell them usually make it tough to qualify because of strict underwriting standards. If you are opposed to network care, see if you can apply for indemnity coverage through an organization to which you belong.

Drawback: While you have complete freedom to use the doctor of your choice, such plans are very expensive. A family of four that chooses a plan with a $200 deductible and reimbursement rate starting at 80% of the first $5,000, and 100% of all expenditures above that, would pay about $850 monthly.

Still Growing

The number of people covered by managed care has been increasing steadily since the early 1980s.

Millions covered

Source: InterStudy Publications, The Competetive Edge 6.2, 1996

CAN YOU COMBINE THE FLEXIBILITY OF AN INDEMNITY PLAN WITH THE COST SAVINGS OF AN HMO OR A PPO?

Yes, a Point-of-Service (POS) plan allows you to decide whether you want to consult a network doctor or an out-of-network doctor every time you require medical care.

Members' costs vary: When you stay within the network, the charge is $5-$15 per visit. If you choose to go out of network for care, your costs will be higher, since insurers will reimburse only 70% to 80% of the cost of a doctor's visit once you meet the plan deductible.

Monthly cost comparison: POS plans cost more than HMOs or PPOs, but less than traditional indemnity plans. A family of four in a major city would pay about $600 per month for an HMO/POS plan and about $630 per month for a PPO/POS plan.

Drawback: In today's insurance market, individuals and their families cannot purchase POS coverage. It's only sold to businesses, which may offer it to their employees.

Opportunity: If you're self-employed, you can apply for POS health care coverage as a business, rather than as an individual.

HOW DO I FIND A GREAT HMO OR PPO?

Because there are many different types of plans and consumer options keep changing rapidly, it makes sense to consult a licensed insurance agent who works with a range of insurers and can help you compare your choices.

Selection priorities: While low cost is important, it should not be your top consideration.

More important: Evaluate the quality of the insurer and its network by contacting present and former policyholders, the Better Business Bureau and your state department of insurance.

Over time, you'll tend to use doctors in the network more and more, so it pays to shop for a plan whose network physicians are conveniently located, and well qualified to meet your family's needs. Networks are growing rapidly as more doctors join them. While your physician may not be a member now, that may change in the near future.

If you don't love the choices your agent has suggested or are concerned that they're too costly, sign up for the best plan that's available now. Then, in three to four months, ask your insurance agent to survey the marketplace to see if better products have become available.

Health care policies are changing so rapidly these days that it is possible something better will come along soon.

WHEN EMPLOYEES NEED MORE INSURANCE

In some cases, people who already receive health care coverage from their employers need additional protection. To decide whether you need more coverage, ask yourself: "Does my policy only provide hospitalization coverage?" If so, it makes sense to buy an HMO or a PPO plan to cover other medical costs. Choose a plan with

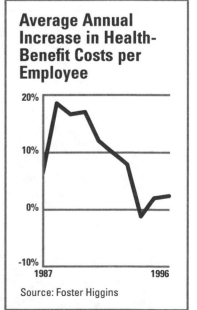

Average Annual Increase in Health-Benefit Costs per Employee

Source: Foster Higgins

the best physicians, but don't worry about its hospitalization feature since you're already covered.

Important: If your decision to seek additional coverage is due to your unhappiness with the doctors who belong to your plan's network, don't despair. A growing number of states, such as New Jersey, have passed "any willing provider" laws. These laws require HMO and PPO networks to accept any willing physician who meets their licensing, training and other standards.

That means your physician choices may soon improve within your existing plan. So it makes sense to wait, rather than to spend money for supplementary coverage.

COVERAGE FOR RETIREES

Retirees often ask whether it makes sense to supplement Medicare coverage with an HMO or PPO plan. The answer is "no." That's because Medicare will cover most of the cost of your basic medical and hospital services. What you need is a different kind of supplementary insurance policy known as Medigap, which pays retirees for any expenses that Medicare fails to reimburse.

Opportunity: The federal government has started working with some HMO insurers to provide in-network medical care to retirees.

Here's how: If retirees sign up and commit themselves to only visiting network physicians, they won't need to purchase Medigap coverage. Instead, they will pay only $10 per doctor's visit and Medicare will

reimburse other expenses. If this option is available to you, it's worth considering.

William Shernoff Unveils the Biggest HMO Traps

In an effort to keep costs down, a growing number of managed-care providers and HMOs are denying or limiting payment in a number of situations.

WORRISOME TRENDS
Increase of bonus incentives
A growing number of HMOs and managed-care systems provide doctors, administrators and claims adjusters with financial incentives to deny or cut back coverage to customers.

Insurance companies seldom disclose these financial arrangements to customers, except when disputes turn into lawsuits.

Hidden arbitration clauses in plan documents
Most people don't realize it, but when they sign up for coverage through some plans, they abandon their constitutional rights to a jury trial in the event of a health care policy dispute or fraudulent business practice.

Instead, they have agreed to file an arbitration

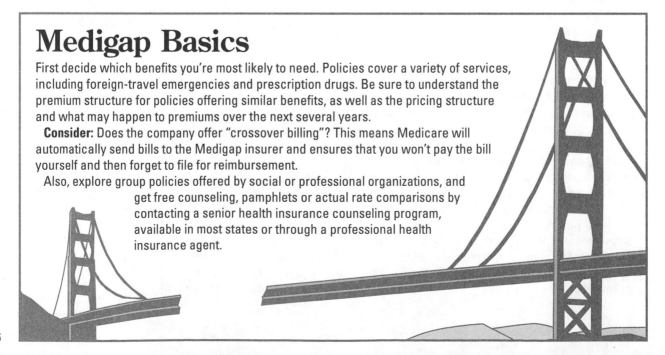

Medigap Basics
First decide which benefits you're most likely to need. Policies cover a variety of services, including foreign-travel emergencies and prescription drugs. Be sure to understand the premium structure for policies offering similar benefits, as well as the pricing structure and what may happen to premiums over the next several years.

Consider: Does the company offer "crossover billing"? This means Medicare will automatically send bills to the Medigap insurer and ensures that you won't pay the bill yourself and then forget to file for reimbursement.

Also, explore group policies offered by social or professional organizations, and get free counseling, pamphlets or actual rate comparisons by contacting a senior health insurance counseling program, available in most states or through a professional health insurance agent.

suit, which is typically decided by administrative panels with strong ties to the medical community. In many states, these panels cannot award consumers more than the cost of contested medical services.

THE IMPACT ON YOU

Specialists

Insurers may discourage doctors from referring patients to specialists. This problem often shows up in cases where consumers require treatments that are expensive or somewhat new or unusual.

Typical problem areas: high-risk pregnancies, cancers, multiple sclerosis and other serious diseases.

Some HMOs and managed-care systems deny full reimbursement to primary care physicians who refer patients to specialists, no matter how severe the patients' illnesses. This means primary care physicians lose money when they recommend specialists, leading to an ethical conflict that patients learn about only if they sue their health care provider.

Solution: The best thing you can do under these circumstances is complain. Start by making an argument in writing to your primary care physician about why you believe you need a specialist's care. The next step is to complain to your HMO's board of directors. If the board isn't sympathetic, consider consulting a specialist and filing your claim, and hope for the best. Your health always comes first.

Acute rehabilitation care

Insurers may discourage doctors from recommending acute rehabilitation care. This problem typically occurs among patients over age 65 following a serious stroke or a serious injury that results in paraplegia, quadriplegia or hip surgery.

Although the problem is widespread, it's most pronounced when Medicare patients receive their care from HMOs.

Solution: Don't succumb to the marketing pitches you hear from HMOs. There's absolutely no reason to assign your Medicare coverage to an HMO. You'll only wind up limiting your freedom of medical choice.

Emergencies

Insurers may refuse to pay for certain emergency treatments. This usually happens when an HMO patient has a medical emergency while traveling and must be treated at a hospital that doesn't belong to the HMO. It's also common in states where people often work more than one hour's commute from their homes and must seek treatment at nonmember hospitals.

Trap: Providers often deny claims on the grounds that the patient should have been treated at a member hospital or could have been transferred to a member hospital.

> Freedom-of-choice waivers now allow states to enroll Medicaid beneficiaries in managed care programs. Forty five states already have waiver systems in place.

Solution: Always request a letter from the emergency room facility documenting that you experienced a medical emergency and were unable to be transferred to another facility without endangering your health.

WHEN INSURERS WON'T PAY CLAIMS

At both HMOs and traditional insurers, more and more medical claims are being challenged on the grounds of being not medically necessary.

In these cases, it's the insurance plan doctor's judgment against any other physician's judgment. Regardless of what your doctor tells you, the decision may be influenced by bonus incentives.

Some HMOs and insurers are even disallowing claims as unnecessary after they have been recommended by physicians and pre-approved.

Example: In one case, a woman stayed in the hospital for five days after a Cesarean section, under doctor's orders. Then her insurance company refused to pay for more than two days' bills, despite the fact that the patient could not have discharged herself early from the hospital.

If your HMO or insurance company tries one of these ploys to deny you or a family member medical coverage, here's what you can do.

OUCH!

Percent of patients reporting problems with certain aspects of their HMO's service.

Continuity and transition	28.7%
Emotional support	26.6
Information and education	23.1
Involvement of family and friends	22.3
Coordination of care	22.9
Respect for patients' preferences	21.8
Physical comfort	10.4

Note: Based on a survey of 23,768 patients.
Source: American Hospital Association

1. **Start by following the insurer's complaint procedure**. Most health care policies require you to report your grievance to a specified person or department.

Don't forget to put your complaint in writing and include all relevant documentation. Retain a copy for your records, then send the complaint by registered mail, and keep the receipt.

2. **If this fails, turn to state regulators**. If your complaint is with an insurer, even a managed-care company, complain to your state insurance department. Be sure to include a copy of your original complaint plus all of the relevant correspondence.

If your complaint is with an HMO, turn to your state department of corporations. You may want to report cases of severe bad faith or fraudulent behavior to your state attorney general or your local Better Business Bureau.

3. **Make as much noise as possible**. Since state regulatory oversight in these areas is often weak, you may improve your chances by also reporting your problem to the local consumer hotlines and consumer affairs reporters at television stations and newspapers.

4. **Seek legal redress if necessary**. If the sum in dispute is small, you may be wiser to sue in small-claims court. Check your state limits to see if this solution will work for you. Otherwise, you may want to consult an attorney.

Important: If a lawsuit seems likely, you are better off hiring a contingency fee attorney so that you'll only be charged if you win your case.

If your policy includes an arbitration clause, you'll still be better off with a contingency lawyer, but finding one to represent you may be difficult since the financial payoff is limited.

Strategy: Interview several contingency fee attorneys who specialize in HMO lawsuits. The initial consultation should be free. Also find out whether your state permits arbitration awards larger than your contested medical claims. That should increase your chances of finding a lawyer to represent you.

Protect your interests
Take these steps before signing up for coverage and long before potential problems can arise.

Step 1: Question potential insurers or HMOs about arbitration clauses and hidden financial incentives for denied claims. If any exist, don't sign up.

Step 2: Check with state agencies and consumer groups to see if the HMO or insurer has a record of complaints. If so, that's another reason to avoid signing up.

Step 3: If you've got no choice because your employer offers only one type of coverage,
● Put your objections in writing.
● Save a copy for your records.
● Send your letter to your plan representative by registered mail as proof that the insurer or HMO has been informed of your objections. Also give a copy to your employer's plan administrator. This may help protect your legal interests in the event that you ever face a policy dispute.

Before Joining An HMO

Check whether it has been accredited by the National Committee for Quality Assurance (NCQA), an independent nonprofit organization now in the process of rating HMOs on their medical treatment, physicians' qualifications, preventative health services recordkeeping and more. To date, HMOs covering 50% of all HMO enrollees have been rated.

Beware: More than half have received less than a top grade because of various deficiencies. To see if a particular HMO has been reviewed and what the results were, call the NCQA at 800-839-6487 and request its free Accreditation Status list, which is updated on the 15th of each month.

Precertify Hospital Procedures

Protect medical insurance claims when facing expensive medical treatment. Have the hospital precertify the procedure as soon as possible. Include the date on which treatment is to begin. This creates a deadline by which the insurer must make a decision. Make sure the insurer has agreed to pay your claim, not just given permission for you to stay in the hospital. Have your doctor and hospital send an information package to the insurer supporting the treatment's necessity and acceptance by the medical community. Keep records of all contact you have with the insurer.

Secrets of Qualifying For Medicaid and Protecting Assets

Americans should be aware of two very frightening statistics.

1. It has been estimated that one in four Americans over age 70, and two in four over age 80, will spend some time in a nursing home. With only minor exceptions, the cost of this care is not covered by Medicare or supplemental Medicare insurance.

2. The average cost of a nursing home stay today is between $50,000 and $60,000 a year, although it can run over $100,000! Additional funds are also needed to maintain the healthy spouse in the couple's residence when the other spouse enters a nursing home.

Due to the high statistical probability of needing long-term care and its exorbitant cost, only people with over $1 million in income-producing assets can afford to shoulder their own costs. For all others, planning is essential.

Information on Aging—Free!

National Council on Aging: 800-424-9046
Offers information on family caregiving, senior employment and long-term care.

National Institute on Aging Information Center: 800-222-2225
Information about healthy aging. Provides literature and referrals to organizations dealing with specific age-related illnesses.

MEDICAID

For many, reliance on Medicaid (Medi-Cal in California), a need-based federal/state program, becomes inevitable. The focus of planning, then, is to ensure eligibility for Medicaid while protecting assets as much as possible.

Medicaid planning is a highly specialized area of the law. It is important to have the help of a com-

Before You Have A Medical Test

Be sure to ask your doctor what it will reveal about your condition that he or she does not already know, what it costs, what risks and side effects the test might cause and what the alternatives are to taking the test. If in doubt about whether to have a test, get a second doctor's opinion.

petent attorney who is well-versed on this topic. The cost of legal assistance to plan properly is relatively inexpensive when compared with costly mistakes that can be made by the uninformed.

Since Medicaid is primarily for needy individuals, be sure to understand the limits on assets and income that a person can have and still qualify for Medicaid. These limits vary from state to state.

Also understand the restrictions on transferring assets to anyone but your spouse. There is a three-year lookback rule for outright gifts and a five-year lookback rule when trusts are involved. This rule lets Medicaid look at all gifts made within three or five years of applying for nursing home benefits (with exceptions noted below).

Gifts within this time frame result in a period of ineligibility. The length of this period depends on the amounts transferred and the locality of the person seeking Medicaid.

DURABLE POWER OF ATTORNEY
When people become incompetent, they can no longer take steps for Medicaid planning, such as transferring assets or buying annuities, without court approval. If a durable power of attorney is signed before the onset of incompetence, however, another person can still act on your behalf. Durable power of attorney is a legal document that names an agent to act in the place of the person granting the power (called the principal). The document gives the agent broad authority to handle the financial affairs of the principal. The power is durable because it continues to be effective despite the incompetence of the principal. The power ends at the principal's death.

Self-defense: Be sure the durable power of attorney is drafted by an attorney. Preprinted forms available at stationery stores may not include all the powers necessary to do Medicaid planning. While an attorney-drafted form costs a little more, it can save you thousands of dollars.

Whom Does Medicaid Serve?
- 18.7 million children.
- 7.6 million adults who care for these children.
- 5.9 million blind and disabled.
- 4.4 million elderly.

How Much Does Medicaid Cost?
- Total 1995 Medicaid expenditures for health care were $152 billion.
- The average expenditure per eligible beneficiary was $3,700.
- States paid 43% and the Federal government paid 57%.
- The Federal government contributes between 50% and 80% of the payments made under each state's program.

Source: Health Care Financing Administration (HCFA) data for 1995

LONG-TERM CARE INSURANCE
Older Americans who are not yet in need of long-term care should consider buying a nursing home policy for long-term care anyway. This type of policy provides a fixed daily dollar amount ($100 or $150 per day) for a pre-determined period of time, usually three to five years. A long-term care policy can be used to pay the entire cost of care or merely supplement an individual's own funds.

Tip: A long-term care policy can be used as a stop-gap measure to allow for additional

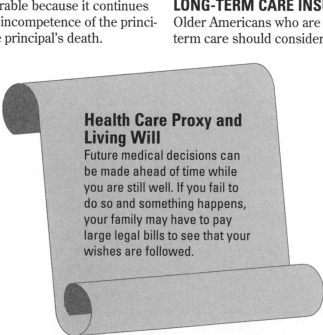

Health Care Proxy and Living Will
Future medical decisions can be made ahead of time while you are still well. If you fail to do so and something happens, your family may have to pay large legal bills to see that your wishes are followed.

planning. A policy that pays benefits for at least three years will give sufficient time to transfer assets and make other arrangements within the Medicaid lookback period.

PROTECTING A HOME

A key item of concern for many older Americans is preservation of their residence. While a residence is treated as an exempt asset for Medicaid (ownership of a home, regardless of value, will not keep a person from qualifying), there are still good reasons for taking action.

Reason: In a number of states, if a single person enters a nursing home and cannot show an expectation of returning to the home, it loses its exempt status.

Even though the home is exempt for purposes of determining Medicaid eligibility, the state has a right to recover against the home after the owner dies. The recovery is limited to the Medicaid funds expended on the owner's behalf. If spouses own a home jointly, consider transferring the home to the sole name of the healthy spouse. Then have that spouse provide in his or her will that the property passes to children or others (not the ill spouse) upon death. There is no lookback period for transfers between spouses, so a deed change just before a Medicaid application will not affect eligibility.

Alternative: Transfer the home to children or other relatives, retaining a life estate, and wait out the three-year lookback period. (A life estate gives the parent the right to live in the home for life.)

Caution: Be sure to understand the legal and tax ramifications before you transfer.

Opportunity: Transfers of a home within the lookback period will not disqualify an applicant if the transfers are to a child who is under age 21, blind or disabled; to a sibling who is a co-owner and who has lived in the home for at least a year; or to a child who has been living in the home for two years and who provided care which enabled the applicant to remain in the home.

Law changes to Medicaid in 1993 severely restricted the use of trusts in Medicaid planning. It is still possible to create a trust that pays only income to the settlor (the person who sets it up), with the assets of the trust passing to others upon the settlor's death.

Key: As long as the trust clearly limits the interest of the settlor to income, the assets in the trust will

not be counted for determining Medicaid eligibility after the appropriate waiting period. The trust must be irrevocable, however, meaning the settlor does not have the right to cancel the trust and reacquire the assets.

Caution: An income-only trust should be used only by those people who are able to wait out the five-year lookback period.

Don't Delay Applying For Medicare Coverage

When you delay Social Security past age 65, you must apply for Medicare if you want coverage to start at 65. You can apply for Medicare as early as three months before your 65th birthday month.

If you apply for Medicare three months before your birthday month, your benefits will start on the first day of your birthday month. If you apply one or two months before your birthday month, benefits should start sometime during your birthday month, but that date is not guaranteed.

> **The HCFA estimates that over 1.7 million people in nursing facilities received care covered by Medicaid in 1996.**

Warning: If you wait until your birthday month or after to apply, you could lose Medicare coverage for up to a year.

The Rising Cost of Medicare

The cost of Medicare has increased dramatically in recent years, and, together with Social Security, encompassed 36% of Federal outlays for fiscal year 1995.

The number of people enrolled in Medicare has increased by 95% over the past 30 years, from 19.5 million in 1967 to an estimated 38.1 million in 1996.

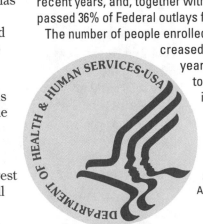

National health expenditures grew from $247 per person in 1967 to $3,510 in 1994.

Source: Health Care Financing Administration (HCFA)

Birthday Bonus

Get an extra month of Medicare if you were born on the first of the month.

Reason: Under Social Security rules, you turn one year older the day before your birthday.

Example: If you were born on February 1, you will officially turn 65 on January 31 and be entitled to Medicare benefits for the entire month of January.

Important: Take this into account when figuring out the month in which to enroll for your Medicare benefits.

How to Protect Your Savings from Catastrophic Illness

With the cost of caring for someone with a catastrophic illness running at $50,000 or more annually, life savings can be wiped out in a very short time. Typical medical policies, including Medicare, may not adequately cover these expenses. However, planning can prevent financial destruction and ensure proper care.

TRANSFERRING ASSETS

States determine the ineligibility period by a formula: the amount of funds transferred divided by the average monthly nursing home bill in the area (a figure set by Medicaid).

Caution: All gifts within 36 months (the lookback period) of applying are examined and used in the formula.

Example: Sam transfers $50,000, and 35 months later applies for Medicaid. Since the average cost of a nursing home in his area is fixed at $5,000, he is ineligible for ten months ($50,000 divided by $5,000).

> **Medicaid is the largest insurer of long-term care for all Americans, including the middle class. Medicaid covers 68% of nursing home residents and over 50% of nursing home costs.**
> Source: HCFA

There is no limit on the ineligibility period. If Sam had transferred $250,000 within 36 months of applying for Medicaid, he would have been ineligible for 50 months ($250,000 divided by $5,000).

TWO QUICK FIXES FOR ASSET PROTECTION

1. If there is not enough time to give all assets away, the "half a loaf" approach can still protect substantial assets.

Example: Sam, with $100,000 in assets, transfers half his property to his daughter. Now he is ineligible for ten months ($50,000 divided by $5,000). But Sam still has $50,000 so he can pay for his own care for those ten months of ineligibility and then get coverage. In addition, he successfully protected $50,000.

2. Assets can be used to buy a single-premium annuity. The income from the annuity will go to the nursing home, but if the owner dies before the end of the payout period, the heirs will receive the balance.

The law limits the assets that the non-Medicaid spouse can keep. This varies from state to state.

Caution: Assets of a married couple are viewed together. Medicaid does not care how assets are titled between spouses or how long assets have been held. Prenuptial agreements do not have any effect for Medicaid purposes.

USING TRUSTS

The federal government has given its okay to shield assets in a trust if certain guidelines are met.

1. It is irrevocable (you cannot get the property back once the trust is set up).

2. It is an income-only trust, one that pays the income earned on the assets in the trust to the person who set up the trust (or that person's spouse) for life.

3. The trustee can't have any discretion to pay out the trust's assets during the life of the person who set up the trust (or that person's spouse).

Caution: This strategy requires preplanning since a 60-month lookback period may apply to assets transferred to an income-only trust.

RETIREMENT AND ESTATE PLANS

Financial and logistical moves made for retirement and estate planning purposes may put your money in jeopardy.

For example, sunny Florida may be a retirement goal, but this destination can prevent Medicaid coverage for some. Florida, New Jersey and some others are cap states. They will not provide coverage if your income exceeds a certain cap.

Asset transfers for Medicaid eligibility can also throw estate plans into havoc.

Tax consequences of gifting assets to children or others must be factored in. While there may be no federal gift tax cost in making these transfers, there may still be state gift taxes. In addition, the income tax consequences to those receiving the assets must be considered.

Married couples must be careful to redo wills after one spouse becomes ill. If the well spouse dies first, his or her will should leave property to children or others. If property is left to the spouse in a nursing home, the funds will be spent on care that would otherwise be covered by Medicaid.

Caregiver Self-Defense

To prevent financial abuse by caregivers, or even family members, do the following.

- Limit powers of attorney. Allow agents only to do specific things, and require an annual audit of what they do.
- Use direct deposit for Social Security and other benefit checks.
- Use automatic bill payment for routine bills.
- Communicate regularly with your bank. Banks are often the first place to spot a pattern of possible abuse.
- Check caregivers' references.

Long-Term Care Insurance Essentials

To offset the future expense of a nursing home or of home health care, many people who are in their 50s and 60s should consider long-term care insurance.

But while long-term care insurance policies have specific benefits, they are not for everyone. Here's what you need to know before you buy.

LONG-TERM CARE INSURANCE BASICS

Long-term care insurance emerged about ten years ago to help people pay for extended health care themselves without wiping out their assets. This type of insurance also protects the assets of family members at a time when they may have other financial obligations.

An insurance policy's annual premium depends on your age and health at the time you apply for the policy, the benefit amount selected, the benefit period, the elimination period (the time that must elapse before a policy begins paying benefits) and any inflation option.

Examples: A basic policy may provide for a $100-a-day benefit for three years with an automatic inflation option. It could also include a 100-day elimination period. If purchased at age 55, this basic policy would cost about $800 a year; at age 60, $1,100 a year; and at age 70, $1,800 a year.

By contrast, a top-of-the-line policy can provide a $250-a-day lifetime benefit with a 5% compound inflation rider and a 20-day elimination period. At age 55, the annual premium would be $2,900; at age 60, $3,970; and at age 70, $7,090.

Staying Old Longer

Life expectancy in the United States has increased dramatically over the past 55 years.

Life expectancy at birth

Year born	Male	Female
1940	60.8	65.2
1950	65.6	71.1
1960	66.6	73.1
1970	67.1	74.7
1975	68.8	76.6
1980	70.0	77.4
1985	71.1	78.2
1990	71.8	78.8
1994	72.4	79.0

Source: National Center for Health Statistics

WHO NEEDS IT?

The ideal candidates for long-term care insurance are healthy and between the ages of 55 and 75 with assets of $500,000 to $2.5 million, not including the value of their homes.

These people usually want to preserve their assets for their heirs rather than use them to pay nursing home or home health care bills. In addition, this group can usually afford to pay the premiums now.

But others should consider long-term care insurance for different reasons.

- Ages 40-65. This group may want to protect their children from having to take care of them when they are older.
- Ages 65+. This age group may want to be able to continue living in their own homes, and understandably they may be reluctant to transfer their assets to their children in order to qualify for Medicaid.

BEFORE BUYING A POLICY

Consider the term of the policy

If you are under age 60, lifetime coverage is preferable. If you're over age 80, opt for two or four years. Those people between the ages of 60 and 80 should buy what they can afford.

Note: A single person may opt to take out lifetime coverage because he or she doesn't have a spouse to handle some of the burden.

Consider the policy's elimination period

The longer the elimination period, the lower the premium will be.

Strategy: Consider the trade-off between price and peace of mind. For most people, a 100-day elimination period may make the most sense because, if they are eligible, Medicare may pay some of the expenses for the first 100 days.

New Long-Term Health Care Option

A new way to pay for long-term health care is single premium insurance. You make a single, up-front premium payment to buy a life insurance policy with a specified death benefit. If nursing care needs arise during your life, the policy pays a monthly benefit equal to 2% of the death benefit, or 1% of the death benefit for home care. These amounts are offset against the ultimate death benefit.

Major advantage: If you don't need the health benefit, you retain the policy as a financial asset that goes up in value, earning investment returns on a tax-deferred basis.

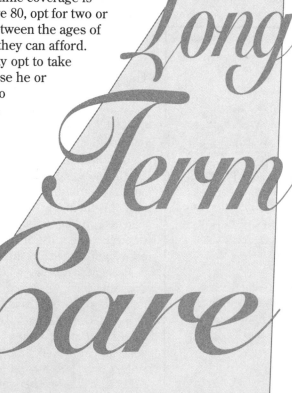

What the Right Policy Provides

- Guaranteed renewability. As long as you pay the insurance premiums, the policy cannot be canceled. The premium can be increased only for the entire group, not on an individual basis.
- Nursing home and home health care. The policy should include both options, and your personal physician should decide what kind of care you need.
- Payment triggered by the policyholder's inability to perform at least two of five basic activities of daily living: bathing, feeding, administering medications, toileting and moving from a chair to a bed.
- Coverage throughout the U.S. You want a policy that provides protection no matter where you live, perhaps even in other countries.
- Coverage in the event that you develop Alzheimer's disease.

Frank Darras Reveals How to Buy the Right Disability Policy

When people ask me whether they really need to buy long-term disability insurance, I ask them, "Could you pay your bills if you were out of work for an extended period of time due to illness or injury?"

Some think for a moment and realize that they could not. Others reply, "My company's long-term disability policy would cover me."

Reality: Most company short- or long-term disability plans do not provide enough coverage. They also do not include the same level of consumer safeguards that individually purchased policies do, nor do they provide the same financial benefits, since they are considered taxable income by the IRS.

The fact is that disability insurance is more important in many cases than life insurance, since you are more likely to be injured or disabled at a younger age than you are to die.

Here's what you need to know when considering long-term disability coverage.

THE BASICS

Disability insurance replaces a portion of your income if you become sick or injured and are unable to perform the substantial or material duties required by your job.

Important: Each policy includes its own definition of a qualifying sickness or injury. Generally, any illness must have begun after your policy was issued in order for you to qualify for benefits.

Whenever you buy long-term disability insurance, your goal is self-protection. To accomplish this goal, you need a policy that offers you the largest amount of coverage and the most flexible options for reimbursement in the event that you ever need to apply for benefits. The rates for such coverage vary, depending on your age and sex.

Example:
A 40-year-old male should expect to pay $500 a year for a good basic policy in order to receive a benefit of $1,000 a month. A 40-year-old female would average $600 a year.

Disability Update

The number of people reporting disabilities more than doubled between 1990 and 1995. Over half of those people became disabled when they were not working.

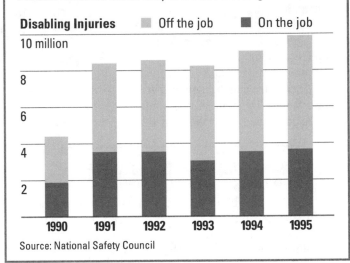

Disabling Injuries   ▢ Off the job   ▆ On the job

Source: National Safety Council

COMPANY TRAPS

Employer long-term disability plans are regulated under the Employee Retirement Income Security Act (ERISA) guidelines. As a result, you lose your individual rights. If you become disabled due to an illness or injury, and your company's insurer unfairly denies or delays your benefits, even after appeal, here is what's likely to happen.

- You will have to sue the insurer in federal court, where your case will likely be decided in 15 months by a federal judge—not by a jury. If the court can find any basis to uphold the insurer's denial of your benefits, you will lose.

- Under ERISA, you are not permitted to sue for emotional distress or punitive or other damages. These restrictions limit your ability to hire a lawyer on a contingency basis, meaning that you'll have to pay for all legal services out of your own pocket, no matter what the judgment.

- Whatever benefits you receive will be considered taxable income.

- During the first year of your illness or injury, your group benefits are reduced by any amounts you receive or are eligible to receive, even if you don't apply for them, from state disability, workers' compensation or Social Security disability benefits. As a result, your group plan could wind up paying you as little as $50 per month, after any waiting period.

Shopping for a Policy

If possible, rely on a licensed and appointed insurance agent, not a broker. Agents give you the highest level of consumer safeguards.

Reason: Insurers are responsible for their agents' errors in taking down application information.

When you buy individual long-term disability insurance through brokers, however, you're not protected from their errors because brokers work for you.

Licensed and Appointed Insurance Agent

Important: Verify the agent's credentials by requiring license documentation issued by your state department of insurance. Then call or write your state insurance department. Give your agent's license number, and request a complete list of all the insurance companies that have appointed him or her. Look for an agent who is appointed by at least several disability insurance companies to ensure a good range of policy options and benefits.

WHY INDIVIDUAL POLICIES MAKE GOOD SENSE

If you're disabled, your monthly payment from most insurers cannot be taxed or reduced by any other benefits you receive, even those that come from an employer's long-term disability plan.

Individually owned policies are not regulated by ERISA and, therefore, offer greater consumer safeguards if claims are being unfairly denied or delayed and you must take legal action. You can sue the insurer for any of the following.

- Denied or delayed benefits plus emotional distress.
- Damages suffered as a result of the delay, such as a repossessed car or home, and punitive damages if the insurer has acted with malice, oppression or fraud.
- Your attorney fees.

The case is decided by a jury from the county in which you live.

GREAT POLICY ESSENTIALS

Here are what I consider to be the best disability insurance policy features, in order of their importance to consumers. Choose as many as you can afford.

1. **Own-occupation coverage**. This guarantees benefit payments if you are unable to perform the substantial and material duties of your profession.

Example: If a heart surgeon with an own-occupation policy develops a heart condition and can no longer operate on cardiac patients but could work as a general practitioner, he would be considered disabled under the policy's terms.

General-occupation coverage is cheaper, but it won't pay up if you can perform any other job for which you are suited by education, training or actual job experience.

Example: If the same heart surgeon could teach in a medical school, he would not be considered disabled or entitled to his benefits.

2. **Waiver of premium rider**. This forces the insurer to waive the premium for your coverage while you are totally disabled.

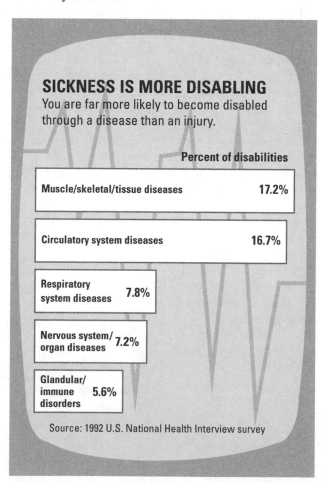

SICKNESS IS MORE DISABLING

You are far more likely to become disabled through a disease than an injury.

Percent of disabilities

Muscle/skeletal/tissue diseases	17.2%
Circulatory system diseases	16.7%
Respiratory system diseases	7.8%
Nervous system/organ diseases	7.2%
Glandular/immune disorders	5.6%

Source: 1992 U.S. National Health Interview survey

3. **Short waiting period**. Look for a waiting period of no more than 60 to 90 days for benefits to begin after you become disabled. Some policies make you wait as long as one year.

4. **Lifetime benefits**. This feature ensures payments for as long as you are disabled.

Problem: While desirable, lifetime benefits are expensive and add 20% to the cost of a policy. In addition, it is increasingly difficult to find an insurer that will provide them.

Second best: benefits that will pay until age 65.

Avoid policies that limit benefit payouts to between two and five years. The longer your benefits last, the longer you will be protected.

5. **Cost-of-living adjustment**. This option guarantees that your benefits will get adjusted annually to keep up with inflation; it costs more, but it's worth it.

6. **Noncancelable–guaranteed renewable**. As long as you pay your premiums on time, you are guaranteed that the contractual language of your long-term disability coverage will not change and that your premiums will not increase, even if your insurer stops selling policies in your state.

7. **Coverage for a psychiatric condition**. Limitations are undesirable, so try to get a policy that pays for at least 24 months of care, should a psychiatric condition disable you.

BOTTOM LINE

Don't try to save money on premiums by accepting a partial or residual benefit option. Some policies will pay part of your benefits if you can perform one, but not all, of the duties of your job.

Example: a surgeon who can consult with patients in the office, but, due to illness or injury, cannot operate, could qualify.

Some buy this option because it increases their chances of receiving some kind of benefit.

Problem: Such policies can be used by an insurer to avoid paying the full disability benefits for which you paid. If you have such an option, the insurer can often find one or more duties that you can perform. That means you will receive only a prorated part of your benefits rather than the full amount.

Strategy: Purchase a straight total disability policy without any residual option or rider. It will pay your full benefits if you are unable to perform the substantial and material duties of your occupation.

How to Find the Best Hospitals in the U.S.

American hospitals are, overall, the safest and most professional in the world.

But when it comes to your health, and your life, there's no point in taking the slightest risk or settling for less than the very best hospitals, doctors, equipment and systems. This is true if it's only for your peace of mind in an era where horror stories abound

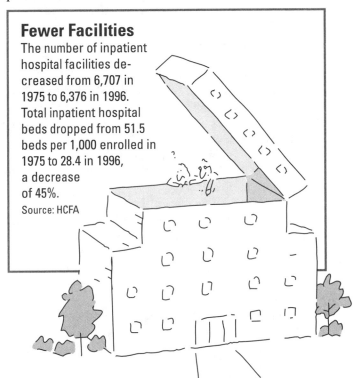

Fewer Facilities
The number of inpatient hospital facilities decreased from 6,707 in 1975 to 6,376 in 1996. Total inpatient hospital beds dropped from 51.5 beds per 1,000 enrolled in 1975 to 28.4 in 1996, a decrease of 45%.
Source: HCFA

(although you can reduce the odds of a mistake by choosing your hospital carefully, even good institutions aren't completely free of accidents).

Choosing a great hospital (as opposed to just a good one) is much easier than you probably believe. Most people have misconceptions about just how wide the choice is.

HOSPITAL MYTHS

1. Your doctor must be affiliated with a hospital for you to be admitted

Reality: While most people want to stay with their own doctors, if a particular hospital is important to you, you can choose to go with its doctors instead. Contact the hospital of your choice. As long as it performs the procedure you need, its own doctors will examine you and treat you according to the results of the examination.

Moreover, since most insurance policies today require a second opinion, they nearly always pay for the second exam as well as whatever portion of the medical procedure is covered by your policy.

2. The best hospitals have such a long waiting list that it's difficult to get in

Reality: Nearly all top hospitals in the country want you to be their patient. In most cases, that's how they make the money that allows them to provide excellent service.

3. Top hospitals charge top prices

Reality: Many of the best are also the least costly.

Example: The Mayo Clinic in upstate Minnesota is one of the world's best medical institutions. It is also modestly priced at $545 a day for a semiprivate room. That compares with a cost of more than $1,000 a day at the University of California Medical Center in San Francisco.

Some hospitals will lower their rates if you can demonstrate a financial need. While smaller regional hospitals can often provide excellent service, it's usually wise to choose one of the relatively new medical centers modeled after the Mayo Clinic system.

Advantages:
- An array of the latest procedures and equipment.
- Treatment by a team of doctors who pool their expertise before deciding which procedure, if any, you need.

Exception: For people with conditions that require highly specialized treatment, it may be best to choose a hospital that concentrates specifically on their ailment.

NARROWING THE CHOICES

In addition to asking your doctor's advice,

research your ailment thoroughly before deciding which hospital is the best for you.

Step 1: Contact the national organization that serves people with your ailment, such as the American Heart Association or the Epilepsy Foundation of America.

If you aren't sure of the proper group, ask your doctor or call the American Medical Association's Answer Center at 312-464-5000. Associations can give you the names of hospitals that treat your condition, including those that are experimenting with new procedures.

Local chapters of associations can often steer you to nearby members who have been patients. Contact these people and ask about their experience in the hospital that you're considering.

Step 2: Read the latest literature about your medical condition. Associations can usually recommend books and articles, which can also be located through computerized services now available at most public libraries.

Through reading medical literature, you can often determine which hospitals have the most advanced and successful treatments. Also, literature usually mentions doctors you can contact for recommendations.

Step 3: Before making a final decision on a hospital, talk with people on its administrative and medical staffs. Inquire about

- **The quality of its nursing staff.** It's usually a good indicator of the hospital's all-around quality. Ask

---

Another Reason Not To Drink and Drive

Drunk drivers may not be insured for medical costs incurred in accidents. Some insurance companies, and a number of corporations that insure their employees directly, will not pay for the medical claims of people who drive while drunk. Companies say employees who do not drink and drive should not be forced to subsidize ones who do, and since drunk driving is a crime, there is no reason to pay for injuries sustained during an illegal act.

Four Sensational Hospitals

Cleveland Clinic
This hospital is best known for its excellence in heart surgery and treatment. Other top-rated specialties include organ transplants, epilepsy, gastroenterology, gynecology, laryngology and pulmonary diseases. A semiprivate room costs $675. The staff includes over 700 physicians, 750 residents and 1,356 nurses. Cleveland Clinic, 9500 Euclid Ave., Cleveland, OH 44195, 216-444-2200.

Johns Hopkins Hospital
Surveys of doctors have given Johns Hopkins top ratings in more specialties than any other hospital. These include allergies, cardiology, dermatology, neurosurgery, pediatrics, psychiatry and rheumatology. It has 901 residents and 1,728 physicians. A semiprivate room costs from $560 to $654. Johns Hopkins has 1,687 nurses. Johns Hopkins Hospital, 600 N. Wolfe St., Baltimore, MD 21287, 410-955-5000.

Mayo Clinic
Mayo is top-rated in many specialties, including cancer, cardiology, geriatrics, rehabilitation and urology. The hospital charges $545 for a semiprivate room. It has 1,720 physicians, 1,515 residents and 3,528 registered nurses. Mayo Clinic, 200 First St. SW, Rochester, MN 55905, 507-284-2511.

University of Pennsylvania Hospital
The University of Pennsylvania Hospital has earned a worldwide reputation in several fields, including early treatment of breast cancer, dental medicine, infectious diseases, radiation therapy, kidney treatment and general surgery. Registered nurses number 1,313. There are 650 physicians on staff as well as 1,006 residents. The price of a semiprivate room is $939. University of Pennsylvania Hospital, 3400 Spruce St., Philadelphia, PA 19104, 215-662-4000.

whether the nursing staff has won any awards, since the staffs at second-string institutions rarely win awards.

● **The job turnover in the nursing staff.** Be wary of a hospital that loses more than 15% to 20% of its nurses a year. In most excellent hospitals, about half of the nursing staff have earned their bachelor's degree.

● **The hospital's quality-assurance program.** This is a computerized program that monitors patient care so that doctors know on an hour-by-hour basis the treatment each patient receives. Eliminate any institution that doesn't have a quality-assurance program. The best programs provide highly detailed data, not just general information, about a patient's condition, location and treatment. Also, look for a program that's administered by doctors instead of nonmedical personnel.

Be cautious about an institution that hesitates in answering your questions. The best hospitals are usually forthcoming.

Former patients are usually reliable information sources on how well the nursing staff communicated with them. That's important because one of the first tipoffs of a second-rate institution is the failure of nurses to communicate.

Another Way to Save On Your Hospital Bill

Hospitals have check-in and check-out times, just like hotels. If you arrive early or leave late, you will be charged for an extra day.

Self-defense: When being admitted for an elective procedure, call ahead to find out the check-in time. When ready to leave, check out promptly. If necessary, wait in a hospital sitting room for someone to pick you up, instead of staying in your room and being charged for an extra day.

Choosing the Best Health Club

More than ten million Americans work out in health clubs and spas across the country. They pay substantial amounts for the privilege, but things don't always turn out as planned. Club members face three common dangers: club insolvency, staff incompetence and personal injuries. Here are the best ways to protect yourself.

1. CHECK WITH CONSUMER GROUPS

Call your state or local consumer protection agency and the Better Business Bureau. Ask whether any negative reports have been filed against the club you have in mind. At least 36 states have enacted legislation designed specifically to protect the interests of health club members.

For more information, contact the International Health, Racquet & Sports Club Association for free at 263 Summer St., Boston 02210 (send a self-addressed, stamped, business-sized envelope).

This trade group investigates complaints against clubs to ensure that they meet minimum standards.

2. CONDUCT A THOROUGH INSPECTION

Go at peak time: at lunch or after work. If the place is wall-to-wall people, it probably lacks equipment or instructors. If it's empty, something else is wrong.

Facilities: The pool, bathrooms, locker rooms and weight rooms should all be clean and well-maintained. Equipment should be in good repair. Faulty or worn equipment can cause injuries.

As you walk around the club, ask members what they like most about it, and what they like least.

3. MAKE SURE THE CLUB IS BONDED

Some states require health clubs to post a minimum bond of $500,000 to protect members against losing their money if the club goes out of business. That's hardly enough for a large club, but it suggests some financial security on the part of the owner. Request evidence of bonding from the club or a consumer protection agency.

4. INSIST UPON QUALIFIED INSTRUCTORS

Though many fine trainers lack formal credentials, competent ones often will be certified by professional groups, such as
- Aerobics and Fitness Association of America: 800-445-5950.
- American College of Sports Medicine: 317-637-9200.
- American Council on Exercise: 800-825-3636.

5. NEGOTIATE YOUR MEMBERSHIP FEE

Annual fees range from several hundred dollars for a family all the way up to $3,500 for an individual. Some clubs tack on a nonrefundable initiation fee of several hundred dollars. No matter what the initial quote, membership fees and conditions are almost always negotiable.

6. INSIST ON A SHORT-TERM CONTRACT

Sad but true, 90% of health club members stop working out after three months. To avoid paying for workouts you never use, arrange to pay on a monthly basis or sign up for a 90-day trial membership.

Important: Don't sign on the spot. Take the contract home and review it with a friend or family member.

7. RESIST HARD-SELL TACTICS

An eager salesperson may offer you a special membership contract that expires "at midnight tonight." Don't take the bait, no matter how interested you are in the club. Instead, say you would like a one-day trial membership.

Cost: no more than a few dollars, perhaps free. If possible, try a sample session with one of the club's personal trainers.

8. READ THE FINE PRINT

A typical health club contract is two pages. Each portion must be scrutinized not only for what it includes, but also for what it omits. Make sure you will have full access to all facilities that interest you, like the swimming pool or squash courts. Avoid contracts that limit the hours you can use the club, unless those hours fit your schedule. If the contract does not include an escape clause, insert one. It should stipulate that you will get a prorated refund if you move or become disabled before the term is up.

Caution: Watch out for the club's escape clause, a waiver of liability in case you are injured. If a club tries to escape liability for injuries caused by its own negligence in the contract, cross off and initial that clause before signing.

Finally, make sure the contract covers everything you've discussed with club employees. Never rely on verbal agreements.

Never join a health club before it opens, no matter how sterling its prospects. Look for a club with at least three years of continuous operation, or a new branch of an established chain.

If you have second thoughts after joining a health club, ask for a full refund. Most states mandate a three-day cooling-off period, during which consumers can back out of contracts.

SOURCES

Sources are listed in the order in which their contributions appear. A source may have contributed part or all of an article, or a series of articles.

Frederick Ruof, National Emergency Medicine Alliance (NEMA)

Glenn S. Daily, insurance consultant

George Biddle, DAHST (Dial a Hearing Screening Test)

Charles B. Inlander, People's Medical Society

Rich Gulling, RPh, MBA, Wright State University

"Health After 50," *The Johns Hopkins Medical Letter*

Art Ulene, MD, medical reporter, WNBC-TV

Lisa Tuomi, PharmD, Stanford University Medical Center

Sam Beller, CLU, ChFC, Diversified Programs, Inc.

David Roll, PhD, University of Utah, College of Pharmacy

Charles Ratner, Ernst & Young, LLP

William Shernoff, Shernoff, Bidart & Darras

Barry Scholl, NCQA

Richard Carter, attorney

Art Ulene, MD, medical reporter, WNBC-TV

Alexander A. Bove, Jr., Esq., author of *The Medicaid Planning Handbook*

Amy and Armond Budish, authors of *Golden Opportunities: Hundreds of Money-Making, Money-Saving Gems for Anyone over Fifty.*

Harley Gordon, Esq., author of *How to Protect Your Life Savings from Catastrophic Illness and Nursing Homes*

Jan Walsh, National Endowment for Financial Education

Howard Klein and Dale Kramer, Klein, McGorry & Klein Ltd.

Alan Nadolna, Associates in Financial Planning

John W. Wright, author of *The Best Hospitals in America, a Guide to the 88 Top-Rated Hospitals in the US and Canada*

Elizabeth Igleheart, Towers & Perrin

Art Ulene, MD, medical reporter, WNBC-TV

Stephen L. Isaacs, JD, Columbia University

Home Finance
Make the Most of Buying, Selling and Living in Your Home

How to Sell Your Home Fast

If you want to sell your home quickly and on your own, here's how to get a great price in just five days.

STEP 1: LOWER YOUR ASKING PRICE

To attract a large number of serious buyers and show that you are flexible, price your home 10% below the price of similar homes in your area. The goal is to make your home seem as attractive as possible when your ad first appears in the local paper. Free enterprise (having potential buyers bid against one another) will take care of the rest.

STEP 2: PLAN TO HOLD AN OPEN HOUSE

Get your home in tip-top shape and gather all the information that you'll need to answer buyers' questions over the phone or in person. This information includes a detailed description of your home, an independent inspection report, a radon report and a copy of your property survey.

STEP 3: ADVERTISE THOROUGHLY

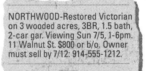

NORTHWOOD-Restored Victorian on 3 wooded acres, 3BR, 1.5 bath, 2-car gar. Viewing Sun 7/5, 1-6pm. 11 Walnut St. $800 or b/o. Owner must sell by 7/12: 914-555-1212.

Run your newspaper ad for the three days before and the two days during the open house. This will attract the maximum number of buyers.

The content of your ad is critical. It should include
- The location of the home.
- A brief description of the home.
- The asking price.
- The times of the open house.
- Your phone number.
- That you're selling it yourself.
- That you'll accept the best reasonable offer.
- That you plan to sell the home by the next week.

When interested buyers call, say your home will be sold to the highest bidder. Expect to hear from between 50 and 100 people.

STEP 4: HOLD THE OPEN HOUSE ON SATURDAY AND SUNDAY

On Saturday morning, put up signs in your neighborhood to help guide those who saw your ad in the paper. These signs may also attract some walk-in traffic.

Be absolutely honest about all of your home's flaws. This is not only ethical but smart. Getting interested buyers to trust you is only part of the reason. You also don't want them to withdraw their bids after they learn the truth about your property.

STEP 5: CONDUCT ROUND-ROBIN BIDDING

Use open bidding. Sealed bidding, which asks people to put their bids in envelopes to keep them secret from others, isn't fair to anyone. You will probably receive many offers. The only way to settle on one offer is to accept the highest bid.

Strategy: Ask interested buyers to submit bids before leaving your home. Then call the bidders on the phone—first the highest bidder, then the next-highest and so on. Be honest and tell everyone exactly how his or her bid fits in with the others.

Repeat this process for each round. One of the remarkable things about this system is how its structure maximizes competition. Bids may start at your asking price, but ultimately they will rise higher and higher.

Don't rush the bidders. Expect to spend about five minutes on the phone with each bidder per round.

When a top bidder emerges, call the other bidders to tell them exactly where they stand.

Tell the top bidder that the house is his or hers. Then tell the next two highest bidders that they'll be able to buy your home at their bid price if the higher bidders back out or do not qualify for financing.

Do-It-Yourself Home Selling

Invest in a professionally printed For Sale sign instead of an advertisement in the classified section of your local newspaper.

Reason: Classified ads are expensive and often unnecessary because those people most likely to buy your home will already

FOR SALE
- 2 Bdr/2 Bath
- $135,000
- Call 555-1212

THE RIGHT PRICE
The most reliable way for a buyer or seller to determine the value of a home is to find out what similar homes are selling for in the same area.

Metro area	Median home price, 1995 (in thousands)	Annual growth 1986-95	Annual growth to 2000 (projected)
Atlanta	$97.7	2.6%[1]	4.3%
Baltimore	111.4	4.7	1.3
Boston	178.2	1.3	2.3
Chicago	147.4	6.2	3.2
Cleveland	103.3	4.9	4.4
Cincinnati	102.6	5.5	4.7
Dallas	96.3	0.3	3.9
Denver	126.2	4.3	5.4
Detroit	98.5	6.0	5.9
Houston	79.4	1.4	3.1
Kansas City	91.1	3.8	3.8
Los Angeles	176.9	3.0	0.4
Miami	106.5	3.1	3.2
Milwaukee	114.3	5.6	4.1
New York City	196.6	0.6	1.7
Philadelphia	117.0	4.0	1.7
Phoenix	96.3	2.3	4.5
Pittsburg	80.6	3.5[2]	1.8
San Francisco	255.3	4.9	2.8
San Diego	172.0	4.2	2.1
Seattle	158.5	8.5[3]	3.2
St Louis	87.4	2.4	3.8
Washington DC	155.8	4.9	1.1

[1]1989-1995
[2]1988-1995
[3]1987-1995

Source: National Association of Realtors

know your neighborhood, either because they live nearby or because they visit the area often.

Strategy: On the sign, list the number of bedrooms and baths, the asking price and your phone number. Including this information will reduce calls from those who wouldn't be interested or qualified to buy.

Prepare Now to Sell Your Home

Fix anything that could become a bargaining chip for prospective buyers. One problem could make them suspicious that there are more problems they haven't discovered.

Roof: Patch any minor problem. Otherwise, you may have to pay for a whole new roof when negotiating a sale.

Kitchen: You will probably regain the cost of renovating an outdated kitchen when you sell, and a new kitchen makes your house more attractive to buyers.

Yard: An ugly lawn may turn people away. It's far cheaper to seed than to sod. Trees and shrubs need time to fill in, so try to plant at least two years prior to selling.

Heating/cooling systems: If your house has oil or electric heat in a neighborhood where all the others have gas furnaces, it probably pays to switch systems. Similarly, if all the homes in your area have central air-conditioning and yours doesn't, install it.

Clean Homes Sell Better

Clean your home from top to bottom before interested buyers come over, and keep it tidy throughout the selling process. This ensures that buyers will see your home at its best.

- **Kitchen:** Keep the countertops free of objects and as clean as possible.
- **Living, dining and family rooms:** Remove any unnecessary furniture to open up the space, and take down any cluttered or garish pictures and plaques.
- **Bedrooms:** Tidy up closets so clothing isn't tightly crammed together, even if this means getting rid of some clothing or storing it elsewhere.
- **Bathrooms:** Keep all countertops and sinks clean, stock fresh, light-colored towels and keep the windows slightly open. Use air fresheners in interior baths.

Also: If your pets have the run of the house, consider calling in professional carpet cleaners to remove any stains or odors.

Home Features that Sell

The most important feature of a house is its location. A house located in a great neighborhood will sell for a lot more than the very same house located in a less popular neighborhood. Here are some other features that help sell a home.

- A large, first-floor family room connected to the kitchen.
- A luxury-appointed, home-within-a-home master suite.
- An eat-in kitchen loaded with the latest in high-tech gear.
- Lots of windows, skylights or a greenhouse.
- A house in excellent condition.

How to Sell Your Oil-Heated Home

Oil-heated homes with in-ground storage tanks are more difficult to sell. Potential buyers don't want to take on the environmental hazard and costly expense of a leaking tank. This impacts on homes with non-leaking tanks, too, since buyers fear what could happen in the future.

Self-defense: Whether or not your in-ground tank has a leak, consider having it removed and installing an above-ground tank in your garage or cellar, or switching to gas heat.

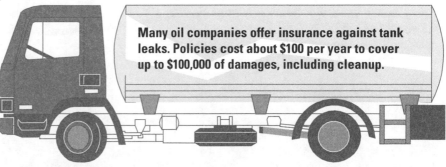

Many oil companies offer insurance against tank leaks. Policies cost about $100 per year to cover up to $100,000 of damages, including cleanup.

Caution: Today's buyers are also concerned about asbestos. Consider having any asbestos removed or at least encapsulated to eliminate future problems.

What to Ask before Buying a Home

If you haven't shopped for a home or purchased one in the past five years, consider yourself a first-time home buyer. That's how much the real estate market has changed in this short period of time.

CHANGES IN THE MARKET

Today's home sellers have become more sophisticated about finding ways to get the most money for their homes.

The last few years have also has seen the emergence of brokers who represent buyers instead of sellers, on-line brokerage services, new types of mortgages and changing rules governing the information that brokers and sellers must disclose to you.

Some of these changes are great for buyers, but you need to know how to take advantage of them. Start by asking yourself these questions.

WHAT DO I NEED AND WHAT DO I WANT?

Start by deciding what features you really can't do without. Otherwise, you are likely to buy a house that satisfies some of your wishes, but not all of your requirements.

Strategy: Sit down with your spouse and make a list of the things you want in a house. That list might include location in a certain school district, proximity to work or family, a certain size or type of house, and amenities such as a pool, a great kitchen or a place for your antique billiard table. Then refine that list down to the things that you absolutely cannot live without.

Keep both lists handy when you're looking at potential homes.

First list what you want.

Then list what you can't live without.

HOW MUCH CAN I AFFORD TO PAY?

Most people overestimate the amount they can afford. The rule of thumb that brokers often cite says that, with 8% mortgage rates, you can pay two and a half to three times your gross income. By that measure, a person with a gross income of $110,000 could buy a home for $275,000 to $330,000. But the rule doesn't take into account other debt or major financial obligations such as paying children's college tuitions.

Strategy: Use the more conservative guidelines that lenders usually rely on. They generally figure that borrowers can spend 36% of their gross income on debt, including mortgage, car loans, credit cards and the rest, and as much as 28% just on a mortgage.

Beware: In recent years, some lenders have stretched those guidelines to let home buyers borrow more. Avoid going beyond the traditional limits, even if your lender says it's alright.

Traditional Lenders' Limits

Lenders usually require that borrowers' debt (mortgage, car loans, credit cards) comprise **no more than**

36%

of gross income.

Lenders generally assume that borrowers can afford a mortgage **that costs up to**

28%

of gross income.

WHAT KIND OF MORTGAGE IS BEST FOR ME?

Mortgages used to come in two varieties: fixed 15-year and fixed 30-year loans. Now you can choose between fixed-rate and variable-rate loans with widely different terms. Some fixed-rate loans even convert to variable-rate loans after a certain period, which can be as long as ten years.

Before you choose a loan, decide how long you are likely to live in the house.

Example: If you and your spouse expect to have children soon, you may need to move into a larger house in a few years. If that's the case, there is no reason to choose a fixed-rate 30-year loan. Instead, go with an adjustable-rate mortgage (ARM), which has a lower rate over the time you'll be living in your home. Chances are, you'll move before the rate rises enough to wipe out the money you saved getting an ARM instead of a 30-year fixed-rate loan.

If you are planning to stay more than five years, a fixed-rate mortgage may make more sense.

Warning: Avoid gimmicky loans that increase your cost by large amounts over time.

Example: Negative-equity loans have a fixed payment, but if interest rates rise, the lender tacks on extra payments at the end. In effect, you end up paying interest on interest, which is a terrible idea.

SHOULD I USE A BUYER'S BROKER?

Traditionally, the broker works for the seller. But during the past few years, buyers' brokers have emerged as a mainstream option for home buyers. A buyer's broker will look after your interests, offering you information about the property and neighborhood that a seller's broker might not provide.

Some home buyers worry about having to pay a commission if they hire a buyer's broker. Most of the time, however, the seller will agree to pay the commission, which will be split between the buyer's broker and the seller's.

HOW DO I NEGOTIATE SUCCESSFULLY?

Many first-time home buyers give up the opportunity

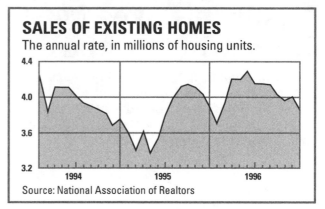

SALES OF EXISTING HOMES
The annual rate, in millions of housing units.

Source: National Association of Realtors

to save thousands of dollars because they don't know how to negotiate properly. The key to a successful negotiation is to have the facts on your side.

For starters, you need to figure out approximately how much a particular house is worth in the current market. You also must figure out what the list price on various homes really means. Home sellers typically build in some negotiating room, but that will change in different markets.

Strategy: Start out by going to see every house on the market that is in your price range. Carry a camera and take pictures. Have your broker give you information about comparable homes that have sold in the market in recent months and note the difference between their list prices and sales prices.

Also, ask a broker to tell you the average number of days homes in the area have been listed on the market, and whether that average is climbing or shrinking. If it's climbing, the market is slowing down and you may be in a stronger position to bargain.

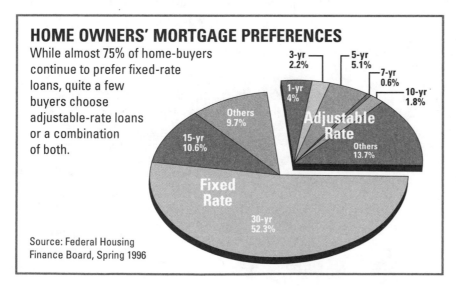

HOME OWNERS' MORTGAGE PREFERENCES
While almost 75% of home-buyers continue to prefer fixed-rate loans, quite a few buyers choose adjustable-rate loans or a combination of both.

Others 9.7%
15-yr 10.6%
Fixed Rate
30-yr 52.3%
1-yr 4%
3-yr 2.2%
5-yr 5.1%
7-yr 0.6%
10-yr 1.8%
Adjustable Rate
Others 13.7%

Source: Federal Housing Finance Board, Spring 1996

Realtors And Model Homes

Don't use a Realtor when inspecting a development with model homes. Instead, ask the developer to reduce the purchase price by the portion of the 6% fee that would be paid to the real estate agent or to add the equivalent amount in interior upgrades.

Costly Mistakes Most Home Buyers Make

Buying the right house at the right price requires skillful bargaining and good judgment. But even buyers who exhibit both can make their biggest mistakes between the time they sign intent-to-buy contracts and the closing dates.

During this period (which often lasts several months), home buyers must juggle dozens of critical details, any one of which, if handled incorrectly, could delay the deal and add costs.

Expert advice: In most cases, your real estate agent, mortgage broker or attorney is responsible for getting you information on these details, but you must be persistent about asking for what you need when you need it.

NOT KNOWING WHAT'S IN YOUR CREDIT REPORT

There are three national credit repositories that receive reports on how you repay your debt. Mortgage lenders depend on these reports to determine the creditworthiness of prospective borrowers.

Obtain a copy of your report from each of these companies several months before you shop for a home (see page 76 for names and numbers).

Reason: If there is a problem and the lender finds out about it first, you may lose your chance to buy the home while trying to work out your credit problem or you may not be able to get a mortgage at all. Getting your reports early allows you to clear up any mistakes or problems.

Common problem: The credit search turns up someone in your community who has a name similar to yours, and that person has an outstanding debt. It will take time, sometimes weeks or even months, for you to correct the mistake and clear your name.

GETTING AN EXPECTED CASH GIFT TOO LATE

If a generous relative is helping you pay your down payment, try to get this money before you apply for a mortgage. Not only could this be required by your mortgage lender, but it will reduce the risk that the relative will back out on you at the last minute, making it impossible for you to come up with the down payment.

NOT UNDERSTANDING THE STATUS OF YOUR MORTGAGE

When you inquire about a mortgage, the lender will let you know in advance whether you've been prequalified or preapproved. There's a big difference between the two.

Prequalified means that a lender tells you how much of a mortgage you can afford based on your income and preexisting debt payments.

Preapproved means that a lender guarantees in writing that you'll receive a loan.

Trap: Many home buyers are not aware of the difference. As a result, prequalified borrowers mistakenly assume they will receive mortgages for which they were never actually approved.

Strategy: Be sure the commitment guarantees that you will get your loan at a specific interest rate, even if rates rise after you sign the agreement.

Important: Avoid making major career moves or large purchases during this period. A change in your loan status after you've applied for a mortgage could jeopardize the loan and cause the entire process to start over. Even a new job that pays more money could be detrimental to your loan because you would lose your history with your previous employer.

Home Ownership Rates by Age
75% of Americans own a home by age 50.

Age	% who are homeowners
less than 35 years	39.1%
35 to 44 years	65.5
45 to 54 years	75.6
55 to 64 years	80.1
65 years and older	79.2

Source: U.S. Census Bureau, 1996

If you just barely qualify at today's rates, a rate jump could disqualify you from the mortgage you've requested. If you are in this category, talk to your lender about locking in your rate. Lenders have many ways to handle this.

ASSUMING YOUR REALTOR WILL HANDLE EVERYTHING

In busy real estate markets, it is hard for some brokers to be attentive to all of their clients. As a result, clients who ask for assistance and attention usually get it before those who do not. It is your responsibility to stay in close contact with the agent.

Self-defense: Request a detailed list of the major events that will occur in the weeks leading up to your closing and what you will be required to do or provide and when. Always stay on top of the details, and do not expect that they will be taken care of for you.

WAITING TOO LONG TO DO A TITLE SEARCH

A title search checks to see if there are any encumbrances against the property that could imperil the deal. The title insurance company or the bank's attorney usually handles the title search.

Strategy: Have your agent or attorney make sure this is done as early as possible. The discovery of a problem late in the process, whether the problem is valid or not, can significantly delay the closing on your new home.

Mortgage Comparison Checklist

To choose between two or more mortgages, compare the numbers from each offer that apply to the categories below.

BASIC FEATURES
- ☐ Fixed annual percentage rate
- ☐ Variable annual percentage rate
- ☐ Index used and current value
- ☐ Amount of margin
- ☐ Current rate
- ☐ Frequency of rate adjustments
- ☐ Amount/length of discount
- ☐ Interest rate caps

Length of plan
- ☐ Draw period
- ☐ Repayment period

Initial fees
- ☐ Appraisal fee
- ☐ Closing costs
- ☐ Application fee

REPAYMENT TERMS
- ☐ During the draw period
- ☐ Interest and principal payments
- ☐ Interest only payments
- ☐ Fully amortizing payments

When the draw period ends
- ☐ Balloon payment
- ☐ Renewal available
- ☐ Refinancing of balance by lender

NOT SPECIFYING THE SELLER'S OBLIGATIONS ON THE CONTRACT

Your attorney or agent should confirm that the seller has complied with the promises outlined in the contract. Such obligations may include repairs or improvements.

If you do not follow up on the progress of these improvements, they may not be completed before the closing. At this point, the seller has the negotiating advantage. Obviously, it is much more difficult to get things done after the seller has moved.

Warning: Never take it for granted that the property description in the listing agreement will be accurate. Put the same details in writing in the sales contract.

NEGLECTING TO TAKE A FINAL WALK-THROUGH

The walk-through is your last chance to look over what you're buying. Take the walk-through as near to the date of your closing as possible, and after the seller has moved out.

The walk-through will allow you to question any previously agreed-upon repairs that have not been made, any damage to the home that occurred after your last visit and the removal of anything that you were told would remain, such as air conditioners, blinds and furniture. The walk-through allows you to postpone your closing until the problems are ironed out.

Strategy: Use a keen eye as you take the walk-through. Concentrate only on major problems or contract violations, not small matters, such as a squeaky door or a window that won't open easily. Such issues are probably not worth postponing the closing or creating ill will between you and the seller.

NOT ANTICIPATING THE TOTAL COST OF CLOSING

Closing costs include the application fee, document preparation fees, appraisal, a survey and a loan origination fee called points. These fees can total between 2% and 8% of the home's selling price.

Important: Your lender is required to provide you with a good-faith estimate of closing costs three days after you submit your loan application. These fees are negotiable. If asked, many lenders will waive some of them. If you plan to negotiate these fees, do so early in the process. At the closing, make sure you compare the fees you are actually paying with those agreed to earlier.

NOT BRINGING THE RIGHT CHECKS TO THE CLOSING

Large sums of money change hands at closings. Some of the checks can be written out at closing, but others must be certified by a bank. In some cases, they'll have to come from an in-state institution.

Ask your loan officer for a list of the checks, how much they must be made out for and what type of check is needed. Try to get this information at least one week before closing.

How to Choose a Real Estate Broker

Find names of top-selling agents through ads placed by their firms or by asking real estate lawyers. Interview one or two top performers and one or two agents recommended by friends or neighbors. Have each agent give one or two other agents' names as references, so you can check how well he or she works with others. Also get the names of other sellers who have used each agent. Ask them how well the agent handled negotiations and closings, and whether they would use that agent again.

Real Estate Broker
References Available

The Cost of Utilities

To check a home's energy consumption, ask to see several months of the seller's utility bills. While you'll have to take into account differences in family size and lifestyle, consider it a warning sign if the winter heating or summer cooling bills run $300 to $400 per month for a typical single-family house.

Beware of Home Warranties

In theory, home warranties cover major design and structural flaws.

Reality: When flaws emerge, a warranty company determines who is at fault, a process that can take months. If the company decides compensation is due, it then seeks payment from the builder, which may entail a long court battle.

Strategy: Don't choose a home solely because it comes with a warranty, and have the structure inspected yourself.

Home Buyers Beware

Buying a home for investment purposes may not be a smart move right now. The outlook for U.S. real estate values isn't bright, with homes appreciating at only 3% to 3.5% each year.

Reasons: Income growth among U.S. workers has been low, resulting in limited demand. In addition, the number of first-time home-buying couples in their early 30s is much smaller than during the baby-boomer wave of the 1980s.

Option: Consider renting in a great neighborhood and investing your down payment elsewhere.

Before You Buy that Vacation Home

Before buying a vacation home as an investment, consider the costs that you would not have if you invested in something other than real estate.

Also be sure you really want to vacation regularly

in the area where you buy the home. If you buy the home now and plan to retire to it later, make sure it is located where you want to retire and will not limit your options for traveling elsewhere.

Need a Down Payment?

If you need cash for a down payment on a new home, use your existing home for a home-equity line of credit. Then, after selling your old home, use the gains to pay off the loan.

Example: You want to buy a $150,000 home and the equity in your existing home is $30,000. Since you have access to up to 80% of that amount, borrow $24,000 for the down payment.

$30,000	**Equity in your existing home**
x .80	**Multiplied by 80% of equity**
=$24,000	**Amount you can borrow to make the downpayment on new house**

Important: Pay the loan back quickly, since the interest rate on the loan is unpredictable.

Condominiums and Cooperatives

When mortgage rates inch higher, people who were thinking about buying expensive homes consider more affordable condominiums or cooperatives, which can be appealing as investments.

Reasons:
- Condos traditionally have been the first properties to decline when the market softens and the last to rise during a real estate boom. As a result, many condos still reflect the lower prices of the recent housing recession.
- The ratio of renters to owners in many condo developments has improved dramatically. The fewer renters in a development, the more desirable it is for owners.

Reason: Renters don't tend to take as good care of their units as owners do.

OWNERSHIP BASICS

The terms "condominium" and "cooperative" are definitions of types of ownership.
- In a condo, you actually own your unit, just as when you buy a house.
- In a co-op, you own stock in the building's corporation, which entitles you to the use of your unit.

STYLES OF OWNERSHIP

	What you own	Your rights	What you pay for
House	The building and the land on which it's built.	You can rent or sell as you choose.	• Mortgage and insurance on the property. • Real estate taxes based on assessed value of house and land. • All maintenance, repairs and renovations.
Condo	Your own living space. (The association owns the building itself and land.)	You can rent or sell as you choose.	• Mortgage and insurance on your unit. • Real estate taxes based on assessed value of your private condo unit. • Monthly maintenance charge for upkeep and real estate taxes on the condo's property.
Co-op	Shares in a corporation that owns the building (and usually the land), which entitle you to live in an apartment.	You can choose a buyer, subject to board approval. Renting may be prohibited.	• Payment of loan used to finance purchase of shares (the equivalent of a mortgage). • Monthly maintenance charge (for real estate taxes, mortgage on the building, fuel, insurance, operating costs) based on number of shares you hold. • Repairs paid by co-op and passed along to shareholders.

In both types of residences, you share common areas such as lawns, gardens and pools with other residents.

Condos and co-ops rarely compete for the same buyers in the same market. When they occasionally do, price differentials are most often determined by location, rather than by type of housing. Co-ops tend to be a bit more difficult to sell, however, because of strong co-op boards that carefully scrutinize every new buyer.

Condos

There are fewer absentee owners today because many of the investors in condos in the 1970s and 1980s bailed out during the housing recession of the early 1990s, and their units were purchased by occupant-owners. As a result, there are now far fewer investor-owners who rent units out to tenants than there are occupant-owners.

Co-ops

The story is a little different for co-ops. They appeal primarily to long-term buyers, not investor-owners, and have far fewer renters. However, because their prices also dropped overall during the last few years, many co-ops offer good opportunities.

Co-ops are mostly found in urban areas on the East Coast.

WHAT TO ASK

Ask the condo homeowners' association or the co-op's board of directors the following questions.

- What percentage of the units are owner-occupied?
- What are the rules and by-laws? All residents must live by these rules. Examine them carefully to see if there are any by which you can't abide.

CO-OP CAVEAT
Be wary when the number of renters rises to **25%** or more of the development.

- Are there any pending lawsuits? In our litigious society, disgruntled owners of many condo developments are increasingly suing the homeowners' associations to settle disputes. In such cases, each owner may be liable for payment of a judgment won against the association.
- What are the fees? Compare fees of different developments. Some condos and co-ops have much higher charges for maintenance and replacements than others.
- Has there been a pattern of large special assessments? Some developments, especially those with low monthly fees, have sporadic high assessments to cover surprise needs, such as roof repairs or repainting. Even one of these can add significantly to your monthly costs.

GET THE BEST VALUE

- Have a competent attorney review the condo or co-op's documents, including the bylaws, rules, regulations, financial statements and sales agreement.
- Buy in the best neighborhood you can afford. You'll enjoy living there more and will have an easier time selling later.

Handling Adjustable-Rate Mortgages

When interest rates on standard 30-year fixed-rate mortgages are high, adjustable-rate mortgages (ARMs) are more popular with home buyers. Here are some of the ARMs that lenders are offering now.

TRADITIONAL ARMs

What makes an ARM particularly attractive is its low rate, often three percentage points lower than a 30-year fixed-rate mortgage.

Unlike a fixed-rate mortgage, an ARM's interest rate changes each year on the date you officially borrowed the money. Most adjustable rates are tied to the average yield on one-year Treasury bills during the past year.

Advantages: A traditional ARM makes more sense than a 30-year fixed-rate mortgage if you plan to move in a few years. The rate on your ARM will likely be lower during that period than the fixed rate. An ARM is also beneficial if its low initial rate is the only way you can afford the monthly mortgage payments on a home.

Strategy: Ask lenders if they offer ARMs with interest rates tied to the 11th District Cost of Funds Index. This index is based on lenders' borrowing costs and tends to fluctuate much less than the one-year Treasury bill rate. The result is that the year-to-year change in your annual rate will be smaller.

HOW INTEREST RATES COMPARE

Here's how typical mortgage rates compared to the interest rates on other loans and investments in September, 1996.

One-year CDs	One-year T-bills	One-year adjustable-rate mortgages	15-year fixed-rate mortgages	30-year fixed-rate mortgages	Car loans	Credit cards
5.1%	**5.9%**	**6.2%**	**8%**	**8.4%**	**9%**	**17.2%**

COMBINATION ARMs

The combination ARM was introduced just a few years ago. It combines an ARM with a fixed-rate mortgage. Borrowers initially receive a special fixed rate that is lower than the prevailing 30-year fixed rate. This discounted fixed rate lasts for the first several years, after which the loan converts to an adjustable rate.

A typical 7/1 ARM gives you a low fixed rate for seven years. Then it converts to an ARM with an annual rate tied to the Treasury bill rate. Combination ARMs also come in 3/1s, 5/1s and 10/1s. The longer the fixed-rate period, the higher the fixed rate.

Advantage: You get a low fixed rate for a set number of years. Then, when the mortgage converts to an ARM, your adjustable rate may still be lower than a 30-year fixed rate.

Consider a combination ARM if you are likely to move before your discounted fixed rate converts to an adjustable rate.

FHA ARMs

One of the great features of a Federal Housing Administration (FHA) loan is that it is less risky than a traditional ARM. That's because an FHA ARM's interest rate cannot increase more than 1% a year. The rate on nearly every other type of ARM can increase a maximum of 2% a year.

With an FHA ARM, the most the rate can increase over the life of the loan is five percentage points. There is a six-point cap on most other ARMs. Any FHA-approved lender can provide you with an application and information.

When to consider an FHA ARM:

- Whenever you can qualify for one. To be eligible, the amount you want to borrow must be less than the FHA limit set for your geographic area. This limit depends on the median cost of a home in your market. The maximum FHA ARM loan for a single-family home in the nation's costliest markets is $151,725.
- If you can afford only a small down payment—as low as 3% of the home's total cost.

ARMs vs. Fixed-Rate Mortgages over Time

Here's how the monthly payments on two different $100,000 mortgages would compare over a four-year period.

1-year ARM (2% adjustment cap & 6% life cap)		Monthly payment	Yearly total	30-year fixed at 9.5%		Monthly payment	Yearly total
Year 1	6.5%	$632.07	$7,584.84		9.5%	$840.85	$10.090.25
Year 2	8.5%	$761.19	$9,134.28		9.5%	$840.85	$10,090.25
Year 3	10.5%	$903.69	$10,837.44		9.5%	$840.85	$10,090.25
Year 4	12.5%	$1054.11	$12,649.33		9.5%	$840.85	$10,090.25
Grand totals after 4 years:			**$40,205.89**				**$40,361.00**

Does the FHA Owe You Money?

Home owners who have paid off FHA mortgage loans are owed a total of $65 million in unclaimed insurance premium refunds. Since 1934, the Federal Housing Authority has provided mortgage insurance on home loans, with premiums paid by the borrower. When the mortgage insurance is terminated, by either paying off or refinancing the mortgage, the borrower is entitled to a premium refund.

But the process of claiming a refund is complicated and many people don't even realize they are entitled to one, so thousands go unclaimed each year. Average amount: $700 to $900, with some as large as $4,000. To obtain a refund, you usually have to file within six years of paying off the mortgage, depending on your type of account.

Home Mortgage Do's And Don'ts

Shop for a mortgage before you shop for a house. Knowing how much financing you can get will focus your search.

Talk with at least three lenders. Have one run your credit reports so you can correct errors. Ask the lender how it views negative items in your record, and prepare explanations.

If you qualify, lenders issue a letter stating the maximum loan you can receive. Having the letter makes you more attractive to a seller who has comparable bids from different buyers.

Strategy: If you plan to spend less than you qualify for, have the letter state the lower amount, so sellers don't know you could spend more.

When You Can't Pay Your Mortgage

If you're having trouble paying your mortgage, take stock of your financial situation and get in touch with your mortgage loan officer to schedule a personal meeting.

Most lenders prefer to reschedule payments and avoid foreclosure because it's an expensive, time-consuming process that would force the lender to deal with selling your home in an uncertain market.

Your Home Can Cost You Much Less

Owning a home is a major part of the American dream. It is also usually a very expensive part, but it doesn't have to be that way. Most Americans needlessly pay too much on their insurance and escrow/impound accounts.

Here are steps you can take to lower your cost of home ownership by $200 to $2,000 or more every year.

ACCELERATE MORTGAGE PAYMENTS
Paying more than the minimum on your mortgage each month guarantees you an increasing amount of long-term savings by putting the power of interest compounding to work for you instead of for your lender. Here's how to do it right.

1. Pay half your monthly mortgage every two weeks
Using this strategy, you will make 26 annual payments, the equivalent of 13 months rather than 12. Most lenders won't let you pay every two weeks, but will let you pay more each month.

**NO POINTS!
NO CLOSING COST!**

High Interest Mortgage Alert
Home loans with no points and no closing cost may look attractive, but beware. They usually carry higher interest rates, incurring more in interest costs over the full life of the loans. Before taking out such a loan, compare the amount you'll save up-front with the amount of extra interest you'll pay over the life of the loan. You'll probably find that if you've got the cash to cover closing costs, a traditional loan will be a better deal.

The Bi-Weekly Advantage

Choosing to pay your mortgage on a bi-weekly basis can save you about one third of the money you'd spend on a monthly mortgage. And you will pay off your mortgage in one third less time.

Terms of the mortgage	Monthly mortgage	Bi-weekly mortgage
Amount financed	$100,000	$100,000
Interest rate	8%	8%
Payment amount	$733.76	$380.02
Number of payments	360	514
Term of loan	30 years	20.8 years
Total financial charges	**$164,160.47**	**$105,214.21**

Save $58,946.26 and pay off your mortgage almost ten years sooner.

Here's how: Determine how much to pay by dividing your monthly payment (excluding taxes) by 12 and adding the resulting sum to each mortgage payment.

Result: You'll make the equivalent of 13 payments per year and pay off a 30-year mortgage in between 18 and 22 years.

2. Prepay a set amount per month

Prepaying just $25 a month on a 30-year, 8% fixed-rate mortgage will save you $23,337 over the life of the loan. Prepay $100 a month and you'll save $62,456 in interest, and own 100% of your home almost ten years ahead of schedule.

REDUCE INSURANCE COSTS

There are several strategies you can use to significantly reduce your home's insurance costs.

1. Get a competitive bid from an outside insurer. If you bought your homeowners' policy through your mortgage lender, your premiums are probably too high.

2. Raise your deductible from $250 to $500 to save 10% or more on your annual premiums.

3. Reduce the replacement cost coverage portion of your policy if the value of your home is now significantly lower than when you bought it.

ELIMINATE PRIVATE MORTGAGE INSURANCE (PMI)

PMI protects the bank in case you default. It is required when the starting equity in your home is less than 20% or if you have blemishes on your credit report. The cost of PMI is $250 to $560 or more annually for every $100,000 borrowed on a mortgage.

Trap: Many home owners are paying costly PMI fees unnecessarily. This is most likely if

● You live in an area where there has been a recent significant increase in property values.

● You have never calculated when you will be able to stop paying PMI.

● You are prepaying regularly on your mortgage.

Unfortunately, lenders don't tell you when you're eligible to discontinue PMI.

Self-defense: Calculate your equity by figuring out your mortgage balance. Get this from your lender. Then subtract that number from your home's current value based on recent sales of similar homes in your neighborhood (or ask a Realtor to give you an

Monthly Payment Finder

Find the intersection of your chosen term and interest rate, and multiply that amount by the number of thousands of dollars you want to borrow. The result will be your monthly mortgage payment (before taxes and insurance).

Rate	10 years	15 years	20 years	25 years	30 years
6.50%	$11.36	$8.72	$7.46	$6.76	$6.33
6.75	11.49	8.85	7.16	6.19	6.49
7.00	11.62	8.99	7.76	7.07	6.66
7.25	11.75	9.13	7.91	7.23	6.83
7.50	11.88	9.28	8.06	7.39	7.00
7.75	12.01	9.42	8.21	7.58	7.17
8.00	12.14	9.56	8.37	7.72	7.34
8.25	12.27	9.71	8.53	7.89	7.52
8.50	12.40	9.85	8.68	8.06	7.69
8.75	12.54	10.00	8.84	8.23	7.87
9.00	12.67	10.15	9.00	8.40	8.05

estimate). If the answer (your equity) exceeds 20% of the present-day value, you should no longer have to pay PMI. When this is so, contact your lender in writing and demand to have your PMI eliminated. This is your right.

Note: In an area where housing prices are very soft, lenders may raise the equity threshold to 25%.

GET REFUNDS AND REDUCED PAYMENTS FROM YOUR ESCROW/IMPOUND ACCOUNT

This is a separate account held by the mortgage lender that you pay into each month for the property taxes and hazard insurance the lender pays for you. It is called an impound account in California and the West. Federal rules introduced in 1995 say that lenders

● Cannot require more than two months' payments as a cushion. Some now require cushions of four months or more, which is illegal.
● Must send you a statement early in the year projecting how much your escrow payments could increase. A year-end statement will compare projected and actual payments.
● Must consider money already in the account when calculating the monthly payment for the coming year, resulting in lower payments for most home owners.

Strategy: Find out how much is in your escrow account by checking your monthly statement or calling your lender. If the lowest balance during the year is more than twice your monthly payment (principal, interest, taxes and insurance) complain to the lender.

MAKE SURE YOU'RE RECEIVING LEGALLY MANDATED INTEREST

Millions of consumers don't receive interest on their escrow accounts, though they should.

Financial institutions in California, Connecticut, Iowa, Maine, Massachusetts, Minnesota, New Hampshire, New York, Oregon, Rhode Island, Utah, Vermont and Wisconsin are now required to make interest payments. The rates range from 1.6% to 5.25%, and payments are usually made annually.

On an average balance of $2,000, 5% interest comes to $100 a year for the life of the mortgage. That could mean a total of $3,000 in your pocket.

Strategy: If your home is in one of these 13 states and you're not getting interest, complain to your lender or contact the American Homeowners Association.

STAY PUT AND SAVE

Some banks encourage borrowers who plan to live in their homes for the long term to agree to a prepayment penalty clause on their mortgage. In return, the banks might waive closing costs or lower the interest rate.

Here are two ways a prepayment penalty might save you money.	WITH PAYMENT PENALTY	WITHOUT PAYMENT PENALTY
Example 1: Lower interest rate		
Amount borrowed	$100,000	$100,000
Points charged	None	None
Closing costs	$1,500	$1,500
Interest rate–First year	7.00%	8.00%
Later years	Variable	Variable
Monthly payment in first year	$665	$734
Prepayment penalty*	$2,500	None

Borrower pays $828 less interest in the first year.
[12 months x ($734 - $665) = $829]

	WITH PAYMENT PENALTY	WITHOUT PAYMENT PENALTY
Example 2: Lower closing costs		
Amount borrowed	$100,000	$100,000
Points charged	None	One ($1,000)
Closing costs	Waived	$1,500
Interest rate–First year	6.50%	6.50%
Later years	Variable	Variable
Monthly payments in first year	$632	$632
Prepayment penalty*	$2,500	None

Borrower saves $2,500 at closing.

* In the first month: It declines gradually each month as principal is repaid, and is eliminated beginning with the fourth year.

Is Mortgage Prepayment for You?

Mortgage prepayment penalties may be good for some borrowers. That is because lenders charge lower interest rates and smaller closing fees on loans that carry prepayment penalties.

Example: On a typical $150,000 loan, a home buyer could lower the interest rate by 0.75%, or reduce the closing costs by $3,000, by agreeing to pay a $2,400 penalty if the loan is paid off within three years.

Strategy: If you are confident that you are not going to move within the first few years after purchasing a home, consider a loan with a prepayment penalty. They are not legal in all states and not all lenders offer them, so check local rules and shop around.

If interest rates drop, the option of refinancing may be expensive.

When Not to Prepay a Mortgage

Prepaying a mortgage isn't always a good idea. Before prepaying, ask yourself these three questions.

1. How long do I plan to own the home? If you expect to sell in the near future and thus get rid of the loan anyway, prepaying probably doesn't make sense.

2. Do other investment opportunities offer yields higher than the after-tax mortgage rate I pay on my home? If so, you'll do better by putting money in the other investments than by prepaying the mortgage.

3. Do I have foreseeable cash needs (such as children's tuition costs) that make it prudent to keep funds liquid?

Prepaying a mortgage may not make sense if it means you will have to borrow funds later.

REFINANCING

When interest rates go down, you may want to refinance your fixed-rate loan to get a lower rate and reduce your borrowing costs. If you're planning to refinance, however, be sure you are going to stay in your home at least long enough to cover your costs.

The Cost of Refinancing

Discount points (prepaid interest)
+ Origination fee (if any)
+ Application fee
+ Credit check fee
+ Attorney fee (yours)
+ Attorney review fee (lender's)
+ Title search fee
+ Title insurance fee
+ Appraisal fee
+ Inspections
+ Local fees (taxes, transfers)
+ Estimate for other costs
+ Prepayment penalty (if any)

= Total cost of refinancing

The Time to Recoup Costs

I. Current mortgage's monthly payment
− New mortgage's monthly payment

= Difference between the two payments

2. Total cost of refinancing
÷ Difference between the two payments

= Number of months to recoup costs

Give Your Homeowner's Policy a Checkup

Most people buy a homeowner's policy and just file it away.

Even if it was the best policy in the world when it was purchased, however, it may now be out of date because of fluctuations in the value of your property: Improvements or remodeling may have increased the value of your home, rebuilding costs may have risen, or you may have inherited or acquired possessions that need special coverage.

Here are the key ingredients of any good homeowner's policy. Make sure your policy includes them.

Help with Property Taxes

- The Consumer Reports Home Price Service (800-775-1212, $10 for 10 minutes) will fax you prices of recently sold properties for most of the United States.
- *How to Reduce Your Property Taxes*, by Frank J. Adler (Genesis Press, $19.95) explains U.S. and Canadian assessment rules and appeals procedures.
- *How to Slash Your Property Taxes and Earn Extra Income* (805-942-8827, $15) is a step-by-step manual that guides readers through the entire assessment procedure.
- *The Real Estate TaxPak USA* (800-382-9725) kit shows you how to have your property taxes reduced.

THINK AHEAD
Don't wait until you need to make a claim to determine if your coverage is adequate.

GUARANTEED REPLACEMENT COST ON YOUR DWELLING

Many homeowner's policies provide replacement cost coverage: what it would cost to replace your property with something of comparable quality. Guaranteed replacement cost is better. This type of coverage will add a little to your existing premium, but it's worth it.

To qualify for guaranteed replacement cost coverage, an insurer will require you to insure 100% of the total replacement value of your home. If this is estimated at $100,000, you will need to buy a $100,000

policy. The replacement value of your home is usu-ally calculated by your insurance agent based on an appraisal and a regional formula for square-foot construction cost for similar homes.

Strategy: Hire a contractor instead for a more precise and beneficial estimate. An insurance agent's estimate is based on houses similar to yours, but you want your house rebuilt, not someone else's.

If you own an older or custom-made home, check the company's replacement policy carefully. Some insurers will only rebuild according to current standards.

Example: You have lath and plaster walls, but the company wants to replace them with plasterboard.

Ideal: If you can, consider going up another level and getting unlimited guaranteed replacement coverage. This means coverage is not limited by the value established in the policy.

REPLACEMENT COST ON THE CONTENTS OF YOUR HOME

Many policies that pay full replacement cost on the dwelling will only pay cash value on the contents of the home.

Solution: Make sure your policy specifies that it pays replacement cost not only on the dwelling but also on the contents of your home (up to the limit of your policy). Also check with your agent to see if you own valuables that must be covered separately.

Beware: Most insurers calculate the coverage on a dwelling's contents, other structures on the prop-erty, landscaping and debris removal as a percentage of the dwelling's coverage. The limits on contents are too low for most home owners. Take the time to review these figures.

UNLIMITED ADDITIONAL LIVING EXPENSE

Most policies limit coverage for living expenses while your home is being rebuilt or repaired to 12 months or a fixed dollar amount. In many cases, this is adequate, but if your home or neighbor-hood suffers a major disaster, these limits can be a problem.

PROPER ENDORSEMENTS

There are conditions and limitations throughout your policy, not just in the section marked Exclusions. In many cases, you may believe something is covered, only to find out that it is not covered under certain circumstances. Many exclusions and conditions can be removed and limitations broadened if you pay a slightly higher premium.

Self-defense: Read the policy and pay special attention to the clause marked Code Upgrade Coverage, Ordinance or Law.

Caution: Many policies do not cover costs incurred due to changes in local building codes, even with guaranteed replacement cost coverage.

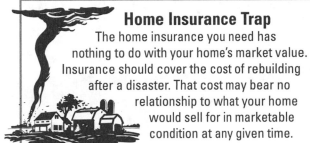

Home Insurance Trap
The home insurance you need has nothing to do with your home's market value. Insurance should cover the cost of rebuilding after a disaster. That cost may bear no relationship to what your home would sell for in marketable condition at any given time.

ADEQUATE LIMITS ON LIABILITY AND MEDICAL PAYMENTS

This coverage is meant to protect your home and assets in the event that you are sued. Most homeowner's policies offer a maximum of $1 million in liability coverage. But what if someone is permanently disabled in a fall on your property and gets a judgment against you for $2 million?

Solution: If you have substantial assets to protect, consider buying an umbrella liability policy. These are quite inexpensive (the premium for $1 million in coverage is about $102 a year) and they also cover liabilities that are excluded on homeowner's policies.

Examples: suits for slander, libel, invasion of privacy and costs of defense against a groundless suit.

Insurance Cost-Cutters

- Buying your home and auto insurance from a single insurer may mean discounts of up to 10%.
- Central alarms that ring at a police or fire station in an emergency can earn insurance discounts of 15%.
- Smoke detectors, fire alarms and deadbolt locks can earn discounts of up to 5%.
- Increasing your deductible can lower your premium.
- Significant upgrades of wiring, plumbing, roofing and so forth may earn you renovation credits.

How Much Insurance Is Enough?

To determine if your house is adequately insured, ask your insurance company to do a free replacement-cost analysis. The company will photograph and measure your home and estimate your rebuilding costs. Ask for a copy of the report. Then check to see if your policy would cover these costs if the house were leveled in a disaster.

Best Way to Insure Personal Property

Use a floater, not an endorsement, when insuring valuable personal property like jewelry. A floater is a separate policy covering valuables. It is usually an all-risk policy, covering all forms of loss except what is specifically excluded when the policy is written. An endorsement of your homeowners' policy will usually offer less coverage than a floater provides.

Reason: Homeowners' insurance is perils coverage: it covers only risks specifically mentioned in the policy.

Important: Before deciding how big a floater to buy, have valuables professionally appraised.

Moving Insurance Solution

Interstate movers are liable for damage done to goods at rates as low as 30¢ per pound; for a smashed 50-pound color television you might recover only $15. Movers will sell insurance, but only for goods they pack, and having the mover pack boxes for you can easily double the cost of a move.

Solution: Most home owner's policies will cover personal property being moved from one home to the next for a period of 30 days, but check with your insurance agent first. If you're switching insurance companies, make sure you let both insurers know your move date to be certain that you are covered.

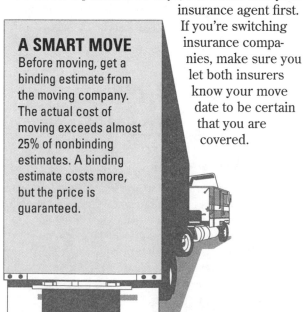

A SMART MOVE

Before moving, get a binding estimate from the moving company. The actual cost of moving exceeds almost 25% of nonbinding estimates. A binding estimate costs more, but the price is guaranteed.

The Big Home Remodeling Mistakes And How to Avoid Them

As people begin to take on the tasks of designing new rooms, choosing materials and hiring labor for the first time, they are likely to fall into traps that cost them time and money. Here are the seven most common errors to avoid when renovating your home.

1. NOT SEEING THE BIG PICTURE

When planning major structural changes, such as adding a room, many people do not take the architectural integrity of their homes into consideration. They need additional space or want their homes to look new, so their main concerns are that the work be done quickly and at a cost that is within their budgets.

Problem: Renovation work that is out of character with the rest of the home sticks out and will be a big turnoff to potential buyers if you decide to sell in the future.

In addition, many people try to do too much without having enough money to do it right. The result is shoddy work.

Note: Redoing the basement may be less important, and ultimately less financially rewarding when selling your home, than adding a high-quality den or family room.

Strategy: First determine how much you can afford to spend on renovating. Then draw up a wish list of what you want done, in order of preference. To find out what your money might realistically buy, invite two architects and two contractors to look around your home and provide you with ballpark estimates. They should do this for free.

Then plan on striking a proper balance between solving your needs and achieving an appropriate level of quality for your type of home while working within your budget. If you can't get to it all, postpone renovations on other parts of the house until the following year or the year after.

Trap: Many people spend too much on renovating

and make their home the most expensive one on the street, thereby pricing it out of competition.

Solution: Choose work that will truly improve your lifestyle and make your home more attractive without putting it beyond the reach of a potential buyer.

2. BEING EXCESSIVELY TRENDY

As the number of colorful home-improvement magazines and TV shows increases, so do home owners' wishes for the fancy things they see.

Examples: Current trends include heavy terra cotta floor tiles in the kitchen, fancy opaque glass walls, geometric fireplaces, and trendy colors and finishes.

While many of these features may look great for a few years, you'll probably outgrow them faster than you think. In all likelihood, you'll also have to live with them, since the expense of redoing what you have done will be higher in the future.

Before you commit to the latest design fad or put a Jacuzzi in the family room, consider the long-term consequences. Ask yourself if you will be comfortable with this new style for the next 20 years. When it comes to selling a house, timeless work, such as functional spaces and generally neutral colors in kitchens and bathrooms, always holds up best.

3. ASSUMING YOU WILL PAY WHAT YOUR NEIGHBORS DID

When home owners go looking for architects, contractors, carpenters and electricians, they usually call their friends for recommendations. They also frequently ask what their friends paid for remodeling or renovation work that was done a few years ago. With those estimates in mind, they are often shocked when they hear what the work will cost today.

Note: During the 1990-1991 recession, business was terrible for architects and contractors and they often worked at distress prices. In addition, the cost of lumber has soared in recent years.

Be prepared to pay **5% to 15%** more for renovations than your friends did a few years ago.

KEEP THIS SLIP FOR REFERENCE

4. NOT HIRING THE RIGHT PEOPLE

Most home owners who set out to hire people to design or build for them wish the job were already finished. It's only natural to want your renovations completed shortly after you imagine them, but it's important to be practical and take the project one step at a time.

Once you've talked to a few architects and contractors, ask three of each for bids, no matter how inexpensive the project. Of course, the contractors' bids are solicited after the architect completes documents for bidding. The contractor will hire electricians, plumbers and other laborers. Ask each for three references, and be sure to contact all of them.

5. NOT DECIDING ON THE DETAILS EARLY

Many delays are the fault of the contractor, but some are caused by home owners who haven't preselected fixtures or colors. Avoid delays by choosing your faucets, tiles and stones ahead of time and making sure everything the contractor needs is in place. Holding up a project for a few days because you have changed your mind about some element can add weeks to the timetable.

Reason: The contractor may have budgeted only two months to complete your job, after which he must move on to another project. A two-day delay may therefore cause him to stop working on your house for several weeks.

You may save money by ordering and picking up finishing materials yourself. Get a list of what you need from the contractor.

Example: Bring tile samples home to make sure they work with the rest of the room. Ripping up newly laid tiles costs time and money.

6. NOT MAKING OTHER HOUSING ARRANGEMENTS

If possible, home owners should move out while extensive interior work is being done. It's not just a question of noise and workmen underfoot. There will be dust, debris and furniture out of place. There may even be hazardous materials around.

Strategy: Arrange alternate accommodations at a residence hotel, which offers lower rates than commercial hotels, or sublet an apartment.

If you do continue to live in your home, be willing to make certain sacrifices.

Example: Try not to make a fuss if you hate the music the workers play on the job. You'll have a happier crew that does better work.

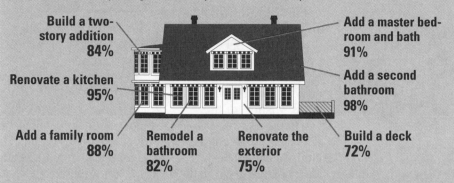

Home Renovation Resale Values

Payoff on home renovations varies by project. Have a contractor add a second bathroom, and you'll recoup 98% of the project cost when you sell your house. Build a deck, and you'll get back only 72% of the outlay.

Build a two-story addition
84%

Renovate a kitchen
95%

Add a family room
88%

Remodel a bathroom
82%

Renovate the exterior
75%

Add a master bedroom and bath
91%

Add a second bathroom
98%

Build a deck
72%

Note: The payoff is greater on do-it-yourself projects (provided the job is well done).

7. NOT OVERSEEING THE WORK PROPERLY

It's important to keep tabs on how the work is progressing. It's your house, and there is a certain joy in seeing your plans come to fruition.

Avoid being bossy and looking over the contractor's shoulder ten times a day, but don't be aloof or inaccessible either. If you're not there to raise an important issue or answer questions, the project may wind up delayed.

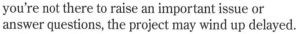

Strategy: Check on the progress every day or every other day. Raise any issues as soon as possible with the contractor.

If there are enormous conceptual issues involved, call the architect first and have him or her help you discuss matters with the contractor. If you need to talk with the contractor about a serious problem, do it away from the crew so you don't undermine his or her authority. It's also a problem if you and your spouse communicate different opinions and information to the contractor. Couples should agree on their wants and needs in advance.

Strategy: Determine who will speak with the contractor and workers. Generally, the same person should handle this task throughout the job.

Whenever possible, hash out you and your spouse's aesthetic disagreements before talking to the professionals who are working on your home. If your spouse has a question that you can't answer or are uncomfortable asking, both of you should sit down with the contractor and calmly discuss the problem.

Steve Gonzales Tells How to Hire the Best Home Contractor

Over the past 20 years, there have been some horrible stories about unscrupulous contractors doing terrible things to home owners.

As the number of home-improvement projects in the U.S. increases, some contractors find it easy to rip off people who have not had enough experience to know better.

A contractor is responsible for hiring others to install a new kitchen, add a new room or make major design changes. Here's how to hire the right one and how to make sure your interests are protected.

SIZING UP THE TALENT
Do some in-depth research before you hire a contractor and it will pay off in the long run.

Ask friends for recommendations
Ask around for recommendations and then get two or three references from each contractor you contact. Visit at least one completed project as well as one project in progress for each contractor.

Strategy: Ask former clients specific questions about each contractor's work and work style.
- Was the job started on time?
- Did workers show up on time?
- Did they complete the job on time?
- Was the contractor always available?
- Did you get what you wanted?
- Were there any surprises?
- Was the contractor responsive to problems after the job was completed?
- What would you do differently if you were hiring a contractor again?

Each of these questions is designed to yield critical information. Negative answers shouldn't necessarily rule out a contractor, but instead raise issues you need to discuss.

Example: You may discover that the contractor you like best isn't prompt about returning phone calls. Knowing this in advance, you can stress how important callbacks are to you and insist on establishing a daily or weekly time to speak.

Ask for bids on the project
Each contractor should provide a free job estimate that is typed, easy to understand and specific. A good bid includes start and completion dates, pro-

consumer clauses like daily working hours and promises to protect existing surfaces.

Important: Make sure there's no clause authorizing the substitution of materials without your written permission.

MAKING YOUR CHOICE
If you find that all the contractors are great and all their bids are similarly priced, the answers to these questions will help you decide among them.

Does the contractor have a clean complaint record?
Call your local Better Business Bureau, which will provide a verbal or written report. Also, call your state's Attorney General's office, Building Department and Licensing Bureau to find out about complaints. More than one recent complaint about a contractor is a red flag.

How many projects is the contractor working on right now?
A contractor working on more than two or three projects at once may be hard to locate and unlikely to spend much time at your job site.

Will the contractor warranty the work for one year?
A written warranty should be part of the contract, and all legitimate contractors will include one. A warranty is important because if something falls apart, it will usually happen within the first year. The warranty should state that the contractor will fix the problem within 10 days.

BEFORE SIGNING THE CONTRACT
Make sure all the details are in place before you sign a contract.

Interview the Candidates in Person
Face-to-face meetings are always best, since you will be able to determine whether you are comfortable with the contractor. You don't want someone who looks impatient or seems reluctant to answer detailed questions.

Important: Before an interview with a contractor, put together a list of your general expected working rules. Give the list to the contractor, so that he or she knows up front what you expect.

Example: If you want to avoid having dirt tracked through your home, insist that the contractor bring a portable bathroom.

Review important documents

Ask for copies of all professional licenses and insurance documents, including the contractor's driver's license to confirm his or her identity. Without it, you can't be sure that the other licenses actually belong to that contractor.

Also make sure the contractor purchases a performance bond, available through a surety company for about $100. A surety company provides a bond to the contractor for one year and pays the home owner if the contractor skips out on the job. The performance bond covers the cost to complete the job if the contractor cannot for any reason.

The contractor should have legible copies of an occupational license from the city, a county license and, in most states, a state license. Ask your state's Attorney General's office for a list of what is required. (A subcontractor needs to have a county license and sometimes a city license.)

The contractor should also have workers' compensation and liability insurance. Request a certificate of insurance. If the contractor is a sole proprietor with no employees, confirm that he or she has personal insurance or workers' compensation and call the agent to confirm the coverage.

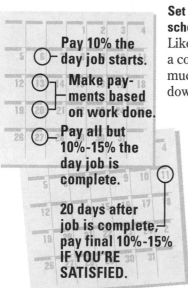

Pay 10% the day job starts.

Make payments based on work done.

Pay all but 10%-15% the day job is complete.

20 days after job is complete, pay final 10%-15% IF YOU'RE SATISFIED.

Set up a payment schedule

Like any businessperson, a contractor will want as much in the form of a down payment as possible.

Ideal: You provide 10% of the project's total cost on the day work starts, not when the contract is signed.

Strategy: Create a payment schedule pegged to specific work milestones. Be fair, but write the contract so that you withhold the final 10% to 15% until 20 days after the job is completed. That will give you time to see if everything was really done as you requested. In addition, it will give the contractor an incentive to finish promptly. It's a bad sign if the contractor balks at this.

Make sure you'll get what you pay for

Have the contract state that you'll have an opportunity to inspect all materials before they are used. Contractors sometimes try to save money by using less than they promise.

Example: Consumers often get gouged on insulation jobs when contractors shortchange them on the amount of insulation that is required.

Solution: Home-repair books or insulation packages can tell you how much you'll need based on the square footage involved. Then count the bags before the insulation is installed. Some contractors bring empty bags to fool people who count this way. If you're in doubt, ask the company to provide a density test.

How Tightwad Amy Dacyczyn Fixed Her Own House

Several years ago, my husband Jim and I bought a house in Maine that needed quite a bit of fixing up. To save money, we decided to do a lot of the work ourselves. We're not done yet, but we're very happy with the results so far.

We're not exactly gifted craftspeople. My greatest skill is attention to detail. Jim is good with tools, but he's not a pro (he calls himself a "wood butcher"). Here's what we've learned from our adventure that can be applied to any type of remodeling project.

FIXER-UPPERS CAN BE SMART BUYS

While economic necessity was the primary reason we bought a house that needed work, getting a great deal was important, too. If you have the vision to see what a house can become after some work, buying one that's not perfect can be a very smart idea.

Example: Our 1890 farmhouse was recently appraised. We were told it is now worth the purchase price, the labor and materials that have gone into it, and as much as $50,000 more.

Time-saver: Tour only those houses you might really buy. We went into only 10% of the 176 houses with For Sale signs that we drove by.

HOW TO ATTACK
Follow these suggestions to make your remodeling job more manageable.

Take your time
Conversations with family and friends convinced us that the biggest renovation mistakes are due to two factors.

1. Rushing a decision. There's less time pressure than you think.

2. Veering away from your personal taste in design.

Example: I like white walls. On a whim, I stained the wooden walls in my home office. Eventually, I repainted them white.

Write a master plan
Writing down everything you want to do to your home helps you set priorities and establish a reasonable schedule.

A plan also helps you spend your money wisely. It forces you to ask, "If I do project A, will project C look good next to it?"

Handle the eyesores and discomfort zones first
Jim and I attacked the grimy kitchen first. We removed the dreadful wallpaper, patched the plaster and painted the walls white. We fixed a small hole in the ceiling with a piece of sheetrock we found on the property and put a piece of plywood down as a new bottom for the woeful sink cabinet.

Our kitchen island was created by using a large, freestanding antique counter we found in the woodshed. We refinished the top, painted it and hauled it into the kitchen.

This renovation took only a few hundred dollars, yet it quickly gave us a sense of accomplishment.

Start with small tasks
This will help you feel good right away about the property you just bought.

We fixed up the kitchen as best we could but stopped work before it was done in the country-living style we wanted. Eventually, we bought a beautiful $350 antique cupboard and other accessories to complete the look. I also bought an antique wood-burning stove. Instead of paying $800 for a restored one at an antique shop, I bought one through a newspaper ad for only $350.

Hold off on desirable but less necessary tasks
They can wait. Only after we took care of the kitchen and put in a small furnace to heat the rooms that were unheated did we go to work on the rest of the house.

We took eight utility trailer loads to the dump. Then we landscaped the property by cutting the grass and weeds for the first time in what must have been decades. This cost no money, but the aesthetic result was remarkable.

When you see water damage, act quickly
If you wait, the problem will be much worse and more costly to fix.

Example: A foundation sill in the back of the carriage house was beginning to rot. We handled this immediately.

Do one room or project at a time
This eases confusion, makes the home livable and allows you to feel a sense of accomplishment. Small triumphs, even just repainting a windowsill, give you the momentum to see the work through to completion. Besides, no one wants to live in a place where almost everything looks unfinished.

Re-Do vs. Rebuild
Look at houses that need cosmetic work, not interior demolition. Avoid older places that have undergone extensive modern renovation in the last 50 years. It's something for which you pay extra but have to rip out completely if you want to restore a home to its original feel.

Keep details consistent
Don't mix old and modern styles. You can buy used items from shops that salvage materials from old houses or you can buy old-looking, but actually new pieces from renovation supply houses.

Browse through *Country Living, Old House Journal* and other publications to find local sources.

Don't assume you can't do something

I refinished many old doors that were unsightly because ancient coats of varnish had become dark and dried. I used an ordinary paint scraper, denatured alcohol and steel wool to smooth off the remainder. How did I learn what to use? I visited someone who was refinishing woodwork and I asked him for advice.

Hire outside help only when necessary

Here are some compelling reasons.

1. There are health risks. We hired professionals to replace our asbestos roof when it sprang a leak.

Important: If someone else is doing the dangerous work, relocate your family during the project or have the work done before you move in.

2. You lack the skills. Although we probably could have made kitchen cabinets ourselves, they would never have looked as good as we wanted them to. The result we wanted required real craftsmanship.

3. You're up to your eyeballs handling the rest of your life. Jim and I had four young kids when we began work on the house. A year later, we had twins. So we hired some carpenters to do work we could have handled ourselves because we didn't have the time or energy.

Protect Your Home While You're Away

Trouble-proof your home before leaving for an extended period of time.

- To prevent a flood from a burst pipe, have a ball valve installed on the water main at the point where the pipe enters the house. The valve lets you turn off all the water with a lever. Cost: about $100.
- Unplug nonessential appliances like TVs, computers, toasters and room air conditioners, which all can cause fires.
- Do not leave clothes spinning in the dryer. Malfunctioning dryers are the leading cause of appliance-related house fires.
- Ask a neighbor to check your home every few days to make sure everything is okay.

SOURCES

Sources are listed in the order in which their contributions appear. A source may have contributed part or all of an article, or a series of articles.

William G. Effros, author of *How to Sell Your Home in Five Days*

Larry Roth, editor of *Living Cheap News*

Robert Irwin, author of *Tips & Traps When Buying a Home*

Kenneth W. Edwards, Real Estate Education Company

Fortune

David Schechner, Schechner & Targan

Ilyce Glink, author of *One Hundred Questions Every First-Time Home Buyer Should Ask*

Gary W. Eldred, PhD, author of *The 106 Common Mistakes Homebuyers Make (and How to Avoid Them)*

The New York Times

Jordan Clark, United Homeowners Association

James Berkovec, Federal Home Loan Mortgage Corp.

Robert J. Garner, Ernst & Young, LLP

James Putman, CFP, Wealth Management, Inc.

Robert Irwin, author of *Tips & Traps When Buying a Home*

Peter G. Miller, author of *The Common-Sense Mortgage: How to Cut the Cost of Home Ownership by $100,000 or More*

Gary W. Eldred, PhD, author of *The 106 Common Mistakes Homebuyers Make (and How to Avoid Them)*

Peter G. Miller, author of *The Common-Sense Mortgage: How to Cut the Cost of Home Ownership by $100,000 or More*

Paul Havemann, HSH Associates

John Dorfman, writer for *The Wall Street Journal*

Richard Roll, American Homeowners Association (AHA)

Robert van Order, Federal Home Loan Mortgage Corp.

Julie Garton-Good, Real Estate Education Company

Ina DeLong, United Policyholders

Jonathan D. Pond, Financial Planning Information, Inc.

David L. Scott, PhD, Valdosta State University

Anna Maria Galdieri, insurance consultant

Barbara Taylor, Insurance Information Institute

Loretta Worters, Insurance Information Institute

James Paragano, RA, AIA, residential architect

Robert Irwin, author of *Tips & Traps When Selling a Home*

Steve Gonzalez, author of *Before You Hire a Contractor: A Construction Guidebook for Consumers*

Amy Dacyczyn, editor of *The Tightwad Gazette*

Tom Fitzpatrick, Chubb Group of Insurance Companies

Automotive Expertise

Keep Down the Costs of Your Car

What Car Makers Don't Want You To Know

One of the best ways to save money is to avoid buying or leasing a new car. Motorists can easily double or even triple the life spans of their present cars simply by performing proper maintenance, practicing good driving habits and avoiding the kinds of mistakes that send most cars to the junkyard. Following are a few mistakes you don't want to make.

FAILING TO OBSERVE THE BREAK-IN PERIOD

Drive gently during a new car's first 50 miles, and vary your speed for the first 1,000 miles of the car's life. Failing to do so results in improper seating of the piston rings, which leads to increased oil consumption throughout the life of the car. Also, change the oil promptly after the first 1,500 miles to eliminate the bits of metal and grit found in a new engine.

MAKING SUDDEN STARTS AND STOPS

Accelerating aggressively only to slam on the brakes at the next traffic light doesn't save time, but it does cause needless wear on your engine, transmission, suspension and brakes. And it wastes gas.

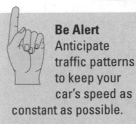

Be Alert Anticipate traffic patterns to keep your car's speed as constant as possible.

DOWNSHIFTING NEEDLESSLY

In the early days of automobiles, brakes were so unreliable that prudent drivers always shifted into a lower gear when descending hills or approaching busy intersections. Today, brakes are very reliable and far less costly to repair than engine and transmission components.

Rule of thumb: Use engine braking only when descending a long, steep grade. At all other times, use your brakes.

DRIVING HARD WITH A COLD ENGINE

Engine wear occurs most swiftly not during high-speed driving, but in the first moments after a car has been started, when the cylinders are starved for oil. Accelerating briskly with a cold engine can cause the engine's head gaskets to fail, and premature use of accessories speeds wear of engine bearings.

To avoid trouble: Before driving off, let your engine idle with your foot off the accelerator pedal for about one minute. Once you're under way, drive slowly and avoid using your heater and other power-hungry accessories until the engine reaches its proper operating temperature, usually after about three minutes.

SHIFTING GEARS HAPHAZARDLY

Manual transmissions cost less and are cheaper to maintain than automatics—if you learn proper shifting techniques. Picking too high a gear for a given speed lugs your engine. Picking an excessively low gear causes it to over-rev. Both waste fuel and damage your engine bearings.

ENGINE STRATEGY

Shift so your engine maintains between 2,000 and 3,000 revolutions per minute (RPMs). Use overdrive settings only for speeds greater than 45 miles per hour.

Common problem: In many cars with manual transmissions, shifting from neutral to first gear causes an audible grinding of the transmission's synchronizer rings.

Remedy: Avoid shifting directly from neutral to first gear. Instead, move the shift lever briefly into second, then shift into first gear. And never rest your hand on the shift lever or your foot on the clutch pedal. Use your right foot for both the accelerator and the brake. Use your left foot for the clutch.

DRIVING WITH DIRTY OR WORN-OUT OIL

For many motorists, oil maintenance means simply adding the occasional quart of 10W40. In fact, 10W30 offers far more protection against engine wear than 10W40 does.

By the time you're a quart low, it's time for an oil change. Change conventional motor oil once every three months or every 3,000 miles, whichever comes first.

To keep oil clean between changes, select the biggest oil filter that will fit. Most cars come equipped with a short filter but will accept either a short or a tall filter. The tall one always provides better filtration.

If you live in a dusty environment, bolting on a bypass oil-filtration system provides an extra measure of protection without void-ing your car's warranty. Cost: About $80 plus labor.

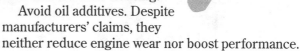

Switch from a disposable pleated-paper air filter to a reusable wetted-foam filter. Cost: $20 to $40. To lock out dirt, apply a thin layer of grease to the seal between the filter and the filter housing.

Avoid oil additives. Despite manufacturers' claims, they neither reduce engine wear nor boost performance.

DRIVING WITH DIRTY FUEL

Although owners' manuals often give it short shrift, clean fuel is essential for long engine life. Replace your fuel filter every 10,000 miles or two years, whichever comes last. Cost: $12 to $50.

In either case, stick to the recommended fuel. Using regular gas in a car designed to run on premium causes knocking, which can quickly destroy the engine. Using premium gas in a car designed to run on regular wastes gas and money.

Caution: If your car has fuel-injection, never let your tank drop below one-quarter full. Cornering on an almost-empty tank can momentarily disrupt the flow of fuel to the fuel pump, shortening its life.

FAILING TO GUARD AGAINST WEATHER DAMAGE

To reduce exposure to sunlight and environmental threats, keep your car garaged or at least covered. If your car must remain outdoors without a cover, put a dashboard-protecting sunscreen in your windshield and park so that the car faces a different direction

GAS GUZZLERS

U.S. gasoline consumption (in billions of gallons per year) is still on the rise.

Source: U.S. Department of Energy

each day. This helps spread out sun-induced damage. To preserve weather stripping and rubber surfaces, use silicone spray twice a year.

IGNORING YOUR ANTIFREEZE

Antifreeze not only keeps your car working in cold weather but also helps prevent rust and corrosion. For optimal protection, use a 50-50 antifreeze-water mix.

Important: Use distilled water, not tap water. Change the fluid every two years or 24,000 miles, whichever comes first.

OVERTIGHTENING THE LUG NUTS ON YOUR WHEELS

Though it sounds trivial, improperly tightened lug nuts or bolts represent a big source of trouble for car owners. If there is too much lug-nut torque, your brake rotors will warp and cause your brake pedal to pulsate. If the lug nuts are too loose, your wheels will not be securely attached.

Problem: Many mechanics tighten lug nuts with air wrenches, which are notorious for overtightening the nuts.

Solution: Get your own torque wrench. Cost: $15. Every time your wheels are removed for maintenance, use the wrench to check the torque readings on your lug nuts against your owner's manual or the specs from your tire dealer.

REGULARLY FAILING TO PERFORM HIDDEN MAINTENANCE TASKS

While owners' manuals usually specify how and when to perform the most crucial maintenance tasks, they often provide incomplete information about other key tasks.

Examples: Manuals typically say nothing about brake fluid, which should be changed once every two years or 24,000 miles, whichever comes first. Brake fluid in antilock systems should be changed annually.

Power-steering fluid should be changed every three years or 30,000 miles, whichever comes first. Timing belts should be replaced every 60,000 miles, timing chains every 100,000 miles.

Without regular use, certain systems quickly fall out of adjustment.

To avoid trouble: Run your air conditioner and your defroster at least once every two weeks. Release and reapply the parking brake daily. Ask your mechanic how to test your antilock brake system safely.

FAILING TO RECHARGE OR REPLACE AN OLD OR WEAK BATTERY

Besides increasing the risk of leaving you stranded, a weak battery causes wear on the alternator and the starter. Both need a good power source to operate properly.

To avoid trouble: Replace your battery six months before it is due to expire. Check the date on the battery's sticker. Choose the biggest, most powerful battery that will fit under the hood.

RUSTPROOFING YOUR CAR

New manufacturing techniques and materials mean that rust is no longer the problem it used to be.

After-market or dealer-applied rustproofing treatment is unnecessary, costly and, in many cases, can void your car's rust warranty.

Best Car Protection
Car covers help prevent scratches, dings, faded paint and interiors, and keep the car clean.

Important: Cover only a clean vehicle. Buy a high-quality cover made of a fabric that repels water and lets trapped moisture escape. If the cover collects dirt, leaves or other debris while on the car, clean it off before removing it. These covers can be washed in a washing machine.

Protect Yourself from Unauthorized Charges

If your car is a lemon, contact the National Highway Traffic Safety Administration at 800-424-9393 or http://www.nhtsa.dot.gov They can issue recalls or warnings if enough people complain.

Make sure the auto mechanic accepts credit cards, and get a detailed written estimate before work begins. One of the top consumer complaints at the Better Business Bureau involves shoddy auto repairs and unauthorized charges. If you use a credit card, you can withhold payment if there is a problem while the credit card company investigates.

Strategy: Ask in advance that your bill state you will not pay anything over the mechanic's written estimated price.

Today's Cars Require Less Maintenance

Twenty years ago, spark plugs had to be changed every 12,000 miles. Today, platinum-tipped plugs can last as long as 100,000 miles.

Warning: Independent mechanics and car service centers may recommend more service than you need. Follow the maintenance schedule listed in your owner's manual.

Airbag Theft Alert

Thieves are stealing airbags in high-crime urban areas. Because driver-side airbags are designed to be easy to replace after an accident, they are also easy to steal. It takes three minutes to remove one. The cost of replacing an airbag is between $700 and $1,000. The street price for stolen airbags is $50 to $150.

Self-defense: Get an effective car alarm.

Note: Insurers say airbag thefts would stop if automakers cut prices and gave each airbag's serial number to the National Insurance Crime Bureau.

TOP RATED AIR BAGS

The National Highway Traffic Safety Commission ranked these 1997 cars as having the best-working frontal and side air bags in their class.

1997 Heavy passenger cars	1997 Medium passenger cars	1997 Compact passenger cars
Ford Crown Victoria	Audi A6	Crysler Sebring
Mercury Grand Marquis	Chevrolet Camaro	Dodge Avenger
	Ford Mustang Convertable	

Source: National Highway Traffic Safety Commission

Car Savers

- Use quick-lube-and-oil-change services and save more than 50% over dealer or full-service garage prices. If you must use factory-authorized parts, buy a factory-authorized oil filter at the dealer's service center and give it to the franchise.
- Don't idle a cold engine. Modern cars need only a few seconds of idling time, unlike models of yore. Any longer than that is wasting gas and increasing engine wear.
- Buy gas in the morning. You'll get as much as 5% more for your money if you buy gas before the day's heat has expanded the gas in the station's fuel tank, especially in the summer. And don't top off your gas tank—expansion will cause it to overflow.
- Save up to 20¢ a gallon by pumping your own gas. The average American household spends more than $1,000 a year on gas alone.
- Replace worn spark plugs and keep the engine tuned for a savings of one mile per gallon, or $53 a year. Save another $53 by replacing air filters. Save 2% to 3% on every gas bill by keeping tires properly inflated.
- Use the air conditioner. Today's cars are aerodynamically efficient. Driving at high speeds in hot weather with the windows open creates drag, which wastes more fuel than driving with the windows closed and the air conditioner running. Do, however, turn off the air conditioner when you are idling or driving short distances at low speeds.
- Take a defensive driving course. Most states now require car insurers to give a discount to anyone who has recently taken a defensive driving course. You can save as much as $150 a year for three to five years, and may avoid an accident.

Air Conditioner Update

Automobile air-conditioner repairs are becoming more expensive because of new environmental laws.

Background: By international agreement, the refrigerant used in almost all car air conditioners built before the 1994 model year stopped being manufactured on December 31, 1995. The refrigerant, R-12, contains chlorofluorocarbons. These have been linked to depletion of the ozone layer.

A newly developed refrigerant, called R-134a, is more environmentally friendly but cannot be used in air-conditioning units designed for R-12.

Result: As R-12 becomes increasingly scarce, the average bill for servicing an older system has increased from $30 to $100.

Alternative: When R-12 is no longer available or cost-effective, consider retrofitting the unit. Cost: $200 to $800. Generally, the newer the car, the less the alteration will cost.

Beware of Improper Charges When Buying A Car

Here are two scams dealers commonly use to make extra money off of unsuspecting customers.

INVOICE
SCAM 1
Charging extra for standard features.

INVOICE
SCAM 2
Charging for dealers' own preparation costs.

KEEP THIS SLIP FOR REFERENCE

SCAM I

The dealer orders cars without some standard equipment, such as carpeting, and then claims you'll have to pay extra for it.

Self-defense: Get a manufacturer's brochure detailing the list of standard equipment. Review it to make sure you are charged properly.

SCAM II

The dealer tries to get you to pay for his or her cost of doing business by passing dealer prep charges along to you.

Self-defense: Refuse to pay them, and be prepared to walk out of the dealership if the charges are not removed.

OPTIONS THAT HELP SELL A CAR

Options that pay off when you resell a car	Options that don't pay off
● **Air conditioning**	● **Heated seats**
● **Power steering**	● **Multidriver memory seats**
● **Larger engines**	
● **Antilock brakes**	● **Dashboard trip computers**
● **Traction control**	● **Digital dashboards**
● **Security and safety options**	● **Exterior wood-grain paneling**

Super-premium sound systems, custom wheels and built-in cellular phones may or may not help you sell your car.

Easy Way To Get a Low Price On a New Car

Find out what dealers paid for a vehicle by consulting a pricing service. Add $200 to $500 for profit. Then, in a polite letter to dealership managers, tell them what you're willing to pay and that you have contacted their competitors. For a swift response, state that you will buy from the first dealer who meets your offer.

The Best Car-Model Years

The best car-model years are the second through fourth that a car has been in production. The first model year often has quality problems, since most money has been spent on research and development. The fifth model year is often the last for many cars, and quality control frequently slips as companies focus on research and development of a redesigned model.

How to Buy a Recreational Vehicle

A recreational vehicle provides all of the freedom, mobility and savings of tent camping, without sacrificing the comforts of home.

Savings: On average, a trip in a recreational vehicle costs a family of four 50% less than if they made the same trip by car and stayed overnight in hotels or motels, and 75% less than an air/hotel/motel vacation. If you take extended vacations every year or have a large family, the travel savings can be even greater.

The Basic Types

There are two basic types of recreational vehicles.
1. **Motor homes** are self-propelled by gas or diesel engines.
2. **Travel trailers** are units that are towed behind a car or truck.

Both types are equipped for comfortable living. Motor homes and travel trailers that are 20 feet or longer have at least a galley with a multiburner range and refrigerator, an enclosed bathroom with a shower, seating, eating and sleeping accommodations for four or more, hot and cold running water, a furnace and plenty of extra storage space.

The most popular add-on options are air conditioners and microwave ovens.

MOTOR HOMES

Class A motor homes are box-shaped and range in length from 23 to 38 feet. Some large Class A models are bus conversions, motor homes that are built on bus chassis.

Starting prices: Bus conversions begin at $250,000. Smaller models begin at $35,000.

Class C motor homes are built on van chassis and range in length from 20 to 30 feet. A distinguishing feature of all Class C models is the forward compartment over the driver/passenger cab. It usually contains a double bunk.
Price range: $20,000 to $45,000.

Camping van conversions are standard vans that have been modified to contain sleeping accommodations, a dining table, a tiny galley and, in some cases, a toilet.
Average price: $33,000.

TRAVEL TRAILERS

Conventional travel trailers are box-shaped and can be towed by any vehicle that can pull their weight. Check vehicle manufacturer's specifications. They come in a range of sizes, from 13 to 40 feet.
Price range: $10,000 to $40,000.

Fifth-wheel travel trailers can be towed only by pickup trucks. They each have a raised front section that extends over the bed, in which the hitch is mounted. Sizes range from 20 to 40 feet.
Price range: $15,000 to $80,000.

Folding-tent trailers have fabric tops that fold down for towing. When set up, the fabric top's ends project outward to form roomy double berths. Folded-down lengths are 11 to 20 feet. Unfolded, they are six to eight feet longer.
Starting price: $3,000.

RV CHECKLIST

- Rent before you buy. By renting first, you'll be able to determine whether an RV is right for you. To locate rental companies, consult the yellow pages under Recreational Vehicles, Renting and Leasing.
- Determine if the costs of insuring, registering and maintaining the vehicle are affordable. Many new buyers forget to add on these costs, which can be substantial.
- Find out if you may legally park the vehicle on or near your property when it is not being used. If local ordinances preclude parking the vehicle on the street, or if there is no suitable place to park it at your residence, you may have to keep the RV in a storage facility.
- Check out the RV's facilities for comfort. Stand in the bathroom with the door closed and see if you can have enough room to move around, try out the bed for size and pretend to make a meal in the galley, especially in a unit in which counter space is minimal. Make a list of all of the things you will take with you in the vehicle, and determine whether the storage space is sufficient.
- Make sure the RV fits your needs. If you like backwoods camping, for example, purchase a unit that is not too long or too low-slung.

Mistakes to Avoid When Buying a Used Car

When shopping for a car today, many people choose a used vehicle instead of a new one.

Reasons:

- The average cost of a new car is increasing faster than inflation. Between 1985 and 1995, the average cost of a new car rose 70%, from $11,500 to $19,500. During this period, however, household incomes increased only about 40%.
- The growth of leasing has increased the supply of high-quality 2-and 3-year-old vehicles in dealers' showrooms. That, combined with today's emphasis on value, has considerably narrowed the status gap between new and used cars.

Here are the most common mistakes people make when buying used cars.

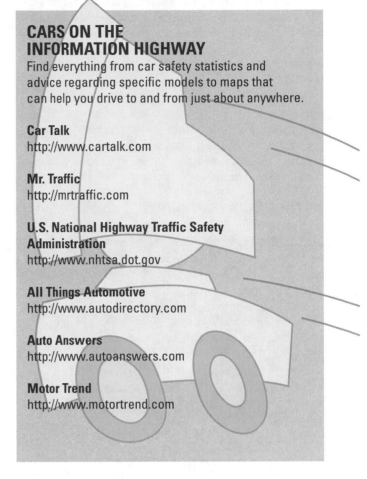

CARS ON THE INFORMATION HIGHWAY

Find everything from car safety statistics and advice regarding specific models to maps that can help you drive to and from just about anywhere.

Car Talk
http://www.cartalk.com

Mr. Traffic
http://mrtraffic.com

U.S. National Highway Traffic Safety Administration
http://www.nhtsa.dot.gov

All Things Automotive
http://www.autodirectory.com

Auto Answers
http://www.autoanswers.com

Motor Trend
http://www.motortrend.com

EXPECTING A BETTER DEAL FROM THE PREVIOUS OWNER

Buy from an owner only if the price is 15% or more below the price a dealer is charging for a similar make and model.

A 2-, 3- or 4-year-old vehicle may still have some warranty protection, but this is transferable only if you buy from a dealer. To find out if a car has this protection, call the regional office of the manufacturer or contact its financing arm.

Caution: If you buy from an owner, you'll have no recourse if you're dissatisfied. In a private transaction, whatever goes wrong is your headache. With a dealer, you can always take your complaint to the state authorities.

Note: The more adept you are at fixing cars, the more incentive you have to seek a deal from an owner instead of a dealer.

NOT DRIVING A VEHICLE BEFORE BUYING IT

More than 60% of used-car buyers never take a test drive. Many believe that doing so constitutes an agreement to buy, but they are wrong. They also worry that if they drive the vehicle, the dealer or owner will start pressuring them.

Strategy: Take a test drive or walk away from the deal. Try every knob, button and option while driving the car. Listen for odd noises. If there are some problems but you still like the vehicle, include in the contract that the problems must be fixed before you put down any money.

BUYING A COMPANY-OWNED CAR

Of the 3.5 million 2- and 3-year-old vehicles that come back to dealers every year, only 1.5 million were owned by individuals. The rest were owned by companies. Avoid these company cars whenever possible. They take much more abuse because they tend to be driven more and maintained less.

Reason: Drivers of company cars simply have less economic incentive than owners to take good care of their vehicles.

How to tell: First, ask the salesperson if the car was company-owned (you may or may not get a straight answer). Then check the mileage. Leased cars average 15,000 to 16,000 miles per year, while company cars average 20,000 miles per year.

NOT BEING ASSERTIVE

If you know what kind of vehicle you want, ask for it—even if you don't see it on a dealer's lot.

Example: Ask three dealers in your area if they have a red Chevy Suburban with a lease that is within a month or two of expiration. This might get you a better price because the dealer will only have to clean up the vehicle and hand you the keys.

Sometimes, a dealer will even contact the current leasee of the vehicle in which you are interested and offer to release him or her from the lease ahead of time in order to lease it to you.

RELYING HEAVILY ON USED-CAR PRICE GUIDES

Most are notoriously out of date. Instead, review the classified ads in your Sunday newspaper for several weeks to get an idea of the prices of the models in which you are interested.

Note: The assumption behind used-car pricing is that the average vehicle is driven 15,000 miles per year. If the mileage on the car you are interested in is greater, you should get a discount of 15¢ to 20¢ for every mile over 15,000. Also, you should be willing to pay more for a car that has been driven less than 15,000 miles per year.

BUYING A CAR WITH WATER DAMAGE

The huge floods in many parts of the country in recent years have generated a lot of water-damaged merchandise.

Tell-tale signs: See if there's a loose corner of the interior carpet. Can you feel water underneath? Check the nooks and crannies in the trunk for signs of moisture. Look beneath the dash and in the seat track as well. Are there water stains around the inside top of the car? These often represent more than aesthetic problems.

If you find any signs of water damage, don't even consider buying the car. Water can corrode the engine, brakes and other parts of the vehicle. On the other hand, surface rust underneath the vehicle is normal and is not a sign of internal damage.

NOT EXAMINING DETAILS CAREFULLY

Tires are usually one of the most expensive parts of a used car that you'll have to replace. This expense can be avoided if you carefully examine the tires and have the dealer replace faulty ones before you sign a contract. Looking the tires over or kicking them is not enough.

Here's how: Rub your hand on top of each tire in both directions. Well-balanced tires should feel smooth. Then put a penny into the tire tread: Insert Lincoln's head first, and run the penny around the tire. If you can see the top of his head at any point, the tires are worn and you will have to replace them.

Also, check the stitching on the seats to see if they have been repaired improperly. If the stitching is stretched, it is likely to tear soon.

NOT CHECKING FOR MANUFACTURER CERTIFICATION

Certification is a guarantee that a vehicle is in tip-top shape. Certified vehicles are more expensive because the manufacturers—not the dealers—have taken responsibility for fixing them up. They are in better condition than average used cars and are worth the extra money (from $300 to $1,000). Such vehicles are available only from dealers, not through private owners.

Used Luxury Cars

A glut of expiring luxury-car leases means these preowned vehicles are now selling for as much as 40% less than new cars of the same model. The dealers keep the best cars, including those with manufacturer-subsidized warranties. There are several tips you should pay attention to when looking for a used luxury car.

- Look for newer cars (3-years-old or less) with mileage of less than 12,000 miles per year.
- Try to find a pampered auto with complete service records.
- Examine three or four cars at different dealers to compare values.
- Go to an independent specialist mechanic for inspection.
- Don't accept the first price—on most luxury cars you can save 3% to 6%, so it pays to bargain.

- Beware of used-car leases. While new-car leases are often subsidized by the manufacturer, leases on used cars are not, resulting in relatively higher monthly payments.

Luxury Car Surprise

A full-size luxury car can cost up to $13,000 more per year to own and operate than a subcompact car. Extra costs include fuel, oil, tires, maintenance, insurance, depreciation, financing, taxes and licensing.

The Six Big Car Financing Traps

To get the best deal on a new or used car, you have to do more than browbeat the dealer into giving you a great price. You also must negotiate the best terms and interest rate on your car loan.

Caution: Many car dealers will give ground on the car's price but dig in when discussing financing. That's because they make most of their money on the financing, not on a vehicle's markup.

Here are six big traps people get into when borrowing to pay for a car.

1. NOT INVESTIGATING THE BEST FINANCING SOURCES

Many people think the best deal on a loan is offered by the dealer who is selling them the car.

Reality: Sometimes it is, but many times it isn't. Dealers are usually financing middlemen between you and the institution lending the money. They'll often try to mark up the interest rate set by the direct financing source, whether it's a credit union or a car company, and pocket the difference.

Solution: Before you begin shopping for a car, research the loan rates offered by local credit unions, which often have better deals. If you don't belong to a credit union, try to join one. If you don't

have a credit union at work, you may be able to join one to which a relative belongs or that is affiliated with your occupation.

Then, over the phone, compare the credit union's loan rate with car loans offered by local banks and savings-and-loan institutions.

Other options:
- Home-equity credit line. The rate on a home-equity credit line might be lower than a car loan rate, and the interest is tax-deductible. Remember, however, that if you default, you could lose your home.
- A loan against your cash-value life insurance policy. Rates charged by insurers vary widely, but you might get a better deal this way, especially if your credit rating is tarnished.

Line up your financing one week before you go to buy the car. The procedure for doing this is the same as that to get an actual loan.

DEALER PROFITS ON NEW VS. USED CARS

Dealers make about the same gross profits on used cars as on new ones. The average gross profit on a used car was $1,250 in 1994. On a new car, it was just under $1,240. Used-car demand has increased as higher prices for new cars have made buying them not affordable for many people.

WHERE THE CAR LOANS ARE

There is more than one place to go for a car loan, so shop around.

LENDERS	ADVANTAGES	LIMITATIONS
Commercial Banks	● **Widely available locations and funds.** ● **Preferred rates for bank customers.**	● **Require good credit rating.** ● **Higher rates than some other sources.**
Savings & Loans	● **Loans often cost less than at commercial banks.**	● **Require good credit rating.** ● **Exist in only some states.**
Credit Unions	● **Can be easy to arrange for members in good standing.** ● **Lowest rates.**	● **Membership required in organization or group.**
Sales Financing Companies	● **Can be easy to arrange.** ● **Good terms during special promotions.**	● **High rates.** ● **Since loan is secured, defaulting can mean loss of item and payments already made.**
Small Loan Companies (Personal Finance Companies)	● **Can be easy to arrange.** ● **Good credit rating not required.**	● **High rates.** ● **Cosigner often required.**

Strategy: State the amount you want to borrow. For a used car, only credit unions will commit to financing if you don't yet know the make and condition of the car you're buying.

2. NEGLECTING TO NEGOTIATE A LOWER RATE

Once you've determined the rates and terms offered by different institutions, call them all back and see if they can beat the lowest bid.

3. BEING THE TYPE OF BUYER DEALERS LOVE TO OUTFOX

Like any good salesperson, car dealers look for behavior patterns in buyers that will give them an opportunity to make money. Here are the buyer types for which dealers look.

● The buyer who goes to a dealer thinking, "I won't pay more than $8,500 plus my trade-in for that new car." By focusing on the car's price, you may be ignoring the real value of your trade-in and shortchanging yourself in the process.

● The buyer who seeks a specific price for a trade-in, like $4,000. The problem is that this buyer is vulnerable to a bait-and-switch ploy. You'll get the price you want for the trade-in, but you won't get the car model you came to buy. For example, a dealer might say, "I can give you $4,000 on your old car, but only if you buy this particular model."

● The buyer who stresses the amount that he or she wants to pay each month in financing. This figure is important, but only if you buy the car of your dreams and the loan is for the time period you requested. All dealers will find a way to give you your desired monthly payment, but in the process you may be saddled with a longer-term loan on a car you don't love.

4. NOT BEING PREPARED FOR DEALER DOUBLE-TALK

If you discuss financing with a dealer, be prepared to be told that your information about how they do business is all wrong.

Reason: By negotiating the financing, you're cutting into the dealer's profits. Here are the most common lines dealers use to throw you off guard when discussing financing.

● "The money we're lending you comes from a credit union, too." That's often true, but it costs you more—perhaps one or two percentage points more—because you have to cover the commission that the credit union pays the dealer for bringing in your business.

● "Our rate is 4.9%—much lower than the credit union's rate of 10%." Not necessarily. The dealer may have forgotten to take any rebate into consideration.

Example: On a $12,000 car financed by a dealer at 4.9% for 48 months, you'll pay $276 a month. But if you use your rebate—let's say it is $1,500—toward your down payment and then finance a loan at 9.5%, you'll pay $264 a month. That's a savings of $576 on a 48-month loan.

Important: Be sure that the manufacturer sends the rebate check directly to your home.

5. BUYING CREDIT LIFE OR CREDIT DISABILITY INSURANCE

Such insurance policies are used to pay your car payments if you die or become disabled.

They are very overpriced. Coverage is almost always optional. No matter what the dealer says, assume it's negotiable. If you decline the insurance and you die, your estate is liable for all future car payments.

Strategy: Check your contract to make sure that the dealer or lender hasn't added the policy without telling you, leaving you with a monthly payment that may be about $10 higher than you anticipated. Using a calculator or loan table, find out your monthly payment without insurance and then make sure this is the figure on which you're signing off.

6. TAKING A LOAN FOR THE LONGEST PERIOD

Car buyers often take the longest period—60 or 72 months—in order to lower their monthly payments.

Problem: You may end up paying far more than the car is worth, which will be disappointing and costly if you resell it.

Strategy: If possible, avoid such easy-payment loans. The payments may be lower and easier to make each month, but they'll seem to drag on forever. You're better off buying a more affordable car.

It's also a mistake to make too small a down payment. If it's financially possible, the best strategy is to take out a loan for no more than 80% of what the car cost the dealer or no more than 80% of the loan value of a used car.

> **TIP**
> **Union Benefit**
> Many credit unions do not charge extra for credit insurance; since their founding, many unions have believed that death cancels loan obligations.

How to Get a Better Car Lease

Leasing a car makes sense if you want to drive a new or expensive model but don't have the money or desire to own the car outright. Leasing is an especially good deal if you do not plan to keep the car for more than five years, do not drive more than 15,000 miles per year, and are careful not to damage the car's exterior or interior.

But while leasing a car is generally less expensive than buying it, most people end up paying more than they should. Keep these tips in mind the next time you lease.

DON'T BE FOOLED BY THE DEALERSHIP'S ADS

To attract customers, most ads stress low monthly payments in large type. In smaller lettering, you may find that you have to make a down payment of several thousand dollars to get that low rate.

Ads that stress low monthly payments also play down the fact that the lease may run for longer than you think, like 36 months rather than 24, so you may wind up paying additional interest charges.

LEASE **$339** A MONTH* **24** MONTHS
*$1,564 DUE AT LEASE SIGNING

***$1,564 due at lease signing.**

***$1,944 due at lease signing.**

OR LEASE **$219** A MONTH* **36** MONTHS
*$1,944 DUE AT LEASE SIGNING

Important: Read the entire ad before going to the dealership. In the case of television or radio ads, call the 800 number that is now legally required to be announced in the ad to learn about all of the lease's details.

BE AWARE OF ALL THE LEASING FEES

All leases charge acquisition fees, which you may be asked to pay up front. You can also expect to be charged a disposition fee of $300 or more. This fee covers the dealer's cost of shipping the car to a used-car dealer or selling it at an auction.

207

Important: If you are a regular customer, these fees are negotiable and may even be waived.

DISCUSS THE WEAR-AND-TEAR POLICY BEFORE YOU SIGN

Unfortunately, there's no industry definition or standard for wear and tear on leased cars. Therefore, a misunderstanding at the beginning of a deal can be costly when the lease expires. Small problems like dents in the frame, dog hair or food stains on the seats, and a broken power seat can all add up.

Strategy: When negotiating a lease, spend an extra 15 minutes with the dealer going over the definition of wear and tear.

If the dealer is vague, ask him or her to join you for a look at cars parked along the sidewalk, or to walk around a used-car lot. Point out specific types of damage and ask what the costs might be. Then have the dealer put these costs in writing.

Ask the dealer about areas that may be unclear.

Examples: Cigarette burns on the upholstery always cost you money. But what about the smell of cigarette smoke in the car or tiny dings in the windshield that were caused by small stones?

NEGOTIATE THE COST OF THE CAR

Most people are unaware that they should negotiate the total cost of a car before discussing their intent to lease with the dealer.

Only about **9%** of people looking to lease bother to haggle, compared with **75%** of those who plan to buy.

Haggling is a smart move because lease payments are based on the car's total price. Here are the steps to take before you negotiate.

Step 1. Research the dealer's cost of the car. To find out dealer costs, check the *Pace Buyers' Guide—New-Car Prices.* Then try to negotiate a price that is $250 to $600 above cost. Also, be sure the dealer is giving a fair residual value. Check the *Automotive Lease Guide's Residual Percentage Guide* to find out.

Step 2. Call several competing dealerships to find the lowest price.

Step 3. Try to negotiate an even lower price. Indicate that you want to get the lowest monthly payment without adding any money to the down payment. Ask the dealer to check leases from various finance sources, including banks and auto companies, to find out who has the lowest rates.

Only then should you discuss the monthly lease payments and other terms of the contract.

CONSIDER USING THE AUTOMAKER'S FINANCE COMPANY

There's nothing bad about obtaining financing for your lease from a national or local bank. All else being equal, however, it's just easier to deal directly with the automaker's own financial group, such as Ford Motor Credit or GMAC.

Car companies make their money producing cars, not lending money. Therefore, they are less concerned about squeezing every dime out of you for excess wear and tear, or whether you drive 1,000 miles over the limit set in your lease contract.

Caution: If you finance a lease through a bank and you plan to move out of state, you'll need the bank's permission to continue the lease.

BUY A GAP-INSURANCE POLICY

Monthly lease payments do not cover the total cost of a car. You're just borrowing the car and paying rent on it. If the car is stolen or totaled while you're leasing it, however, you are liable for the car's entire cost.

This is why you need gap insurance, which covers the difference between what the car is worth and what you still owe on the lease. Some lessors include gap insurance in the cost of your lease. Be sure to ask the dealer about it before signing the papers.

BUY EXTRA MILES WHEN YOU SIGN THE LEASE

The number of miles you expect to drive and what you actually will drive over three to five years probably will be different. About 35% to 40% of people who lease cars take 12,000-miles-per-year deals, and most of these people exceed the limit, resulting in higher mileage costs.

Example: One excess mile costs 10¢ to 15¢ if you don't buy it up front. Buy in advance, however, and the per-mile cost is only 8¢ to 9¢.

Strategy: Purchase an excess-mileage package when you lease. If you don't use the miles, the fee is usually refundable.

THREE WAYS TO PAY

People choose how to pay for their cars depending on their unique economic and personal circumstances. Any buyer, however, should be able to compare the costs of different payment methods. Here are three ways you might pay for an $18,000 car.

THREE YEAR LOAN

	$3,000	Down payment
+	$1,260	7% Sales tax
+	$20,126	Monthly payment at 10% ($559 x 36)
=	**$24,386**	**Total cost (before resale)**

THREE YEAR LEASE

	$500	Leasing fee
+	$317	Prepayment
+	$11,412	Monthly payment ($317 x 36)
=	**$12,229**	**Total cost**

CASH

	$18,000	Purchase price
+	$1,260	7% Sales tax
=	$19,260	Cost
+	$4,860	Loss of investment interest at 9% (purchase price $18,000 x 9% x 3)
=	**$24,120**	**Total cost (before resale)**

TAKE CARE OF THE REPAIRS YOURSELF

Have any excess wear and tear repaired yourself. An independent mechanic will charge you considerably less than the dealership's mechanic.

Tip: Never take a lease for longer than 42 months. You may end up making costly repairs that are not covered by the warranty. Instead, choose one for 36 months or less.

Tire Saver

If you're leasing a front-wheel drive car, be sure to rotate the tires every 10,000 to 15,000 miles, switching the front tires for the back tires so that they wear more evenly. This can save you a tire charge.

DON'T ACCEPT A DEALER'S OFFER TO TERMINATE EARLY

The offer is fine if it suits your needs at the time. Just be aware that the dealer probably has a motive: In most cases, such an offer means that your car is a hot seller and the dealer can make money reselling or releasing it to another customer.

Important: If the dealer can sell your car at a profit, so can you. Turn down the deal. Then, when the lease runs out in a year or two, consider buying the car so you can sell it and pocket the difference. In all likelihood, the car will still be popular.

To Buy or to Lease?

If you can afford to put a lot of money into a car, buy it. If you do choose to lease, don't be talked into making a large up-front payment to obtain a lower monthly payment. The benefit of leasing is that you reduce your immediate cash cost, but a large up-front payment increases it.

Comparison: You wouldn't sink a big down payment into a house you were going to lease for only two years. Don't do it with a car.

Bargain Car Leases

Used-car leasing is becoming popular as more cars are turned in after their new-car leases run out. Used-car leases cost much less than new-car ones, and bargains can be found among models that are not currently in demand.

Caution: Be sure the car will be under warranty for the full term of the lease. Have an independent mechanic check parts that normally wear, such as brakes and tires; if they wear out during the lease term, you may have to replace them.

And remember, it may be cheaper to buy a used car than to lease one.

Before Your Car Lease Ends

When the end of a car lease approaches, many people are faced with critical choices but aren't sure what to do. Here is a list of your options and some suggestions on how to make the decision that makes the most sense for you.

OPTION 1
KEEP THE CAR

About 65% of Americans buy their leased cars. It pays to buy when
● You've incurred more than the maximum mileage allowed on the car, and it has given you no problems.
● You love the vehicle.

Note: Before you buy the car, there's important math to consider. Buying a car after leasing it winds up costing more than it would have to buy it new. In addition, after a car has 30,000 miles on it, the average consumer spends $1,200 a year on routine maintenance: tune-ups, new brakes, tires, belts and hoses. It may be cheaper to lease a new car than to finance and repair a used one.

OPTION 2
SELL THE CAR YOURSELF

This option makes sense if your leased car is of greater value than its purchase option at lease end. Why shouldn't you, rather than the dealer, take advantage of an equity situation?

Also, if you have a lease-end inspection 30 to 60 days before your lease is over, you may discover that there are damages to your vehicle that you will have to pay for. By buying the vehicle and selling it outright, you will void the lease's normal depreciation clause.

Strategy: Invest about $50 to have someone clean the vehicle inside and out. This is also known as detailing, and it can add $300 to $500 to its selling price. Then run a classified ad. Advertise the car for a little less than everyone else is asking for similar models and years.

Example: If the purchase-option price is $12,000 and the car retails used for $14,000 to $15,000, advertise it for around $13,000.

Begin this process about 60 days before the lease ends.

OPTION 3
TURN IN THE CAR

This is a logical choice if you don't like the car, want to drive a newer model or know that the car you're driving hasn't held its value as expected. But first take these steps to avoid additional charges.

1. Make sure the car is absolutely clean. Detailing isn't necessary, but it might be a good idea and a simple time-saver.

2. If there are any scratches or dents, get an independent estimate of the repair cost. Compare the estimate with what you'll have to pay the dealer for wear and tear. You'll almost always come out ahead by taking the car to a body shop yourself.

3. If the vehicle needs new brakes or tires, find out the cost before turning it in. You'll profit by having the work done before the lease ends.

4. Take pictures or a video of the vehicle in case of a dispute.

How to Cut Your Car Insurance Costs

Every year, thousands of drivers spend more than they need to on auto insurance premiums. By shopping around for the cheapest—and best—insurance company and taking a hard look at your policy, you can trim your premiums by as much as two-thirds.

Example: Across the U.S., the average cost of car insurance is about $750 a year. By shopping around, you can easily cut that amount by a few hundred dollars. If you have a young driver in the family and live in a major city, the savings can amount to several thousand dollars.

Here's how you can reduce the cost of your car insurance.

BUY THE RIGHT CAR

The more expensive the car, the more expensive it is to insure. This is particularly so for sports cars, such as Corvettes and Porsches, which tend to get stolen more frequently.

The Price of Pizazz
It can cost three to four times as much to insure a Porsche as to insure a Buick.

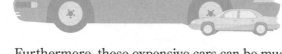

Furthermore, these expensive cars can be much more costly to repair than other cars.

If you're satisfied with your current insurer and are in the market for a new car, call your agent before you buy and ask what the insurance costs are for several different models. That way there will be no surprises.

TAKE A LARGE DEDUCTIBLE

Plan to pay for fender benders and other small claims yourself rather than paying for coverage for them. By paying for these damages on your own, you can save a bundle on premiums and use your coverage only for the purpose for which it was intended: large claims.

Example: By raising your deductible from $100 to $500, you can save 10% to 15% on your total premium, and by raising your deductible from $100 to $1,000, you can save an extra 25% to 30%.

Analysis: If you still believe that a low deductible makes sense, ask yourself whether you would submit a claim for $200. Chances are you wouldn't. It's so small that you would probably pay for the damage yourself rather than risk higher premiums in the future. If that's the case, then why are you paying for coverage that you're not going to use?

DROP COLLISION COVERAGE ON OLDER CARS

Collision covers the cost of repairing your car if you are in an accident, regardless of whether or not you are at fault.

Collision coverage can cost $300 to $400 or more, depending on the type and age of your car. For older cars, the cost of collision coverage can be a lot more than the cost of repairing the car.

Strategy: Drop collision if the premium is equal to 10% or more of the value of your car. To check the value of your car, look in the *National Automobile Dealer's Association Official Used Car Guide*, also called the Blue Book.

DON'T DROP COMPREHENSIVE COVERAGE

Unless the coverage is very expensive, comprehensive covers damage to your car from all other types of incidents, such as fire, theft and storms. Typically, the cost of this coverage is modest—about $50. The chance of a total loss due to theft is greater than the chance of a total loss due to a collision.

DROP COVERAGE FOR MEDICAL PAYMENTS

Medical-payments coverage pays for medical expenses resulting from an auto accident, regardless of who is at fault. It's redundant if you have medical insurance.

DROP COVERAGE FOR TOWING, LABOR AND CAR RENTAL

While the annual cost of these provisions isn't great—perhaps $15 to $25—these charges can add up, particularly if you insure more than one car. And they are usually poor values.

MAKE USE OF ALL THE DISCOUNTS FOR WHICH YOU QUALIFY

Many insurance companies give discounts for a variety of reasons.

- Insuring more than one car with the same company (15% off).
- Having your home owners' policy with the same company (15% off).

VEHICLES MOST LIKELY TO BE STOLEN

Here are the top ten cars that were stolen more than any others in 1996. Honda Accords, some of the best-selling cars in the United States, held 11 out of the top 25 spots.

1. 1994 Honda Accord EX
2. 1988 Honda Accord LX
3. 1992 Honda Accord LX
4. 1987 Oldsmobile Cutlass Supreme
5. 1995 Ford Mustang
6. 1986 Oldsmobile Cutlass Supreme
7. 1995 Honda Accord EX
8. 1990 Honda Accord EX
9. 1989 Toyota Camry
10. 1992 Honda Accord EX

Source: CCC Information Services

AUTO INSURANCE DANGER

A growing number of auto insurers are using credit reports to determine the riskiness of applicants. A bad credit report can result in higher premiums.

Strategy: Clear up your credit before applying for a new policy: Call TRW (800-682-7654), Equifax (800-685-1111) and Trans Union (800-916-8800) for your credit reports, and examine them for problems and mistakes.

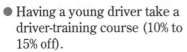

- Having a young driver take a driver-training course (10% to 15% off).
- Having good grades (10% off for young drivers, although some states have disallowed this discount as discriminatory).

Call your insurer to ask about other discounts that may be available.

Caution: Never lose sight of the total cost of coverage. A company that offers you ten different types of discounts can still charge more for the same amount of coverage than a company that offers you no discounts.

USE A DIRECT WRITER

These insurance companies sell coverage directly to the public, not through insurance agents.

Benefit: Your premium could be about 10% lower than rates charged by the major companies because you won't have to pay extra for an insurance agent's commission.

You won't have to sacrifice service if you use a direct writer. Surveys show that direct writers often provide better service than companies that depend on a network of agents for sales.

Two large direct writers with good reputations are Amica (800-242-6422) and GEICO (800-841-3000).

Important: If the insurer is a mutual company, an insurer that is owned by its policyholders, call the company and ask about its dividend history. What percentage of its premiums has it returned to policyholders in the past? Only with that information can you accurately compare policy costs.

Example: The premiums charged by Amica may seem high compared with the premiums charged by Allstate. But Amica has regularly paid annual dividends of about 20% to policyholders. These dividend checks, usually distributed on the anniversary of the date you started coverage, reduce the actual cost of insuring your car.

Car Insurance Trap

Insurers in most states are not required to disclose their underwriting guidelines.

Result: Applicants don't know why they're rejected and policyholders don't know what's required to stay insured. Many unwittingly lose coverage.

If you've been treated unfairly, contact your state insurance commissioner. If coverage was suspended, ask that the commissioner have the company reinstate your policy until the dispute is resolved.

SOURCES

Sources are listed in the order in which their contributions appear. A source may have contributed part or all of an article, or a series of articles.

David Solomon, editor of *Nutz & Boltz*®

The Family Handyman

Barbara Berger Opotowsky, Better Business Bureau of Metropolitan New York

Bill Brauch, Iowa Consumer Protection Division

Kim Hazelbaker, Highway Loss Data Institute

Lee Simmons, coauthor of *Penny-Pinching: How to Lower Your Everyday Expenses Without Lowering Your Standard of Living*

Douglas E. Mark, General Motors Corp.

Stephanie Gallagher, author of *Money Secrets the Pros Don't Want You to Know*

Jan Ocean, editor of *National Automobile Dealers Association Official Used-Car Guide: Retail Consumer Edition*

Amy Dacyczyn, publisher of *The Tightwad Gazette*

Kurt Allen Weiss, author of *Have I Got a Deal for You!*

Bill and Jan Moeller, authors of *RVing Basics*

Art Spinella, CNW Marketing/Research

Ashly Knapp, Auto-Advisor

Runzheimer International

Tom Webb, National Automobile Dealers Association

Art Spinella, CNW Marketing/Research

Kurt Allen Weiss, author of *Have I Got a Deal for You!*

Robert Hunter, Consumer Federation of America

Gerri Detweiler, author of *The Ultimate Credit Handbook*

Robert Hunter, Consumer Federation of America

Paying for College
Plan for Your Child's Higher Education

Last-Minute College Aid Opportunities

Parents frequently go into sticker shock after they receive the first bill from their child's college. If your current cash flow and financial aid are insufficient to cover the cost, here are some ways to make up the difference.

While you are considering these last-minute strategies, don't forget the importance of long-term planning to maximize your eligibility for financial assistance in the future.

Stafford Loans

For dependent undergraduate students*

Loan limits
$2,625—1st year
$3,500—2nd year
$5,500—remaining years

Aggregate loan limit
$23,000

*1996-97 numbers

FEDERAL GOVERNMENT STAFFORD LOANS

You can apply to borrow money for a given school year up until May of that same year. Undergraduates can borrow up to $2,625-$5,500 per year, depending on their year in college. Graduate students can borrow up to $18,500. Virtually all college students qualify for this type of loan.

Benefits: The interest rate on the Stafford Loan is variable with an 8.25% cap for 1997. That is a lot lower than most credit card and bank loans. For students who demonstrate need, interest will be paid by the government while they are in school. Those who don't demonstrate need can elect to defer interest payments until after college graduation, although interest will be added to the principal balance. The college will advise you as to whether you will borrow through a bank or its financial aid office.

Opportunity: If you must borrow through a bank, consider one affiliated with the Student Loan Marketing Association, Sallie Mae. If you make the first 48 monthly payments on time, the bank will reduce your interest rate by two full percentage points.

Important: Other government aid programs for which any student can apply include the Perkins Loan, the Work Study Program, the Supplemental Educational Opportunity Grant and the Pell Grant. The college's financial aid office can tell you about the filing requirements for each and provide application forms.

PARENT LOANS FOR UNDERGRADUATE STUDENTS (PLUS)

Apply for PLUS to make up the difference. PLUS allows parents to borrow the total cost of tuition less the amount of financial aid the child is eligible to receive from the school. The 1997 interest rate on a PLUS is variable, with a 9% cap. Unlike the Stafford Loan, interest payments on a PLUS cannot be deferred until a later date. But, like a Stafford Loan, the college will tell you how you will borrow the money.

DEFERRED-PAYMENT

Most colleges bill students twice a year, but many also offer monthly payment plans to spread out the cost. The two plans that are most widely used by universities are offered by Academic Management Services (800-635-0120) and Knight College Resource Group (617-267-1500).

HOME-EQUITY LOANS

The rate for these loans is variable and usually tied to the prime lending rate. Most banks charge the prime plus one-and-a-half points.

Benefits: In most cases, the interest on the loan is fully tax deductible. In addition, the loan reduces your equity in your home, which can improve your chances of getting more financial aid in the future.

Risk: If you can't make the loan payments, you could wind up losing your home.

BORROW AGAINST YOUR PENSION

Federal laws allow you to borrow against the assets in your tax-deferred pension, profit sharing and 401(k) plans if you need money for college.

By borrowing against your pension assets, in most cases, you will be borrowing from yourself.

BORROW FROM YOUR IRA

If you need a lump sum in a hurry, consider borrowing the funds from your IRA. Federal regulations allow you to make this type of withdrawal once a year on the condition that you replace the funds within 60 days of removal. This resource could be especially important when you are paying the first semester's bill.

Caution: Borrowing from your IRA is a desperation move, and only for obtaining funds for a short term. If you cannot replace the funds in 60 days, you'll be taxable on the funds. But, starting in 1998, there is no 10% penalty on funds used for qualified higher education purposes.

> **TIP**
>
> ### Another College Financing Option
>
> The William D. Ford Federal Direct Loan Program lets college students borrow money directly from the federal government. Turnaround time is faster than with other student loans, there's less paperwork and repayment is tailored to a student's capabilities. Direct Loan is a new program available at 1,400 colleges.

Consider your alternatives thoroughly before using this option. If you decide to go ahead, make sure to consult a financial adviser to set up a payback strategy.

Qualifying for Need-Based Assistance

- Avoid realizing large capital gains to pay this year's bills. Those gains show up on your tax return as income. You want to avoid taking any significant capital gains during the years you hope to qualify for aid.
- If possible, avoid cashing in U.S. Savings bonds. Receiving the interest in a lump sum will inflate your Adjusted Gross Income (AGI) and reduce the size of your financial aid package the next year.

  While it's true that the interest on U.S. Savings bonds that is used to fund education costs is deductible for many taxpayers, the gains constitute income for purposes of the financial aid formula.

Could Saving for College Be a Bad Idea?

Some people fear that if they save to finance college, they will be penalized by having to pay more while those who did not save at all receive extra financial assistance.

Reality: Financial aid formulas weigh income more heavily than assets. If you have good income but no savings, you will still be expected to make a substantial contribution to college costs. Plus, a significant amount of aid is in the form of loans, which have to be repaid. The more cash you save before college, the less debt you and your children will have to pay off afterward.

Top Ten College-Aid Application Mistakes

While it's important to meet the application deadlines, many parents are not careful enough when filling out financial aid forms. They also don't weigh their college options strategically when their children receive financial aid.

Here are the biggest mistakes that parents are making now while they are seeking financial aid for their college-bound children.

1. RUSHING THROUGH THE APPLICATION PROCESS

Many people believe that financial aid is first come, first served. That is really not the case.

The reason many students are turned down for financial aid is not because their parents make too much money, but because they rushed through the aid application process and committed one or more errors.

Take your time. It's the tortoise that wins the race, not the hare. It's better to submit a complete application the day that it is due than to hastily complete the forms and make mistakes while trying to be one of the first to submit them. You'll be rewarded for paying attention to details.

Important: Send all your financial aid applications and correspondence by certified mail. Some schools suggest you send it by first class, but, if a piece of certified mail is lost, the post office can trace it directly.

2. UNDERESTIMATING YOUR FINANCIAL AID ELIGIBILITY

Some families assume that they make too much money to qualify, or think that because their children's friends applied and didn't receive any aid, they won't either.

Those who underestimate their eligibility tend to limit their search to colleges they can afford even if they do not receive aid, such as state schools or community colleges, rather than those that may be best for their children.

3. OVERESTIMATING YOUR FINANCIAL AID ELIGIBILITY

Other families assume they will get tons of financial aid and, therefore, apply only to the most expensive schools. When the aid doesn't come through, they can't afford the schools to which they applied.

Solution: In addition to investigating aid options, always apply to one financial safety school, a college for which your child meets the admission criteria and you can afford to pay for even if you get little or no aid. Usually, this will be a

FINANCIAL AID FORMULAS

The Department of Education uses a standard formula, the Congressional Methodology, to determine how much you're able to contribute to your child's education and whether your family qualifies for federal aid. You will receive a Student Aid Report (SAR) within a month of your application, stating your Expected Family Contribution (EFC).

Congressional Methodology takes several factors into account.

- Parental income, including nontaxable income and money contributed to IRAs and Keogh plans.
- Parental assets if taxable income is over $50,000 (not including the family home or money in retirement accounts and annuities).
- Child's earnings, investments and savings.
- Family size and the number of students attending college simultaneously.

state-supported school in your home state.

It is also wise to apply to your child's dream school with the clear understanding that it might not be financially possible for him or her to attend.

Important: Some high schools limit the number of colleges to which students can apply to five or six. If this is the case, and once the safety and dream schools are out of the way, apply to two pairs of schools—similar schools that attract the same types of students.

Reason: Schools that look for students with similar grades and SAT scores often compete with each other for applicants. If your child is accepted at two similar schools and wants to attend the school that expects you to pay more money, you can use the other college's more attractive financial aid package to bargain with the school your child prefers. Although schools often deny that they engage in such bargaining practices, it happens all the time.

4. THINKING THAT ALL STATE SCHOOLS ARE INEXPENSIVE

During the past few years, the gap between tuitions at out-of-state public colleges and private schools has narrowed. Take a careful look at the tuition for out-of-

The Rising Cost of College

COST OF 4 YEARS OF COLLEGE

Top private schools

Private schools

Public schools

$275,000
$250,000
$225,000
$200,000
$175,000
$150,000
$125,000
$100,000
$75,000
$50,000
$25,000
$0

1991 1995 2000 2005 2010

state public colleges. You'll see that they are no longer the bargains they once were.

Example: The University of Vermont and the University of Michigan each cost more than $20,000 a year for out-of-state students. This is about double what in-state students pay.

5. COUNTING ON RELATIVES

One student's grandparents promised to pay her tuition. Then, the grandfather died and the grandmother needed the money, so she retracted the promise. Although the student was eligible for quite a lot of aid, she had not applied for it by the school's priority filing deadline. Therefore, she received less than she could have gotten had she applied sooner.

Self-defense: Apply for financial aid even if you anticipate that you will not need it, and meet each school's priority filing deadline.

6. NOT APPLYING TO EXPENSIVE SCHOOLS

Applying to and selecting colleges based solely on their sticker prices rather than the discount prices you'll pay after receiving financial aid can be a big mistake. A college education is one of the biggest purchases most families ever make. However, many will choose a school without first investigating all their financial options.

Example: College A costs $30,000 a year and College B costs $15,000 a year. Under the aid formula, let's assume a family is expected to contribute $10,000 per year. Need for aid is based on the difference between the school's cost and what the family is expected to pay. Therefore, this family would be eligible for $20,000 in aid from College A and $5,000 from College B.

Because of the way financial aid packages work, it may not cost more to attend a school with a higher sticker price than to attend a lower-priced school.

Caution: Out-of-state public schools are a poor choice for families that demonstrate high financial need. That's because most state colleges prefer to give aid to in-state students.

Solution: If you can demonstrate financial need, you will usually do better at a more expensive private school than at a less expensive out-of-state public institution.

7. TAKING OUT A PERSONAL LOAN

Taking out a personal loan through a bank for the additional money you need could be an expensive mistake. Check first with the aid office of the college that your child will attend regarding various options. The federal government, some commercial organizations and the schools themselves will usually offer much more attractive financing arrangements.

8. BEING AFRAID OF DEBT

One of parents' biggest fears is forcing their children to pay off college loans in the early part of their careers.

Recommended: The Perkins Loan and the subsidized Stafford Loan are very attractive because there is no interest charged and no repayment of principal until a few months after the child graduates, leaves school or drops below half-time status. This is much more attractive than a home-equity loan or other types of credit which charge interest immediately.

9. RESPONDING TO A COLLEGE'S OFFER TOO SOON

A student was offered a financial aid package early in the year with a deadline of May 1 to respond. The family accepted immediately because the college was the child's first choice. A few weeks later, a comparable school offered a better package. There was nothing they could do, however, since the student had already committed to the first school.

Strategy: Keep your options open as long as possible. Don't disclose your intentions to any school until you have to. If you're going to negotiate a better deal, your strongest leverage is a competitive package from a similar-caliber school. There's no advantage to responding to the school before its deadline. Had this student waited, he could

have used the second aid package as a bargaining chip to get a better deal from his first choice.

10. WAITING TOO LONG TO THINK ABOUT FINANCIAL AID

By senior year, parents and students may get nervous and make important financial aid decisions emotionally and in haste.

Solution: Start thinking about your financial aid eligibility when your child is in 10th or 11th grade. Try to determine how your income, assets, debts, expenses and retirement provisions will affect your eligibility. Hire an independent aid consultant or consult one of the financial aid/college money guidebooks. Make sure it contains worksheets and formulas used to determine eligibility as well as

Begin Investing Early

Here is an indication of what you will need to put away each month in order to afford the cost of your child's college education.

Years until student begins college	School year (fall)	Projected total 4-year cost		Monthly savings required	
		Public	Private	Public	Private
1	1997	$44,743	$94,416	$3,570	$7,533
2	1998	47,428	100,081	1,817	3,834
3	1999	50,274	106,086	1,232	2,600
4	2000	53,290	112,451	939	1,982
5	2001	56,487	119,198	764	1,612
6	2002	59,877	126,350	646	1,364
7	2003	63,469	133,931	562	1,187
8	2004	67,277	141,967	499	1,053
9	2005	71,314	150,485	450	950
10	2006	75,593	159,514	410	866
11	2007	80,128	169,084	378	798
12	2008	84,936	179,229	351	740
13	2009	90,032	189,983	328	692
14	2010	95,434	201,382	308	649
15	2011	101,160	213,465	290	613
16	2012	107,230	226,273	275	580
17	2013	113,664	239,849	261	552
18	2014	120,484	254,240	249	526

Note: Cost figures assume 6% annual increases and use College Board survey data for the current school year as a base. Savings figures assume investments yield 8% annually until the student enters college, at which point saving and investment income cease.

Source: T. Rowe Price Associates Inc.

specific planning strategies. Also, start looking into how different types of schools distribute aid.

Example: The criteria for state schools are very different than those for private schools.

Big College Financing Mistake

Putting college savings in a child's name could significantly reduce your eligibility for financial aid.

Reason: Standard college tuition aid formulas consider 35% of a child's total assets to be available to pay tuition, compared with only 5.65% of a parent's total assets. So putting assets in a child's name can reduce, or eliminate, your eligibility for tuition aid.

Solution: Keep tuition savings in your own name. If you've already put money in a child's name, consider transferring it back to yourself or to another trusted family member—through a gift—before applying for tuition aid. Annual gifts of up to $10,000 each to as many separate recipients as desired can be made free of gift tax. However, if you've put the money into certain accounts, like UGMAs, it legally belongs to your child.

Less Expensive Tuition Option

Sending a child to college abroad may be cheaper than sending him or her to a comparable school in the U.S., even including the cost of trips home, international phone calls and the like. Tuition is often cheaper abroad, and students who become legal residents of a foreign country may be entitled to valuable benefits, such as national health insurance in Great Britain.

Winning the College Aid Game

Here are the crucial steps to ensure that your college-bound child receives the best possible financial aid package.

STEP 1: GET THE RIGHT FORMS
Free Application for Federal Student Aid
Every family can fill out a Free Application for Federal Student Aid (FAFSA). Since there is no income cutoff for applying for federal aid, any family that sus-

---

Getting Help and Information
The Federal Student Aid Information Center offers information and assistance in navigating the federal student aid process.

Helpful Phone Numbers
Call 800-433-3243 if you want an information specialist to
- Assist you in completing the FAFSA.
- Identify whether a specific school participates in the federal student aid programs and provide that school's student loan default rate.
- Explain eligibility requirements.
- Explain the process of determining financial need and awarding aid.
- Send you federal student aid publications.

People with hearing impairments may call TDD 800-730-8913.

Call 319-337-5665 if you want an information specialist to
- Find out if your federal student financial application has been processed.
- Send you a copy of your Student Aid Report (SAR).
- Make a change in your mailing address.
- Send your application information to a specific school.

Helpful Websites
- www.ed.gov/prog_info/SFA/StudentGuide (Provides *The Student Guide* on-line)
- www.ed.gov/prog_info/SFA/FAFSA (Provides help completing the FAFSA)
- www.ed.gov/offices/OPE/t4_codes.html (Lists Title IV school codes that you may need to complete the FAFSA)

Source: U.S. Department of Education

> The cost of a four-year private college exceeds $100,000 at many schools today. At those prices, nearly everyone will need financial aid.

pects it will need aid should complete a FAFSA for each student seeking aid.

The FAFSA is also required to determine your eligibility for a Stafford Loan or Parent Loan for Undergraduate Students (PLUS). The FAFSA can be obtained from your child's high school guidance counselor. Make sure you get the proper version for the year you are seeking aid.

PROFILE

The College Scholarship Service Financial Aid PROFILE Application may also be required, especially by private colleges. This form is more detailed than the FAFSA.

The PROFILE can only be obtained by registering with the College Scholarship Service, a private needs-analysis company. The registration fee is $5, plus $14.50 for each school you designate to receive the data. High school guidance offices can provide information on how to register.

STEP 2: MEET YOUR DEADLINES

Missing a financial aid deadline is worse than missing a mortgage payment. Your bank will likely give you another chance, but colleges will probably not.

Review the admissions and financial aid materials for each college under consideration to determine the financial aid deadlines and which forms must be completed. Be sure to sign the forms, make copies of everything, and then send the documents by registered mail, return receipt requested, to the appropriate address.

Important: Don't wait to be accepted by a college to apply for financial aid. At some schools, you may even need to complete financial aid applications before the admissions deadline.

STEP 3: DO YOUR TAXES EARLY

Colleges determine how much financial aid you should receive based in part on your previous year's income. So financial aid for the current academic year will be based on your previous year's tax information.

Early deadlines: Because the deadlines for many colleges come so early, most parents will probably have to estimate their tax figures on the aid forms. It's better to estimate now and revise your figures later than to miss a deadline while waiting for your tax returns to be completed.

When your tax returns are complete, send copies to those colleges that require them. At many colleges, you will not get your final financial aid package until the admissions office receives copies of your returns, so try to get your taxes done as soon as possible.

STEP 4: NOTE ANY SPECIAL CIRCUMSTANCES

In some cases, your previous year's finances may not be an accurate representation of your family's current financial situation.

Examples: If a parent has lost a job or received an unusually large bonus, or there were large nonrecurring capital gains, such as the sale of a house, you should let the schools know.

Here's how: Explain such circumstances in a separate letter to each school's financial aid office. Be brief and to the point. Remember, these schools must deal with thousands of aid applications in a very short time.

Double Check Your Deadlines

Financial aid deadlines listed in college guides sold in bookstores are often inaccurate. To avoid missing the official deadline, refer to each university's application packet.

STEP 5: COMPARE PACKAGES

Once you've compared the relative merits of the schools that have accepted your child, you may want to try to improve your financial aid packages.

Strategy: Don't accept any college's offer of admission until your financial aid package is set. Otherwise the college won't have much incentive to improve the deal. However, you must accept or reject the admission offer by May 1.

Many colleges, especially selective ones, have become more flexible about their financial aid offers.

What to do: Be cordial and frank. Call the college's financial aid officer to briefly explain your situation. Most likely you will have to mail or fax a letter outlining your reasons for appealing the aid package. Before you call, know the precise amount of increased aid you're seeking. If you've received a better offer from a comparable school, this can be an excellent bargaining chip. Be prepared to furnish a copy of the better aid package as proof.

Easier Way to Repay Student Loans

The Federal Direct Loan Program allows all loans to be consolidated into one simple payment. Payments can be tied to the graduates' income levels, so they pay less when entering the job market and more as their income rises.

Tax-Free College Aid

Grandparents can avoid gift tax by making payments for tuition directly to the institution. A special provision of the Tax Code exempts such payments from gift tax. Tax-free tuition payments can be made in addition to tax-free $10,000 annual gifts.

College Freshmen And Computers

Don't buy a computer for a college-bound freshman without first asking someone at the university's computer center what type of system it uses. Most colleges use a DOS-based system for IBM-compati-

ble units or a Macintosh-based system for Apple models, but not both. Students with compatible computers can work at their dorms or the computer center using the same floppy disks.

Helpful: A laptop model, which can be transported easily to lectures or the library, can be a big plus. Also consider a modem with send/receive fax capabilities for on-line and research purposes.

Cheaper College Housing

Cut the cost of college housing by buying an apartment or small house for your child to live in. Hire your child as building manager for free rent, and rent out the extra bedrooms.

Payoffs: Your mortgage payments give you equity in an asset of value while payments for a dorm or apartment would be lost forever. Rental income may offset the cost of the property or provide a profit. By treating the property as an income-producing asset, you can deduct expenses, such as insurance, maintenance, depreciation and the management fee paid to your child.

Best Way to Pay Off Your Student Loans

Spouses can consolidate their student loans.

Benefits: Consolidating can mean monthly payments that are as much as 40% lower, extended repayment terms and a graduated repayment schedule.

Information: Call Sallie Mae at 800-524-9100.

SOURCES

Sources are listed in the order in which their contributions appear. A source may have contributed part or all of an article, or a series of articles.

Kalman A. Chany, Campus Consultants, Inc.

David Jaffe, College Pursuit and Associates

David Hicks, parent of a college-bound student, quoted in *The New York Times*

Kalman A. Chany, Campus Consultants, Inc.

U.S. Department of Education

Randy Bruce Blaustein, Esq., Blaustein, Greenberg & Co.

Adam Robinson, author of *What Smart Students Know: Maximum Grades, Optimum Learning, Minimum Time*

Jonathan Pond, Financial Planning Information, Inc.

Estate Planning
How to Keep the Most for Your Family

The Biggest Estate Planning Mistakes

You have worked hard to build up your assets. Now you want to be sure that your property will go to your heirs for their benefit and enjoyment.

To do this you need to keep taxes and expenses down. You must look to minimize not only your estate taxes, which can run up to 55% or more, but also to minimize income and estate tax consequences to your heirs. Gift taxes may also come into play. In order to keep the most for your heirs, beware of these common estate planning mistakes.

FAILING TO REDUCE THE SIZE OF AN ESTATE ON A TAX-FREE BASIS
Even wealthy individuals may be reluctant to part with assets while they are alive, despite having more than enough to maintain their lifestyles indefinitely. The result is that Uncle Sam will become their biggest heir.

Solution: Make maximum use of the annual gift tax exclusion. You can give up to $10,000 annually to each person you choose. A married couple can give $20,000 each year. There is no limit to the number of people each year who can receive these gifts.

Caution: Give away first those assets that are likely to appreciate in value in order to decrease the future appreciation of your estate. Don't give away assets needed to provide income for the rest of your life.

BELIEVING THAT A LIVING TRUST WILL SAVE ESTATE TAXES
Living trusts set up during your lifetime with the right to amend or revoke them provide nontax advantages: savings on probate costs and privacy. They do not provide any special estate tax savings.

USING THE RESIDUARY ESTATE TO PAY TAXES AND EXPENSES
Don't have estate taxes and administration expenses automatically paid out of the residuary estate. This is the portion of the estate that remains after paying off all specific bequests, income taxes and estate expenses. When specific bequests and other property

REDUCE YOUR ESTATE TO SAVE TAXES

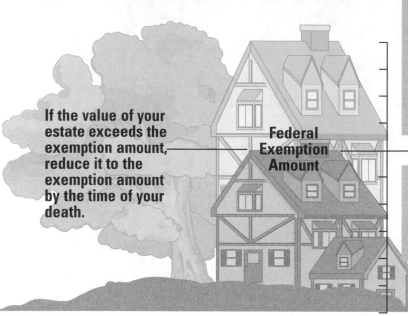

If the value of your estate exceeds the exemption amount, reduce it to the exemption amount by the time of your death.

Federal Exemption Amount

Estates Valued Over Exemption Amount

Estate-tax rates on taxable estates valued at over $625,000 in 1998 range from 37% to 55%. There is an additional 5% surcharge on estates valued over $10 million. Heirs may be able to deduct certain estate expenses, however, and receive a credit for state estate and inheritance taxes.

Estates Valued Under Exemption Amount

There is no federal estate tax on estates valued at under the applicable exemption amount.

passing outside the will are substantial, the heir of the residuary bequest may get little or nothing.

Solution: Understand the impact of taxes on the residuary estate and what it means to the person who will inherit this portion. If you want to protect the interests of the residuary heir, provide that taxes are to be apportioned. Then each bequest will be diminished by its share of the tax bill.

FAILING TO SKIP A GENERATION ON A TAX-FREE BASIS

If you leave assets to your children who have their own sizable estates, the assets will be taxed again in their estates.

If you leave assets to your grandchildren, the tax will skip a generation. However, if too much money is transferred to grandchildren, it could trigger an additional estate tax, known as the generation-skipping transfer tax.

Solution: There is a $1 million exemption from generation-skipping tax. Thus, grandparents can transfer up to this amount to their grandchildren, thereby saving substantial estate taxes for their children.

WASTING YOUR ESTATE TAX EXEMPTION

Each person is allowed to leave an exemption amount before paying estate taxes ($625,000 in 1998, increasing to $1 million by 2006).

Many married couples waste this type of exemption in the estate of the first spouse to die by leaving everything outright to the surviving spouse.

Solution: Instead, married couples whose combined estates exceed two times the exemption amount should use a credit shelter trust (also called a bypass trust) in the estate of the first spouse to die.

Under this trust, assets totaling the exemption amount are held in trust for the benefit of the surviving spouse, who is entitled to all the income earned by the assets for the rest of his or her life. Upon the surviving spouse's death, the assets in the trust pass automatically to named beneficiaries, typically the couple's children. There is no estate tax on the assets in this trust when the surviving spouse dies. Tax savings from using this trust add up to more than $250,000.

Alternative: In very large estates where the surviving spouse is otherwise provided for, the exemption amount can be left directly to children or others.

LEAVING ASSETS TO A NONCITIZEN SPOUSE TO SAVE TAXES

No marital deduction is allowed for property passing to noncitizen spouses.

Solution: Set up a qualified domestic trust to hold assets for the benefit of a noncitizen spouse. This trust must have a U.S. trustee and meet other requirements. The spouse can enjoy the income earned on the assets and the trust will qualify for the marital deduction.

Also: Make lifetime gifts to a noncitizen spouse. While there is no limit on gifts to spouses who are U.S. citizens, there is a $100,000 annual limit on gifts to noncitizen spouses.

HOLDING ALL ASSETS IN JOINT NAME WITH A SPOUSE

These assets pass automatically to the joint owner. The terms of your will do not affect the transfer of these assets.

For couples who want to take advantage of the $625,000 in both estates, see that sufficient assets are held in each spouse's name.

Solution: If a couple has a joint brokerage account, ask the broker to divide the assets into two separate accounts, one for each spouse. The same can be done with bank accounts. Even titles to real estate holdings can be changed to eliminate automatic survivorship rights.

OWNING A LIFE INSURANCE POLICY ON YOUR OWN LIFE

The value of the policy will be included in your estate if you own the policy or if you possess incidents of ownership (the right to borrow against it, cancel it or change beneficiaries). The result will be estate taxes on the policy.

Solution: Set up an irrevocable life insurance trust to own the policy. As long as the policy is transferred to the trust at least three years prior to your death, the proceeds will not be included in your estate.

If you can, set up the trust and have it buy the policy. In this case, there is no three-

year waiting period. If you plan to pay premiums through the trust, make sure it has a Crummey power, which will allow gifts to the trust to qualify for the annual gift tax exclusion. This power requires special language in the trust document giving the beneficiary the right to withdraw contributions to the trust. Without it, your contributions to the trust to cover premiums are considered to be taxable gifts.

NAMING A LIVING TRUST OR ESTATE AS THE BENEFICIARY OF YOUR IRA

This makes all of the IRA benefits immediately subject to income tax upon the event of the owner's death.

Reason: Benefits are taxed according to the life expectancy of the owner and, in some cases, the beneficiary, but neither a trust nor an estate has a life expectancy.

Solution: Name a spouse or other individual as beneficiary of the IRA. A spouse will be able to roll over the IRA benefits to his or her own IRA and defer payment of income tax until age 70½, when minimum distributions from the IRA must begin. Other named beneficiaries cannot roll over inherited IRAs to their own IRAs, but they can enjoy a period of deferral until they must pay income tax on the benefits.

LEAVING RETIREMENT PLAN BENEFITS TO HEIRS

This strategy is costly when retirement plan benefits are substantial because estate taxes on the benefits can cost up to 70% of the benefits.

Example: If benefits were $1 million, heirs might get only $300,000.

Solution: Set up a private foundation and leave the benefits to the foundation. Name heirs to run the foundation. Income on the retirement benefits can be used to pay not only charitable causes but also salaries to your heirs that, over the years, will more than exceed what they would have received had the retirement benefits been left directly to them.

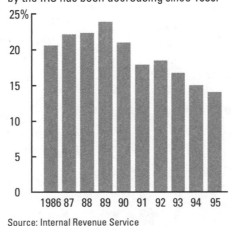

Audit Odds Are Looking Up
The percentage of estate tax returns audited by the IRS has been decreasing since 1989.

Source: Internal Revenue Service

GIVING A PERSONAL RESIDENCE AS A GIFT

Many home owners have seen real estate values rise considerably over the years. A home that they paid $30,000 for years ago may be worth $300,000 today. If they give the home to their children while they are still alive and their children decide to sell, the children will pay capital gains tax on all $270,000 of the appreciation.

Solution: If the home is held until the parents' death, the children's basis when they sell will be the market value of the home at the time of the parents' death.

Note: The same stepped-up basis rule applies to all assets transferred at death, so stocks and bonds, artwork or other appreciated assets should be held until death if it is anticipated that the heirs will sell the property at that time.

THE ADVANTAGE OF BEING TENANTS IN COMMON

If your estate is worth more than the exemption amount ($625,000 in 1998) and your house makes up most of it, you can save taxes by putting the house in the names of your spouse and you as tenants in common rather than as joint tenants. By doing this and setting up a credit shelter trust in your will, you can save a substantial amount of estate tax on the death of the surviving spouse.

When a house is owned in joint tenancy, it passes outside the will of the first spouse to die. But when the house is owned in tenancy in common, you have the right under your will to direct it to go to a trust and be exempt from estate tax.

I.R.S

TIP

Better Way to Leave Your Heirs' Inheritance

Put money into a mutual fund rather than a deferred annuity. If a $10,000 mutual fund investment grows to $50,000, heirs inherit a stepped-up basis of $50,000, which means they pay no taxes to liquidate or withdraw the funds. But in a deferred annuity, taxes are paid when money is withdrawn. If $10,000 grows to $50,000, heirs must pay taxes on the $40,000 gain.

Do Not Underestimate the Value of Your Estate

The amount that is exempt from federal estate tax ($625,000 in 1998) may sound like a lot, but it is easy to exceed that figure without realizing it.

Reason: Your estate includes the value of your pension benefits, proceeds from life insurance, appreciation in the value of your house and similar items that you can't spend now but which will be subject to tax if you die.

Solution: Avoid leaving part of your wealth to the IRS out of negligence. Survey your assets with an estate-planning expert and adopt a plan to avoid future taxes.

Be Skeptical Of Variable Annuities

Variable annuities let you invest in the stock market with the guarantee that if you die before taking your money out, your heirs will receive at least 100% of the amount that you invested—a lure used to attract conservative investors who are afraid of a stock market drop.

Catch: This guarantee typically costs about 1.4% of your annuity assets annually, and you are unlikely ever to collect on it.

Reason: It does not protect you against losses if you live and withdraw your money.

And the longer you live, the less likely it is that when you die the stock market will be at a price below where it was when you bought the annuity.

Buy Insurance To Pay off Future Estate Tax Bills

The sooner you do it, the less you will pay and the more you'll save for your heirs.

Trap: If you don't buy insurance to pay estate taxes, your estate will have to finance the tax bill by paying cash, liquidating assets or borrowing and then repaying the lender. All three options will leave your heirs much poorer. By using life insurance to pay future estate taxes, you may greatly cut their real cost.

Example: If you and your spouse are each age 60, a single-premium, second-to-die insurance policy costing $1 million could buy a $10 million benefit, and cut the cost of a $10 million estate tax bill by 90%.

Family Limited Partnership Benefit

A family limited partnership can enable you to pass business or investment properties to the next generation while valuing them at a discount to minimize taxes.

Here's how: The property owner acts as the general partner who manages the property and makes gifts of limited partnership interests in the property to children or others who become limited partners. Because the gifted interests lack management control and are subject to transfer restrictions, they are valued at a discount of up to 50%. Gift taxes are reduced or eliminated.

If the property appreciates in value, a large amount of potential estate taxes may be avoided on the transferred interests.

Caution: In light of recently-issued partnership anti-abuse regulations, care must be taken in the formation and transfer of partnership interests between family members.

What's in a Will?

Here are the most commonly asked questions about the will, probably the most important financial document you will ever have.

WHAT HAPPENS IF I DON'T HAVE A WILL WHEN I DIE?

If you die without a will, you die intestate. In such cases, the state in which you live makes a will for you. State law dictates who will inherit your property and in what proportion, who oversees your estate and who becomes the guardian for your minor children.

Having a will allows you to make disproportionate distributions to heirs. It also helps avoid family conflicts by appointing an executor to settle your estate. A will can be used to protect a surviving spouse by leaving sufficient property to maintain his or her current lifestyle. It also enables you to control death-tax consequences.

IF I HAVE A LIVING TRUST, DO I ALSO NEED A WILL?

Many people rely on a living trust as a will-substitute. The trust is used to name a person, or trustee, to manage the trust's property, pay debts and death taxes, and distribute the assets to heirs according to the terms set forth in the trust instrument.

Setting up a living trust does not eliminate the need for a will, however. Not everything a person owns may be in the trust. For example, you may have a pending lawsuit that is settled after your death. The award, as an asset belonging to your heirs, is not in the trust. A will can say who will inherit the award.

You Can Use Your Estate Tax Exemption Amount During Lifetime

The estate tax exemption amount can be used before you die to offset gift taxes. If you expect property that you own to appreciate in value, consider giving it to children or other heirs before you die. Appreciation in the property's value that occurs before your death will then escape estate tax. Taxes will be reduced even though your estate tax exclusion is reduced by the amount that is applied against gift tax.

HELP YOUR HEIRS WHEN THEY NEED IT MOST

When planning your estate, make sure to compile a list of the following information which will be invaluable to your heirs and executors when you are gone.

- ☑ Location of will and deeds.
- ☑ Location of stock, bond and mutual fund accounts.
- ☑ Location of valuable property such as boats, time shares, land, jewelry and silver.
- ☑ List of homes owned and caretakers thereof.
- ☑ Name and number of all insurance policies.
- ☑ Number and locations of all bank accounts and safety deposit boxes.
- ☑ Information on annuity and royalty accounts.
- ☑ Details of any businesses owned.
- ☑ Location of essential keys.
- ☑ Name and address of your lawyers, accountants and brokers.
- ☑ Issuers of credit cards with account and phone numbers.
- ☑ List of outstanding debts.
- ☑ Location of birth, marriage, military and naturalization certificates.
- ☑ Your Social Security number.
- ☑ Personal instructions or important messages.

CAN I DISINHERIT A SPOUSE OR CHILD?

You can't disinherit a spouse. All states have laws protecting surviving spouses. With community property laws and what is known as the right of election against a will, surviving spouses are entitled to a portion of the deceased's estate (from 25% to 50%, depending on state law).

However, a prenuptial or postnuptial agreement can be used to waive state-granted rights of protection to surviving spouses. Generally, for such an agreement to be valid (and override state law), there must be full disclosure of assets by both parties and each party must be represented by a separate attorney.

A child does not have the same protection as a spouse and can be disinherited. A will need not leave anything to a child, but should specifically mention the intention to disinherit.

DOES HAVING A WILL SAVE ESTATE TAXES?

The will, by itself, does not save estate taxes. However, it can be used for this purpose.

Examples: A will can be used to make maximum use of the unlimited marital deduction (which allows spouses to leave each other an unlimited amount of property estate-tax-free). It can also be used to allow both spouses to make full use of their applicable estate tax exemption.

DO I NEED AN ATTORNEY TO WRITE A WILL?

No, but it's a good idea to use one. An attorney will see to it that the will meets state requirements. An attorney can also suggest tax-saving measures.

Generally, an attorney will charge under $500 for a simple will. You can save some money by knowing what you want before you make an appointment. Decide who you want to inherit your property and whom you want to name as executor.

A Letter is Better

List your miscellaneous personal property and the people you want to inherit it in a letter —not in your will—and keep it with your important papers. Then you can avoid the expense of revising your will each time your property changes. Just don't forget to destroy all previous letters each time you write a new one.

Note: The executor must report all miscellaneous property to the IRS and pay any taxes on it.

For Unmarried Couples

Unmarried couples should take steps now to make sure the courts won't dispose of their assets in a manner contrary to their wishes.

Here's how: Draw up a will that distributes your property as you desire. If you are not leaving assets to family members who would inherit by law, specifically say so to minimize the risk of a challenge to the will. Review beneficiaries named on insurance policies, retirement accounts and annuities. Review who holds the title to real estate and other valuable property.

Also establish both a durable power of attorney that names a person to manage your assets and a health care power of attorney to name the person you desire to make medical decisions on your behalf if you become incapacitated.

Providing for Pets

To provide for pets in your will, do not name them as beneficiaries. In all states except California and Tennessee, pets are considered property and cannot own other property.

What to do:
- Use your will or living trust to leave your pets, and some money for expenses, to someone whom you trust to take excellent care of them.
- Never make the gift of pets a surprise. Be sure the recipient will be willing to care for your animals.
- Consider making veterinary-care arrangements for your animals by leaving money to a vet who agrees to provide the care in exchange for a lump sum.

The More the Merrier
Have extra witnesses observe the signing of your will, even more than the law requires. If your will is ever probated, one or more of your witnesses may have died or moved away. Also, use witnesses you know personally so they will be easy to locate.

Trusts Are Not Only For the Rich

Too many people mistakenly assume that trusts are only for the fabulously rich and not for those with just a family home, a company pension and a life insurance policy. But even these people can benefit substantially from trusts.

Reason: Trusts save thousands of dollars in gift and estate taxes and provide a way to manage assets when the original owners are no longer around. They also can protect assets from creditors and malpractice suits.

Trusts need to be set up properly if they are to be effective, so be sure to consult a knowledgeable attorney. Here are five basic types of trusts and what they can do for you.

1. LIFE INSURANCE TRUST

Let's say you own your home and have some modest investments, a pension and a $500,000 life insurance policy. If your children are the beneficiaries of the insurance policy, your family could owe the government hundreds of thousands of dollars in additional estate taxes.

Reason: Life insurance proceeds, while not subject to federal income tax, are considered part of your taxable estate and are subject to federal estate tax at rates of 37% to 55%.

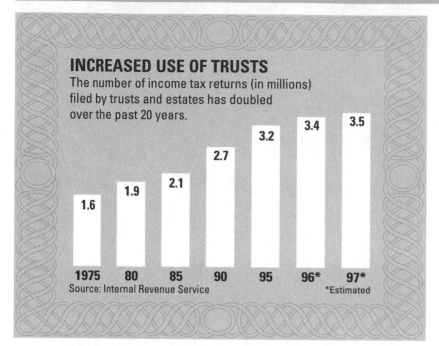

INCREASED USE OF TRUSTS
The number of income tax returns (in millions) filed by trusts and estates has doubled over the past 20 years.

1975	80	85	90	95	96*	97*
1.6	1.9	2.1	2.7	3.2	3.4	3.5

Source: Internal Revenue Service   *Estimated

Solution: Create an irrevocable life insurance trust which will own the policy and receive the cash payout upon the policy owner's death. There are several benefits to doing this.

- **Income for the beneficiaries.** The irrevocable life insurance trust can be structured so that your survivors receive some or all of the annual income generated by the trust. The survivors can even receive the principal—subject to certain restrictions.
- **Avoidance of estate taxes.** If it's properly structured, such a trust ensures that insurance proceeds escape taxation in your estate as well as the estate of your surviving spouse. In addition, because the proceeds are not included in your taxable estate or your spouse's taxable estate, they are not part of the public record and escape publicity. They also are not affected by probate costs.
- **Protection of assets.** The trust protects insurance proceeds from creditors and malpractice actions.
- **Reliable management.** By naming a family member and an outsider, such as a bank or accountant, to manage the trust assets, you eliminate the problem of relying on inexperienced or incapable beneficiaries to handle the trust's money.

2. CREDIT SHELTER TRUST

The primary purpose of a credit shelter trust is to preserve the applicable estate tax exemption that all individuals get in their estates.

Under the law, everyone can give away $10,000 a year to individuals and a certain amount ($625,000 in 1998, increasing to $1 million by 2006) during his or her lifetime or upon death tax-free. Most couples own all their property jointly and have wills in which the husband leaves everything to the wife and the wife leaves everything to the husband. This may not be the best arrangement.

Reason: Let's assume that a couple jointly owns an estate worth $1.3 million. When the first spouse dies, there will be no estate tax because of the unlimited marital deduction. But when the second spouse dies, the estate, which is now larger, will owe more than $225,000 in estate taxes.

Solution: When your joint estate exceeds twice the applicable exemption amount, divide all joint property equally between you and your spouse. For example, change a joint brokerage account into two separate accounts with half the assets in each. Then create a credit shelter trust under each spouse's will. The trust will allow the estate of each spouse to escape tax by taking maximum advantage of the applicable exemption amount.

Example: When the first spouse dies, the assets valued up to the applicable exemption amount go into a credit shelter trust for the benefit of the second spouse. (When the second spouse dies, those assets pass directly to the children or other heirs, with no estate tax).

Whichever spouse survives can have the right to receive all the income produced by the trust. That spouse also has the right to take principal from the trust to maintain his or her standard of living. It's almost like having the assets in your own name.

Important: It's not enough to just create the trust. Retitle your joint property in separate names so that, upon your death, the property can be transferred to the trust in order for it to save your family additional estate taxes.

3. QTIP TRUST

A Qualified Terminable Interest Property (QTIP) trust defers taxes and helps families attain personal goals. Its aim is to ensure that, after a spouse's death, assets exceeding the applicable exemption amount pass first to the surviving spouse tax-free and then to the individuals for whom they are ultimately intended.

Benefit: The trust is often used in second marriages to provide lifelong support for a current spouse. Then, after the second spouse's death, the Q-TIP funnels assets to the children from the first marriage.

Under this arrangement, your current spouse receives all of the income annually from the trust for life. Even though your spouse's interest in the trust property terminates upon death, the initial transfer of property to the trust still qualifies for the unlimited marital deduction.

4. CHILDREN'S TRUST

This trust is designed to provide for your children and addresses a problem that occurs with gifts to children under the Uniform Gifts to Minors Act (UGMA) and Uniform Transfers to Minors Act (UTMA).

Problem: Under UGMA and UTMA, once children reach age 18 or 21 (depending on the state in which they reside), they can do whatever they wish with the money in their custodial accounts. If they want to use it to support a commune or buy a sports car instead of finishing college, there's nothing you can do about it.

Solution: By transferring assets to a children's trust, such as a Crummey trust, the trustee can determine how the money in the trust is to be used and how much the child can receive.

5. GRANDPARENT'S TRUST

This trust is similar to the children's trust, except that the grandparents establish it to help pay for their grandchildren's college expenses.

A separate trust can be created for each grandchild. There is a $10,000 per grandparent limit on the amount that can be placed gift-tax-free in each trust per year.

As with a children's trust, the trust document and the trustee define how much money can be used for which purposes.

Important: Avoid setting up a single trust that names more than one grandchild as a beneficiary. Otherwise, you will run into the expensive generation-skipping transfer tax, which, in many cases, applies to transfers of more than $1 million.

Protect Children from A Previous Marriage

Don't own major assets jointly with a second spouse if you wish to use these assets to help provide for your children from a prior marriage.

Trap: Assets that pass to your spouse may never reach your children, especially if your spouse remarries.

Solution: Establish a family trust to hold your assets after you die, pay income to your surviving spouse for life, and then distribute the assets to your children. This way you can provide for the future financial welfare of both your spouse and children, and eliminate the risk that a third party will gain control of your assets, either by marrying your surviving spouse or otherwise. Also, consider a prenuptial agreement prior to a second marriage.

Ten Most Frequently Asked Questions About Living Trusts

Living trusts avoid probate and legal fees while allowing you to maintain control of your property during your lifetime and after death.

1. WHAT ARE LIVING TRUSTS?

A trust is a legal form of ownership in which property is held for the benefit of another person or persons. Simply stated, a living trust is a type of trust created by individuals or couples during their lifetimes to benefit themselves and their families.

You can name yourself as trustee so that you have complete control over the property placed in a living trust.

Advantages of a trust

● It avoids costly and time-consuming probate for assets held in the trust's name. This is especially valuable when you own property that would otherwise go through probate in more than one state.
● It helps to ensure continuity of your business.

- It lets you keep your affairs private—whereas probate documents are public.
- It provides for you and your spouse in the event of disability, or for minor children if you have them.

Disadvantages

- Trust assets are subject to creditors' claims.
- Property must be transferred from your name to the trust's.
- Because you avoid probate, you forfeit court supervision of your estate upon your death.

Cost: Living trusts are more expensive to create than wills. They cost $500 to $2,000, depending on the attorney and the work involved. There are no ongoing fees if you act as your own trustee.

2. WHY CAN'T I JUST USE A WILL?

Wills do not accomplish as much as living trusts. For example, when you die, property held in joint tenancy, retirement benefits and insurance proceeds are paid to named beneficiaries regardless of what your will says. You are able to control how all of these assets are distributed if they are left to the trust.

Bonus: Wills can easily be contested by unhappy heirs, but living trusts are difficult to contest.

3. HOW DO I PUT MY PROPERTY INTO A LIVING TRUST?

List your property in the trust documents. Put titles to bank accounts, real estate, cars, stocks, bonds and other assets in the trust's name. You can instruct that jewelry, art or other personal items pass through the trust and go to specific individuals.

Trap: Any property omitted from the trust must pass through probate. Some states have minimums ($500 or so), while others do not.

4. HOW DO I CHOOSE A TRUSTEE?

The initial trustees are usually you and your spouse. To avoid having to amend the trust when a trustee

WHAT TO LOOK FOR IN A TRUST COMPANY

Check trust companies carefully before selecting one to administer your estate. Look at investment records, qualifications and tenure of key employees. Consider costs, but know that bank trust departments don't necessarily charge more than you would pay friends or family.

Alternative to an institution: Name two individuals as trustees (they can keep an eye on each other), making sure each has the honesty and basic financial knowledge to serve well. Or name an individual as cotrustee with an institution, making sure to specify each trustee's duties and responsibilities.

dies, list successor trustees to take over when the initial trustees can no longer serve.

Best candidates: Adult children, relatives, friends or financial institutions. You can name individual or joint trustees.

5. HOW DO LIVING TRUSTS SAVE ESTATE TAXES?

In general, they don't. But you save significant probate and legal fees.

Instead of leaving everything to your spouse on your death, you can leave assets valued up to the applicable exemption amount ($625,000 in 1998, increasing to $1 million by 2006) for the benefit of your spouse, ultimately passing to your children or other beneficiaries. By using this technique, called a bypass trust, in the living trust, you can save more than $225,000 in estate taxes. You can, however, accomplish the same tax-saving result by including a bypass trust in your will.

6. HOW CAN I MAKE CHANGES TO MY LIVING TRUST?

Because living trusts are revocable, you can change any term of the trust at any time. It's best to use a lawyer, although you can do it yourself. The most common changes are switching trustees and changing how trust assets are distributed at death.

Note: People who set up joint trusts with their spouses cannot change provisions that become irrevocable at the first death, such as bypass provisions. Changes must be made before a spouse's death.

7. DO I HAVE TO FILE ADDITIONAL INCOME TAX FORMS FOR MY LIVING TRUST?

Not usually. As long as you and your spouse are still alive, you file taxes on **Form 1040**, using your Social Security number for all accounts even though they are held in the name of the trust. However, when the first spouse dies, trusts that have bypass provisions must file a fiduciary tax return, **Form 1041**.

IRS FORM 1041

8. WILL MY LIVING TRUST BE VALID IF I MOVE TO A DIFFERENT STATE?

Yes, a living trust typically is valid anywhere in the entire U.S.

Caution: Louisiana has unusual laws, so consult a financial adviser if you move there.

If you move to or from California or another community-property state, consult an adviser to make sure your trust includes the proper language. You will also need a new will that conforms to the laws of your new state of residence.

9. IF I CREATE A LIVING TRUST, DO I STILL NEED A WILL?

Yes, you need a pourover will. This puts into the living trust any property that is not already there at your death.

Example: If you die in an airplane crash and your estate receives $1 million of insurance, the proceeds are paid to your estate, not the living trust. The pourover provision in the will shifts the money into trust, although it must initially pass through probate.

You also need a will to name a guardian for any minor or disabled children.

10. WILL A LIVING TRUST PROTECT MY ASSETS IN THE EVENT OF A LAWSUIT?

No. Because you have total control over the property in trust, assets are not shielded from lawsuits or creditors. Nor are assets protected should you consider an extended stay in a nursing home.

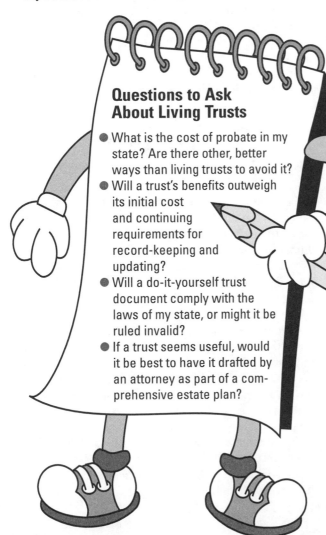

Questions to Ask About Living Trusts

- What is the cost of probate in my state? Are there other, better ways than living trusts to avoid it?
- Will a trust's benefits outweigh its initial cost and continuing requirements for record-keeping and updating?
- Will a do-it-yourself trust document comply with the laws of my state, or might it be ruled invalid?
- If a trust seems useful, would it be best to have it drafted by an attorney as part of a comprehensive estate plan?

Before Buying a Life Insurance Policy

Few areas of life insurance today are more difficult for people to understand than insurance policy illustrations. These are the numbers that insurance agents show to people interested in buying cash-value policies.

The data in an insurance policy illustration project what the consumer can expect to pay in premiums, what the policy's cash value will be worth and what the death benefit will be throughout the insured's lifetime.

Problem: The total cash values of policy illustrations are based mostly on interest rates. Since these rates have declined over the past few years, many people who bought policies in the 1980s are disappointed that their policies' cash values and death benefits are not returning what was anticipated in the original illustrations.

UNDERSTANDING ILLUSTRATIONS

If you are considering taking a new or supplementary whole-life, universal-life, variable-life or variable-universal-life policy, here are two strategies to use when studying policy illustrations.

1. Ask each company the same, specific questions

Ask the agent for an illustration that shows three different scenarios. The illustration should show how the policy will grow at

- The minimum interest rate contractually guaranteed by the insurance company.
- The interest rate the company currently pays, which is usually higher than the guaranteed rate.
- A projection that is one or two points below the current interest rate and slightly above the guaranteed rate, to illustrate what will happen if the current rate drops unexpectedly.

Exception: For whole-life policy illustrations, ask for projections that are one or two points below the current dividend scale. That's because the total cash available in a whole-life policy depends on the amount of dividends the insurer pays out.

2. Compare apples and apples

When comparing the illustrations of two or more policies with similar death benefits and premiums, be suspicious if one company's policy projects considerably greater cash value over ten years than the others. That company may be assuming different interest rates than the other companies.

Self-defense: Ask what assumptions the company makes about future rates when it prices its product

Extra Insurance Tip

For extra health or life insurance, buying supplemental coverage through your employer's group policy often is not a good deal.

Reason: Group plans must supply coverage to all employees regardless of their health and other risk factors, so group plan premiums often are higher than those elsewhere in the market. Insurance is like other consumer products: you find the best deal by shopping around.

LIFE INSURANCE FORMULA

To determine how much coverage you need, assume surviving dependents need 80% of your current income. Divide that number by the interest you would expect to earn over time on a lump-sum insurance payout.

	$50,000	Your annual income
x	.80	You need to provide 80%
=	$40,000	Income needed
÷	.05	Interest you'd earn
=	$800,000	Insurance you'll need to avoid eating into principal

and makes projections about the future.

Also, be sure that similar types of policies have illustrations that run to the same age. For instance, you can't compare one illustration that runs to age 80 with another that runs to age 100. If you choose the first policy because the premiums seem lower, you could be in a bind if you decide to continue the coverage beyond age 80.

Reminder: Pay more attention to values during the first ten years.

Reason: They are more predictable, and most people drop policies within ten years of purchase.

The Hot Insurance Product Now

Variable life insurance is a hot insurance product today. It's the only kind of cash-value insurance that allows the owner to choose the type of investment in which the policy will invest. This is a big advantage. It's like having a mutual fund with the added benefit of tax-deferred growth. In an equity fund that's performing well, you might get a return of 10% or more before expenses.

Caution: There are expenses within an insurance policy that don't occur in a mutual fund. You should understand these before you buy. The sales expenses run from 20% to 45% of the first year premium deposit, dropping to 3% to 5% in subsequent years. The expenses must be clearly described in the prospectus.

Variable life insurance makes the most sense if you expect to hold the investment for at least ten years, so it is better for people who are in their 50s than it is for those in their late 60s.

Cash-Value Life Insurance Alternative

A low-load variable-universal policy charges little commission, so more of your premium ends up in the cash portion of the policy. You also have access to your cash.

Reason: The mutual funds in which the insurers invest are managed separately in case the insurer becomes insolvent.

Strategy: Compare policies' loads and the mutual funds in which they invest.

Life Insurance Trade-In Trap

Beware when an insurance agent encourages you to trade in one cash-value life insurance policy for another, even if it was indeed a mistake to buy the policy you now own.

Reason: If you drop a policy during the first few years that you own it, you forfeit the large up-front fees and commissions that you paid to buy it. Years five through ten are when most begin paying good returns, so that's also a poor time to drop one.

Best: In most cases, if you need more coverage than is provided by a cash-value policy, simply supplement it by buying extra term insurance or another cash-value policy.

Insurance for the Uninsurable

If your health prevents you from buying life insurance, you can still obtain insurance protection for your family.

Here's how: Select a surrogate insured. This person usually is a member of your family (an aunt, uncle or sibling) who is insurable. You create a trust for your children or other beneficiaries, and give the trust the money to buy an insurance policy on the surrogate insured. Eventually, the policy proceeds will pass to the trust's beneficiaries free of estate tax, providing a substitute for the insurance benefit you couldn't obtain on your own life.

SHOULD YOU REPLACE YOUR LIFE INSURANCE?

Before replacing a life insurance policy, ask yourself these questions.

- **Will you have full protection during the transition period?** A gap in coverage could put your family at risk.
- **Will the new policy fully protect dependents?** If you swap a term policy for a cash value policy, you're likely to get less protection at the same price in early years before the policy builds up significant cash value.
- **Are you still insurable?** Illness or advancing age may cause a new insurer to charge you much more than you paid for the old policy.
- **Does the swap help you or the insurance agent?** An agent who is anxious for a commission may try to talk you into borrowing against an old policy to buy a new one, leaving you with a loan to repay that will eat up policy proceeds.

Better Estate Planning with Your IRA

When you leave an employer, you may have the option of leaving your money in the employer's retirement plan or taking a lump-sum distribution of your benefits and rolling it over into an IRA. If so, you should almost always choose the IRA. Here are some reasons why IRAs are a good choice.

SECURITY

Many corporate pension plans are underfunded. Even if your employer's plan is fully funded today, you can't be sure what its status will be years from now. With an IRA, you know where your money is. It's in cash, under your control and won't be put at risk by bad investments.

INVESTMENT CONTROL

You can invest your IRA funds in almost any way you wish: aggressively, cautiously or taking advantage of special opportunities available to you. But funds left in an employer plan are controlled by the plan's trustee. If you have any say at all about how the funds are invested, it's very, very limited.

CONTROL OVER DISTRIBUTIONS

A company pension plan typically will provide you with fixed annuity payments on a set schedule. But an IRA gives you many more choices about how to receive your money. You can take

● The same type of annuity payout.
● Minimum distributions to keep as much money as possible in the IRA for as long as possible to get larger, tax-deferred investment returns.
● Early distributions in any amount you wish to meet personal needs.

BEQUEST PLANNING

If you have substantial savings and wish to leave some of them to children or grandchildren, an IRA offers great advantages over a company plan.

Example: Your spouse is legally required to be your beneficiary of a company retirement account unless he or she signs a waiver of spousal rights. This can be a complicating factor when trying to leave funds to children, especially from a prior marriage.

No such rule applies to IRAs. In fact, you can divide your funds among several IRAs, each with a different beneficiary. This is a clean way to distribute funds among heirs. It may provide children with tax-favored investment accounts from which they will reap benefits for their entire lives. This isn't possible with funds left in a company plan.

Important: When you make a rollover to an IRA from an employer plan, set up a new IRA to hold the rollover funds. Don't mix the rollover money with funds in other IRAs.

Reason: It is possible that the state may have a law making IRA funds immune from creditor claims when the funds were received in a distribution from a qualified retirement plan. A segregated IRA is needed to be able to trace all funds back to the plan distribution.

BENEFICIARY PLANNING

After you've funded an IRA, leave funds in it for as long as possible to reap the greatest benefit from compounding tax-deferred growth.

Because mandatory IRA withdrawals are determined by life expectancy, you can use an IRA to build family wealth by naming the youngest beneficiaries to take the IRA: children or even grandchildren.

ADVANTAGES OF ROLLING OVER YOUR PENSION INTO AN IRA

Company pension lump sum → IRA

● **More financial security.**
● **More investment choices.**
● **Power to determine distribution schedule.**
● **More estate planning options.**
● **More choices of beneficiaries.**
● **Better planning options for your spouse.**
● **Options for longer tax-deferred investing.**
● **Ability to divide money into separate accounts.**

CHILD BENEFICIARIES

If you die before reaching your required beginning date (RBD) for taking mandatory withdrawals from the IRA (age 70½), a child beneficiary can elect to take annual distributions from an inherited IRA over his or her own life expectancy. That is so even if this is 30 or 40 years or more. All the while, the account will reap tax-deferred investment earnings. It's easy to see that even a small bequest can build up to a huge amount when invested on a tax-deferred basis over such a period.

If you do reach your RBD, having a child beneficiary reduces the minimum you must withdraw from the IRA each year because required distributions are computed on the basis of joint life expectancy. A nonspouse beneficiary is treated as being up to ten years younger than the IRA owner for this purpose. The slower payout leaves more for the child to inherit, and again, once the child does inherit, further distributions are made over the child's own life expectancy, so funds can remain in the account for decades.

SPOUSE BENEFICIARY
Of course, you must provide for your spouse's financial security first, planning ahead to make the most of your IRA.

Typical method: A surviving spouse takes an IRA as a beneficiary and simply receives payouts over his or her life expectancy. Upon the spouse's death, any amount remaining in the IRA is taxed and distributed to heirs. That's the end of the IRA benefit.

Better method: The spouse can elect to take an IRA as his or her own, rolling over the inherited funds into a new IRA. The surviving spouse can then name a child as a beneficiary of the account. Thereby the minimum required annual distribution is reduced. In addition, the child eventually will inherit the IRA intact, take minimum payouts based on his or her own life expectancy and receive years, perhaps decades, of tax-deferred IRA earnings.

Problem: The election to treat an IRA that's inherited from a spouse as one's own is often overlooked, at great potential cost to the family. Plan now so your spouse will know to make the election.

JOINT BENEFICIARIES
If you wish a child to inherit IRA funds, do not name your spouse and the child as joint beneficiaries of one IRA which holds all your retirement money.

Trap: The spouse's much shorter life expectancy is applicable to the child and will increase the mandatory payouts and leave less for the child.

Solution: Open a separate IRA for each of your beneficiaries.

THE VALUE OF GOOD ADVICE
Your IRA may be the largest part of your estate, but many estate planning experts are not experts on

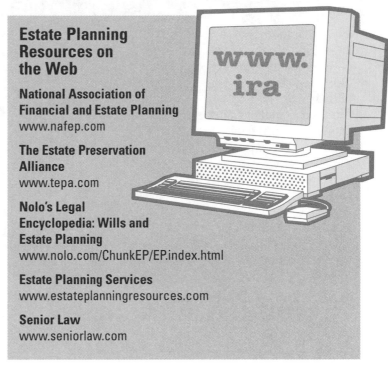

Estate Planning Resources on the Web

National Association of Financial and Estate Planning
www.nafep.com

The Estate Preservation Alliance
www.tepa.com

Nolo's Legal Encyclopedia: Wills and Estate Planning
www.nolo.com/ChunkEP/EP.index.html

Estate Planning Services
www.estateplanningresources.com

Senior Law
www.seniorlaw.com

IRAs. As a result, costly mistakes take place.

Solution: Make sure the person handling your estate has a solid understanding of IRAs.

QTIPs, REVOCABLE TRUSTS AND IRAs
Two types of trusts are currently used frequently by estate planners: revocable trusts and QTIPs. Many estate planning advisers automatically recommend that these trusts be used to hold family assets.

Problem: They can cause the loss of all future benefits from an inherited IRA if the IRA is in the trust.

Reason: When an IRA owner dies, the life expectancy of a revocable trust or QTIP trust becomes zero, so all the money in the IRA must be paid to the trust by no later than the end of the calendar year following the IRA owner's year of death, and is then subject to tax.

QTIP trusts face a second set of difficulties. They are required by the Tax Code to pay out all their income to the spouse beneficiary annually. When a trust fails to do so, its assets become ineligible for the marital deduction and are subject to estate tax.

But few if any IRAs require the distribution of all current income to a QTIP trust. Thus, leaving such an IRA to a QTIP trust will disqualify the trust and incur a surprise tax bill.

Note: Voluntary distribution of all IRA income to the trust does not meet the requirements of the Tax Code. The IRA must be legally required to make such distributions. And even if an IRA should be required to pay out all current income to a QTIP trust, the goal of leaving as much money as possible in the IRA for as long as possible would be defeated.

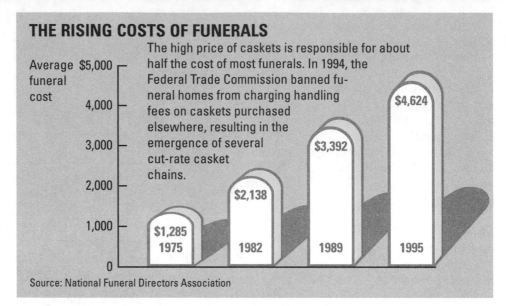

THE RISING COSTS OF FUNERALS

Average funeral cost

The high price of caskets is responsible for about half the cost of most funerals. In 1994, the Federal Trade Commission banned funeral homes from charging handling fees on caskets purchased elsewhere, resulting in the emergence of several cut-rate casket chains.

- $1,285 — 1975
- $2,138 — 1982
- $3,392 — 1989
- $4,624 — 1995

Source: National Funeral Directors Association

Prefunded Funerals Can Be a Bad Deal

People frequently pay the full cost of their funerals ahead of time, putting money in a trust that matches inflation. Often the funeral director keeps any net interest earned. This is a poor investment, because it locks them into using a particular funeral director years in advance.

Other people buy an insurance policy designed to pay funeral costs, but the terms usually are such that they get very little return on their money.

Strategy: Visit a funeral director, make your plans well in advance and set aside funds to pay for them.

Avoid High Casket Charges

There is no evidence that any type of casket preserves a body better than a wooden one, but funeral directors can push expensive caskets by making such a claim. Shop around. The casket constitutes 40% to 60% of the cost of most funerals.

A 1993 survey by the National Funeral Directors Association listed the average prices for different types of caskets: wood caskets averaged $194, steel caskets averaged $907 and bronze caskets averaged $6,000.

SOURCES

Sources are listed in the order in which their contributions appear. A source may have contributed part or all of an article, or a series of articles.

Sidney Kess, consultant to *Financial and Estate Planning Guide*

Martin Shenkman, author of *The Complete Book of Trusts*

Melody Kollath, CFP, Colorado Society of the Institute of Certified Financial Planners

Irving Blackman, Blackman Kallick Bartelstein, LLP

Harold Evensky, investment adviser

Barry Kaye, author of *Die Rich and Tax Free*

Jeff Saccacio, Coopers & Lybrand, LLP

Joseph Toce, Jr., Arthur Andersen

James Jurinski, Esq., CPA, author of *Keys to Preparing a Will*

Martin Shenkman, author of *The Complete Book of Trusts*

Denis Clifford, Esq., coauthor of *Plan Your Estate*

Larry Burkett, author of *Women Leaving the Workplace*

Martin Shenkman, author of *The Complete Book of Trusts*

Stephen M. Rosenberg, CFP, Rosenberg Financial Group, Inc.

Martin Shenkman, author of *The Complete Book of Trusts*

David Klein, Seattle Attorney General's Office

Sam E. Beller, CLU, ChFC, Diversified Programs, Inc.

Thomas Ford, Ford and Associates

Diane Pearl, Moneywise

Lee Slavutin, Stern Slavutin-2, Inc.

Glenn Daily, insurance consultant

Barry Kaye, CLU, author of *Die Rich and Tax Free*

Jersey Gilbert, author of *Life Insurance Handbook*

Seymour Goldberg, professor at Long Island University

Lee Norrgard, American Association of Retired Persons

Dollar Stretchers
Get the Most for Your Money

How to Get the Best Deal on Everything

There are few ways to make money faster than by negotiating. If five minutes of haggling knocks $100 off the price of your new car, you have made money at the rate of $1,200 an hour.

Whether you're buying a car or a house, asking for a raise, or trying to get a discount on a hotel room, it's helpful to know how to negotiate.

Here are some strategies to help you become a better, more successful negotiator.

GET THE OTHER SIDE TO COMMIT TO A PRICE FIRST

Start the negotiations by immediately asking for the other side's best offer.

Example: If you're buying a car, tell the dealer that you don't want to haggle. Say you just want to see if a deal is possible and that you would like to know his or her best offer up front.

Aim: Push the other side to make concessions without your having to make any in return. By using this strategy, you haven't said, "I'll buy from you if you give me such-and-such a price." Instead, you have pinned down the other side to a price in case you do buy.

NEVER SAY YES TOO QUICKLY

Whether you're buying or selling a house or negotiating a new job, a fast yes raises two thoughts in people's minds.

1. I could have done better. This has nothing to do with price. If one party immediately says yes, the other thinks it got taken.

2. Something is happening that I don't understand. An immediate yes raises suspicions on the other side. Is the product damaged or inferior? Once suspicions are aroused, negotiations can stall over minor points.

Strategy: Whenever possible, respond to that first offer with the following strategy. Simply say, "I'm sorry, but you'll have to do better." Then say nothing. Silence typically brings a second, better offer.

MASTER THE FLINCH

You make an offer to buy a house, and the other party counteroffers. Whatever the counteroffer, react with mild shock or pause for a few seconds. This is known as the flinch.

Reason: In most cases, the other party puts a proposal on the table assuming you probably won't accept it. If you don't flinch, the other side will assume you're weak or naive, and will hang tough. The flinch should bring a more realistic counteroffer.

Don't worry if the other party spots the flinch for the bargaining device that it is. It only means that the other party knows something about negotiating. You're always better off negotiating with someone who knows how to negotiate.

Caution: Don't let the flinch or any other gambit lead to confrontational negotiating. Then you may not be able to agree on anything.

Be wary of establishing too much of a rapport with the other side. It may help you to win concessions, but you are also more likely to make concessions you don't want to make.

BE A RELUCTANT BARGAINER
Never appear eager to put a deal together or show that you enjoy bargaining.

Example: You are in the auto showroom, talking to the salesperson just to be polite. If you immediately seemed like a hot-shot bargainer, the salesperson would surely take a harder negotiating stance with you. Instead say, "I'm really not interested in dealing. But just to be fair, because you have spent so much time with me already, give me your best price."

By doing this, you have ended the other party's expectations about getting any deal done. Because we want what we can't have, the other side may give away more to make the deal.

At the very least, you have successfully narrowed the negotiating range before even starting to bargain seriously.

KNOW HOW TO SPLIT THE DIFFERENCE
Splitting the difference may sound like an easy way out.

Example: You want to sell something for $10,000, but the other party offers only $8,000. The other party says, "Let's split the difference at $9,000." Don't do it. There is a better way to proceed that can bring you more money.

Strategy: Be the one who first proposes to split the difference, subject to your getting approval from some "higher authority" to accept the split. The higher authority should remain vague, but it can be your spouse, another family member or a friend.

Example: A $9,000 split is proposed. Say you have to run it by your spouse. The other side agrees.

Now the other side has committed itself, but you still have an out. A day later you return and explain that your spouse won't take $9,000 but will split the difference at $9,500. The other party probably will go along. After all, the other party agreed to split the difference, which you are doing. But your take is now $500 higher.

ALWAYS ASK FOR A TRADE-OFF
Never make a concession without getting something in return. It doesn't have to be a concession of the same size, but it must be a concession. Counter every offer with, "If I do that for you, what will you do for me?"

Example: You'll agree to the seller's price for the boat but say you expect him to include the inflatable dinghy for free.

As long as you keep swapping trade-offs with the other side, you are a negotiator. When you stop doing that, you are a pushover. You'll never know if you got the best deal until the other side walks away and means it.

ALWAYS GIVE YOURSELF OPTIONS
Don't enter into a negotiation feeling that you can't afford to lose.

Example: If you absolutely love a house and will accept no other, you must agree to whatever the other side asks.

You will be a tougher negotiator if you have Plans B and C in case you can't work out a deal on Plan A.

Keep Your Options Open
If you find one house you love, find two more almost as good in case negotiations for the first fall through.

1st Choice   **2nd Choice**   **3rd Choice**

BE PREPARED TO WALK AWAY
Options only work if you are prepared to walk away from negotiations that aren't going your way. If you say, "That's my final offer," and then continue to bargain, the other party will immediately recognize that he or she has the advantage.

Strategy: If possible, combine the walk-away with the good guy/bad guy strategy. Having someone

Try the good guy—bad guy strategy

negotiating with you who has a different temperament or personality lets you double team the other side.

Example: A husband and wife go car shopping. The husband greets the salesperson's best offer with an angry walk-away. The wife stays behind and tells the salesperson, "We're really not so far apart. I'm sure I can get my husband back if only you will be a little more flexible."

MAKE IT EASY FOR THE OTHER SIDE TO SAY YES

If you give away too much, then you're a poor negotiator. If you don't give away something, the deal won't get done. Let the other person feel good about making concessions to you.

Strategy: Keep small concessions in your pocket to be offered at the last minute to clinch a deal. Say, "If you do this, here is something else I'll do for you." The concession should be just enough for the other party to say, "Fine, if you do that for me, I'll go along with the deal." You don't have to give away much, just enough so the other party doesn't feel defeated.

Little Ways to Save Big Bucks

We all want to save money, but no one wants to spend time washing old aluminum foil or tending a goat so they don't have to mow the lawn. Here are some practical, easy ways to save real dollars.

GROCERY SAVERS

- Avoid convenience stores, gourmet shops and specialty markets. Specialty items are very expensive and convenience store prices are high.

- Weigh all produce. Individually wrapped heads of lettuce can differ in weight by as much as half a pound. The actual weight of prebagged carrots can be less than the weight printed on the bag. You might do better buying loose, fresh carrots. Get the most for your money.
- Buy dry staples by the case. Many supermarkets will give regular customers a discount when they buy in bulk.
- Shop once a week—with a list—alone. By avoiding impulse shopping, you can save 15% a year or more on groceries. Buy only what is on your list, and leave grandchildren and spouses at home.
- Stretch and bend. Supermarkets stock the most popular items at eye level. These are also more expensive due to marketing costs, and are designed to encourage impulse buying. Shop the upper and lower shelves.
- Buy store-brand products. Don't pay extra for brand-name sugar, salt, flour, vinegar, bleach or other staples. Most store brands are made by brand-name manufacturers. The only difference is the label and the price.
- Avoid convenience foods. This includes fruit and salad bars, prechopped cabbage, presliced carrots, pregrated cheese and precooked boil-in-bag rice. The premiums you pay for a few minutes' preparation time are exorbitant.
- Don't buy more meat or produce than you need. Just because there are six pork chops or tomatoes in a package doesn't mean you must buy six when you only want three. Ask the butcher or produce clerk to package the amount you need.
- Ask if your supermarket will accept other stores' coupons and advertised specials. Many stores do this, but don't advertise it.
- Buy grocery items in quantities you will use. A gallon of spaghetti sauce may be cheaper, but if you pour half of it down the drain because it gets

Bulk is Better

Ask the manager privately what discounts are offered on cases of paper towels, toilet paper, canned goods, pasta, detergents, soap and toothpaste. Be prepared to shop elsewhere if you are not satisfied.

WHERE OUR MONEY GOES

The Consumer Price Index (CPI) tracks the cost of living in the United States. Each month, the Bureau of Labor Statistics shops for a specific basket of goods and services that is representative of the typical consumer's lifestyle. The monthly CPI reflects the changes in the prices of each item in the basket.

The following numbers indicate the cost of each item as a percentage of the total CPI.

Source: Bureau of Labor Statistics, December 1996

Housing
41.2%

Food & Beverages
17.5%

Transportation
17.1%

---

moldy before you can use it, you've wasted more than you saved.

- Don't buy health and beauty products at the supermarket. It's usually cheaper to go to a discount drugstore.
- Save 35% to 75% a year on pet food and supplies by ordering from a mail-order discounter. Free catalogs are available from The Pet Warehouse (all pets, 800-443-1160), R.C. Steele (mainly dogs, 800-872-3773) and Doctors Foster & Smith (veterinary products for dogs and cats, 800-826-7206).

KITCHEN SAVERS

- Cut down on paper products. Rinse out coffee filters and reuse them several times. Use cloth napkins, dish towels, tablecloths and handkerchiefs. It's cheaper to throw them in with the laundry than to pay top dollar for paper towels, napkins and tissues.
- Pizza stays hotter longer when it's unsliced. If you are ordering a pizza to be delivered or to take home, order it uncut and slice it yourself at home.
- Keep vegetables crisp in refrigerators by lining refrigerator drawers with paper or cloth towels. The lining absorbs moisture that would otherwise cause vegetables to wilt.

Cut Down on Wasted Food

A recent study found that Americans waste about 15% of the food they buy. If your family grocery bill is $500 a month, that adds up to $75 a month, or $900 a year, wasted.

- Milk container expiration dates indicate when milk should be removed from the supermarket shelves and can no longer be sold. Milk generally has another week in the home refrigerator before it is no longer fresh enough to drink.
- Drink more water. It's very good for you, and you'll save a bundle on fruit juice, soft drinks, coffee and tea. Buy frozen juices rather than those that are ready to drink.
- Grease a measuring cup to keep honey or molasses from sticking to it when adding ingredients to a recipe. If the recipe also calls for oil, simply measure the oil first.
- Experiment with odds and ends in your cupboard. Combine the small quantities at the bottom of several cereal boxes for homemade trail mix. Put heels of bread, leftover toast or rolls in a blender or food processor to make bread crumbs.
- Serve smaller helpings at the dinner table. You can always take seconds if you are still hungry. Clear and store leftovers as soon as possible to prevent spoilage.
- Be creative with leftovers. Have a leftover picnic by candlelight. Challenge the others at home to invent new uses for leftovers.

HOUSEHOLD EXPENSE SAVERS

- Know which home appliances are energy hogs, and cut back on using them. It is all right to turn off lights, but savings may not be substantial: Burning a 100-watt bulb for one hour costs less than a penny, whereas one hour's use of a clothes dryer costs 44¢.
- Look into two-tier electricity pricing. In most parts of the country, electricity costs less at night. Run

Medical Care
7.3%

Apparel & Upkeep
5.3%

Entertainment
4.4%

Other
7.2%

Dry cleaning
Babysitting
Haircuts
& more

the dishwasher, do the laundry and clean your oven in the evening when the rates go down, rather than during the day.

- Don't overdry your clothes—it wears them out faster (lint collected in the dryer's filter is clothing fabric particles). Overdrying also makes clothes shrink more, causes elastic to deteriorate and wastes energy.
- Clean the clothes dryer's outside exhaust vent. Like a clogged lint screen, a stopped-up exhaust vent extends drying time and wastes energy. Check the vent regularly and remove any built-up lint.
- Use glass baking dishes and lower the heat called for in recipes by 25 degrees to lower your cooking bill. Use a timer for oven cooking rather than peeking; you lose 25 degrees every time you open the door.
- Pour hot coffee into a thermos or insulated carafe rather than using the coffee maker's keep-warm feature.
- Use a microwave instead of the stove to boil a small amount of water.
- Let dishes air dry. You'll save up to 10% on the cost of running the dishwasher.
- Keep a pitcher of ice water on the kitchen counter. This will greatly reduce the number of times the refrigerator is opened.

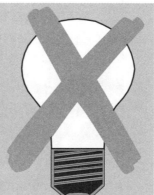

Use Fluorescent Bulbs
One screw-in compact fluorescent bulb uses 75% less electricity to produce the same amount of light as the ten to 15 incandescent bulbs it replaces. The amount saved, even with the higher initial cost of fluorescent bulbs, is about 50%.

- Move the refrigerator away from the oven or dishwasher. Both radiate heat and force the refrigerator to work harder. If it's not possible to separate them, put insulation between the appliances.
- Install a timer on your electric water heater to save $150 per year in most parts of the country. Set the timer to turn the heater off as you go to bed and back on two hours before you wake. Have it do the same when you leave for work.

Surprise: Fiberglass water heater blankets do little, especially with newer heaters that are already well insulated.

- Cut heating bills 10% a month by keeping your furnace in top condition. Have it professionally inspected once a year. Cost: Approximately $50, including a filter change. Then change filters monthly. They cost about $1 each but can save $40 to $100 in heating bills each year.

Also: Arrange furniture so heating vents are not blocked. Keep the door of the fan compartment tightly closed.

- Wear a sweater indoors. Most people are as comfortable in a sweater with the thermostat set at 66° to 68° as they are with no sweater at 68° to 70°.
- Use ceiling fans year-round. In summer, a ceiling fan will make a room feel up to seven degrees cooler. Use them alone or with air conditioning. In

Life Spans of Household Products

People replace household products for a variety of reasons: breakage, aesthetics, the convenience of a newer model or the desire for additional features. Below, data from manufacturers and trade associations indicates the length of time people keep certain items before replacing them.

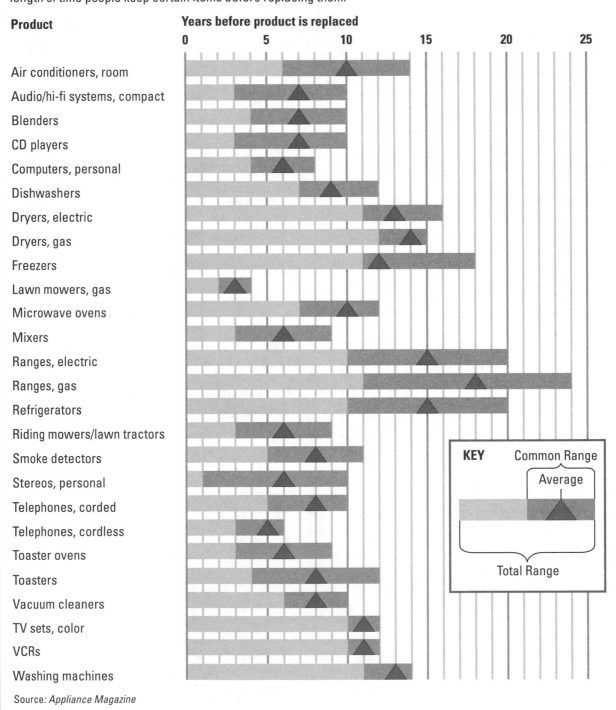

Product

Years before product is replaced

0   5   10   15   20   25

- Air conditioners, room
- Audio/hi-fi systems, compact
- Blenders
- CD players
- Computers, personal
- Dishwashers
- Dryers, electric
- Dryers, gas
- Freezers
- Lawn mowers, gas
- Microwave ovens
- Mixers
- Ranges, electric
- Ranges, gas
- Refrigerators
- Riding mowers/lawn tractors
- Smoke detectors
- Stereos, personal
- Telephones, corded
- Telephones, cordless
- Toaster ovens
- Toasters
- Vacuum cleaners
- TV sets, color
- VCRs
- Washing machines

KEY

Common Range

Average

Total Range

Source: *Appliance Magazine*

242

winter, reverse the fan blades to keep rising warm air lower in the room, and adjust the heat accordingly. The higher the ceiling, the greater the savings will be.

- Aim air conditioner vents up. Cold air falls. Aiming vents upward increases the efficiency of air circulation and lowers costs.
- Plant bushes or trees so their shade falls over air conditioners, which run 10% more efficiently in the shade.
- Cut down on water usage. Install a water-saving shower head, put a brick in the toilet tank (to reduce the amount of water in the tank each time), and don't run water while brushing your teeth or doing dishes. Run only a full dishwasher.
- Drop a denture-cleanser tablet in the toilet bowl and let it bubble away stains. Tablets are cheaper than in-the-tank blue toilet cleaners.
- Make inexpensive curtains from twin sheets on sale. They are already hemmed, and inexpensive.
- Buy white appliances. They are usually cheaper than appliances in colors. Consider buying floor models for an even bigger discount.
- Use less laundry detergent. You will probably find your clothes come out just as clean if you use 10% to 20% less than the package recommends. If you have soft water, you may only need half the amount suggested on the package.

ENTERTAINMENT

- Avoid record, CD and book clubs. Prices are just as good at local discount stores, and you don't have to worry about returning unordered merchandise or buying unwanted selections.
- Go to movie matinees. Bring your own snacks.
- Go to the library. Not only can you save money on books, newspapers and magazines, but most public libraries now lend records and CDs, artwork, videos and computer games. Many also offer free concerts, lectures and paperback book exchanges.
- Use your video equipment. If your VCR and camcorder go unused for an extended period, they can develop a variety of mechanical problems, such as failure to load or eject a tape, rewind malfunctioning and squealing noises. Using the machine helps keep parts lubricated. At least once a month, fast-forward and rewind a complete tape and play it for a few minutes on your VCR.
- Remove loose or curled-up stickers from a videocassette before inserting it into your VCR. Stickers

January Checklist

The beginning of each new year is a good time to re-establish your control over the varied areas of your life. Here's a list of ways you can prepare for the year to come.

- ☑ Set up new tax files for the new year, so you can begin putting records into proper files immediately.
- ☑ Review your estate documents to decide if any changes are necessary due to marriage, birth of a child or retirement.
- ☑ Check the air pressure in your tires. Tire pressure drops as the temperature goes down, and low tire pressure means worse gas mileage and faster tire wear.
- ☑ Update your medicine cabinet. Get rid of all products that are past their expiration dates.
- ☑ Revise your resume. Job openings pick up after the holiday lull.
- ☑ Plan for Valentine's Day.

can fall off inside the machine and damage its delicate inner workings. Exposed glue can also damage the VCR mechanism. Use glue solvent to remove the stickers and any residue, being careful not to get any on the tape itself. Wipe away remaining solvent or wait until it evaporates before inserting the tape into the machine.

- Companies that sell discounted sporting goods advertise in targeted magazines. To find them, pick up a copy of *Golf Digest*, *Tennis* or other publication devoted to your favorite sport.

WARDROBE AND COSMETICS

- Be sensible when buying shoes. Most people have a closet full of shoes, but only one pair they wear all the time. When you find shoes you live in, buy a few pairs.
- Buy shoes at midday or later, so your feet have had a chance to swell. Try on shoes with the kind of socks or stockings you'll be wearing with them.
- Buy accessories to vary your wardrobe. Scarves, costume jewelry, ties, vests, hats and belts can add a lot of mileage to an existing wardrobe.
- Store lipsticks, blush sticks, perfumes and colognes in the refrigerator. They will last much longer.

Shop Seasonally

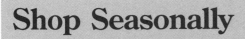

 Buy winter holiday supplies (ribbons, ornaments and cards) and toys in January.

 Buy winter clothing, including parkas, rain gear, sweaters, leggings, boots, hats and gloves, as well as leather goods, in February.

 **Purchase appliances in March and April.**

 **Get indoor furnishings in May and June.**

 Shop for bathing suits, jewelry and major appliances in July.

 **Look for summer clothes, lawn furniture and sporting goods in August.**

Buy lawn and garden equipment in September, which is also the time to put in a pool.

Purchase school supplies in October.

 Scan the classified ads in November and December for deals from people trying to raise cash before the holidays.

New Uses for Household Items

Most of us have been forced at one time or another to use a common household item in an unconventional manner, for instance, a bobby pin for unlocking the bathroom door when your 3-year-old is throwing a tantrum on the other side.

VINEGAR

Replace your $2 to $3 window cleaner, bathroom cleaner, carpet cleaner, drain opener, insect spray and weed killer with a 60¢ bottle of vinegar.

- Clean windows with a mixture of half warm water and half vinegar. When you are done, dry the windows with crumpled newspapers.
- Wash kitchen surfaces with half vinegar, half water to deter ants.
- Use one cup of vinegar per gallon of water on carpet spots, then blot dry.
- Use vinegar to remove bathtub rings and rinse with water.
- Clear drains with a handful of baking soda followed by a half cup of vinegar. Cover, then flush with cold water.
- Spray weeds with a quarter cup of vinegar to one cup water.
- Kill sidewalk or driveway weeds by pouring undiluted vinegar in cracks.
- Add a teaspoon of vinegar per quart to pets' drinking water to help keep away fleas and ticks.

BAKING SODA

Baking soda is a great non-abrasive cleanser for fine china, porcelain appliances, stainless steel, enamel and cast iron. Use it as a deodorizer by placing an open box in the trouble area, sprinkling it directly on a spot or mixing it with a little water and rubbing it on your hands to remove odors.

You can also use it as a facial scrub, toothpaste, mouthwash (one teaspoon in a glass of water) or antiperspirant (applied like powder). One-half cup in the bath water soothes sunburns, insect bites, poison ivy and chicken pox.

HAIR DRYERS

Hair dryers are amazingly versatile. They can be used for drying salad greens (cool setting), removing old shelf paper from kitchen shelves (warm setting

PAINTBRUSHES

These can be used for basting and brushing on sauces (natural bristles are best), for dabbing detergent onto stains, for removing sand from beach chairs, shoes, blankets and bare feet, and for dusting wicker furniture, baskets, typewriter keys and other hard-to-reach crevices. The small sponge paintbrushes are great for applying calamine lotion to bug bites and rashes or the chicken pox.

MILK CARTONS

Heavy furniture can be moved more easily if you place crushed cartons under the legs to create a sliding action.

MUFFIN TINS

Muffin tins can be used as containers for children's paints, as condiment holders, as a divider system in your desk drawer or in the workshop, as trays for cold drinks or as stable oven containers for baked apples, stuffed peppers or potatoes.

TOOTHPASTE

Toothpaste removes stubborn smells from hands (even fishy smells), removes some stains on clothing and dress shoes, works as an emergency white filler for little nail holes left in the wall and removes tar from the bottom of bare feet. It can also be used to clean chrome and silver, to scrub crayon marks from painted walls, to clean jewelry, to remove yellow stains on your fingernails and to dry up pimples.

TOOTHBRUSHES

Use toothbrushes to clean combs (just dip the toothbrush in alcohol and scrub each side), scrub toenails and fingernails, clean faucets and between tiles in the bathroom, scrub stains on cloth before washing and as chew toys for teething babies.

PIZZA CUTTERS

Pizza cutters are great for trimming the crusts from bread, cutting up French toast, pancakes and spaghetti for children, loosening sticky or painted-shut sash windows, and for tracing a sewing pattern as you cut the fabric.

loosens the glue), defrosting frozen pipes or clearing up diaper rash (use on cool to air-dry baby's bottom between changes).

Clever Ways to Pinch Your Pennies

Examine your routine expenditures. Say you get a $12 haircut every two weeks. By extending your routine by just four days to an 18-day interval, you'll cut your hair expenses from $312 to $240 a year.

A person who wears disposable contact lenses that must be replaced weekly can lower the annual cost by almost 25% by wearing eyeglasses for two or three days between lens changes, a reduction from 52 to 40 pairs of lenses per year.

	Time Frame	Cost
Get a $12 haircut	Every 2 weeks	**$312** per year
	Every 18 days	**$240** per year
Replace your contact lenses	Every week	**52** pairs per year
	Wear glasses 2-3 days between changes	**40** pairs per year

Use the MESS Shopping System

M. **Make a list** before shopping to force you to decide in advance what you need and what you don't.

E. **Evaluate** what are truly necessities and what you can live without.

S. **Shop the ads** which can alert you to where the best buys are.

S. **Stick to your agenda** and don't get distracted by impulse items.

Share Tasks, Tools And Time

Organize exchanges and bargaining co-ops with friends and neighbors.

Examples: You buy the electric drill and they buy the leaf-blower. You agree to baby-sit in exchange for help with chores. When contracting for services such as lawn care, carpet cleaning, window washing or driveway resurfacing, coordinate with neighbors and negotiate a group discount.

TIP

Low-Fat Diets Can Save Money

A typical low-fat diet, with 30% of total calories coming from fat, costs 75¢ less per person per day than a typical higher-fat diet.

Result: Low-fat shopping can save a family of four almost $1,100 a year.

The Top Ten Shopping Mistakes

Shopping for the best deal on a major purchase means more than simply finding the lowest price. Today's best shoppers must also prioritize their shopping needs, balance quality against price and seek superior service from merchants and manufacturers. A mistake in any of these areas can be troublesome. Here are the ten most costly mistakes shoppers make, and how to avoid them.

1. FAILING TO ASK QUESTIONS

Shoppers who don't ask questions risk making the most costly mistake of all—buying something they won't use.

The most common reasons shoppers don't question salespeople are fear of appearing stupid, fear of challenging or offending the salesperson, reluctance to take the time and not knowing what to ask.

Important: If you feel intimidated or pressured by a salesperson, shop elsewhere.

When considering a major purchase, ask to speak with the owner, manager, buyer or in-house expert on the product. Let the store know you'll be a repeat customer if you are satisfied.

2. ASKING YES AND NO QUESTIONS

You want to discuss your needs and which item best meets them, not which item the store wants most to sell you.

Don't ask: "Is this a good product? Does this look good on me?"

Ask: "How does this product compare with its competitors? May I see your other casual shirts and jackets? Is there anything else I should have asked that I didn't?"

3. STOPPING AFTER ONE QUESTION

Shoppers often address their key concern and then stop asking questions.

Example: "My last washer didn't have a delicate cycle. Does this one clean delicate fabrics?"

Strategy: Continue by asking, "What won't it clean? What's the advantage of a top loader versus a front loader? How much noise does it make?"

4. FAILING TO ASK YOURSELF QUESTIONS

Shoppers who don't clarify their purpose and prioritize their needs risk overspending on unnecessary features, or not buying the ones they need.

Tip: Before deciding on a major purchase, take the time to ask, "What do I need this item to do? What is my budget? Which features are necessities? What are wish-list features worth to me?"

Examples: An automatic ice-maker or exterior ice/water dispenser can add $300 to the cost of a refrigerator. Are these features you need, or simply ones you want? How much extra are you willing to pay? An automatic bleach/softener dispenser may seem unnecessary, but not if your washing machine is in the basement.

5. NEGLECTING TO DO RESEARCH

Shoppers who don't do their homework are more vulnerable to impulse buying and smooth-talking salespeople.

Frequent victims: older people buying their first computer or younger people buying their first car.

Shop Smart

If you are not a person who enjoys reading *Consumer Reports*, interviewing salespeople and comparison shopping, consult friends or advisers whose expertise you trust.

Online Information for Consumers

Better Business Bureau
www.bbb.org

Consumer Information Center
www.pueblo.gsa.gov

Consumer Partners
www.mindspring.com/~mjc4/partners

Consumer Product Safety Commission
www.cpsc.gov/cpscpub/pubs/cpsr.html

Federal Trade Commission
www.ftc.gov

House of Representatives Law Library
www.law.house.gov

National Institute for Consumer Education
www.emich.edu/public/coe/nice

7. FAILING TO READ GUARANTEES AND WARRANTIES

Many people buy unnecessary service contracts or extended warranties because they don't understand the coverage they have already paid for as part of the vendor or manufacturer's warranty.

Example: Cars usually come with three- to seven-year protection plans. Extended warranties, plans that begin when the manufacturer's warranty expires, are typically filled with small print and exclusions.

Caution: Be aware that most manufacturer's warranties are sufficient. Read the fine print before spending hundreds of dollars on coverage you're not likely to use.

8. PRACTICING MISGUIDED BRAND LOYALTY

Many shoppers automatically buy the same brand they have bought for years, regardless of price. But corporations have changed radically in the past decade.

9. NOT FACTORING IN THE VALUE OF SERVICE

If the two discount appliance stores in your area match each other's prices, why not choose the one with free delivery?

10. RELAXING YOUR JUDGMENT WHILE TRAVELING

Don't be seduced into overspending while you're on vacation. Remember that even reasonably priced goods can turn out to be expensive once customs and shipping charges are added.

6. PAYING FOR IMPROVED TECHNOLOGY

Many shoppers believe it's always best to buy the latest technology. This may be true when buying a high-tech item, such as a computer, but do you really need to program your VCR for months in advance? Improved electronics can even be a drawback, especially with cars or appliances.

Examples: Electronic touchpad controls add to the cost of dishwashers, washers, dryers and stoves. Automatic windows and locks add to the price of a car even though they malfunction more often than dials or knobs, don't improve performance and can be costly to repair.

Strategy: Try the mechanical controls. If you are bothered by arthritis, the convenience of touchpad controls may be worth the extra cost. Otherwise, why pay more?

Get It in Writing

Beware 0% interest financing deals offered by retailers. They often come with strings attached that are not disclosed by salespeople.

Self-defense: Read all the small print in newspaper advertisements. Ask the retailer to give you a written description of all terms and conditions that apply.

Just in Case It Breaks

Write the date, place of purchase and warranty expiration date with a permanent marker at the bottom of each new appliance or any other equipment you purchase. Having this information at your fingertips will save time should you need to call a repairman or order replacement parts.

Home Shopping Channels Trap

Home shopping channels prey on viewers' hunger for friendship and luxury.

Because order-takers talk to them, viewers who are lonely and alienated, especially the elderly, often fall victim to the need for companionship. They then buy more, sometimes much more, than they could ever need.

Others fall prey to the lure of opulence, and these channels sell truckloads of low-quality jewelry, rugs and other accessories.

Much Shrewder Outlet Shopping

Remember these tips to get even bigger bargains at bargain outlets.

BE READY TO BARGAIN

Bargaining with the manager is acceptable. If you find an item that you like but feel that the price should be lower because of a flaw, talk to the manager. Explain what is wrong with the merchandise and make a counteroffer.

Example: Ask to have $5 taken off for a missing button or $10 for a more serious problem.

Look in Back

The best bargains are often found in the back of the store. In many stores, there is a table or rack with clearance merchandise priced below everyday sale items.

CALL AHEAD

Call ahead if you are looking for a specific item. You can call some outlet stores and ask if they have a particular dress or sports jacket that you found for full price at a retail store.

In most cases, you won't be able to buy the item over the phone, but some stores will hold it for you.

BRING A GROUP

Going with a group can get you red-carpet treatment. If you are planning a bus trip to an outlet center with a group of 25 people or more, call the center's manager. Many centers will help subsidize the trip, greet your group personally, give out refreshments and even offer special group savings.

How to Tell if a Sale Is Really a Bargain

Go through your newspaper's Sunday circulars and make calls to several stores. Sales have become so common that it is impossible to tell if 50% off is an actual bargain or a decrease in an artificially inflated list price.

Strategy: Ignore promises of 30%, 40% or 50% off and focus on what you will actually pay for an item. A store advertising 20% off may actually have a lower price than one claiming 50% off.

The Secrets to Not Overspending

Here are some reasons that we overspend, and how to limit your debt.

THE URGE TO SPLURGE

We are a nation of overspenders. In 1994 alone, Americans charged $611 billion on credit cards, up 23% from the year before. Here are the primary reasons for such excess.

Seduction by hard-to-resist advertising

Everyone is influenced to spend money by the promises of enhanced status and improved self-image that are made in TV and print advertising. It is natural to respond to these enticements, but you can get into financial trouble if you spend more than you can afford.

Sense of entitlement

Credit cards enable us to buy what we want and not deal with the consequences until later. We may feel we deserve something whether we can afford the item or not.

Need to combat emptiness

In our high-speed culture, we spend money whether we have it or not to counteract feelings of loneliness or depression, or even as an outlet for feelings of elation.

Fear of looking cheap

When buying gifts for others or throwing holiday parties, many people overspend on food and accessories because they don't want others to think they are stingy. Once you confront these self-defeating behaviors, you'll be on the road to recovery.

HOW TO AVOID OVERSPENDING

Follow these guidelines to begin to reduce your everyday spending.

Get an overview of your money

Write down how much you earn each day after taxes, and list all of the money you owe, including credit card debt and car loans.

By calculating your earnings and listing your debt, you are becoming more aware of how long it takes to earn what you're thinking of spending, and how hard it is to pay off what you already owe. Consider taking the list of debts along when you shop.

Before you go shopping, make a list of what you intend to buy and set a limit on how much you are going to spend.

In 1993, Americans paid $36 billion in credit card interest alone.

70% of all credit card holders carry a balance.

The typical credit card holder pays 17.6% interest.

Source: Federal Reserve Board; Bankcard Holders of America

Keep a spending diary

Before a shopping trip, write down your feelings about what you're interested in buying. During and after your trip, the more honestly you record your thoughts and feelings, the better you'll understand what tempts you to overspend and how you can stop it.

Avoid your points of temptation

Many overspenders tend to be more tempted in certain predictable places, such as malls. Others begin by planning to shop for friends but end up buying many items for themselves.

Hold on to Your Receipts
Developing this habit means you will always have them if a problem arises.

KEEP THIS SLIP FOR REFERENCE

Rethink Traditional Gift-Giving

Going into debt is not what the holidays should be about. If the pleasure of exchanging gifts threatens to turn into the pain of payments you can't afford, agree with friends and family members to limit how much you'll spend.

Instead of a display of extravagance, make gift-giving an exercise in creativity. A photograph, a poem or a small family heirloom is a truly personal gift that conveys more love and caring than a costly, store-bought item ever could.

How to Cut Holiday Shopping Bills in Half

- Get family members to agree not to buy each other presents. Instead, exchange items you own that your relations have long admired.
- Take a hard look at your current credit card bills before going shopping. There's nothing like a debt reminder to bring a spending spree down to earth. Try writing the balances on tiny Post-Its and sticking them on your credit cards.
- Make a list and check it twice. Set a budget. To

avoid going overboard, shop early in the season. You're more likely to find what you can afford.

- Don't go wild treating yourself. Remember it's time for sharing joy with others, not for spending money on your own desires.
  - Tipping is important, but don't play Santa. Giving cash says "thanks," but don't go broke doing it.

'TIS THE SEASON FOR TIPPING

Everyone uses different criteria when tipping service providers during the holiday season. Remember that a tip is your way of thanking someone for a job well done (and hopefully a job that will continue to be well done), so use your own discretion when choosing a number. Here are some typical amounts.

Baby-sitter	One to two nights' pay	Housekeeper	One to two weeks' pay
Building superintendent	$50-$100	Nanny	One to two weeks' pay
Doorman	$20-$25		
Garbage collector	$15-$50	Newspaper carrier	$15-$50
Garage attendant	$20-$100		

PRESSED-FLOWER STATIONERY

This is extremely expensive to buy at a store, but you can make it cheaply yourself. Buy flowers and press them between layers of newspaper or inside a phone book with a heavy weight on top. Use small whole flowers or single large petals. The flowers will take two to three weeks to dry before they're ready to arrange on cards or folded paper. Use white glue to attach flowers.

THEME GIFT BASKET

This is ideal for someone who is passionate about cooking, gardening, sports, the outdoors or any hobby. Fill the basket with items related to that person's interest.

Time for Do-It-Yourself Gifts

Have fun and save money making special holiday presents for your friends and family.

A GIFT OF SELF

This homemade coupon can be redeemed for a day of baby-sitting, a meal (the gift-giver cooks, serves and washes the dishes), a car wash or chores. This is a particularly good gift for a child to give a friend or relative because it costs little or nothing.

HOMEMADE FAMILY VIDEO

To thrill grandparents at little expense, make a copy of parts of home videos taped during the past year. Copies can be made at electronics or stationery stores or your local library. Or hook up two videotape machines to the television and make copies yourself.

PERSONALIZED PHOTO ALBUM

Assemble a scrapbook based on a friend or relative's life. These are invariably a big hit with children and adults alike.

Tipping at Expensive Restaurants Can Be Confusing

If you were happy with the service, tip 20% of the bill, excluding the tax. If there was a captain (the person who took your order and managed the waiter), give him or her 25% to 30% of the total tip. The sommelier (the person who recommended and served the wine), should receive 10% of the cost of the wine in cash ($5 minimum).

FIGURING YOUR TIP

$100 food
+ $100 wine
= $200 bill (before tax)

Server	Tip	How it's figured
Waiter	$40	20% of $200 bill (before tax)
Captain	$10-$12	25%-30% of waiter's $40 tip
Sommelier	$10	10% of $100 wine bill

Better Fine Dining
Instead of fighting for reservations at that hot, new restaurant that everyone's talking about, try going there for lunch. It'll be easier to get a table, and you'll often pay less for the same food.

Put on a Yard Sale That Sells

Take time to prepare. Don't decide today to have a yard sale tomorrow. Planning is the key to a successful yard sale.

Helpful: If you regularly hold a yard sale, set aside a closet or out-of-the-way corner in which to store items you want to sell. Price items as you put them away so you'll be well-organized when the time comes to hold the sale.

- **Gain power in numbers.** Try to get someone else on the block to hold a sale at the same time; shoppers like to go to multifamily sales.
- **Give buyers time to get there.** Hold your sale over at least a two-day period to give as many people as possible the chance to shop your goods.

Even better: Hold a three-day sale, with the first day on a Friday (when you get fewer, but more serious, shoppers).

- **Protect yourself.** Check your home-owner's insurance to make sure you are covered in case of accidents.
- **Be ruthless.** Don't be sentimental with items that once meant something, but that you no longer use or need. Let somebody else develop an emotional attachment to your junk.
- **Know what sells.** Try wooden chairs and tables, lamps, wicker

baskets, patio furniture, lawn and garden tools, overcoats and appliances, especially in their original boxes.

Caution: Old toys, dolls and other items might be collectibles, so don't give them away.

Also: Campy is chic, so don't be afraid to put out your old bowling shirts, celebrity mementos, lava lamp, club pins, ties and hats.

- **Respect your customers.** Don't try to pawn off stained or broken goods. You'll only drive away potential customers.
- **Price items reasonably.** Shop for similar items in antique and thrift stores, and then price your goods 25% to 50% lower than the stores do.

Fabulous Freebees

Take a good look before you respond to an offer for anything free. If you have to pay for shipping and handling, you've paid for the item. There are many worthwhile companies who really will send you valuable products, guides and information—absolutely free. Here are some of the best.

EARRINGS
Simply Whispers makes lightweight, earrings for supersensitive ears. Silver styles are polished surgical steel. Gold styles are electroplated 24-karat gold.

Free offer: a pair of earrings plus catalog.

Simply Whispers, Roman Research, 430 Court St., Dept. 94P4-0406, Plymouth, MA 02360, 800-445-9088 (Ask for operator 94P4-0406).

HARMONICA LESSONS
Hohner, Inc. demands that even their least expensive harmonicas meet rigorous standards of craftsmanship.

Free offer: a 24-page beginner's guide to playing the harmonica.

Send a stamped, self-addressed, business-size envelope to Hohner, Inc., Box 15035, Richmond, VA 23227, 804-550-2700.

TOY FADS	
1960's	**1990's**
Hula Hoops	Virtual Pets
Silly Putty	Beanie Babies
Slinkies	Tickle Me Elmo

VITAMINS

Daily's Food Supplements offers vitamins and minerals that have been formulated by a renowned cardiac surgeon who combed the findings of more than 100 scientific studies on the benefits of vitamins, minerals and antioxidants.

Free offer: an antioxidant chart.

Daily's Food Supplements, 3665 Kearney Villa Rd. #301, San Diego, CA 92123, 800-483-2459.

Information on Anything

Free or low-cost information on hundreds of health, family and consumer issues is available through the U.S. Consumer Information Center. The center's free catalog offers more than 200 publications.

Subjects: health and nutrition, cars, children, federal programs, money, small business, travel and hobbies. Send your name and address to *Consumer Information Catalog*, Pueblo, CO 81009.

Fun (and Funny) Government Freebees

Strictly speaking, these items aren't really free because your tax dollars pay for them. So why not order yourself a few?

FUN FOR EVERYONE

- **Assorted pamphlets** that prove the government does not lack a sense of humor include *Fiber: Something Healthy to Chew On* and *Question: When Do You Need an Antacid?*, both from the FDA (301-827-4420), and *Citizen's Guide to Pest Control* from the EPA (800-490-9198).
- **Copies of UFO sighting reports** the government investigated for the Project Blue Book. An index is available from which you can order reports. Textual Reference Branch, National Archives at College Park, 8601 Adelphi Rd., College Park, MD 20740-6001, 301-713-7250.

- **U.S. Postal Service Coloring Book** (Notice 71). In addition to this coloring book, the U.S. Postal Service will send you free mailing labels, handbooks, posters, publications or an SDA consumer protection packet. Congressional and Public Affairs Branch, U.S. Postal Service, 475 L'Enfant Plaza SW, Washington, DC 20260.
- **Changes in the One Dollar Bill Since July 1929.** An information sheet describing the value of a buck. Maybe this isn't so funny. Bureau of Engraving and Printing, U.S. Department of the Treasury, 14 and C Sts. SW, Washington, DC 20228, 202-874-3019.
- **Civilian astronaut application.** For private citizens who dream about participating in the Space Shuttle program. Perhaps you'd like one for an annoying neighbor? NASA, Lyndon B. Johnson Space Center, Mail Slot AHX, Houston, TX 77058, 281-483-5907.
- **Free photo of Socks,** the first cat. You can also get free photos of the president or first couple. Write to The President, The White House, Washington, DC 20500, Attn: Photo Request.
- **Massage Your Cat** video. This is only one of the many titles listed in the free catalog of videos available through your local library, *Audio-Visuals Related to Animal Care, Use and Welfare*. Animal Welfare Info. Center, National Agricultural Library, 10301 Baltimore Blvd., Beltsville, MD 20705, 301-504-6212.

ESPECIALLY FOR KIDS

- ***Save Our Species*** is a fun-filled coloring book that introduces children to 21 endangered plants and animals found in the United States. EPA Pub-

Free Books

The Library of Congress gives away thousands of duplicate or unneeded books to nonprofit groups.

Important: You will need to travel to the Library to select the books.

More information: Exchange and Gift Division, Madison Building, 101 Independence Ave. SE, Room B-03, Washington, DC 20540.

lisher's Clearinghouse, PO Box 42419, Cincinatti, OH 45242, 800-490-9198.

- *Earthquakes, Safety and Survival in an Earthquake* is just one of several free publications offered by the United States Geological Survey to answer children's questions regarding earthquakes. U.S. Geological Survey, Box 25046, MS-967, Denver Federal Center, Denver, CO 80225, 303-273-8500.

- *Fun Facts about Money* is one of several free information sheets that teaches children about money and how it is printed. Other information sheets cover engravers and engraving, the history of money and how the value of the dollar has changed over the years. Bureau of Engraving and Printing, U.S. Department of the Treasury, 14 and C Sts. SW, Washington, DC 20228.

- *Tree Rings: Timekeepers of the Past* is a booklet that explains how past environmental conditions have been recorded in tree rings and how this information is interpreted by scientists. U.S. Geological Survey, Box 25286, Denver, CO 80225, 303-236-5900.

- **Solar System Puzzle Kit** is an activity for grandparents and children to enjoy together. Kids are asked to assemble an eight-cube paper puzzle which, when solved, becomes a miniature solar system. National Aeronautics and Space Administration Educational Publications, Code FEO-2, Washington, DC 20546, 202-554-4380.

Free Hobby Booklets

Dozens of free publications are available from hobbyists' organizations and private companies. Also check your local library for the Encyclopedia of Associations, to look up your area of interest.

CALLIGRAPHY

- **Information on calligraphy** is available from Hunt Bienfang Paper Co., 2020 W. Front St., Statesville, NC 28677, 800-879-4868.

CHESS

- *Ten Tips to Winning Chess.* Send a self-addressed, stamped envelope for this free booklet from the U.S. Chess Federation, 186 Rt. 9W, New Windsor, NY 12553.

MODEL RAILROADS & MORE

- *Introduction to Model Railroading* includes sample track layouts. This and other booklets, including *Discovering Miniatures*, *Welcome to Amateur Astronomy*, *Those Amazing Birds* and *Guide to Making Bead Jewelry,* are available from Kalmbach Publishing Co., 21027 Crossroads Circle, Waukesha, WI 53187, 800-446-5489.

PAPER MAKING

- *How You Can Make Paper* is a booklet available from the American Forest & Paper Association, Information Center, 1111 19 St. NW, Ste. 800, Washington, DC 20036, 202-463-5179.

BREATH DEEP AND SAVE

Good News for Smokers over 50
The good news in this pamphlet is that you will see great improvement if you quit. Office on Smoking and Health, Centers for Disease Control and Prevention, 4770 Buford Hwy. NE, MS K-50, Atlanta, GA 30341, 770-488-5705.

Want Help Once You Get the Good News?
Get the free booklet, *Clearing the Air: A Guide to Quitting Smoking.* National Cancer Institute, Bldg. 31, Rm. 10A18, 9000 Rockville Pike, Bethesda, MD 20892, 800-422-6237.

PHOTOGRAPHY

● *Tips for Better Pictures* and *Picture Taking in Five Minutes* are booklets available from Kodak Information Center, Dept. 841, 4545 East River Rd., Rochester, NY 14650-0811, 800-242-2424.

STAMP COLLECTING

● *Mystic's Guide to Stamp Collecting* is a booklet for beginners available from the Mystic Stamp Co., 9700 Mill St., Camden, NY 13316, 800-433-7811.

● *Stamps Etc.* and *Introduction to Stamp Collecting* are books on stamp collecting available at your local post office or from the U.S. Postal Service, Philatelic Sales Div., 475 L'Enfant Plaza SW, Rm. 4474-EB, Washington, DC 20260, 202-268-6338.

How Neale Godfrey Taught Her Children To Value Money

I was in a board meeting eight years ago when I first realized that my children had a money problem. My secretary interrupted to tell me that my daughter Kyle was on the phone saying it was an emergency.

I took the call in the meeting. The emergency? Kyle had seen a toy on TV and needed money so she could buy it.

When I asked Kyle later if she understood where money came from, she said that it grows in the bank vault where I work and that I pick it and bring it home at night. It hit me that even though I was a bank president, my kids, then ages 4 and 1, didn't understand money. So I set out to change that.

Here's how I taught my kids about financial responsibility. These concepts can work for anyone's children.

MONEY MUST BE EARNED

In my house, we post an allowance chart on the refrigerator. As citizens of our house, my kids have certain mandatory responsibilities, such as keeping their rooms relatively clean. But they also can earn a weekly

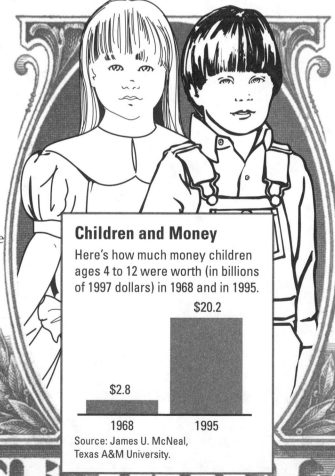

Children and Money

Here's how much money children ages 4 to 12 were worth (in billions of 1997 dollars) in 1968 and in 1995.

$20.2

$2.8

1968   1995

Source: James U. McNeal, Texas A&M University.

allowance by completing other chores, such as feeding the cats or taking out the garbage.

Important: Rotate the chores so that no one child feels stuck with the worst ones. As jobs are completed, check them off on the chart.

If my children complete their chores, I pay each of them up to $1 for each year of their ages. Parents sometimes gasp when they hear figures this large, but you have to make the amount large enough so your kids will take an interest. Besides, the child is really only keeping about half of this amount. The other half goes into a series of savings jars.

If any of your children are too young for some jobs, do the chores with them until they are ready to handle them on their own.

SAVE YOUR MONEY

As soon as my children began earning allowances, I had each of them divide their weekly income among three jars.

1. Quick cash
The children can spend this money as they wish—within my parameters, of course. If I don't want them buying candy or toy guns, I say so.

2. Medium-term savings
This is for luxury products the kids want, such as in-line skates or a CD player. In some cases, they pay for the full expense of the item, while at other times, I help.

3. College
Even though coins and bills won't amount to much, this jar forces children to think long-term. To encourage more enthusiasm for savings, offer to match the funds they set aside. About once a month, deposit the money in this jar into a savings account or CD.

Strategy: Put a picture of the item for which they are saving on each jar.

Note: Young children may have trouble with delayed gratification. Set more modest savings goals, so they take only a few weeks to attain rather than a few months.

TAXES ARE A REALITY

When I received my first paycheck as an adult, I remember thinking, "Who is FICA?" I would rather my kids grow up with an understanding of how earnings and taxes really work.

For my kids, the family is their larger community, so 15% of their allowance goes in the Family Tax Jar. Later, there's a house vote to decide how to spend it. Originally, my kids voted for a trip to Disneyworld. Then they did the math and determined it would take about 75 years to reach that goal. Instead, we use the money for pizza and video nights.

IRRESPONSIBILITY CAN RESULT IN FINES

I give each child a jar containing $10 in quarters at the beginning of the year, and I start a similar jar for myself.

When they leave a light on or a window open when the air conditioning is on, a quarter comes out of their jar and goes into mine. If they catch me, the quarters go the other way. If they have quarters left at the end of the year, they can keep them. The quarters in my jar help pay the utility bills.

Important: I don't allow them to get into finger-pointing. If there's an argument over who left the light on, both kids owe quarters.

THE IMPORTANCE OF CHARITY

Learning values is an important part of learning about money. I have my children give 10% of their allowances to a charity jar and we conduct a family vote to choose a charity. My children contribute their allowance, so it's important for them to have a say in where it goes.

RESPECT WHAT MONEY CAN BUY

Part of appreciating money is taking care of your possessions and your environment.

Solution: If my kids leave toys lying around the house, the toys go into a Saturday Box and don't come out until Saturday. Consider starting preschoolers with a Tomorrow Box. A week can be too long for a 3- or 4-year-old to wait.

CHECKING ACCOUNTS

Ever since my oldest daughter turned 12, I have given her money and let her handle her own budget for school clothes and discretionary spending.

Naturally, I'm still in charge of visits to the doctor and other necessities. But she's in charge of her own budget and writing her own checks. If she spends it all on designer clothes, she doesn't get any more for the movies. Kids might mess this up at first. Even if they don't overdraw the account, there's a tendency to underestimate needs.

Example: A parent who tried my system told me her child felt rich with $200 in an account and blew it in the first week. The parent held firm, however, and the child made it through to the end of the year with very little in the account. Now the child shops sales instead of looking for brand-name products.

Government Auctions Are Still Great Opportunities

Key: The best auctions are those that are not heavily promoted and, therefore, have fewer bidders competing.

Government auctions are not what they used to be. In the late 1980s and early 1990s, many different federal agencies were flush with confiscated assets, such as real estate, luxury cars and furnishings, and they sold them off to the public.

Today it's harder to find great bargains at government auctions, but they're still out there if you know where to look.

WHERE THE AUCTIONS ARE

Here are the hottest auctions now and what to do when attending.

1. Department of Defense

Like anyone who has gone on a supermarket shopping spree, the Pentagon often buys more goods than it can use and winds up selling off its surplus.

Much of the surplus is offered in bulk, such as dozens of tires or pairs of boots, and bought by dealers who resell the goods at flea markets.

Amid the piles of merchandise, however, are often individual items, such as stereos, VCRs, used cars and Rolex watches. Since dealers survive on profit margins, which are best generated through bulk purchases, they are not likely to compete with you for these items when the bidding starts.

Defense auctions are usually held at military bases around the U.S. and at another 20 or more locations worldwide. They are generally held every month, but frequency varies at each base depending on the availability of surplus merchandise. The condition of the goods that are sold ranges from scrap to brand new.

More information: Call the Department of Defense (800-468-8289) and ask for a list of the bases that will be holding auctions in the near future.

2. United States Postal Service

Ever wonder what happened to those holiday presents that never arrived? It is more than likely your unclaimed and undelivered merchandise was sold to the highest bidder at a U.S. postal auction. These auctions are conducted frequently at the postal headquarters in the cities of Atlanta, San Francisco and St. Paul.

Auction-goers bid on bins, which can contain anything from compact-disc players and camera equipment to books, designer clothes and small appliances. Prices for these bins are frequently less than $100. Many auction-goers buy the lot, keep one item for themselves and resell the rest or give away the surplus as gifts.

The condition of merchandise is often excellent, since many of the goods are new.

More information: Call the Mail Recovery Center at one of the postal headquarters in the three cities mentioned above. Ask to be placed on the mailing list so that notifications of upcoming auctions will be sent to you. A catalog of the merchandise is available at the site of the auction for a nominal fee.

3. Internal Revenue Service

The IRS is a great source of deep discounts on cars, boats, furniture and collectibles. Each local IRS office conducts its own auctions, so there are no regular schedules.

Note: Last-minute cancellations of these auctions sometimes occur when owners pay taxes at the last minute and their assets are returned.

More information: Look in your local newspaper's classified section under Auctions. Also check the notices posted in the lobby of your county courthouse. A phone number to get more information appears at the bottom of the notice. Before you travel, call to check that the auction has not been canceled.

The IRS does not maintain a mailing list, but you can call the IRS at 800-829-3676 regularly and ask for **Form 2434**, which is issued for every auction it holds.

IRS FORM 2434

Form 2434 details what will be sold at a specific auction.

Larger IRS auctions use private auctioneers, and you can obtain a catalog directly from the auctioneer whose number appears on the courthouse notice.

4. City, county and state auctions

Every sector of the bureaucracy, from the local police department to the division of motor vehicles, utility companies and state purchasing departments, auctions off surplus or confiscated merchandise.

Goods range from cars and bicycles to boats and computers. Jewelry and real estate also wind up on the block.

The frequency of these auctions varies with the size of the city or community. For information, call each local branch of the government.

Caution: Avoid any state or local auction that is publicized in large print or media ads. These will likely be too crowded, and novices routinely overbid, pushing prices up beyond what the items are really worth.

More Information: A good source in which to find all types of little-known government auctions is the *National Auction Bulletin* ($49 per year). It lists about 200 auctions and contact phone numbers around the country. 4419 W. Tradewinds Ave., Fort Lauderdale, FL 33308, 800-327-2049.

Before You Bid

Learn these basic rules before you attend your first auction.

1. Examine the goods in advance

The secret is to preview goods that will go on the block. Amateurs neglect the importance of this step, but professionals take great care to inspect auction goods.

Strategy: Visit the auction site the day before the actual auction. Professionals traveling a distance usually book a motel room and attend several auctions each trip. Carefully examine the goods and take notes. Then quickly comparison shop against similar items advertised in the local newspaper's classified section. This will give you an idea of what the goods would cost on the open market.

2. Write down a set price and stick to it

Public auctions are designed to get people excited and carried away. When they do, prices rise rapidly.

To keep from getting swept up in the frenzy, write down the highest price you're willing to pay. This may prevent you from exceeding the amount you planned to spend, and from paying too much.

3. Make plans in advance to transport the merchandise

Auctions do little more than let you see the merchandise in advance and then let you bid on the goods. Getting the items home is your problem.

4. Find out what forms of payment the agency accepts

Though more government auctions will now accept credit cards, many still insist on cash or cashier's checks and will not accept personal checks.

Strategy: Bring just the right amount of cash or a number of cashier's checks made out for your maximum prices, and not a penny more. This is a smart strategy when traveling out of town, even if the auction agency accepts credit cards. Carrying a signed check is less risky than carrying cash, and security is fairly tight at the auctions. Agencies and auctioneers can issue refunds on the extra amount by mail.

TIP

Better Sealed-Auction Bidding

Most auction-goers bid even amounts of money, like $10, $500 or $1,000. Bidding an uneven number, like $11, $505 or $1,025, increases your chances of making the winning bid.

GUERRILLA BIDDING STRATEGIES

Here are some strategies to help you get more for less at any auction.

1. Offer a ridiculously low bid

This should make other bidders question the value of the merchandise and avoid competing.

Example: One fisherman bid $15 and bought a $55,000 fishing trawler. Other bidders were so busy laughing and remarking to each other that he won.

This strategy works best when used on the first item offered at the auction because there is tension in the air and everyone is a little uncomfortable. It works less frequently after the auction gets rolling because it is less shocking or surprising. To be first, shout your bid as soon as the auctioneer starts describing the merchandise.

2. Offer a high bid

Open by shouting out a higher price than the initial one asked by the auctioneer. This will unsettle the auctioneer and demonstrates to other bidders that you really want the item.

Caution: This technique only works once per auction, as others catch on to its cleverness and power. It's also important to shout out a high bid that is your best offer. Otherwise, you'll get caught up in a bidding war and exceed your maximum.

3. Bid a fraction

Catch the auctioneer offguard by bidding one-half or one-quarter of what he or she is asking. This tactic is acceptable but mildly disruptive and may anger the auctioneer. It will also slow down the bidding by cutting the auctioneer's asking price by half.

Or increase your bids by only $1 or $5 increments, even if the auctioneer is already jumping in higher increments.

Examples: If the auctioneer starts by asking $100, you can respond with a bid of $50. Or if bidding is in process and the auctioneer asks for bids in $500

increments, you can respond with an increase of $100, $250 or whatever your pleasure above the previous bid.

Be prepared. The auctioneer may ignore or needle you in return, causing you some embarrassment. But the auctioneer also may give in to you in an effort to generate bidding activity.

Before Buying Your First Computer

Buying a computer can be a relatively painless procedure if you know what you want. Here are the questions you need to ask yourself and the salesperson in order to make the right decision.

WHAT SOFTWARE PROGRAMS WILL I BE USING?

To the uninitiated, this question may seem to be putting the cart before the horse. But smart consumers choose their software first, and then buy a computer to run it.

To determine what type of software you'll need, ask yourself what you hope to accomplish with your computer. Will you use it exclusively for writing? Will you need it to produce sophisticated graphics? Do you want it to print your checks or figure your taxes?

Before you decide on software packages that will satisfy your needs, you must decide whether to buy software that operates on a Macintosh computer or software that works on a PC system, which is used by IBMs and IBM-compatible units.

How to choose: Consider what software you are already familiar with and which format, Macintosh or PC, will be most useful for your family. What programs do you or your spouse use at the office? What do your kids use at school? Will you be sharing data with a friend?

HOW MUCH MONEY DO I WANT TO SPEND?

After you select the type of software you'll need and the type of computer to run it, your next step is to consider which computer model is best for you.

The good news is that computer prices continue to drop as technology advances. While any purchase hinges on your needs, you can probably find an adequate unit for less than $1,200. That price will buy you a package that may include

- A CD-ROM drive, which operates CDs that are packed with data and information.
- A built-in modem, which allows you to access on-line services and communicate with other users over the phone lines.
- A color monitor.
- A sound card, which enables your computer to play music.
- A basic software package.

Caution: A laptop can be a valuable second computer, but isn't recommended as a first purchase. Laptops have drawbacks, such as smaller keyboards and screens, higher price tags for equivalent computing power and limited expandability.

What You Could Get for About $1,200

14" color monitor (sometimes sold separately)

16 bit stereo audio

8x CD-ROM Drive

28.8Kbps data/14.4bps fax modem

- 133–200 megahertz microprocessor
- 2 gigabyte hard drive (ROM)
- 16 megabytes RAM

- Pre-installed software & CD-ROMs
- Internet software

Keyboard and mouse (sometimes sold separately)

HOW FAST SHOULD MY COMPUTER'S MICROPROCESSOR BE?

The microprocessor is the small chip that directs all the computer's activities. The larger the megahertz (MHz) number, the faster the computer will process your work and commands.

Buy the fastest microprocessor you can afford. The standard chip is called the Pentium.

HOW MUCH MEMORY DOES MY COMPUTER NEED?

Computer memory comes in two forms.

1. Short-term, random-access memory, commonly referred to as RAM, is needed to run your software and handle the file on which you're currently working. To run today's software, home-computer users will need at least 16 megabytes (16MB), which is roughly equivalent to eight million typed characters. Most programs run better with 32MB.

2. Long-term, storage memory, which enables the computer to store files and recall them, is contained in the hard disk drive. The size of your hard disk drive should be dictated by the demands of your software, which are listed on the packages. To determine how much long-term memory you'll need, add up all of your software requirements, add another 40MB, and then double the total.

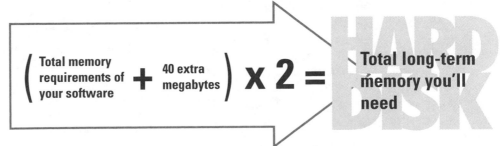

$$\left(\text{Total memory requirements of your software} + \text{40 extra megabytes}\right) \times 2 = \text{Total long-term memory you'll need}$$

HARD DISK

Should You Choose a Mac or PC?

If you're in the market for a computer, a big decision you will have to make is whether you want to buy a Macintosh system or a PC.

The PC system was designed by IBM and is now sold by IBM and the many competing computer companies that have cloned IBM's technology. All PCs can use the same operating systems, most commonly DOS or Windows.

Macintosh was created by Apple Corp., which recently decided to license its technology to other manufacturers. The operating system it uses is MacOS. PowerMacs, however, allow you to run DOS and Windows with the purchase of additional software.

To help you decide which type is best for you, here's how each system fares in various key categories.

MACINTOSH uses the MacOS operating system.

New PowerMacs can run PC systems with some added software.

EASE OF USE

Despite improvements in PC technology, Macs are still easier to operate, particularly for nontechnical users.

Reason: Since the Mac was designed originally for graphic operation, its software tends to be easier to use than equivalent PC programs. PCs, designed to handle text, still struggle to provide a user-friendly working environment.

MULTIMEDIA

This term refers to a computer that can display many types of media, including text, photos, audio and video. Both PC and Macintosh have models that can do all of this, though these models tend to be more expensive, around $1,500 and up. Lower-end models can be upgraded with all of these components, but buying them separately may prove to be more costly in the long run.

SOFTWARE SELECTION

There's no contest here. There are many more PC programs than those produced for Macintosh. Even in education, desktop publishing and multimedia software, PC programs far outnumber Macintosh offerings.

Important: Before buying a computer, carefully consider what types of programs you and your family will need. Then see which of the two systems offers them.

COMPUTING POWER

If your biggest consideration is that the computer be extremely fast and able to handle large amounts of data and programs, it makes little difference which type of computer you buy. Apple's new high-end Power Mac models are as powerful as PCs that have the new Pentium microprocessor chip.

WHEN TO GET A GOOD DEAL

Shop at the end of the quarter, when hardware and software makers stuff retail channels to reduce inventory, and retailers offer discounts to move the extra products. Don't insist on advertised prices; in-store prices may be lower, so ask for the best price. Consider older models that may be available at a deep discount when the difference in performance compared with newer models is minimal. Don't be seduced by a lot of preloaded software, since most people never use most of it.

MARCH 31
JUNE 30
SEPT 30
DEC 31

COMPARATIVE COST

While the price gap between PCs and Macs has narrowed in recent years, Macs still cost slightly more than approximately equivalent PC models.

This situation is likely to change, however, as the Macintosh clones hitting the market spark a price war among competing manufacturers. Already available from Power Computing in Austin are three high-end Apple clones—all at slightly lower prices.

PCs can use the DOS and Windows operating systems.

BOTTOM LINE

If you're looking for easy installation and operation, the Macintosh beats the PC hands down. If you want a system that offers extensive hardware and software compatibility, go with the PC.

Get New Life from Your Old Computer

Technology is evolving so quickly that many personal computers purchased just two years ago may not be powerful enough to fulfill owners' needs today. Rather than spending several thousand dollars on new equipment, you may be able to upgrade your existing unit (for much less), depending on your needs.

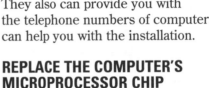

Important: Upgrading a computer yourself takes patience and substantial knowledge of your equipment. Many computer retailers will provide free or discounted installation with the purchase of an upgrade kit. They also can provide you with the telephone numbers of computer clubs that can help you with the installation.

REPLACE THE COMPUTER'S MICROPROCESSOR CHIP

A more powerful chip will help your computer handle a greater range of complex programs and commands.

Many people who bought IBM-compatible computers with 386 or 486 microprocessor chips can install the new 586 chip. Owners of Macintosh IIs and Macintosh Quadras may be able to upgrade to PowerPC microprocessors. There are several upgrade kits available.

Price range: around $250 to $400.

Important: Though upgrade products are available for older computers that use 286 chips, these models suffer from so many other performance limitations that it's more cost-effective to buy a new computer.

Seniors On-line

This computer network on America On-line links thousands of people ages 55 and older. SeniorNet also has 105 Learning Centers throughout the U.S., where volunteers teach computer classes to older people.

SeniorNet (800-747-6848, www.seniornet.org) also counsels members about buying new equipment, going on-line or using specialized software.

TIP
Computer Upgrades for Less

Software upgrades are available even if you do not have an earlier version of a program. Manufacturers offer competitive upgrades at far lower prices than the full cost of a new program. These packages allow users to buy at the upgrade price if they have any of a variety of similar programs listed on the outside of the box. Even if you do not have any of the listed programs, you can often buy an older version of one of them, plus the upgrade, for less than the cost of the full-price version of the program you want.

ADD MORE MEMORY

Additional memory will allow your computer to run newer programs and make many of your current programs run faster. Today, eight megabytes (MB) of Random Access Memory (RAM) will let your computer run most off-the-shelf programs.

Price range: As low as $29 for 2MB and $200 for 16MB.

INSTALL A LARGER HARD DISK

Before Windows and multimedia software, a 100MB hard disk was considered adequate. Today, you need a hard disk with at least 500MB to 1,000MB of storage.

Price range: $200 to $400.

PURCHASE A MULTIMEDIA UPGRADE KIT

These packages, which include a CD-ROM drive, a sound card and stereo speakers, will let your computer run the latest interactive software. Most come with entertainment and educational CD-ROMs.

Price range: $400 to $800.

Important: For best performance, purchase a kit that provides an 8x or faster CD-ROM drive and a 16-bit sound card. You'll also receive more realistic sound output if the card features wavetable synthesis, which features recordings of musical instruments.

BUY A NEW HIGH-SPEED MODEM

The current standard for computer modems is 28.8K bits per second, although 14.4K bits per second is fine for day-to-day faxing. Most new modems come with fax send/receive capability.

Price range: $100 to $300.

Cellular Phone Secrets

The biggest surprise is that your cellular phone bill will be higher than your home phone bill. Many first-time buyers think the two bills will be similar, and that they'll have to pay only a monthly fee plus any long-distance charges.

Cellular phones carry a number of other charges.

- A monthly access fee for the privilege of making calls.
- Per-minute charges, even for local phone calls.
- Fees of as much as $1 or more per minute, plus a $2 to $3 usage fee per day for calls made from outside your local calling area.
- Charges for calling toll-free numbers.
- Charges for incoming calls.

Not all cellular service providers are the same. In every market, there are at least two cellular-service providers available.

Strategy: While most offer similar service plans, get a list of what each plan offers and charges. Compare them. Based on how you expect to use your phone, select the plan that best serves your needs.

When you purchase a cellular phone, you are locked into a service provider for at least one year.

- If you want a cellular phone solely for security, or don't expect to use it more than a few minutes per month, choose a plan that offers the lowest monthly access fee, even though it will probably have higher per-minute rates.
- If you expect to use your phone frequently, look for a plan with a higher access fee and lower usage

rates. For really high users, some plans offer up to 500 free minutes per month and discounted rates that improve with usage.

- Choose a service provider that charges less for calls made during off-peak periods, such as evenings and weekends, if you will be making calls then.
- Look for a plan that bills in 30-second increments rather than in one-minute increments or longer. This could save you as much as 10% on your bill.
- Limit your calls. Every time you pick up the phone, ask yourself, "Is this call really necessary?" If it isn't, wait until you're back home or at your office to make the call.
- Be stingy about giving out your phone number. Most providers charge for incoming as well as outgoing calls.
- If you are a heavy user, consider getting a pager. After seeing the incoming number on the display, you can decide whether to return the call immediately or later.

Phone Card Tip
If you use a prepaid phone card, keep the cost down by limiting calls to under four minutes and using the card during daytime hours, when other rates are highest.

Prepaid Phone Card Call Trap

Prepaid phone card calls tend to be more costly than collect or credit card calls.

Example: AT&T, MCI and Sprint prepaid phone cards may charge up to 60¢ per minute for calls anytime of day to anywhere in the U.S., Puerto Rico and the U.S. Virgin Islands, compared with 20¢ to 75¢ for collect or credit card calls. Fees vary depending on the credit card used, length of call and long distance carrier.

Added problem: If you are on a call and you use up your allotted funds on a prepaid phone card, the call is terminated. Calling cards let you talk for as long as you need.

Costly Phone-Card Mistake

Don't assume that all long-distance calls charged on the card receive the issuer's rates.

Reality: Rates are set by the different carriers that provide service to publicly used phones.

Solution: When making calls from a hotel or pay phone, dial "00" and ask the carrier's long-distance operator for the rates. If they seem unreasonable, use the access number on the back of your card to receive your card issuer's rates.

CALLING LONG-DISTANCE

Before you choose a long-distance telephone company or calling plan, take a look at how many calls you make and when you make them. Then choose the plan that's best for you.

COMPANY	STANDARD PLAN	TOLL-FREE NUMBER
AT&T	**One Rate:** 15¢ per minute on any long-distance call in the U.S. 24 hours a day. For $4.95 per month, you can receive a flat rate of 10¢ per minute.	800-222-0300
LCI International	**All America:** 19¢ per minute from 8 a.m. to 5 p.m., 14¢ from 5 p.m. to 11 p.m., and 12¢ from 11 p.m. to 8 a.m. and all weekend. **Flat Rate:** 15¢ per minute around the clock. **Two Rate:** 25¢ per minute 6 a.m. to 6 p.m., and 10¢ per minute 6 p.m. to 6 a.m. and all weekend.	800-746-3767
MCI	**MCI One:** 12¢ per minute if you spend over $25 a month, and 15¢ per minute if you spend less than $25. Minimum charge of $5 monthly.	800-444-3333
Sprint	**Sprint Sense:** 10¢ per minute 7 p.m. to 7 a.m. Monday through Friday and all weekend. Weekday rates are 25¢ per minute out-of-state and 22¢ per minute in-state.	800-524-4685

Foil Car Phone Bandits

Turn off your unit when driving near airports, bridges and tunnels.

Thieves pirate phone numbers with electronic scanners in areas where traffic moves slowly. The owner is not responsible for false charges, but working out the bill can be a hassle. See if your company will add a free line-protection feature.

Shrewd Advice from Real Burglars

Author Beth Spring corresponded with dozens of imprisoned burglars to learn why they targeted some homes and avoided others. Their advice for burglar-proofing your home follows.

MAKE BURGLARS THINK THAT YOU ARE HOME

Even though many thieves know the tricks people use to make it look as if they are at home, they're still more likely to pass up your house if it appears occupied. The risk of being wrong and getting caught isn't worth it to most burglars.

- Have at least one light on a timer. It should go on in the evening and stay on all night, or at least until you come home.
- Leave a radio on in a bedroom or living room when you're out of the house. Tune it to an all-talk station. From a distance, a burglar's first impression may be that the conversation is coming from people in the house.
- Arrange for a neighbor to pick up your newspapers and any advertising flyers when you're away for more than a day (offer to do the same in return). Burglars often check curbside mailboxes before exploring the premises.
- Have the lawn mowed in your absence when you're away for a week or more. Tall grass is an invitation to crooks.
- Never leave a note on the door explaining that you're not home.
- Don't leave anything outside your home that might attract a thief, such as tools, toys, bikes or equipment, and lock your garage.

TAKE A BURGLAR'S-EYE VIEW OF YOUR HOME

Thieves strike where they think they won't be seen. They would also prefer to gain access to your home without making any loud noises.

- Make sure obscure openings, such as pets' swinging doors, crawl spaces or ventilation openings, are locked or blocked.
- Cut back overgrown bushes that hide doors or windows. Also, prune any branches that offer access to second-story windows.
- Illuminate a dark driveway or side yard with floodlights. If you install an energy-saving motion detector, the floodlight will go on whenever there is movement in your yard or driveway.

WHAT TO HIDE

- Store valuables in places burglars seldom look. For example, don't keep your best jewelry in a bedroom jewelry box. Put it in a plain box in a bedroom closet, on a basement shelf or in the back of a seldom-used kitchen cupboard—places where a thief won't look.
- Never hide a spare key. Burglars know all the hiding places. Instead, give a key to a trusted neighbor.

GET A DOG

If you don't like dogs or are allergic, consider these alternatives.

- Record an hour-long tape of a dog barking intermittently, and have it play while you're out. Of course, it shouldn't be so loud that your neighbors complain.
- Put a large dog bowl near the front door. The point is to make a burglar think twice about striking your home. The more doubts you provide, the less likely it is you'll be victimized.

PARTICIPATE IN AN OPERATION IDENTIFICATION

Make a complete inventory of all your possessions, which is beneficial for insurance purposes. Keep your list in a bank safe-deposit box. Then, mark your valuables with an engraving tool, which you can borrow from a police station or library. Engrave the items in obscure locations so that a thief can't mar the number. Marked items are worth less to a burglar because they can't be sold as easily as those that are unmarked.

After you return the engraving tool to the police, you will receive stickers that can be pasted to your windows or front door. This isn't a burglary alarm system, but it tells thieves that you've taken precautions.

SECURE YOUR DOORS

The safest types of doors are made of metal, steel or solid wood. A hollow-wood door can be kicked in or pulled apart easily by a burglar. A door with glass window-panes also makes your home more vulnerable.

● If you have a sliding glass door, secure it with a tight-fitting metal or wooden pole and a keyed lock.
● Buy an anti-shim device, which prevents a plastic card from opening the latch. They are available at hardware stores.
● Install a deadbolt lock. Three basic types are effective.
    1. Double-cylinder deadbolt.
    2. Single-cylinder tubular deadbolt.
    3. Rim-mounted lock.

If you already have a deadbolt lock, check the strike plate, which holds the sliding bolt in place when the door is locked. If the strike plate is thin-gauge metal, replace it with a heavy-duty one. Anchor the plate with three-inch, number-12 wood screws. If you're unsure about the safety of your locks, or any aspect of your home, ask the police to point out the safety flaws.

SECURE YOUR WINDOWS

Nearly every window in your house can be secured, no matter how large, expensive or exotically designed. If your windows are not traditional, call a locksmith or ask the window's manufacturer for advice.

● Basement windows, in particular, offer easy access for burglars. Replace the regular pane glass with Plexiglas or polycarbonate. Consider using security bars, a heavy-duty screen or ornamental grillwork.
● Check the latches on all casement windows to be sure they work properly. The crank handle should feel tight, not wiggly.
● Louvered widows, which open out like awnings, can be very difficult to secure. Think about replacing them with safer, double-hung windows that slide up and down.

IS YOUR HOME AN EASY TARGET?

The Best Home Safes

Burglars hate safes. They take too long to crack, and a good one is too heavy and secure to move. But some safes are safer than others. Here's what you need to ask before you buy one, and the different types to consider.

WILL YOUR VALUABLES FIT INSIDE?

At home, put all your valuables in a box. If there's room left inside, fold all the sides down around your valuables. Remove your valuables, and take the empty box along with you to slip inside different safes.

WILL YOUR VALUABLES SURVIVE A FIRE?

A tag on the safe will indicate whether temperatures inside will remain below 451 degrees, the point at which paper burns.

TYPES OF SAFES

No matter which safe you decide to buy, a combination lock is better than one that requires a key. Consider safes with labels from Underwriters Laboratories, Inc. (UL), an independent product-testing lab.

1. Wall safe

One great advantage to a wall safe is that it can be easily hidden behind a painting or other wall hanging.

Drawback: Most walls in newer homes are thin, so these safes are small and may not hold all your valuables. They can hold jewelry, coins and papers, but not much else.

A good wall safe has sides made of half-inch solid steel with a one-inch-thick door. The combination lock should have a device that freezes the bolt mechanism in the locked position if someone tries to drill a hole through the lock. In addition, you can make the safe harder to pry out of a wall by using larger screws when you install it.

Best location: away from the master bedroom, which is where thieves look first. The safest location is the basement.

2. Floor safe

Safes that stand on the floor and are bolted into either the floor joists or a wall are ideal for a large amount of possessions. They can hold all of your jewelry, important papers and small objects. A floor safe can be bolted into a cement floor.

Drawback: Bolting a safe into the floor makes it very difficult to remove if you ever want to redecorate or relocate.

3. Gun safe

These safes are the size of a large wardrobe and are very heavy. They are designed to keep guns out of children's hands and prevent guns from being stolen, but they can also hold other valuables.

Gun safes have more sophisticated locking mechanisms and thicker doors. They're not disguised. These safes can weigh up to 1,000 pounds, so the basement may be best able to support them.

Note: Some gun safes have quick-open locks, which are designed to allow you to access a loaded weapon quickly. These quick-open safes can hold one or several guns, but they are not intended to hold other valuables.

The Latest Consumer Frauds and How to Protect Yourself

Telemarketing scams are the fastest growing type of consumer fraud, and people over age 50 are frequent victims. Watch out for these scams.

TELEFUNDING

The caller asks for a donation to a cause that sounds worthwhile, and promises a lavish prize if you contribute.

You'll be asked to make a large donation, perhaps $1,000. In return, you'll be promised that you will win one of five prizes: typically a big screen TV, new car, diamond ring, gold ingot or Caribbean vacation.

Trap: This prize offer is what is known as a one-in-five scam. The prize you'll win if you send in money is the "diamond" ring, which actually will be worth only $10.

INVESTMENTS

Telescammers are always pushing some investment, often precious gems, gold or oil leases.

One big investment scam involves wireless cable franchises. This type of technology exists to transmit cable programming without having to wire a house.

But there's little evidence that wireless cable can be profitable. You'll be asked to pay thousands of dollars for the right to bid in federal auctions for wireless cable franchises.

Trap: If you decide to invest in wireless cable, you don't need to pay anyone for help. You can bid on your own by doing some paperwork and paying a small fee. Even if you do it yourself, you can't be sure of winning, or of making any money if you do win.

BUSINESS OPPORTUNITIES

There are many business opportunity scams. People over age 50 are easy targets because many want to run businesses after retirement.

A common scam involves pay telephones. The crook will offer to sell you pay phones with the promise that you can install them anywhere and make huge profits.

Reality: Losses of $10,000 and up are common.

Trap: You'll pay far more for pay phones than they are worth, with little chance of recovering your money. The average pay phone generates a mere $200 a year in net profits for their operators. And legitimate phone companies will install and maintain the phones for you in return for a share of the profits.

HEALTH PRODUCTS

You'll be offered vitamins or other health-care products, "specially formulated for someone your age."

Trap: You'll pay very high prices for products of minimal or no value. Take medical advice from your doctor, not from a scam artist.

INTERNET

The same phony investment and business opportunity deals that have long been pitched over the telephone are now turning up on the Internet.

Warning: A scam is a scam whether it is pitched by phone or computer. Don't let your guard down because an offer appears on your computer screen.

AFFINITY FRAUD

This refers not to the type of scam but to the way victims are picked. Computer-generated phone lists can be drawn very precisely, enabling crooks to pinpoint targets.

Trap: Older people will be called by someone soliciting funds to help finance a "Save Medicare" cam-

Tell-Tale Signs

No matter how legitimate the offer seems, here are four signs you are dealing with a crook.

1. The promise of prizes
Something is wrong if you haven't entered a contest but someone calls and says you have won a prize. It is absolutely a scam if you must buy something or send in money to collect your prize.

2. Pressure to do it now
Beware of any special deal good for only that one day. No legitimate deal requires you to decide or act immediately.

3. Requests for personal financial numbers
Since most people know better than to give credit card numbers over the phone, the caller will ask for the numbers on the bottom of your check, "so your money can be put to work faster." Armed with those numbers, the crook can empty your checking account, and you won't know about it until your checks begin bouncing.

4. Demands that payment be sent by overnight delivery service
Telling you your money will be picked up in just a few hours is another way of reducing the time you have to think the deal through. Also, the crook avoids mail fraud by using a private package delivery service instead of the U.S. Postal Service.

paign. Alternative scams involve health-care books or products aimed at 50-plus users.

WHAT TO DO

Be prepared to fight back if you are the victim of a scam. Complain to your local Better Business Bureau, state attorney general, and city or state consumer affairs department. Write to newspapers and TV stations in the area where the fraud began.

Ask regulators for names of anyone else who has complained about the same fraud. The more victims you get to complain, the more likely regulators will take action.

More information: National Fraud Information Center, Box 65868, Washington, DC 20035, 800-876-7060.

If Your Wallet Is Stolen

Know exactly what is in your wallet at all times, so you can report if something is lost or stolen.

Strategy: Arrange your credit cards so you can immediately see if one is missing.

Carry no more than two or three cards at a time, and keep a photocopy of all your credit cards at home, along with a list of whom to call in case of a problem.

SOURCES

Sources are listed in the order in which their contributions appear. A source may have contributed part or all of an article, or a series of articles.

Roger Dawson, Roger Dawson Productions, Inc.

Rochelle LaMotte McDonald, author of *How to Pinch a Penny Till It Screams: Stretching Your Dollars in the '90s*

Melodie Moore, editor of *Skinflint News*

The Family Handyman

D. Stephen Elder, home inspector

Bessie Berry, U.S. Department of Agriculture

Kathryn Marion, editor of *Reality Check Gazette*

Dean King, author of *The Penny Pincher's Almanac Handbook for Modern Frugality: Hundreds of Simple Ways to Spend Less and Get More*

Vicki Lansky, author of *Another Use For 101 Common Household Items*

Lee Simmons, coauthor of *Penny-Pinching: How to Lower Your Everyday Expenses Without Lowering Your Standard of Living*

Neale S. Godfrey, Children's Financial Network

Dean King, author of *The Penny Pincher's Almanac Handbook for Modern Frugality: Hundreds of Simple Ways to Spend Less and Get More*

Thomas Pearson, MD, Bassett Healthcare's Research Institute

Dorothy Leeds, author of *Smart Questions for Savvy Shoppers*

Priscilla Douglas, Department of Consumer Affairs

Melodie Moore, editor of *Skinflint News*

Amy Waldman, staff writer at *The Washington Monthly*

Dawn Frankfort, editor of *Joy of Outlet Shopping*

Barbara Berger Opotowsky, Better Business Bureau

Olivia Mellan, author of *Overcoming Overspending*

Rochelle LaMotte McDonald, author of *How to Pinch a Penny Till It Screams: Stretching Your Dollars in the '90s*

Wayne Dyer, PhD, author of *No More Holiday Blues*

Terry Savage, finance columnist for *The Chicago Sun-Times*

Jackie Iglehart, editor of *The Penny Pincher*

Letitia Baldrige, author of *Letitia Baldrige's New Complete Guide to Executive Manners*

Consumer Reports Travel Letter

Dean King, author of *The Penny Pincher's Almanac Handbook for Modern Frugality: Hundreds of Simple Ways to Spend Less and Get More*

Library of Congress

Matthew Lesko, coauthor of *1,001 Free Goodies & Cheapies*

Mary Ann Martello, author of *Gobs of Really Neat Stuff the Government Gives Away to Anyone!!*

Amy Dacyczyn, editor of *The Tightwad Gazette*

Neale Godfrey, Children's Financial Network

George Chelekis, author of *The Official Government Auction Guide*

Dan Gookin, author of *Buy That Computer!*

John Edwards, computer industry analyst

Lise Buyer, T. Rowe Price

Bradley Haas, SeniorNet

John Edwards, computer industry analyst

Neil Sachnoff, TeleCom Clinic

Kathleen Wallman, Federal Communications Commission

Neil Sachnoff, TeleCom Clinic

Beth Spring, author of *Staying Safe: Prison Fellowship's Guide to Crime Prevention*

David Alan Wacker, Smart Systems

Fred Schulte, investigations editor for the *Fort Lauderdale Sun-Sentinel*

Christine Dugas, author of *Fiscal Fitness—A Guide to Shaping Up Your Finances for the Rest of Your Life*

Retirement
Live Well without Working

Gordon K. Williamson's Retirement Savings Strategies

Not everyone can save a fortune by the time he or she reaches retirement. With the many expected (and unexpected) expenses that people face during their working years, it is hard to squirrel away as much as many experts insist is needed for a comfortable retirement.

Don't despair. If your home mortgage and college bills have been paid, you can make do with far less: 40% to 60% of your preretirement income rather than the 75% to 90% goal set by many experts.

STEP 1: CALCULATE THE MINIMUM ANNUAL SAVINGS YOU NEED TO RETIRE

Let's assume you and your spouse now have a combined income of $100,000 a year. If you had to, you could live relatively well when you retire on an after-tax income of $4,000 a month, or $48,000 a year in present dollars. After you both retire, Social Security benefits will bring in $1,000 per spouse per month, or $24,000 combined a year, starting at age 65. (This Social Security figure assumes that each spouse earned at least an average of $40,000 in income in each of the five years before retiring.)

Therefore, you will need another $24,000 a year during retirement. To determine how large an amount is necessary to generate this annual income, divide $24,000 by 12%, the average annual return on U.S. stocks over the past 50 years, to get $200,000.

You can do even better by using foreign stocks, which have performed better than their U.S. stock counterparts over the past 25 years.

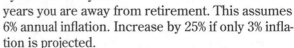

STEP 2: FACTOR IN INFLATION

Multiply the lump sum by 50% for every six years you are away from retirement. This assumes 6% annual inflation. Increase by 25% if only 3% inflation is projected.

Grand total: In the case of our example, if you were six years from retirement you would need at least $300,000 when you retired. Invested at 8%, $300,000 will produce the needed $24,000 a year.

STEP 3: PLAN TO ACHIEVE THIS GOAL

You can save the money you need to retire if you follow these tips.

Use the stock market for fast growth

The good news is you could probably save enough to live well during retirement just by investing in stocks, even if you started at age 50. That's because growth stocks and other fast-growing investments historically produce high returns over ten years, assuming all gains and dividends are reinvested.

THE RULE OF 72

$$\frac{72}{\text{Rate of return}} = \text{Time it takes to double your money}$$

The Rule of 72 shows how long it takes money to double. Divide 72 by the rate of return. At a rate of 14%, your principal will double in 5.2 years (72 divided by 14). If you earned just 10%, your money would double in 7.2 years.

Take your employer's tax-deferred retirement plan seriously

Through a 401(k), Keogh, SIMPLE, SEP or 403(b) plan, you can set aside pretax dollars. The money will grow without being taxed until you begin to withdraw it, which you can begin to do at age 59½.

Consider variable annuities

As an alternative to mutual funds, you may consider putting savings in a variable annuity later in life. Start shifting your money out of mutual funds and into variable annuities when you reach your early 50s. Then, as you approach retirement, you may want to transfer up to 75% of your nonretirement assets into annuities.

What You Should Make, Save and Spend

There are three important numbers you need to know to be in control of your retirement savings: the amount you will need to receive from your investments each year, the total lump sum you and your spouse will need to retire comfortably and how much of your savings you can spend during your retirement. This example illustrates an easy way to find those numbers.

Step 1: What Your Investments Need to Produce

	$100,000	Your current income after taxes
x	.80	Percent of current income you will need during retirement
=	$80,000	Annual amount of money you will need during retirement
–	$33,000	Annual pension plan income
–	$23,868	Anticipated Social Security benefits
=	**$23,132**	**What you will need annually from investments**

Step 2: Lump Sum You Will Require

	8%	After-tax rate of return you anticipate earning (considering your risk profile)
–	3%	Anticipated rate of inflation
=	5%	After-tax rate of return adjusted for inflation
	$23,132	What you will need annually from investments
÷	5%	After-tax rate of return adjusted for inflation
=	**$462,640**	**Minimum amount of savings you need to retire without diminishing your principal**

Step 3: What You Will Be Able to Spend

	$750,000	Total amount of savings at retirement
–	$462,640	Minimum amount of savings you need to retire
–	$35,000	Money you will set aside for emergencies
=	**$252,360**	**Total amount of your savings you will be able to spend without diminishing your principal**

Annuities are similar to mutual funds but have some important advantages over them.

1. **Tax-deferred status.** Annuity investments enjoy tax-deferred status until the funds are withdrawn. There is a 10% penalty, however, on the growth portion of the tax-deferred money if you withdraw funds prior to age 59½ (unless a special exception applies).

2. **Mutual fund-type investment options.** You can switch from one investment to another, but only within your variable annuity company's family of investments. In a regular mutual fund, such a move could trigger a capital gains tax. Not so in an annuity.

3. **Death benefits.** Say you have put $100,000 into the annuity and, due to investment reversals, this $100,000 is worth significantly less at your death. Your heirs will still collect $100,000, no matter how much your investments have declined. But if your $100,000 is worth more at your death than you originally paid, say $200,000, your heirs still will receive the full $200,000.

Caution: Shop carefully. Annual fees on some annuities can be high, and performance may be poor enough in some annuities that you would do better holding shares in a top growth fund, even after paying taxes on the gains.

Strategy: Look for an annuity that has a strong track record and has been managed by the same manager for at least five years. The annuity should have finished in the top 50% of its category during each of the past five years.

ASSET ALLOCATION

If you're just starting to invest at around age 50, you should build a mutual fund or variable annuity portfolio with

- 20% in fast-growth, small-cap stock funds.
- 40% in slower-growth, blue-chip stock funds.
- 40% in an international stock fund.

With this portfolio mix, you can expect to have annual gains of approximately 14% compounded.

If you invest $100,000 at age 50, you could have $750,000 at age 65.

Important: I don't like to use bonds for this part of retirement savings. The 1980s were great for bonds, which posted 13% gains. Yet even then stocks still outpaced them, with gains of 17.5%.

Bonds and bond funds are ideal for those conservative investors who are only a few years from retirement, or who have already retired.

Get on Track

Here's how to figure out whether you're on the road to a comfortable retirement. Take your total current savings as a percentage of your current annual salary and compare it with the table below. Then see whether you have saved the appropriate amount for your investment style and the number of years before you retire.

Investment style	Years to retirement							
	0	5	10	15	20	25	30	35
Aggressive	957%	675%	463%	307%	193%	109%	48%	3%
Moderate	1,046	773	558	393	268	172	98	42
Conservative	1,148	890	676	505	369	261	174	105

Source: T. Rowe Price Associates

DETERMINE IF YOU ARE ON TARGET

- At age 35, you should have roughly 10% of your goal.
- At age 40, you should have roughly 20% to 25% of your goal.
- At age 45, you should have 35% of your goal. (In the years leading up to age 45, you may move slowly due to college expenses or costs of caring for parents.)
- At age 50, you should have accumulated at least 45% of your goal.
- Between ages 50 and 60, as family costs ebb, you should be investing much larger amounts to reach 50% to 60% of your target.

Good news: If you have just 50% at age 60 and the money earns 12% a year compounded, your money will double in the next six years. You'll also have a cushion because you'll still be adding some money through ages 60 to 65. This strategy will help to offset any market corrections during that period and can be a hedge against inflation.

GOLDEN RULES

1. Never invest in something with which you are uncomfortable. No projected return or broker's assurance can take the place of a good night's sleep. Discovering your risk level will help you decide which investments to use.

Here's how: Ask yourself how much of your portfolio you could stand to lose in one year—5%, 10%, 20%? You'd have to be pretty aggressive to lose more than 20% in one year.

2. Don't worry if you are behind your target. Take heart and start saving anyway. Reduce your future retirement needs dramatically by improving your cash flow today.

Better Retirement Investment Allocation

Ignore the common advice to keep a portion of your investment portfolio in stocks equal to 100 minus your current age.

Using this rule, a 65-year-old would have 35% of his or her investments in stocks (100 – 65 = 35).

Problem: This strategy has become too conservative as life expectancies have increased. Today's retirees need to continue increasing, not just preserving, their capital until at least their mid-70s.

New rule of thumb: Multiply your age by 80% (0.80), and put at most that percentage in bonds or bond funds and the rest in stocks.

Example: A 65-year-old should have at most 52% in bonds (65 x 0.80 = 52), and the rest in stocks.

Considering Early Retirement?

Early retirement for people in their 60s may not be as costly as they think. Do a projection of your current income after taxes and compare that with your retirement income after taxes. Note that you may be in a lower tax bracket after retirement and, in some cases, many of your expenses will be lower.

How to Plan for Early Retirement

More and more people are dreaming of retiring early. A recent survey of more than 1,000 Americans found that 83% of the respondents planned to retire before they reached age 65.

The reality for most people, however, is that early retirement will remain a dream. Barring a major financial windfall, early retirement requires an enormous amount of discipline and an aggressive savings plan. It's also essential that you and your spouse agree throughout your working years to try to retire early, since you both will have to make many choices and at least some sacrifices.

WHAT YOU'LL NEED TO HAVE SAVED

Very few 50-year-olds can save enough money in five or six years to retire early. You'll need at least 15 or more years to amass a nest egg that will provide you with enough income to last you at least 40 years in retirement.

First, determine how much money you will need. Conservatively speaking, your retirement savings should be equal to between 20 and 25 times your desired pretax income in your first year of retirement.

Formula: To determine your desired pretax income, multiply your current annual spending (gross income minus savings) by about 75%. Then factor in inflation, which will likely average 3.5% per year until you retire.

When doing these calculations, do not include income that you expect to earn from working part-time during your retirement. If you continue to make money by working at a hobby or consulting, this income will be supplemental. Do not depend on it for your basic needs.

Reason: You may intend to stay busy, but a job (and its subsequent income) may not materialize, or your health, or that of your spouse, may not permit you to continue working.

CUT WAY BACK ON SPENDING

Once you've determined how much you'll need, set up an ironclad budget that diverts as much of your income as possible to your savings.

Most successful early retirees make a conscious choice to live below their means for years before retirement. They become experts at delayed gratification. Not everyone is psychologically equipped to do this. It means you probably won't be able to keep up with the Joneses or latest trends.

Strategy: Realize that all major spending decisions and lifestyle choices have retirement implications. Don't spend more than you need to on housing, vacations and dining, even if you can afford top-drawer purchases. The best savings method is to pay yourself first, making long-term investments your first priority every month.

Here's how: Have one of your mutual funds debit your savings or checking account each month, or have the fund take money right out of your paycheck. That way, you can't spend the money and it begins compounding sooner.

Trap: Many savers go astray because initially they find it impossible to save as much as they want. They get discouraged and give up. Even if you can't save as much as you would like, save something. The process is addictive, and eventually you'll begin to save more.

POUR MONEY INTO RETIREMENT PLANS

It goes without saying that would-be early retirees must make maximum contributions to their 401(k) plans.

Equally important: Make the most of your Individual Retirement Account (IRA).

Strategy: Make the maximum allowable contribution to your IRA ($2,000 per year) even if you don't get any tax deduction. Use Roth IRAs over deductible IRAs if you're eligible. You will still get one of the best tax breaks around: Your investments will grow tax-deferred until you retire and begin withdrawing your money.

Some people choose employers based on pension plans. They look for companies with 401(k) plans that match employee contributions. Such plans grow quickly because they compound tax-deferred.

TAKE ON RISK

Far too many people who intend to retire early don't give any thought to making their savings outpace inflation. Even if inflation averages only 3.5%, the cost of living will double every 20 years. Only an investment strategy based on growth, rather than capital preservation, will enable you to reach your goal.

Strategy: Most people who want to retire early should invest their savings primarily in stocks and stock mutual funds. As a result, they will have to choose more aggressive investments than the average long-term investor.

OTHER WAYS TO CUT BACK AND SAVE

● Consider canceling life insurance policies once your nest egg is large enough. Once your net worth grows to the point at which you have savings to cover emergencies and you have no more financial dependents, you may not need life insurance. At the very least, you can reduce the amount of your coverage.

● Invest in several rental real estate properties and devise a plan to pay off the mortgages by the time you retire. Once the mortgages are out of the way, you will have a dependable, increasing income stream with minimal expenses for your retirement. If you don't want to be bothered with property management duties once you've retired, hire someone else to do it. Your cash flow will still be substantial.

Accounting for the Rate of Inflation

Don't forget to take into account the unpredictable rate of inflation. If you create a retirement plan that relies on a low rate of inflation and then inflation soars, your money will be worth far less than you anticipated.

13.5%

2.3%

1980   1995

Source: Standard & Poor's, a division of the McGraw Hill Cos.

● Develop sensible car-ownership habits. If you routinely keep each of your cars for ten years instead of three, you'll save well over $100,000 during your working life.

● Consider the long-term impact of modifying everyday habits.

Example: Save $5 a day by eating breakfast at home and brown-bagging your lunch during the week. Do this for 25 years, investing the savings at 8.5%, and you'll save around $100,000.

- Finally, beware of early retirement incentive plans if you haven't amassed a sizable nest egg. Many people have accepted these buyouts only to discover a few years later that they really couldn't afford early retirement. Before accepting an incentive plan to retire, always compare what you would get under the plan with what you would get if you stayed for a few more years.

Example: At some companies, a person retiring at age 59 might receive 60% less per year in pension money than someone retiring at age 65.

The company is betting it will save money because you'll probably live a long time in retirement. That's what the actuarial tables tell them, and these tables are fairly accurate.

Free Help Managing Your Money

Low-cost money-management assistance is available in many areas through the American Association of Retired Persons. AARP (800-424-3410) cooperates with state and local agencies and nonprofit groups to help seniors set up budgets, pay routine bills and keep track of finances.

Clients usually must have incomes below $16,902 for individuals or $23,917 for couples, and no more than $25,000 in liquid assets. Some state and local agencies also help seniors directly. To obtain the name of the agency nearest you, call the Eldercare Locator at 800-677-1116.

MAX OUT YOUR 401(K)

Here's what a person making $75,000 and contributing 6% (the average contribution) to a 401(k) would have after five years vs. the same person putting in 15% (the maximum the government allows up to a cap of $9,500). Assume the employer matches half of contributions up to 6%.

Source: Fidelity Investments

$85,535.04

$42,767.52

6% Contribution (Plus 3% employer contribution)

15% Contribution (Plus 3% employer contribution)

David J. Jepsen Makes 401(k) Investing Simple

As more and more companies turn the responsibility of running their 401(k) plans over to large financial institutions, employees are being offered a growing mix of investments. The result is information overload, confusion and, in some cases, inaction.

To simplify the decision-making process, here are some common mistakes people make with their 401(k)s and how to determine the best asset-allocation for your needs.

BIGGEST 401(k) MISTAKES

Not saving enough

It is important to contribute as much as you can to harness the enormous power of tax-deferred compounding. Many companies match employee contributions, making such plans even more valuable. The maximum amount you can contribute for 1998 is $10,000, regardless of how large your salary is. This excludes employer contributions.

Investing too conservatively

Too many employees put their 401(k) investments in money market or bond funds because they want very little risk.

Reality: Low-risk money doesn't grow as fast as investments with higher risk. History shows that stocks, not bonds, are the only investments that have consistently outpaced taxes and inflation. Even if you are close to retirement and have only ten years to invest, the chances are very good that you're going to earn more by investing at least some of your money in stocks.

Constantly shifting your investments

Research shows that people who fiddle with their 401(k) plan investments, trying to sell when markets are high and buy when they are low, don't do as well as those who settle on an investment strategy and examine it annually. Yearly review will allow you to rebalance your portfolio to your original allocation.

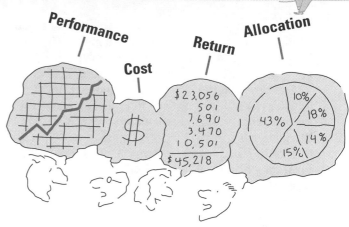

YOUR INVESTMENT PROFILE

How do you formulate a strategy for your own 401(k) plan account? First, you need to know where you are on the investment lifestyle track.

Once, conventional wisdom assumed that people moved along a career path, finishing college and then going on to jobs where they could count on spending the rest of their working lives.

Reality: The economy and lifestyles have changed. Now there are 40-year-old managers starting new jobs, 40-year-old executives with toddlers and 70-year-old entrepreneurs.

Here are the three different investment types that exist today. See where you fit in.

401(k) Beginners

Regardless of age, they have little or no retirement savings.

401(k) Middlers

They have accumulated about half the savings they need for retirement, through company savings plans, inheritances or independent investing.

401(k) Preretirees

They have accumulated most of the savings needed for their retirement. You belong in this category if you have saved almost enough to provide for a financially comfortable retirement and are five to ten years away from leaving the world of work.

YOUR RISK TOLERANCE

Now that you know where you fit in, you must evaluate how much risk you can accept without losing sleep over market swings.

Questions to ask yourself
- Is it important to earn the highest return, even if I must take higher risk to do so?
- Will I accept short-term losses if I believe the long-term returns will be good?
- Do I want my investments to grow steadily and avoid sharp ups and downs, even if this reduces my long-term returns?

If you answered yes to the first two questions and no to the third, you're a risk-taker who is comfortable pursuing a fairly aggressive investment strategy. By contrast, if you answered no to the first two questions and yes to the third, you prefer a conservative investment strategy.

If your answers to the above questions were in between, you're likely a moderate whose investment stance straddles the two extremes.

YOUR ASSET ALLOCATION

Once you've determined your profile and risk tolerance, here are some suggested asset allocations.

Beginners who are
- Aggressive investors: 100% stocks.
- Moderate investors: 80% stocks and 20% bonds.
- Conservative investors: 60% stocks and 40% bonds.

Middlers who are
- Aggressive investors: 80% stocks and 20% bonds.
- Moderate investors: 60% stocks and 40% bonds.
- Conservative investors: 40% stocks and 60% bonds.

Preretirees who are
- Aggressive investors: 60% stocks and 40% bonds.
- Moderate investors: 40% stocks and 60% bonds.
- Conservative investors: 20% stocks and 80% bonds.

CHOOSING THE RIGHT FUNDS

If the information from your company's plan is comprehensive and provides you with a variety of respected funds, you're in luck. Some companies offer funds that are so well-known they are household names. But others offer obscure funds with names that make it hard to determine their investment strategies.

Before you can decide in which funds to invest, determine in what types of stocks or bonds each fund invests, and how well each fund has performed compared with other funds in the same category.

Strategy: Call the 401(k) plan's sponsor to find out in what types of stocks each fund invests. Look over reports from an independent source, such as Morningstar Mutual Funds or Value Line to see how it rates the funds in your plan. Both are available through a broker or at many libraries. Choose the highest-rated fund in a category.

Smarter 401(k) Investing for Couples

Working couples unable to fully fund both of their retirement plans should concentrate on maximizing contributions to the better one. Focus on plans at companies that make contributions, that allow employees to control those contributions, that offer a wide range of investment options, and where you intend to stay long enough to keep the company's contributions when you leave.

Examine Your 401(k) Plan Carefully

If the investment options it offers aren't sufficient, speak up and ask for others. If the plan provides projections of future earnings from investments, be sure they reflect what will be left after fees and management costs are subtracted, and are expressed in today's dollars. Compute what you'll keep from investments after paying tax on withdrawals, and see if it will be enough for you to live on.

ASSET ALLOCATION FOR YOUR 401(K)

Assuming one of the broad asset allocations outlined on page 275 works for you, here are some investment allocations by asset type. They represent how you could build a portfolio if all of the options were available to you.

100% in stocks	80% in stocks and 20% in bonds	60% in stocks and 40% in bonds	40% in stocks and 60% in bonds	20% in stocks and 80% in bonds
● 60% in funds that invest in large-cap U.S. companies.	● 50% in funds that invest in large-cap U.S. companies.	● 45% in funds that invest in large-cap U.S. companies.	● 40% in funds that invest in large-cap U.S. companies.	● 20% in funds that invest in large-cap U.S. companies.
● 15% in funds that invest in small-cap U.S. companies.	● 10% in funds that invest in small-cap U.S. companies.	● 5% in funds that invest in small-cap U.S. companies.	● 60% in funds that invest in U.S. government and corporate bonds.	● 80% in funds that invest in U.S. government and corporate bonds.
● 25% in funds that invest in major non-U.S. companies.	● 20% in funds that invest in major non-U.S. companies.	● 10% in funds that invest in major non-U.S. companies.		
	● 20% in funds that invest in U.S. government and corporate bonds.	● 40% in funds that invest in U.S. government and corporate bonds.		

Where the Returns Are

Up to 94% of investment returns result from asset allocation, according to a study by Beinson, Hood and Beebower. What matters is the type of asset invested in, such as stocks, bonds or money funds, rather than the particular investments within the type.

COMPOUND ANNUAL RATES OF RETURN BY DECADE

	1920s*	1930s	1940s	1950s	1960s	1970s	1980s	1990s**
Large company	19.2%	-0.1%	9.2%	19.4%	7.8%	5.9%	17.5%	13.0%
Small company	-4.5	1.4	20.7	16.9	15.5	11.5	15.8	15.3
Long-term corp.	5.2	6.9	2.7	1.0	1.7	6.2	13.0	11.3
Long-term govt.	5.0	4.9	3.2	-0.1	1.4	5.5	12.6	11.9
Inter-term govt.	4.2	4.6	1.8	1.3	3.5	7.0	11.9	9.0
Treasury bills	3.7	0.6	0.4	1.9	3.9	6.3	8.9	4.9
Inflation	-1.1	-2.0	5.4	2.2	2.5	7.4	5.1	3.4

*Based on the period 1926-1929 **Based on the period 1990-1995

Source: ©Computed using data from Stocks, Bonds, Bills & Inflation 1997 Yearbook™, Ibbotson Associates, Chicago (annually updates work by Roger G. Ibbotson and Rex Sinquefield). Used with permission. All rights reserved.

Result: Many investors would do better to spend more effort finding the right mix of investments for their needs, and less on seeking the best stock or bond funds among many high-quality candidates.

Retirement-Savings Mistake

Many employees over age 40 who leave their companies use their lump-sum 401(k) distribution checks to pay everyday bills.

Caution: If you're under age 59½, you will owe a penalty as well as taxes on the amount you withdraw, and you will have spent your retirement savings.

Solution: Always move the lump sum into a rollover IRA or a new 401(k) plan. If you need money, take out a home-equity loan or a 401(k) loan, or explore taking monthly distributions from your IRA without tax penalty.

Emergency Funds

If you must withdraw money from a 401(k) retirement savings plan before age 59½, do so early in the year so other interest-earning accounts can help offset income tax and the 10% tax penalty charged by the IRS on early 401(k) withdrawals.

If your withdrawal is for buying your first house, time the purchase so that you close early in the year during which you take the withdrawal.

The mortgage interest and real estate tax deductions can help offset the taxes you will have to pay on the 401(k) withdrawal.

General rule: Withdrawing early from a 401(k) account should be a last resort.

Is Your Pension Plan In Trouble?

Are pensions at risk, or are they safe? The media reports that the nation's retirement income programs are in both jeopardy and fine shape.

Reality: Most pension programs today are sound, but trouble spots do exist.

HOW PENSIONS WORK

There are two basic types of plans.

1. Defined benefit

This is the old-fashioned kind. It promises you a set income throughout retirement. The amount you'll receive varies according to how long you've worked and how much you've earned. Typically, employers make all of the contributions to these plans, and they appoint themselves or others as plan trustees to invest the money. If investment earnings are better than expected, the employer will contribute less money to the plan in future years. If the fund's performance is poor, the employer contributes more money to make up the difference.

2. Defined contribution

With this type of plan, your benefit depends on how much money is contributed and how well it is invested. Your pension will be the amount accumulated in your account, which is often paid as a lump sum.

There are different kinds of defined contribution plans. (Sometimes employers have more than one.)

a) In profit-sharing and money-purchase plans, the employer usually makes the contributions.

b) In 401(k) and 403(b) savings plans, employees themselves are responsible for putting money into the plans, although employers often match their employees' contributions.

PENSION PROBLEMS

While most media attention has focused on underfunded defined benefit plans, the government insurance program protects most of these benefits.

Defined contribution plans, however, are not insured and may be mismanaged. You can become your own pension watchdog by reviewing the financial information that is given to you by your employer's plan.

IRS FORM 5500

Figuring Your Pension Plan's Rate of Return

Here's how to figure out your pension plan's rate of return using Form 5500, which can be obtained by contacting the U.S. Department of Labor, PWBA, Public Disclosure Facility, Room N5638, 200 Constitution Ave. NW, Washington, DC 20210, 202-219-8776.

Income from interest (items 32b(1)(H))
+ Income from dividends (items 32b(2)(C))
+ Income from rents (item 32b(3))
+ Gains/losses from sale of assets (items 32b(4)(C))
+ Unrealized gains/losses (items 32b(5))
+ Gains/losses on special investments (items 32b(6) through (10))
+ Other income (item 32c)
_____
= **Total annual gains/losses**

÷ (+ Total annual gains/losses Net assets at beginning of year (Form 5500 31l, col.(a)))

= Rate of Return

Source: U.S. Department of Labor

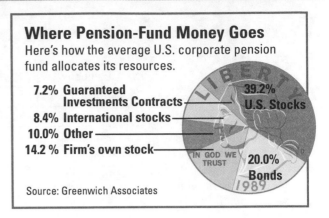

Where Pension-Fund Money Goes

Here's how the average U.S. corporate pension fund allocates its resources.

7.2% **Guaranteed Investments Contracts**
8.4% **International stocks**
10.0% **Other**
14.2 % **Firm's own stock**
39.2% **U.S. Stocks**
20.0% **Bonds**

Source: Greenwich Associates

Here's how: Federal law requires larger company and union plans to provide an overview of the plan's finances each year. This usually takes the form of a one-page Summary Annual Report (SAR) that is either handed out or mailed to all plan members.

The SAR tells you how much money is in the plan and whether plan investments have performed well or poorly. It also says how much the plan trustees have paid out in administrative costs. Large losses and excessive costs can be red flags that signal problem areas.

Important: The SAR will tell you how to get a copy of the detailed financial statement the plan is required to file with the federal government. This statement is called **Form 5500.** Form 5500 will disclose the types of investments (stocks, bonds, real estate and the like) your plan has made and how much money these investments have gained or lost. If yours is a larger plan, you are likely to find attached to Form 5500 a detailed listing of all the investments held by the plan, along with a report by a certified public accountant and information showing the amounts paid to people providing services to the plan.

If the plan trustees have entered into unlawful transactions with company or union officials, their relatives or those with close connections to the plan, this should also appear on Form 5500.

Tip: To help employees analyze their Form 5500s, the Pension Rights Center has published a 42-page guide called *Protecting Your Pension Money* ($8.50, Pension Publications, 918 16 St. NW, Suite 704, Washington, DC 20006-2902).

Strategy: If you discover any questionable transactions or other alarming information in your plan's Form 5500, contact the Department of Labor's Pension and Welfare Benefits Administration field office for your area. If you can't find the listing in the phone book, call the national office of the Department of Labor at 202-219-8840.

Pension Choices

Employees often are offered the choice of an enhanced pension or a lump-sum severance payment as an incentive to take early retirement. It can be difficult to decide which is most valuable.

Rule of thumb: Multiply the increase in your pension by 100 and compare it with the cash payment. An extra $500 per month added to your pension would be the equivalent of a severance payment of around $50,000.

Note: The 100 multiplier is based on a series of complex calculations that take into account such factors as life expectancy, age of retirement and present value of the payment.

Integration Trap

If your pension plan is an integrated plan, your retirement income may be less than you expect.

Reason: Your calculated pension benefit is offset by your Social Security benefits, instead of being in addition to them.

Nonintegrated Pension Plan	Integrated Pension Plan
A nonintegrated pension plan will pay you $1,000 per month. If you also receive $400 from Social Security, your total monthly retirement income will be $1,400.	Under an integrated plan your $400 Social Security benefit will offset about $300 of your pension benefit, making your pension only about $700 monthly. This and the $400 from Social Security will total only $1,100.
You receive monthly: 　$1,000 Pension 　　　　 payment +　 $400 Social Security	**You receive monthly:** 　$1,000 Pension 　　　　 payment +　 $400 Social Security -　 $300 Offset by 　　　　 Social Security
= $1,400 Monthly total	= $1,100 Monthly total

Make the Most of Your IRA

No one likes to save for retirement. In fact, most investors will use any excuse to avoid socking away money now that they won't be able to use for 20 years or more. There are just too many demanding ways to spend extra income: on a new home, a car, children's college educations or credit card debt.

Safety Net
An IRA is just as important as a 401(k). The uncertainties of the workplace mean that you may not have a 401(k) throughout your career, and Social Security is no longer the sure thing it once was.

As a result, most Individual Retirement Accounts (IRAs) have been sorely underfunded compared with 401(k)s. Investors view the 401(k) as the better choice because it takes money directly out of their paychecks in the form of pretax dollars. A 401(k) also allows for higher contributions than an IRA, and its contributions are often matched by employers.

DON'T UNDERESTIMATE THE REWARDS
One of the reasons people don't contribute the annual maximum amount, $2,000, to their IRAs is that they don't think it will add up to a significant portion of their retirement savings. They feel that their other savings accounts are really where the action is. They're wrong.

Reason: Assume you invest $2,000 a year from age 25 to age 35 and then stop making contributions. If your investment earns 12% annually, the S&P 500 Index's annual return over the past 50 years, your money will grow to $1.26 million by the time you turn 65. Assuming your spouse is the same age and also contributes to an IRA, you'll have a total of $2.52 million. If you each continue to contribute until you reach age 65, you will accumulate a total of $3.07 million for your retirement years.

Inflation will chip away at the value of your IRA over 30 years, but that should not stop any investor from making contributions.

DON'T ASSUME YOU CAN'T DEDUCT YOUR CONTRIBUTIONS
It is a common misconception that contributions to IRAs are no longer deductible.

IRAS: HOW MUCH CAN YOU DEDUCT IN 1998?

Many people don't realize that tax deductions for IRA contributions are gradually phased out (not cut off) for single people making $30,000 to $40,000 and married couples making $50,000 to $60,000. Take advantage of any deduction for which you are eligible.

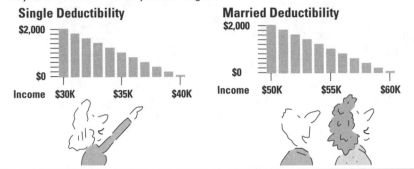

Single Deductibility

$2,000

$0

Income $30K $35K $40K

Married Deductibility

$2,000

$0

Income $50K $55K $60K

INVEST HALF OF YOUR IRA IN FOREIGN STOCKS

Over long periods, foreign stocks have beaten U.S. stocks, and studies suggest that a blend of U.S. and overseas stocks can reduce your risk by as much as half that of a portfolio of only domestic stocks.

Strategy: Put 80% of your foreign portfolio in overseas funds whose managers spread their assets among different countries.

Important: Devote about 20% of your foreign-stock portfolio to an emerging-markets fund, which invests in countries that are just starting to expand economically. Typically, such funds are volatile. But since this is retirement money, time is on your side.

Include a broad mix of four domestic stock funds. Your domestic-fund choices should include funds that buy small-, midsize- and large-company stocks. To determine what types of companies a fund invests in, ask what the average market capitalization is in its portfolio. Less than $1 billion is a small-cap fund, $1 billion–$5 billion is a mid-cap and $5 billion or more is a large-cap fund.

Up until 1986, almost anyone could deduct his or her annual $2,000 IRA contribution. Then the law changed to eliminate some deductions, and many people stopped funding their accounts.

Reality: Most investors still qualify for deductible contributions. Only those who are covered by employer-sponsored retirement plans and earn more than $40,000 in 1998 ($60,000 for married couples filing jointly) cannot claim any deductions.

Important: For many investors, the actual cost of funding an IRA is much lower than $2,000 a year. For example, a fully deductible $2,000 contribution costs only the equivalent of $1,440 if you are in the 28% tax bracket.

DON'T TREAT BONDS AS LONG-TERM INVESTMENTS

If you won't need the money in your IRA for ten years or longer, avoid bonds, even at 7% to 8%. The chances that stock returns will trail bond returns over any ten-year period are very small. Over longer periods, the advantage to owning stocks is even greater.

Example: The best 20-year period for bonds during the past 200 years was barely better than the worst period for stocks. During the past 50 years, there were 41 rolling ten-year periods: 1945 to 1954, 1946 to 1955 and so on. Government bonds beat inflation in only 14 of those periods on a pretax basis. And government bonds beat inflation during only seven of 31 twenty-year periods. Bonds had their best-ever decade in the 1980s, but they still trailed stocks.

IRAs are for long-term investors, and bonds are not great long-term investments.

DON'T WASTE THE TAX BREAK

Occasionally I see people who invest their IRA money in tax-sheltered annuities. Annuities are issued by insurance companies, and annuity returns are tax-deferred. You pay an extra one or two percentage points in fees to get that tax break.

There is no reason to do that if your returns are already sheltered, as they are in an IRA.

HOLD INCOME INVESTMENTS IN YOUR IRA

If bonds or high-yield stocks are part of your long-term investment strategy, hold them inside the shelter of an IRA or other tax-sheltered account.

Reason: Outside an IRA, you will pay tax on the income from a bond every year. But if you hold growth stocks outside an IRA, you don't have to pay tax on capital gains until you sell the stocks for a profit. That way, you are taking advantage of tax-deferred compounding, both inside your IRA and outside of it, which is a little like having your cake and eating it too.

SEP-IRA Alert

Simplified employee pension plans make sense, even in the early phases of a new business when cash flow is tight. The plan known as an SEP-IRA gives you the comfort of knowing a cushion is being set aside even as you endure the trials of making a new business succeed.

Establish a SEP-IRA with **Form 5305-SEP**, available from banks and mutual fund companies. You may contribute up to 15% of net self-employment earnings from the previous year, up to a maximum of $30,000.

Alternative: You can also establish a Keogh retirement plan, which is more complicated but allows you to save 25% of self-employment earnings up to a maximum of $30,000.

Early IRA Withdrawal

Many Individual Retirement Account agreements let you have your balance paid over your lifetime in equal yearly payments. And, you can ask that payouts start at any time. The company holding your account will use IRS tables to determine your life expectancy and start sending you the money. You will pay taxes, but no penalties, on the withdrawals.

Caution: Once started, the arrangement cannot be stopped until you reach age 59½ or the plan has run for at least five years, whichever is longer.

IRA Tax Strategy

All funds distributed from an IRA are taxed as ordinary income at rates up to 39.6%, even if they are derived from long-term capital gains that would be taxed at no more than 28% and maybe much lower!

Strategy: If you want a portfolio that contains both taxable bonds (or other income-producing securities) and appreciating stocks, buy the bonds in your IRA and keep the stocks outside the IRA.

The bond income that normally would be taxed at top rates will obtain tax deferral from the IRA, and the capital gains tax break will be preserved for the appreciating stocks.

When to Withdraw From Your IRA

You can put off the first withdrawal until April 1 of the year following the year you reach 70½.

Caution: If you delay taking the first distribution until April 1, you are still required to make a second withdrawal by December 31 of that year.

Trap: Taking two withdrawals in one year can push your income to the point where you pay tax on 85% rather than 50% of your Social Security benefits.

Self-defense: Take this into account when deciding whether to put off your first withdrawal until April 1.

Answers to Your Elder-Law Questions

As we age, issues relating to money management and health care are of paramount importance.

These concerns are often handled by elder law attorneys, specialists in the areas of law that deal with the issues of aging. Here are the questions most frequently put to elder law attorneys.

WHO WILL MANAGE MY AFFAIRS IF I BECOME INCAPACITATED?

If a person fails to make arrangements to deal with this issue and becomes unable to handle his or her finances, often a court is called upon to act. Guardianships or other court-monitored procedures may come into play. These procedures are not only potentially embarrassing and time consuming, but costly. And they may result in the appointment of someone the impaired person would not choose.

If a person takes action before the onset of incapacity, then he or she can determine who will handle financial matters. Two tools that will help you do this are a durable power of attorney and a living trust.

Durable power of attorney

This is a document used to name someone to act as an agent (called the attorney-in-fact) for the person signing the form (called the principal). It lists a wide range of financial items that the agent can handle, such as banking transactions, selling real estate and trading stocks and bonds. The agent can also be authorized to file tax returns, make gifts on behalf of the principal and transfer property to trusts set up by the principal before incapacity.

The agent can be a spouse, adult child, friend or paid agent, such as an attorney or accountant. Since the agent has virtually unfettered discretion on money matters, the person named should be one in whom the principal has complete trust. It's wise to appoint more than one agent so there is a system of monitoring. And a successor should be named to ensure that there will always be someone available to act.

TIP **Springing Power of Attorney**

Consider using a springing power of attorney. It becomes effective only after a physician certifies you have a disabling incapacity.

Living trust

These trusts are sometimes referred to as inter vivos trusts. You transfer your property to the trust and it is then managed according to the terms of the trust and state law. For example, you could change the title of your stocks and house to the name of the trust.

The manager of the trust is called a trustee. Usually, the person who sets up the trust also acts as trustee for as long as he or she is able, although in some states a co-trustee is necessary.

Generally the trust is revocable, meaning that the person setting it up (the grantor or settlor) retains the power to cancel the trust or change its provisions. Once incapacitated, however, the grantor can no longer act. In this case, another trustee named in the trust by the grantor takes over. The trustee can be a spouse, family member or, in the case of large trusts, a bank or trust company (which can serve alone or with a family member).

In general, for someone whose finances are straightforward, a durable power of attorney may be all that is needed for satisfactory money management. For those with more complicated financial situations (with investment properties, business interests and more), a trust may be advisable. The trust can be used to coordinate a person's estate plans and designate who will inherit the property when the grantor dies.

WHO WILL MAKE MY HEALTH CARE DECISIONS IF I CAN'T?

The U.S. Supreme Court has recognized that all competent adults have the right to refuse unwanted medical treatment if they clearly express this desire.

Example: A person can refuse to have a breathing apparatus used in the event of an incurable or irreversible mental or physical condition with no reasonable expectation of recovery, a state of permanent unconsciousness or profound dementia, or an injury from which there is no reasonable expectation of recovering or regaining a meaningful quality of life.

The clearest way to express your wishes about medical care is by signing a living will. Some states allow an adult to name a spouse, relative or friend to make medical decisions when the person is unable to through a health care proxy or durable power of attorney for health care.

Both the living will and health care proxy must be witnessed or notarized according to state law.

HOW CAN I GET THE BEST CARE ON MEDICARE?

Patients must learn to be their own advocates regarding their medical treatment. It is a patient's right to be given respect, informed of the benefits and risks of procedures, and informed of the cost involved with each procedure. Attorneys generally do not intercede between a patient and doctor.

Ask if your doctor accepts assignment. This means that the doctor has agreed to accept as the entire fee the amount approved by Medicare as the reasonable charge.

If the doctor accepts assignment, the patient need only pay the 20% copayment (plus the amount of the deductible if it has not already been met). Additionally, the patient is relieved of having to submit bills for reimbursement. The patient's Medicare Supplemental Insurance (called a Medigap policy) will cover the coinsurance and deductibles.

If the doctor does not accept assignment, fees are still subject to a limiting charge. The doctor can charge no more than a certain percentage (generally 115%) of what Medicare considers a reasonable charge for the service. Medicare still covers only 80% of what it considers a reasonable doctor's fee. The patient must pay the balance.

IF MEDICAID PAYS FOR MY NURSING HOME, WILL MY SPOUSE BECOME POOR?

Medicaid is a government program designed to provide medical care to help those who cannot help themselves. State law sets dollar limits (within federal parameters) on how much income a person can earn and how many assets one can own while still qualifying for Medicaid. For many, Medicaid is the only way to pay for the high cost of long-term nursing care.

Medicaid rules, however, are also intended to protect spouses of Medicaid recipients from becoming impoverished. The spouse who does not go into a nursing home can keep a certain amount of assets and income without jeopardizing Medicaid eligibility for the other spouse. In fact, the spouse at home can even receive income (such as investment income or Social Security) from the spouse in the nursing home if needed for support.

Medicaid planning is complicated. In the quest to preserve assets for family members while qualifying for Medicaid, some may postpone or prevent eligibility by unadvisedly transferring property. It is important for prospective Medicaid recipients to get the advice of an elder law attorney.

How to Avoid Costly Social Security Mistakes

Despite ominous media coverage, Social Security remains a reliable source of retirement income. You can't expect Uncle Sam to track you down, however, and throw a fat check into your lap each month.

It's up to you to follow the prescribed paper trail if you want to collect every dollar you're entitled to receive. To make the most of Social Security, you must avoid these mistakes.

ASSUMING THAT YOU'LL QUALIFY FOR BENEFITS

If you were born in 1929 or later, you need 40 quarters of coverage to receive full benefits. For most workers, that's ten years of employment at four quarters per year. (Older retirees may qualify for full benefits with as few as 32 quarters.)

Recommendation: A few years before you plan to retire, request a Personal Earnings and Benefit Estimate Statement (PEBES) from the Social Security Administration (800-772-1213), which summarizes your earnings history. If you'll be a few credits short of qualifying for a full retirement benefit, keep working until you make up the shortfall.

LETTING ERRORS IN YOUR EARNINGS HISTORY GO UNCHECKED

The Social Security bureaucracy is huge and, consequently, fault-prone. Information lapses relating to your work history can shortchange you when it's time to collect benefits.

Solution: Request a PEBES every three years while you're working. Any errors in your earnings record must be corrected within three years, three months and 15 days of the error.

Backup: If you miss the deadline, you still can rectify the mistake by using an old W-2 form as proof of earnings.

Last resort: If you can't prove an error with an old W-2 (employers don't have to hold on to them for more than three years), try to get a copy of your tax return from the IRS (800-829-1040). The process becomes more complicated if you wait more than six years.

BLINDLY ACCEPTING THE AMOUNT OF YOUR BENEFIT

Even if your earnings history is accurate, Social Security may miscalculate your benefit.

Solution: Get a well-written book on Social Security and go through the worksheet to check the math. If you know someone who is an actuary, ask him or her to crunch the numbers with you. The manager of your local Social Security office may be willing to help you.

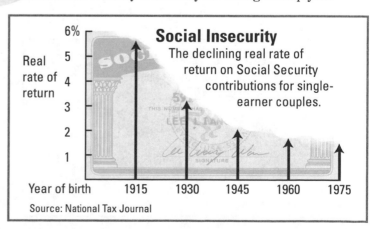

Social Insecurity
The declining real rate of return on Social Security contributions for single-earner couples.

Real rate of return (6% scale)

Year of birth: 1915, 1930, 1945, 1960, 1975

Source: National Tax Journal

MISTIMING YOUR APPLICATION FOR BENEFITS

A few days' difference can cost you hundreds of dollars.

Reminder: You'll need your Social Security card (call in advance for a replacement if you've lost yours), proof of age such as a birth certificate, and your W-2s for the past two years.

RETIRING TOO LATE

You can retire at 62 with a reduced benefit, at 65 with a full benefit and after 65 with an enhanced benefit. (For people born after 1937, these retirement ages will gradually increase to age 67 for full benefits.) Many people delay retirement to get a larger benefit.

Catch: Delaying retirement means continuing to work. In turn, that means continuing to pay income tax and Social Security tax. The amount you add to your benefit by working additional years seldom compensates for the income deferral and taxation in the interim.

Strategy: Unless you have to work or want to work, retire at age 62 and begin collecting Social Security benefits. Early retirees get 80% of their full retirement benefits.

You would have to live until age 77 before the benefits from retiring later catch up to the benefits of retiring earlier. Even then, the early retiree has the edge because money is worth more if you get it sooner rather than later. Collecting benefits early also reduces the risk that you'll die before you have the chance to collect.

WAITING TOO LONG FOR SPOUSAL BENEFITS

Some spouses can claim benefits based either on their own earnings or on their mate's earnings.

Example: Jack and Melissa are husband and wife. Melissa has always earned more money than Jack.

Predicting Your Life Span

How long will your retirement savings have to last you? It may be longer than you expect.

40% of Americans die by age 75.

40% of Americans live to age 82.

Source: U.S. Census, 1990

Jack retires before Melissa, but does not start collecting benefits on his own earnings record. He decides to wait until Melissa retires to start collecting Social Security because he knows that, as the spouse of the high-earning retiree, he will be entitled to a larger benefit amount.

Trap: Instead, Jack might start collecting his own benefits at 62, then keep collecting his lower benefit, missing out on the higher benefit based on Melissa's earnings.

Solution: Jack can start collecting his own benefits at 62. When Melissa retires, Jack can switch to a benefit based on her earnings, if that is to his advantage.

Note: Jack will have to make a new application in order to switch.

Taking the Insecurity Out of Social Security

Social Security pays out about $380 billion each year in benefits. But unless you're older than 62, the age at which you first become eligible to receive the checks, you probably have not given your benefits much thought.

If you or someone you know is about to become eligible for Social Security benefits, keep these tips in mind.

CHECK THE NAME ON YOUR SOCIAL SECURITY EARNINGS RECORD

It's very important for the name that appears on your payroll records to match the name that appears on your Social Security card. Some people may change their names because of marriage or divorce. Others may change them because of personal preference, perhaps by adding or omitting a middle initial.

If there is a discrepancy between the name that is listed on your W-2 form and the name that appears on your Social Security card, notify the Social Security Administration as soon as possible.

While there's no statute of limitations for correcting Social Security records, you must have some evidence, such as W-2 forms or other payroll records, to support your claim. If you wait too long to clear up a discrepancy, your employer may not have the old payroll records to back you up when you finally file for benefits.

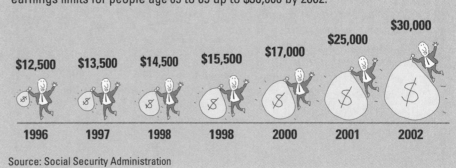

TIP **Before Taking Early Retirement**

Early retirement may reduce Social Security benefits beyond the 20% hit you take if you start benefits at age 62 instead of age 65.

Reason: The basis of your benefit is calculated on the basis of the amount of income you earn in your 35 highest-earning years. Most people earn their highest incomes during their last years of work, so retiring early can reduce their benefits.

SOCIAL SECURITY FORM
7004

Strategy: Call Social Security at 800-772-1213 to ask for an estimate of benefits, **Form SSA-7004**, with which you request a detailed statement of earnings record and estimates of the benefit you will receive based on different retirement ages.

DON'T TAP YOUR RETIREMENT ACCOUNTS TOO SOON

Many people who decide to wait until age 65 to receive benefits sell off some of their retirement investments to meet expenses, sacrificing years of tax-deferred growth by yanking those assets from an IRA, Keogh or 401(k) account.

Strategy: If you have significant assets and can afford to retire early by living off your regular investments, it may make sense to delay your Social Security benefits. On the other hand, if you can invest your benefits rather than spend them, the initial advantage of receiving a smaller check early will be enhanced.

CONSIDER THE TAX ADVANTAGES OF TAKING BENEFITS EARLY

Social Security benefits are tax-free for single people who earn $25,000 or less, or married couples filing jointly who earn $32,000 or less. If you earn between $25,001 and $34,000 as a single person or between $32,001 and $44,000 as a married couple filing jointly, you may have to pay income tax on up to 50% of your benefits.

But if you earn more than $34,000 as a single person or $44,000 as a married couple filing jointly, you may have to pay income tax on up to 85% of your benefits.

These taxes, however, are still lower than those on all your income from sources such as stocks and bonds. And bear in mind that as long as your money remains in retirement accounts, such as IRAs and Keoghs, the earnings accumulate free of tax.

The moment you pull money out of those accounts, it generally becomes fully taxable.

APPLY FOR BENEFITS ON TIME

Many people do not apply as soon as they reach age 62 because they assume that they will earn too much and be penalized. If you continue to work after you start drawing benefits, your benefits will be reduced if you have excess earnings.

Earnings limits for 1998

- People under age 65 lose $1 of benefits for every $2 of income they earn above $9,120.
- People between 65 and 69 lose $1 of benefits for every $3 they earn over $14,500.
- People who are 70 and older can earn any amount without sacrificing any benefits.

Strategy: Apply in January of the year in which you plan to commence receiving benefits, but not more than three months before age 62, regardless of how much you expect to earn. This is particularly true if you think you may just work a few months and not an entire year.

Reason: The earlier in the year you apply, the more months you will have over which to spread your excess earnings.

Increased Earnings Limits

The Social Security Administration plans to gradually increase the annual earnings limits for people age 65 to 69 up to $30,000 by 2002.

$12,500	$13,500	$14,500	$15,500	$17,000	$25,000	$30,000
1996	1997	1998	1998	2000	2001	2002

Source: Social Security Administration

INFORM SOCIAL SECURITY IF YOU EXPECT TO EXCEED THE EARNINGS LIMIT

Having benefits withheld is less painful than having to give back benefits you have already received.

Important: If benefits are incorrectly paid, you will have to repay them. Also, there are penalties for intentionally failing to report your earnings or reporting them incorrectly. Contact your local Social Security office if you are concerned.

TAKE YOUR INVESTMENT STYLE INTO CONSIDERATION

If you're knowledgeable about investing and have a significant portion of your portfolio in stocks, you'll probably do better by taking early benefits rather than selling securities. Invest the benefits aggressively for high future returns if you do not need the income. Your investment gains over three years will probably outpace the larger Social Security checks that you would receive by waiting.

If you're a conservative investor, however, and limit yourself to low-risk, low-return bank certificates of deposit and Treasury securities, you'll probably do better by delaying your benefits until you reach age 65 and receiving more annually.

Reason: Your investment gains will be relatively low compared with the rate of inflation. They also won't equal the benefit increase you would get by waiting until age 65.

DON'T IGNORE THE IMPORTANCE OF YOUR SPOUSE'S AGE

It often makes sense to wait until age 65 to take Social Security benefits if you are married to someone who is much younger than yourself.

Example: Let's say you are 62 and your spouse is 40. If you retire this year and apply for benefits, not only will you get smaller benefit checks than if you had worked three more years, but your spouse will also receive a much smaller survivor's check if you die.

  Social Security says if you work less than 15 hours a month, you're retired.

If you work over 45 hours a month, however, you're not retired.

How Working Affects Social Security

People who work while collecting Social Security benefits face the possibility of a partial reduction of their Social Security check. There is a limit to the amount you can earn from wages or self-employment income while still collecting your full benefit.

Exception: People who are age 70 and older are exempt from these limits.

The limits: The amount that you may earn before your Social Security check is reduced changes every year and depends on your age.

Tip: There is a special monthly rule that applies during the first year that you receive Social Security. During 1998, if you are under age 65 and earn less than $760 in any month ($1,208 for those age 65 to 69), you will receive your full benefit for that month.

THE TWO TYPES OF INCOME

Income that counts toward your earnings limits	Income that doesn't count toward your earnings limits
● Bonuses.	● Investment income.
● Commissions.	● Interest income.
● Fees.	● Veterans' benefits.
● Vacation pay.	● Annuities.
● Pay in lieu of vacation.	● Capital gains.
● Cash tips of $20 or more a month.	● Gifts or inheritances.
● Severance pay.	● Rental income, in most cases.
● Some non-cash compensation, such as meals or living quarters, can also count under certain circumstances.	● Income from trust funds.
	● Jury duty pay.

More Work, More Social Security

Even after your retirement, any income from a part-time job counts toward Social Security entitlements. Social Security automatically refigures your benefit amount after additional earnings are credited to your earnings record.

Result: A Social Security recipient working part-time can be paid wages and additional Social Security, as long as earnings do not exceed the annual limit.

Bigger Social Security Benefits

People who reach age 66 to 69 in the year during which they plan to retire from work should make a claim for Social Security benefits no later than July of that year. A quirk in the law may let them receive retroactive unreduced benefits back to the beginning of the year after such an early filing. A later filing, however, will result in a smaller benefit for the entire year.

1. Proof of your income from the last year you worked

The Social Security office has records of most of the income you have earned over your lifetime, but they may not yet have your most recent (and perhaps your highest) income records. When applying for benefits during 1998, bring your 1997 W-2 or self-employment tax return. This way your 1997 income will be added to your account immediately, instead of when Social Security finally gets around to it, and your benefit will grow.

2. Your birth certificate

Your claim may be delayed if you show up at the Social Security office without a certified copy of your birth certificate.

Get a certified copy from the proper authority in advance and bring it with you on the day you apply for Social Security. It will be returned to you at a later date.

3. Family information and documents

If you are married, bring your spouse's Social Security number and birth certificate (if your spouse is at least 62 years old). Your spouse may get benefits on your record.

Your divorced spouse may also be entitled to benefits. Inform Social Security that you were previously married and the Social Security office will handle the claim from there. You will be asked for your ex-spouse's Social Security number and last known address, if available.

NEW SOCIAL SECURITY REPORTS

Workers 60 and older should automatically receive annual benefits statements from the Social Security Administration. The statements list an estimate of your benefit if you retire at 62, 65 or 70, how much you would receive if you became disabled and what your survivors will receive.

Social Security Tips

Guarantee smooth and fast processing of your Social Security retirement application by remembering this advice.

DON'T WALK INTO THE SOCIAL SECURITY OFFICE UNANNOUNCED

Save time and aggravation by scheduling an appointment ahead of time with your local Social Security office. You will avoid the potentially long wait at the office for walk-ins.

Bonus: You may be able to complete your application by telephone. (You will be given directions for mailing supporting documentation.)

COLLECT ALL THE NECESSARY RECORDS

Bring all your important documents to the meeting so that you won't have to go back again.

Social Security Decisions Are Never Final

You have the right to appeal any decision made by the Social Security Administration. There are four levels of appeal, and you can take your case as far as the federal courts.

Important: Read all correspondence from Social Security very carefully. Although you're allowed 60 days to file an appeal, don't wait. The sooner you get moving, the sooner your case will be considered and decided.

HOW TO APPEAL A SOCIAL SECURITY DECISION

Step 1
The first step is reconsideration, in which you request a review of your original case, complete with any new evidence.

Step 2
If you disagree with the reconsideration, you may request a hearing before an Administrative Law Judge (ALJ) in which you may submit new evidence.

Step 3
If that decision goes against you, ask for an Appeals Council review. The Council may review, refuse to review or return the case to an ALJ for further consideration.

Step 4
If all else fails, take civil action in a Federal District Court.

Act Quickly
You have only 60 days to appeal after getting notice of a decision.

You can represent yourself or hire someone to represent you throughout the appeals process. The representative, who might be a lawyer, but doesn't have to be, must get written approval from Social Security to charge a fee, which is limited to 25% of the back benefits you receive if you win, or $4,000, whichever is less. Social Security (800-772-1213) will provide a list of representatives if you request it.

You can never submit too much evidence. A representative can help you navigate the bureaucracy you may not be familiar with and help secure evidence. If you are disabled, your representative can go to hearings for you. You don't pay the representative if you don't win.

Important: Maintain a file on your appeal and keep a record of everything you do concerning it.

SOURCES
Sources are listed in the order in which their contributions appear. A source may have contributed part or all of an article, or a series of articles.

Gordon K. Williamson, CFP, CLU, Gordon Williamson & Associates

Jonathan Pond, Financial Planning Information, Inc.

Sidney Kess, CPA and attorney

Jonathan Pond, Financial Planning Information, Inc.

Julie Beckley, National Association of Area Agencies on Aging

David J. Jepsen, Frank Russell Co.

Ted Benna, The 401(k) Association

Karen Ferguson, Pension Rights Center

Alexandra Armstrong, CFP, Armstrong, Welch & Macintyre, Inc.

Anthony Gallea, Smith Barney

Ted Benna, The 401(k) Association

Karen Ferguson, Pension Rights Center

Bill Mischell, Foster Higgins

Peter E. Gaudio and Virginia A. Nicols, John Wiley & Sons, Inc.

Gordon K. Williamson, CFP, CLU, Gordon Williamson & Associates

Louann Nagy Werksma, Wordwerks Communications

David J. Silverman, David J. Silverman & Co.

Lewis J. Altfest, CFP, L. J. Altfest & Co.

Laurence Foster, KPMG Peat Marwick, LLP

Peter J. Strauss, Esq., Epstein Becker & Green PC

Nancy Levitin, author of *Retirement Rights*

J. Robert Treanor, William M. Mercer, Inc.

Kiplinger's Personal Finance Magazine

Herbert Loring, Social Security Administration

Karen Tatum, Social Security Administration

John Clark, New York regional Social Security Administration

Alex W. Bussey, New York regional Social Security Administration

Michael Bosley, coauthor of *How to Get Every Penny You're Entitled to from Social Security*

Travel
Go Far on a Little

How to Plan the Perfect Vacation

There is no such thing as a trouble-free vacation. It doesn't matter whether you're off on a weekend jaunt or a worldwide sojourn.

Good news: The right type of planning can help. It not only makes any vacation easier, but makes it a lot more enjoyable too.

Here's the best way to go about planning the perfect vacation.

CHOOSE THE RIGHT VACATION FOR YOU

Make sure you're choosing the right type of vacation for your particular needs at the moment. There is no reason to go on a vacation, be it to Bermuda or Bangkok, simply because your parents or neighbors are raving about it. Before you even consider where to go, think about your needs.

- Do you need to get away and relax?
- Do you want to cut loose and try something new?

 Taking the time to figure out what you need out of a vacation is 90% of the battle. Unfortunately, it is also the 90% that is most frequently overlooked.

CHOOSE YOUR TRAVEL AGENT

Good travel agents have several things in common. They take the time to get to know you and your needs, and offer counseling and advice. Move on if the agent you're dealing with is just reading from a brochure or a computer screen.

Beyond getting a good feeling for a travel agent based on the interest the agent shows, you should always ask whether he or she is familiar with the type of trip you're seeking, be it adventure, education or relaxation. Ask if the agent has been on any of these trips and is personally familiar with the newest vacations being offered.

Caution: Avoid schemes that promise everything at unbelievable prices. Remember, if it seems too good to be true, it is. That's why it is important to work through a travel professional, someone who is well-informed about the range of vacations available. Obviously, not all travel agents are equal. Make sure to work with someone you're comfortable with and who is familiar with the type of vacation you're seeking.

PLAN AHEAD

You don't need to lock yourself into anything, but it is desirable to start thinking about your needs as early as six months before you may want to leave. This gives you plenty of time to examine all the options

The best travel agents use all the resources available to them to find a vacation that matches your needs.

WHILE YOU'RE AWAY

Once you've decided what you need and where to go, the biggest challenge you'll face is determining how much detailed planning you will need once you're at your destination.

Too much planning and scheduling will make your vacation seem like a job, eliminating any chance for exploring and spontaneity. Too little planning may mean you'll miss out on the special attractions at your vacation spot. While everyone has different needs, some wise travelers never plan more than half of their time.

It may sound simple, but a good attitude is the first thing you need to take on a vacation. You're supposed to have fun. Unexpected problems will surface, but they don't have to ruin your vacation. Here are some common problems, and how to handle them.

available and hunt for the best bargains. Set a budget so you know what you can spend. Be enthusiastic about your upcoming vacation, but don't create unrealistic expectations. Such expectations are almost never met, and you'll only be frustrated by the inevitable shortcomings of any trip, ruining what could otherwise be a great getaway.

Usually, the best way to save money on hotels, car rentals and airfares is to book ahead. Use a qualified travel agent to help you get the best deals.

Travel agents should also help you negotiate your way through the maze of airline fares. However, if you're interested in saving money on airfares, consider staying at your destination over a Saturday, taking an indirect route or leaving from a secondary airport. Don't worry about locking in a low airfare early. If you find out about better discounts later on, it is usually possible to have a ticket changed for a small fee.

Accommodations vary widely from luxury hotels and resorts to chain motels to bed and breakfast inns. The most important thing to remember is that no hotel will be as comfortable and familiar as your own home.

Match the hotel to the type of trip you're planning. Above all, you want to be comfortable and relaxed. That may mean an expensive suite in a hotel for some, while for others it means a moderately priced room in a clean motel or a stay at a charming bed and breakfast.

Start planning your vacation six months in advance— especially if you want the best deal.

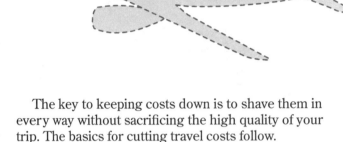

Lost or stolen airline ticket
Immediately file a Lost Ticket Application with the airline that issued it. The matter could take 90 days to resolve, however, so you'll have to purchase a replacement ticket.

Lost luggage
File a claim immediately with the baggage service people, showing them your ticket and baggage stubs. Usually, the luggage shows up on a different flight and will be forwarded to your hotel. Otherwise, the airline will issue a refund for your lost goods within a period of two to six weeks.

Delayed and canceled flights
Often, the airlines will attempt to accommodate passengers by putting them up in hotels or rerouting them. Stay calm. Losing your cool won't get you out of the airport any faster.

Travel Insurance Money Saver

Travel insurance is included in many other policies and under many credit card agreements.

Examples: Accident insurance is automatic when tickets are charged with the American Express card ($100,000 coverage) or Visa Gold card ($150,000). Many homeowner's policies protect personal belongings during travel, including passports, tickets and sometimes cash. Car insurance often covers damages to rental cars in the U.S. and Canada.

Before you travel: Check your coverage to avoid buying unnecessary travel policies.

Save Big Money on Travel Costs

Most people love to travel and would do a great deal more of it if they could just figure out ways to reduce their travel expenses.

The key to keeping costs down is to shave them in every way without sacrificing the high quality of your trip. The basics for cutting travel costs follow.

AIRFARES
Make sure your travel agent uses computer programs like Fare Assurance or Aqua. Fare Assurance searches constantly for the newest, lowest fares, while simultaneously double-checking your ticket until the last minute to see if you might qualify for a better deal.

Special savings: Don't pay for your ticket until the deadline, especially if your ticket is non-refundable or incurs charges for any changes. That way you'll be able to rebook easily.

ACCOMMODATIONS
Call hotels directly. Skip the toll-free 800 number to a central booking service. On-site reservations personnel usually offer better rates. Consider a home exchange if you're staying a month or more. For an $83 fee, you can list your home in Homelink (800-638-3841), and receive five issues of its publication between December and July.

TOURS
Decide how much you can spend, and contact a travel agency specializing in personalized tours. For example, Journeys! (800-344-8890) will arrange a budget-minded one- to two-week walking tour of a historic city.

You can also contact tour operators close to their cancellation deadline and ask to be wait-listed. When they call, negotiate up to 50% off. Most tours have final payment/cancellation deadlines. When cancellations occur, last-minute bargains may appear.

TRAINS
Buy a round-trip ticket even if you don't intend to use both halves. For example, you can pay Amtrak (800-USA-RAIL) $204 for a one-way ticket from New York City to Orlando, or you can ask about discount availabilities and pay as little as $146 for a round-trip ticket, which costs you only $73 each way.

Travel Bargains Galore

FreeFlier, a new service, will enroll you in more than two dozen award programs operated by airlines, car rental firms and hotels, including all major travel award programs now in operation and all new ones that open within 12 months. It also puts you on mailing lists to receive information about travel discounts, upgrade opportunities and special promotions.

More information: FreeFlier, Inc., Bowling Green Station, Box 844, New York, NY 10274, 212-727-9675. Cost: $9.95. Cost for students, seniors, people over 50, retirees and groups of four or more: $7.50.

TOUR BOOKING SELF-DEFENSE
To protect your deposit when signing up for a tour, make sure the tour company belongs to the National Tour Association or U.S. Tour Operators Association. Both have consumer-protection plans. Pay with a credit card if possible. If you must use cash, get a receipt.

Overseas ATM Withdrawls

Notify your bank if you will be using your ATM card to make cash withdrawals overseas and you are not a frequent traveler. A series of withdrawals from unexpected places might lead your bank to block your account.

Cardholders should also check with their banks to be sure a primary account has been designated (checking or savings). Many banks outside the U.S. do not allow you to choose which account to make your transaction from. If your primary account is not designated by the U.S. bank, the overseas bank will make the decision as to which account the transaction will affect, or, in some cases, deny the request.

Tip: Many keypads of machines outside the U.S. have only numbers, not letters. Before going overseas, learn the numeric equivalent of your PIN.

Important: If your ATM card is lost or stolen, notify the bank within two business days in order to limit your liability to no more than $50.

ATM Bonus
Automated Teller Machines (ATMs) give better exchange rates than hotels or airport money counters for travelers who need to convert U.S. dollars to foreign currencies when traveling abroad. One survey found ATM rates to be 43% lower than airport money-counter rates and 57% lower than hotel rates.

Bonus: ATMs are usually available 24 hours a day.

Overseas Credit Card Purchases

Overseas purchases on a credit or charge card can eventually be more, or less, expensive than expected. It all depends on exchange rate fluctuations and how long it takes for the card company to process the paperwork.

Rule of thumb: When the value of the dollar is increasing, the longer it takes to post and clear a charge, the cheaper the purchase becomes. When the dollar is falling, you want the paper-work cleared quickly.

Clearing times:
- American Express: 0 to 7 days.
- Diners Club: 1 to 5 days.
- MasterCard: 0 to 3 days.
- Visa: 3 to 6 days.

Larger retailers in big cities tend to process paperwork daily, or even immediately, electronically. Purchases made from smaller merchants and those in remote villages can take up to a week to clear.

Great, Little-Known National Parks

BIG BEND NATIONAL PARK

320 miles southeast of El Paso, Texas, Big Bend offers some of the most diverse terrain in the U.S., ranging from desert to 8,000-foot mountains. Visitors can find desert flowers and cactuses in bloom just a few miles away from forested mountain slopes. The park can be toured by car or raft, or by hiking the numerous trails.

More information: 915-477-2251.

Overseas Credit Card Trap

When traveling abroad and using a credit card, watch out for the conversion fee that many banks charge to convert charges in foreign currencies to dollars. As with traveler's checks, some banks don't and some banks do charge a fee, generally 1% of the purchase amount. So if you have several cards, it's worth checking with the issuers to see which one offers the best deal on foreign currency conversion. Then weigh this against other relevant factors.

Note: The conversion fee is not included in the legally required disclosure box that appears in credit card promotional material.

BRYCE CANYON NATIONAL PARK

Bryce Canyon National Park, near Panguitch, Utah, is a remarkable sight. Actually, it isn't a canyon at all but a stunning series of natural amphitheaters and rock formations. The colors in the pinnacles, spires, arches and bridges are breathtaking; the landscape almost seems to come alive with pinks, reds and

TOP TEN BUSIEST NATIONAL PARKS

Over 265,796,160 people visited U.S. National Parks in 1996.

At right are the ten most frequently visited national parks and the number of people who passed through them last year.

Blue Ridge Parkway, VA	17,169,062
Golden Gate National Recreation Area, CA	14,043,984
Lake Mead National Recreation Area, NV	9,350,847
Great Smoky Mountains National Park, TN	9,265,667
Gateway National Recreation Area, NY	6,381,502
George Washington Memorial Parkway, VA	6,126,490
National Capital Parks, D.C.	6,094,875
Natchez Trace Parkway, MS	6,088,610
Cape Cod National Seashore, MA	4,901,782
Delaware Water Gap National Recreation Area, PA & NJ	4,657,735

Source: National Park System

rusts that change color as the sun moves across the sky. The park can be visited by car, on foot or on horseback. Accommodations and camping facilities are located in the park.

More information: 801-834-5322.

CANYON DE CHELLY NATIONAL MONUMENT

Two hundred miles northeast of Flagstaff in northern Arizona, Canyon de Chelly has been the home to Native Americans for more than 2,000 years. A Navajo reservation sits at the base of the 21-mile-long canyon, while ancient cliff dwellings perch just below the canyon's rim. The cliffs are up to 2,000 feet high. Visitors must be accompanied by a Navajo guide. Accommodations are available in nearby Chinle.

More information: 520-674-5500.

COLORADO NATIONAL MONUMENT

Colorado National Monument near Grand Junction is 32 square miles of mesas and red rock canyon. Visitors drive along the 23-mile Rim Rock Drive. Of particular note are the Coke Ovens and the Pipe Organ, natural formations that have been shaped by erosion over the centuries. They now rise more than 500 feet from the canyon's floor. Accommodations are available in Grand Junction and Fruita.

More information: 970-858-3617.

HELLS CANYON NATIONAL RECREATION AREA

Near Lewiston, Idaho, on the Oregon-Idaho border, Hells Canyon is best seen by boat. The Snake River runs along the canyon' s walls, which rise 8,000 feet. Since the canyon is particularly narrow in certain places, the high walls can give the whole place a dark and forbidding look, adding to its fascination. Boat rides can be arranged in Lewiston. There are one- to three-day trips that include camping, hiking and fishing excursions, or half-day jet boat trips. Accommodations are available in Lewiston.

More information: 509-758-0616.

ROSS LAKE NATIONAL RECREATION AREA

Near Mt. Vernon, Washington, Ross Lake is a stunning wilderness surrounded by ice-covered mountain peaks, glaciers, rushing rivers and brilliant green mountain lakes. To fully explore the park, you must do so by backpacking. However, four-hour boat tours of the park can be arranged through the Seattle City Light Co., which operates a hydroelectric plant on the lake. The tour includes a railroad lift ride, a boat

tour of Diablo Lake and dinner at the base of the mountain. Accommodations are available in Burlington, about one hour away.

More information: 360-856-5700, ext. 515.

FREE STATE VACATION GUIDES

State tourism departments publish maps, lists of activities and historic sites, and sometimes even magazines on local history and customs.

More information: For your own state, check under Department of Tourism in the state listings in the telephone directory. For other states, call 800-555-1212 to get toll-free numbers.

Caution: Plan ahead. It often takes up to four weeks to receive the materials you request.

Winter Adventures For Seniors

Winter does not have to be a time to sit back and wait for spring. There are increasing numbers of snow-covered adventure vacations specifically geared toward people over 50. And they are not limited to skiing, or to the U.S. for that matter.

THE OVER-THE-HILL GANG

The Over-the-Hill Gang International was started in Colorado many years ago as a ski club for people over 50 who wanted companionship on the slopes. Since then, it has grown to include many other activities. Every year it organizes many senior ski weeks, both downhill and cross-country, at ski areas all over the world with packages that include transportation,

TIP There are often substantial travel savings, such as airline coupons and hotel discounts, for older vacationers that aren't available to younger people. These make the journey not only fun but relatively cost-efficient.

lodging, lift tickets and social activities. Its local "gangs" or chapters also run their own ski trips and all members are invited.

More information: 3310 Cedar Heights Dr., Colorado Springs, CO 80904, 719-685-4656.

SILVER STREAKS OF WATERVILLE VALLEY

Silver Streaks is a club for skiers who have reached their 55th birthday. What you get Mondays through Thursdays for a fee of $40 for the season is reserved parking, coffee and pastries every morning, a different ski school clinic each day, NASTAR races and guided ski runs. Additional happenings include après-ski parties and banquets. Single-day guest passes are also available.

More information: (After October 1) Waterville Valley Ski Area, NH 03215, 800-468-2553, ext. 3133.

SKI NEW ZEALAND

Ski New Zealand provides a unique twist on winter adventure vacations. One reason is that it schedules four trips a year specifically for skiers over 50 to New Zealand's Southern Alps. The other reason is the timing. New Zealand, in the southern hemisphere, has its winter during our summer. The 14-day ski packages take you to seven different ski resorts. Prices include airfare from Los Angeles, accommodations, ground transportation and sightseeing.

More information: 150 Powell St., San Francisco, CA 94102, 800-822-5494.

SENIOR WORLD TOURS

Senior World Tours offers yet another kind of winter adventure for people 50 and older. Its six- or eight-day vacations take you on snowmobile tours, starting at about $1,200, in Yellowstone National Park, or on sleigh rides in the National Elk Refuge. Snowmobiles, snowmobile suits with boots and helmets, lodging and meals are included. No experience is necessary, but participants should be in good physical condition.

More information: 2205 North River Rd., Fremont, OH 43420, 888-355-1686.

ELDERHOSTEL

Elderhostel is the world's leading specialist in low-cost learning vacations for people older than 55 (companions may be younger). Its packages world-wide include many winter tours that offer cross-country and downhill skiing, snowshoeing, animal tracking, dogsledding, sleigh rides, survival strategies and winter nature explorations. The list of programs changes constantly, so send for the voluminous Elderhostel catalogs.

More information: 75 Federal St., Dept. KP, Boston, MA 02110, 617-426-8056.

Over 50? There are great winter sport vacations designed just for you, including

- Downhill skiing.
- Cross-country skiing.
- Snowmobiling.
- Sightseeing.
- Snowshoeing.
- Dogsledding.
- Sleigh rides.
- Survival training.
- Nature hikes.
- Ice skating.
- Snowball throwing.

SENIOR WINTER GAMES

Senior Winter Games at the Summit are open to anyone who is over 55 and looking for winter sports, competition and a good time. Held in the quaint Victorian town of Breckenridge, Colorado, the first week in February, the games include downhill and cross-country skiing, speed skating, figure skating and snowshoe races, among other wintry activities. There is a small entry fee.

More information: Box 1845, Frisco, CO 80443, 970-668-5486.

CONNECTICUT SENIOR WINTER OLYMPICS

In March, these senior winter games featuring downhill, giant slalom, cross-country and snowshoe races, take place at Ski Sundown in New Hartford, Connecticut. Open to amateurs age 50 and up, the games currently require a $35 entry fee to cover costs. Preregistration is recommended.

More information: c/o Ski Sundown, Box 208, New Hartford, CT 06057, 203-272-9890.

GRANITE STATE SENIOR WINTER GAMES

The Games are usually held for three days in the White Mountains of New Hampshire every February and provide perhaps one of the most complete ranges of winter activities for men and women age 50 and over. The competitors are grouped by age and compete in dual slalom, giant slalom and cross-country skiing. Other events include speed skating, snowball throwing and snowshoe races. Call to see if the Games will be held this year.

More information: Box 1942, Rochester, NH 03866, 603-868-7880.

Exotic Outdoor Sports Vacations

YEAR-ROUND: SALTWATER FISHING ON CHRISTMAS ISLAND

Located 1,200 miles south of Honolulu, Christmas Island is one of the most exciting places in the world to fish. Accommodations for the six-day trip are at the Captain Cook Hotel. Sporting options include flats fishing, surf casting, lagoon trolling, blue-water fishing and scuba diving.

Dates: weekly, from Tuesday to Tuesday.

Cost: $2,395 per person (does not include round-trip airfare to Honolulu).

SPRING AND AUTUMN: TREKKING IN NEPAL

This 18-day trip takes hikers into Nepal's Kathmandu Valley. Hikes average four to six hours per day.

Try a Home Exchange
Evergreen Bed & Breakfast Club (800-383-7473) for singles and couples over age 50 offers members home exchanges at 700 locations in the U.S., Australia, Canada, England, Germany, France, the Netherlands, New Zealand and South Africa. The club supplies a directory with information on each host facility, nearby attractions, and hosts' occupations and interests. Annual membership fee: $50 for couples, $40 for singles.

Porters carry heavy gear, so hikes are for anyone moderately fit. Hikers spend the night in guest lodges managed by former Gurkha servicemen.

Itinerary: Spend one day rafting on the Modi Khola River and two days at Royal Chitwan National Park, where you'll search for wildlife from atop an elephant. Nights are spent in a tented camp.

Dates: March to April, or October to November.

Cost: $3,350 per person. Includes everything but round-trip airfare to Kathmandu.

SUMMER: FISHING IN ALASKA

Eight-day fishing trips are held on the Goodnews River in Togiak National Wildlife Refuge. Up to 16 anglers stay in walled-and-floored, two-person tents with propane heat and electricity. Jet boats transport guests to fishing spots along the river. Fish for rainbow trout and all five species of Pacific salmon.

Note: Anglers use barbless hooks and keep only

those salmon that are prepared for dinner. They can take home up to 20 pounds of fillets on the final day.

Dates: Saturday to Saturday, from late June through mid-September.

Cost: $3,550 per person. Includes everything but round-trip airfare to Anchorage.

More information on all sports vacations: Frontiers International Travel, 800-245-1950.

Bargain Family Winter Vacations

You don't have to spend a fortune on a Caribbean vacation to escape the chill. Here are some favorite U.S. destinations that are warm, comfortable and affordable.

ALABAMA

Gulf State Park Resort, in Gulf Shores, Alabama, offers the choice of a resort hotel on a 2.5-mile-long, white-sand Gulf of Mexico beach, or rustic, woodsy cabins on a freshwater lake. Some hotel rooms have kitchenettes and all of the cabins have kitchens. Activities include a championship golf course, tennis, boat and canoe trips, bike trails, nature programs and superb fishing—both salt and freshwater.

More information: 334-948-7275 for cabins, 800-544-4853 for resort.

CALIFORNIA

Santa Barbara is a posh, classic California coastal resort, yet its Miramar Resort Hotel offers a rare combination: true beachfront accommodations and affordable prices. It's a casual, compact place with a beach, two heated pools and four tennis courts on 15 acres of semitropical luxuriance. The Miramar has oceanfront, balcony and standard rooms, as well as cottages.

More information: 800-322-6983 in California, 805-969-2203 elsewhere.

FLORIDA

St. Augustine is a wonderful town for families. There is a lot to do besides go to the beach. Activities range from tourist attractions to the truly historic. The St. Augustine Ocean and Racquet Resort is the place to stay. Just a seven-minute drive from downtown, it is located on a gorgeous, wide beach. Two-bedroom/two-bathroom units sleep up to six.

More information: 800-448-0066.

SOUTH CAROLINA

State park cabins and resorts are among the best-kept bargain secrets in the travel business. The five Edisto Beach State Park Cabins on the lovely South Carolina coast are wonderful. The beach two miles away is well off the beaten track and lined with towering palmettos. The area is laced with hiking trails, playgrounds and picnic grounds.

More information: 803-869-2756 for camping and cabins, 803-869-2527 for resort.

TEXAS

Kids adore the Mayan Dude Ranch in Bandera. It's amid the rolling, lovely hill country of West Texas, and there's plenty for parents to do as well. Mayan is run by a family that has 11 kids of its own. It has a warmth that many other dude ranches are too busy to foster. Guests can enjoy the pool, river tubing, trail rides, cowboy cookouts and hayrides. Some of the accommodations are in cottages, while others are in a lodge with plenty of adjoining rooms.

More information: 210-796-3312.

Explore China in Orlando

Splendid China (800-244-6226) is a 76-acre theme park containing reduced-scale replicas of every major Chinese site, including The Forbidden City, the Great Wall and Terra Cotta Warriors. Because this park has only been open since 1993 and isn't nearly as heavily advertised as nearby Disney World, the crowds tend to be sparse and the lines short.

Caution: There is not much shade, so bring an umbrella or wear a wide-brimmed hat in hot weather.

Fascinating Factory Tours

Working factory tours are interesting to children and grandchildren of all ages—including you. The tours listed here are free, unless noted, and many give away free samples. Call ahead to make reservations.

- **Basic Brown Bear Factory**, 444 DeHaro St., San Francisco, CA, 415-626-0781. There is a charge for teddy bears or other animals if you want to stuff them yourself.
- **Bureau of Engraving and Printing**, 14th & C Streets SW, Washington, DC, 202-874-3188. See paper money being printed—no free samples.
- **Chicago Tribune**, 777 W. Chicago Ave, Chicago, IL, 312-222-2116. Receive a free sample of famous front pages or a special anniversary edition.
- **CNN**, One CNN Center, Atlanta, GA, 404-827-2300. See how television news is produced. $7 adults, $5 seniors, $4.50 ages 6 to 12.
- **Herr's**, 20 Herr Dr., Nottingham, PA, 800-63-SNACK. Sample warm potato chips right from the production line.
- **Hillerich & Bradsby**, 800 Main St., Louisville, KY, 505-585-5229. Visit this baseball bat factory and receive a free 16-inch bat.
- **Intel Corporate Museum**, 2200 Mission College Blvd., Santa Clara, CA, 408-765-0503. You cannot enter the super-clean factory, but you can see how computer chips are made.
- **Mystic Color Lab**, Mason's Island Rd., Mystic, CT, 800-367-6061. Witness mail-order film processing.
- **Tom's of Maine**, Lafayette Center, Railroad Ave., Kennebunk, ME, 207-985-2944. See how a natural toothpaste factory operates.

Alternative Travel Programs

Combine travel with education, voluntary service or a little of both.

Archaeological Tours, 271 Madison Ave., Suite 904, New York, NY 10016, 212-986-3054. Offers tours with university or museum specialists focusing on archeology, history and art.

Earthwatch, Box 9104, Watertown, MA 02272, 800-776-0188. Volunteers assist scientific expeditions in 50 countries and around the U.S.

Delightful Vacation Tax Deductions

Vacations are even more enjoyable if you adopt strategies that let you deduct part of the cost.

NATIONAL TRAVEL

The key to deducting travel expenses is to take a trip that combines business with pleasure, so you can claim a business deduction for your expenses. You may be able to deduct most of the cost of bringing your spouse along on a trip as well, even if it is for purely pleasurable purposes.

Basic rule: When your primary motive for making a trip within the U.S. is business, you can deduct the full cost of travel to and from your destination, along with the cost of lodging and 50% of the cost of meals incurred at your destination.

This is true even if you engage in substantial recreational activities at your destination, like visiting friends, attending sporting events and so on.

Specific nonbusiness expenses, such as the cost of theater tickets or nonbusiness side trips, are not deductible.

Travel for two often costs only a little more than

TIP

If you drive to your destination, you can deduct 100% of your driving costs, even if your spouse rides with you, because you would incur the same costs alone.

travel for one, so you may be able to deduct most of the cost of a trip on which your spouse joins you.

Other deductions:
- A single airfare, even if you obtain a family-fare discount by traveling together.
- A single hotel room at your destination, even if a double room would cost only a few dollars more.
- Basic car rental charges that you would incur at your destination if you traveled alone, even if your spouse uses the car.

You cannot deduct separate expenses incurred by your spouse on the trip, such as for meals or miles put on a rental car during nonbusiness driving.

If you and your spouse extend your stay after your business is done, you can't deduct meal or lodging costs incurred during the additional period. But you'll keep your deductions for travel to and from your destination and for expenses incurred during the business part of your stay.

FOREIGN TRAVEL
Tougher rules apply to travel outside the U.S. You can deduct all of your business-related expenses for such trips only if
- The trip lasts seven days or less, not counting the day you leave but counting the day you return, or
- You are an employee and did not have substantial control over the trip, or
- You otherwise establish that a personal vacation was not a major consideration for the trip, or
- You spend less than 25% of the trip on nonbusiness activities

The percentage of time spent on business activity is the number of business days on the trip divided by the total number of travel days. Business days are

1. Spent traveling directly to or from your business destination, not counting days spent on side trips.

2. Those days for which your presence is necessary for a business purpose, even if you spend most of the day engaged in activities that are considered nonbusiness, such as sightseeing or shopping.

3. Days on which your principal activity during work hours is business.

Business days include weekends and holidays that occur between business days.

Useful: Keep a diary of your daily activities.

Example: You arrive at your destination for a business meeting on Friday, sightsee over the weekend and then work on Monday. All four days are considered business days. But if you worked only on Friday or Monday, it would count as only one business day.

When 25% or more of your travel days are nonbusiness days, you can deduct only the percentage of travel costs that corresponds to the percentage of travel days that are business days.

SPECIAL TRAVEL RULES
Conventions
The cost of attending a business convention qualifies as a deductible business expense, but the costs of attending investment, political or social conventions are not deductible. The cost of attending a business convention outside the North American area is

---

Deducting Foreign Travel

At least 75% of your one-week or longer foreign business trip must be spent on business activities for your entire trip to be deductible.

For example:

6	business days	6	business days
÷ 8	total days	÷10	total days
75%	of trip spent on business	**60%**	of trip spent on business
Full deduction allowed		**Partial deduction only**	

---

deductible only if the meeting is directly related to your business and it is as reasonable for the meeting to be held outside the U.S. as within it.

Cruises
The cost of attending a business convention on a cruise ship is deductible only if the ship is registered in the U.S. and all ports of call are located in the U.S. or its possessions. The maximum deduction is $2,000 per year.

Luxury water travel
If you travel to a business destination by ocean liner, your maximum travel deduction is twice the highest per diem seasonal travel allowance for employees in the executive branch of the federal government, currently $180 to $204.

Get Paid To See The World

If you enjoy traveling and making extra money, consider an opportunity that nearly all travelers overlook: starting a small import business. If you do it right, you can travel as much as you want, take a tax deduction for your expenses and earn a second income. For those at or near retirement, the venture can especially make sense.

Reason: Once people leave their first career, they usually have the time and desire to travel plus the experience that it takes to become a successful importer.

GETTING STARTED
How many times have you been overseas and spotted an item that you wished you could buy back home? Chances are, if you want the item, other consumers would, too.

So the next time you visit another country, bring back a few sample items.

Best bets: textiles, folk art, specialty clothing, decorative items and unusual kitchen appliances. Many countries, for instance, have cooking utensils

that American consumers would have difficulty finding, such as manual food mills from France. Others have clothing that isn't normally found in this country, like heavy wool socks from Afghanistan.

Caution: Stick with items that you know something about. If you don't, there's a risk that you'll buy something that catches your eye overseas, only to discover later that it's either of low quality or already available in the U.S.

WHERE TO GO
The best places to look for importable goods include developing countries, especially China, India, Indonesia, and parts of Africa and South America. These places are excellent for finding folk art, hand-made products and low-priced manufactured goods. Europe is still a resource for household items not normally seen in the U.S., and Eastern Europe is turning out inexpensive manufactured items.

Added advantage: Most developing countries have

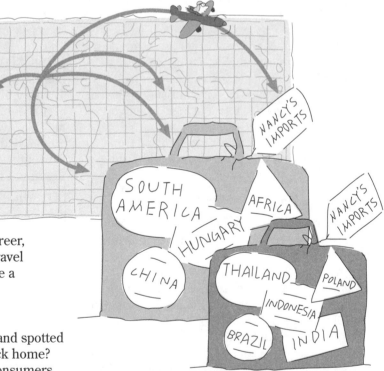

been granted preferential tariff treatment, meaning that goods can be imported at a low rate or even duty-free in some cases. These countries include Indonesia, India and China. A few more highly developed countries, such as Hungary and Thailand, enjoy this tariff treatment as well.

HOW TO SELL YOUR GOODS

When you bring back samples, show them to different types of retailers you think might be interested in selling them. Don't overlook outlets where your product could be an attractive sideline.

Examples: small decorative items that a florist might want for filling out the overall line, or artwork that an interior decorator could sell.

If a retailer is unsure, offer to put a few items on consignment.

Don't be afraid to go to the buying offices of major department stores. It's usually easier than you think to get an appointment because buyers are always on the lookout for small items that will catch customers' attention.

It pays to tell as many people as you think appropriate that you're in the importing business. Word will spread.

BRINGING HOME THE GOODS

Once you have an overseas supplier and a domestic buyer, it's time to put in an order and arrange to ship the goods to the U.S.

It's essential to line up a representative in the foreign country who can make sure that your supplier is complying with the volume and specifications of your order. If you order 10,000 brass bells to be shipped December 15, for example, a representative can make sure the manufacturer doesn't ship 5,000 iron bells on February 1.

To find a reliable overseas representative, ask for recommendations from the American consulate, a local bank or law firm with which you're now doing business, or members of the business community, especially Americans who do business in the country.

YOUR GROWING BUSINESS

As business increases, it also makes sense to tie shipments to some monetary assurance, such as letters of credit. Essentially, this means that your supplier doesn't get paid until he or she provides documentation that your order has been filled and shipped to your specifications.

Representatives are usually paid a percentage of the total order, so it's in their interest to handle the shipment well in order to get larger jobs from you in the future.

Also helpful: A freight forwarder can oversee the actual shipment from the time your foreign supplier puts it on a ship or plane to the time it arrives at your home or warehouse.

Since many forwarders don't like handling small shipments, it's smart to learn the process yourself.

How it works: Your supplier is responsible for packaging and putting your goods on a ship or plane. You receive a bill of lading when the shipment is made. The bill of lading tells you what is being sent, how it's being sent, and when and where it's scheduled to arrive.

If the goods are coming by ship, for instance, you go the pier named on the bill of lading, locate a

TIP

SAFEST MOVE
Test the reliability of an overseas supplier and representative by first placing a small order. Increase the volume as your confidence grows.

customs agent and open the shipment for inspection.

If duty is owed, you pay it at the pier and then claim possession of your goods.

THE PAYOFF

Even though your initial imports may be small in number, the profit may be impressive. In many cases, you may sell the goods you import for twice your total outlay. Moreover, once you begin importing as a business, your outlays, or a portion of them, can qualify as expenses for tax purposes. This includes the cost of travel as well as meals and lodging.

In many cases, you can even bring along a companion whose travel costs may also be expensed, depending on the amount of work the companion does on the trip.

Save Big on Hotel Rooms

Consolidators, also called discounters, book blocks of rooms months in advance and at steep discounts. In exchange for agreeing to buy rooms on slow nights, consolidators also get their pick when the hotel would otherwise be sold out. Most consolidators work with only one or two deluxe hotels in a city, although some also handle midprice and discount properties.

- A room that normally goes for $245.83 at the Drake Hotel in Chicago was recently available through Accommodations Express (800-444-7666) for $234.40 (5% off).
- A $181.17 room at Loews L'Enfant Plaza Hotel in Washington, DC, went for $165.35 (9% off) through Capitol Reservations (800-847-4832).
- At the Rihga Royal Hotel in New York, a $334.09 per night room was available through Quikbook (800-789-9887) for $245.49 (27% off).

WORLDWIDE BUSINESS TRAVEL COSTS

The average daily costs for a business traveler vary widely by city.

City	Cost per day
The Most Expensive	
Hong Kong	$474
Tokyo, Japan	$440
Moscow, Russia	$392
Buenos Aires, Argentina	$383
Paris, France	$377
The Least Expensive	
Hamilton, Canada	$99
Monterrey, Mexico	$129
Bordeaux, France	$133
Panama City, Panama	$135
Penang Island, Malaysia	$143

Per diem prices include breakfast, lunch and dinner in business-class restaurants and single lodging in business-class hotels.

Source: Runzheimer International, March 1997

Hidden Hotel Discount

When business is slow, independent hotels and chain properties are often happy to negotiate discounts, provided you guarantee your loyalty and volume to the hotel. Speak directly with the front desk manager or sales manager.

Best Hotel Rates

Don't try to obtain a discount hotel rate
- After bringing your heavy luggage into the lobby. It's obvious you aren't going anywhere else.
- After 9 pm—night clerks rarely have authority to give discounts.
- By calling the hotel chain's 800 number. The agent there reads off a computer screen and doesn't have authority to negotiate with you.

To get a bargain rate
- Call the hotel's front desk directly.
- Book your room well in advance, so the hotel agent knows you have time to shop around.
- Mention any affiliation that may entitle you to a discount, such as with a professional group, travel group, AAA or AARP.
- Don't accept the first rate offered to you. Many hotels have a fall-back rate that they will quote if, and only if, a customer is reluctant to accept the standard rate.

Get Your Money's Worth

Hotel renovations are a growing annoyance for travelers.

Self-defense: Before booking, call the hotel directly. Ask if there will be any construction done during your stay. Answers may not be straightforward, so listen for words like "redevelopment" or "refurbishment." If your stay is interrupted by construction noise, mess or limited facilities, and it's too late to make other arrangements, request a lower room rate or future discount.

House Calls When Traveling

Doctors make hotel room calls to treat travelers. The doctor brings necessary supplies and medications to the room. The $150 cost of the in-hotel visit is covered by most insurance companies and can be paid by credit card. This service is available in major U.S. cities through Hoteldocs.
More information: 800-468-3537.

We got a 30% discount by booking early.

I got a 30% discount by booking late.

Get the Best Price On a Cruise

Use a cruise-only travel agency. There are more than 800 of these. Their agents are much more likely to have personal knowledge of the ships they book.

Make reservations early or late. By booking a cruise nine months to a year in advance you may get a discount of up to 30% on your choice of staterooms. By booking within the last two months, you may obtain discounts of 25% to 50% on staterooms that are still available.

Cruise Passengers Have Few Rights

Be sure to read the extensive disclaimers on all cruise-line tickets. Cruise lines do not guarantee the condition of their ships or the food and drink served on them. They assume no liability for loss of or damage to passenger luggage unless negligence is proved, and liability then is severely limited. They also reserve the right to change ports.

Single Men Can Travel Free

VOLUNTEER CRUISE HOST

Become a volunteer Cruise Host by contacting your local travel agent and asking for a letter of recommendation to a cruise line. Gentlemen Hosts, usually single men over age 50, receive free passage and sometimes airfare, but no salary. They dance with passengers and otherwise make sure the people on the cruise are having fun. The usual required dances are the fox trot, rumba and cha-cha.

Defend Yourself Against Deposit Loss

Keep these tips in mind when signing up for a tour.
- Make sure the tour operator belongs to a reputable trade association like the National Tour Association, or U.S. Tour Operators Association. Both of these groups have consumer-protection plans. Remember that the tour company is the firm packaging the tour—not your travel agent.
- Pay with a credit card if possible. If the tour company does not provide service, you can refuse to pay the bill.
- If you must use cash or a check, be sure to get a receipt, and get all details of the tour in writing.

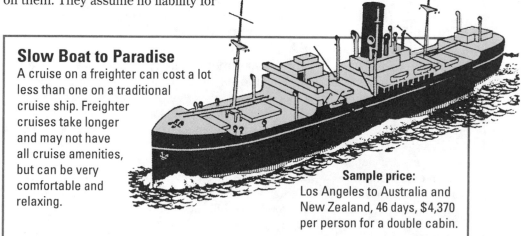

Slow Boat to Paradise
A cruise on a freighter can cost a lot less than one on a traditional cruise ship. Freighter cruises take longer and may not have all cruise amenities, but can be very comfortable and relaxing.

Sample price:
Los Angeles to Australia and New Zealand, 46 days, $4,370 per person for a double cabin.

- Contact at least one hotel listed as a tour stop to be sure rooms are really reserved.
- Ask about omissions and liabilities insurance; reputable tour firms have it.

How to Fly for Much, Much Less

Imagine you're flying the Miami-Tokyo route, sipping coffee, happily reading the newspaper and looking forward to a great vacation. Suddenly, you overhear a conversation between fellow travelers sitting in your section. What a great deal they got: only $698 for a round-trip ticket! You put your newspaper down. You can't believe what you heard. You paid $1,325 for the exact same ticket, and you thought that you had gotten a good deal.

Did the ticketing agent make a mistake?

No. On any given flight, any number of different people could be paying any number of different fares for the exact same flight.

People who aggressively pursue inexpensive fares, rather than passively accepting an airline reservationist's or a travel agent's first suggestion, get the best fares. These are the travelers who make it their business to understand the air-travel marketplace, have a certain amount of flexibility in their travel plans, carefully select the airline, know where the best place is to buy their tickets and take the time to be savvy shoppers.

NO-FRILLS TRAVEL AGENCIES

If you know where you are going, when you want to get there, and what airline you want to fly, you will be able to get an additional discount off an already discounted ticket price because no-frills agents rebate you part of their commission and charge a flat fee.

Example: Travel Avenue (800-333-3335) will issue you a ticket at the lowest possible price the airline allows, mail you the ticket and include the rebate in the envelope as well. The profit for the agent is a $15 fee for domestic tickets and $25 for international tickets. Additional passengers receive even more of a discount.

AIR TAXIS

If you are traveling as a group of three or more, consider hiring a small, private plane for your group. There are an estimated 3,000 independent, federally licensed operators with around 6,500 planes ready to take off at any hour you like. Add up the total cost of the group's tickets on a scheduled airline and see if the approximately $1 per mile round trip an independent would charge you makes sense. Then look in the yellow pages under Aircraft Charter or Aircraft Rental and call every listing to compare costs with the major airline and each private operator.

CONSOLIDATORS

During the course of the year, about one-third of the available seats on planes are empty. In anticipation of this, airlines sell batches of deeply discounted seats to consolidators, who, in turn, sell the tickets at great discounts to the public. There are no advance registration requirements, and you'll realize savings of up to 65% on national as well as international flights.

If you tell the consolidator your preferences for major versus lesser-known airlines, whether you want a non- or minimum-stop flight with direct routing versus indirect multiple-stop routing and the lowest possible price versus higher price with frills, you'll get what you want. Call Travel Bargains (800-872-8385) or look for advertisements for discount brokers in your Sunday newspaper.

BANKS

Many banks offer travel rebates as a way to build customer loyalty and encourage the use of their credit cards. Even if you think you've zeroed in on the lowest possible price for your ticket, check with your bank to see if you can shave off an additional 5% to 10%.

GIMMICKS

Cereal boxes, detergent products, statement stuffers in credit card bills and coupons in the back of travel

---

TIP **Look for Status Fares**

You can get up to 75% off your ticket price if you are:

- A student under age 26.
- An active-duty member of the military (or a dependent thereof).
- A child traveling with an adult.
- Part of a family flying together.
- A senior citizen.

To get a status fare, you've got to let the booking agent know you're eligible.

guides have all been known to offer discount certificates for up to 25% off fares.

Some stores have teamed up with airline marketing departments to offer merchandise that comes with an airfare discount ticket. Some mail-order catalogs will sell you a discount certificate good for 25% off your airfare for just $25!

city (a major city with a national or international airport) is within comfortable driving distance.

Last-minute clubs:
- Last Minute Travel, Boston (800-527-8646).
- One Travel Place, Illinois (800-621-5505).
- Vacations to Go, Texas (800-338-4962).

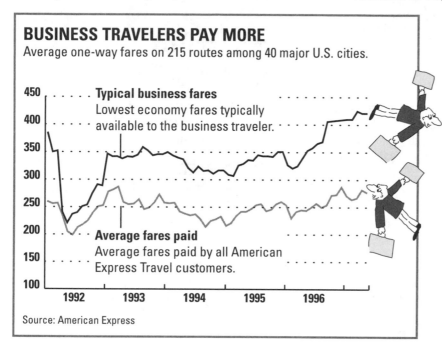

BUSINESS TRAVELERS PAY MORE
Average one-way fares on 215 routes among 40 major U.S. cities.

Typical business fares
Lowest economy fares typically available to the business traveler.

Average fares paid
Average fares paid by all American Express Travel customers.

Source: American Express

AIRLINE ADS
When major airlines announce extraordinarily low fares, reach for your telephone fast. Virgin Atlantic Airways once offered a $99 New York-London round-trip ticket. Within nine minutes, all $99 seats were booked. Continental once offered a bargain $99 New York-Honolulu fare!

INTERNATIONAL LOW-FARE AIRLINES
Foreign-owned airlines like Air Jamaica (800-523-5585), Cathay Pacific Airways (800-233-2742), Icelandair (800-223-5500), Thai Airways (800-426-5204) and Virgin Atlantic (800-862-8621) fly international routes that include stops in major U.S. cities and

Supermarkets occasionally sell, at rock-bottom prices, a redeemable certificate to customers who spend $50 to $100 a week on groceries. These gimmicks can be a source of extraordinary bargains! Watch for them and take advantage.

THE INTERNET
If you've got a modem-equipped personal computer, you've got immediate access (for an hourly usage fee) to the latest airfares as they are updated.

The Official Airline Guides (OAG) Electronic Edition, Eaasy Sabre and Travelshopper publish airfares. These databases are available through the CompuServe (800-848-8199) and Delphi (800-544-4005) networks.

LAST-MINUTE TRAVEL CLUBS
These clubs get fabulous bargains when an airline sells its last-minute inventory directly to the club at discounted prices.

Make sure when you join a club that its gateway

sometimes offer extraordinary bargains compared with better-known, better-advertised airlines.

Dialing to Save Dollars

There are more than 250,000 airfare changes daily. These changes happen so quickly that you can get a price from an airline reservationist, hang up the phone, call the same airline back and be given a completely different price.

Strategy: You must be a persistent caller. When you call, always ask questions like "Could I get a lower fare if I buy my ticket further in advance?" and "Would it be less expensive to fly off-peak or on a different day?"

Keep calling around, making and canceling courtesy reservations that will hold a seat for you for 24 hours. It's the folks who look for a better deal right up to the day of departure who swap the best "deal of the century" stories.

Airfare Cost-Cutter

Save thousands of dollars on airfares by studying a map before you purchase tickets. Circle the area surrounding your destination and make a list of the cities with airports that are within driving distance of your destination. Ask your travel agent about the fares to those cities.

Example: A recent round-trip fare from Chicago to Cincinnati was $307. Round-trip fare to Louisville, only one hour's drive from Cincinnati, was $59, a savings of $248.

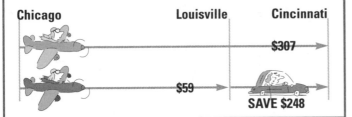

Chicago	Louisville	Cincinnati
		$307
	$59	SAVE $248

Know When to Fly

To be sure of the lowest airfare, ask your travel agent if it would be cheaper to fly on a different day, at a different time of day, during a different week of the month, on an earlier departure date or at designated off-peak times. Also ask your travel agent if there are any special seasonal or promotional fares available.

Be sure to ask about other airlines. Travel agents may promote particular airlines unless you specifically ask for quotes on others. Before finally agreeing to a flight, ask directly if the agent knows any way you could get a lower fare.

Get Better Seating On Airplanes

To get better seating in coach class on wide-body planes, ask for an aisle seat in the center section. Middle seats in that section are considered the least desirable, so this increases the chance that you will have an empty seat next to you, which means more room to get comfortable.

For couples traveling together: If most seats are in groups of three, specifically request an aisle and window in the same row. There is a good chance the middle seat will not be assigned. If you do not specify, one person will sit in the middle.

More Airfare Opportunities

Besides the 10% discounts almost all airlines routinely offer anyone over 60 or 62, there are two major ways to save on airfares.

1. COUPON BOOKLETS

American Airlines, America West, Continental, Delta, Northwest, United and U.S. Air sell booklets containing four or eight coupons. Each coupon is good for a flight on most of that airline's domestic routes. A booklet of four coupons costs from $495 to $596 and a booklet of eight coupons costs from $920 to $1,032, depending on which airline you use. So you can fly up to eight times a year for $115 to $129 each way.

2. SENIOR PASSES

Continental Airlines sells a Freedom Passport to travelers age 62 and older. You can fly routes in the U.S., Canada and the Caribbean (140 destinations) as often as once a week for four months ($999), or once a week for one year ($1,999).

You can buy inexpensive add-ons to Mexico, Central Amer-ica, Hawaii, Europe and the South Pacific. Renew for a second year within up to 90 days after the expiration of the one-year pass and get a special price of $1,799.

Airlines also sometimes offer seniors spur-of-the-moment,

Too Good to Be True
Airline two-for-one deals are not necessarily based on the lowest fares available.

Example: A recent fare from Washington, DC, to Seattle was $484 for one person, but the individual fare used in the two-for-one deal was $658.

Self-defense: Ignore heavily promoted special offers. Have a travel agent check for the lowest fares available.

additional discounts when new routes open or during particularly slow periods.

Caution: These deals are top secret until the last minute. Then, once you break through the busy signal to a reservation clerk, the seats might be taken.

Strategy: Combine the 10% discount with discounts from coupons and Continental's passport. Despite some restrictions, including advance bookings and refunds, these discount fares will get you where you want to go, inexpensively.

When You Can't Stay over Saturday Night

Back-to-back tickets are a way to evade the Saturday night stays often required for inexpensive air travel. Instead of buying a costly round-trip ticket that does not require a Saturday night stay, buy two cheap round-trip excursions: one from your home city to your destination and the other from the destination to your home. Use the first part of each ticket for your trip. Discard the return portions or save them for a future trip. This saves money whenever the cheapest coach excursion is less than half the cheapest coach round-trip that does not require a Saturday night stay.

Round-Trip To Europe: $100

Air couriers get super discounts in return for not checking bags on overseas flights. Couriers take important documents or machine parts to overseas destinations. They usually can take only carry-on luggage for themselves. In return, an air courier pays as little as $100 to $150 for a round-trip ticket to Europe from New York, and $100 to $250 for a round-trip ticket to Asia from California. Couriers must travel on courier companies' timetables.

Round-the-World Fares

These fares include stops in a number of cities on flights that are continuing eastbound or westbound until you circle the globe and return to your starting point.

Example: A single, round-trip San Francisco-Johannesburg business-class ticket might cost $6,848, while an around-the-world ticket with stops in Switzerland, Johannesburg, Singapore and Tokyo could cost only $4,018.

Caution: All your flights might not be on the same carrier. Fare restrictions may include minimum and maximum stays, minimum and maximum numbers of stopovers and no doubling back.

Your Rights if Your Flight Is Overbooked

Even though airlines have the right to bump you from a flight, they'll do so only as a last resort. There are also several ways that can reduce your chances of this ever happening to you.

● Avoid traveling at Thanksgiving and Christmas. Most bumpings take place during those periods.
● Fly airlines with low bump rates. American and United have the lowest rates, while Southwest has the highest.
● Secure an advance boarding pass and seat assignment when you buy your ticket. This puts you in a better position than ticket holders without seat assignments.
● Arrive early at the boarding gate and check in. Late arrivers are at the top of the list to be bumped.

WHEN TO GET BUMPED

If you're not in a hurry and your flight is overbooked, you can volunteer to be bumped, often in exchange for a free ticket or monetary voucher good for a year, and a seat on the next flight to your destination.

When you do fly, some airlines will try to upgrade you to first class as a compensation for your having been bumped. Delta is particularly generous with upgrades.

Caution: Before you volunteer to be bumped, ask when the airline will get you on another flight. If there's a long wait until that flight, ask if the airline will provide free meals, telegrams and phone calls, as well as any ground transportation necessary.

If the airline needs several people to volunteer to be bumped and gets only some of them, they may offer cash, usually starting around $200, in addition to a free ticket. Then, if they still don't get enough volunteers, they may raise their offer as high as $500.

Another Way to Earn Free Miles

Frequent-flier programs and tie-ins are expanding so fast that many people overlook ways to earn free miles. The most-overlooked source is long-distance phone calls made from your home. Each of the three major long-distance carriers credit customers with

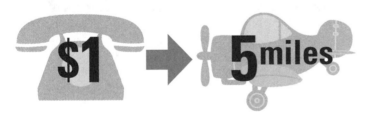

Lost-Luggage Reimbursement Update

The Department of Transportation has recommended increasing airline liability for checked luggage from $1,250 to $1,850 per passenger. However, reimbursement would be based on the depreciated value of clothing and packed items, not replacement value. Passengers would not be reimbursed for losses above that limit or for items for which airlines may deny liability, such as jewelry or fragile items not in their original packaging

Self-defense: Purchase a replacement value rider on your homeowners' insurance, carry on valuable items and leave extremely valuable items at home. Check with the airlines before leaving home if you have any questions about what is covered.

five miles for every $1 spent on calls. Miles are good on different airlines.

Caution: You won't receive miles unless you sign up for the phone company's program.

Shrewder Car Rentals

Reserve a compact car at the lowest rate. You can almost always upgrade to a larger car when you arrive, and the upgrade will often be free.

Reason: Most car-rental companies have more large cars than small ones. If a compact is not available when you arrive, ask that you be upgraded to a larger car at no charge. The agent should comply.

Save on Car Rentals

Don't get a Collision Damage Waiver (CDW) for car rentals. It costs too much, does too little and is unnecessary for at least 60% of car renters, who are already protected by their own auto insurance. CDW is supposed to protect the customer if a rented vehicle is damaged or stolen. If the cause of an accident can be interpreted as being in violation of anything in the rental contract, however, the CDW is void and the customer must cover damages.

Ticketless Travel Alert

Ticketless travel can leave you without paperwork in case of lost reservations or overcharges. United and Southwest, which both offer ticketless travel, will issue itineraries and ticket numbers to passengers who request them. This could be valuable in case of disputes. Ask other airlines if they provide documentation on request.

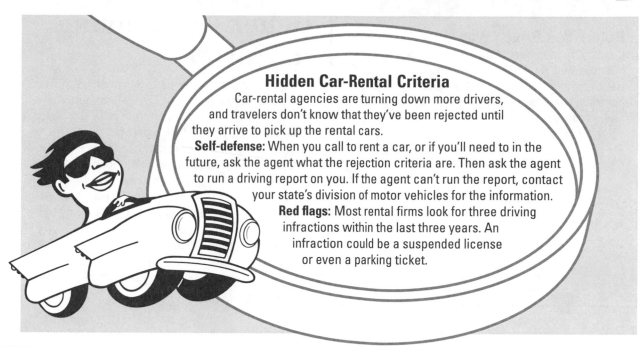

Hidden Car-Rental Criteria
Car-rental agencies are turning down more drivers, and travelers don't know that they've been rejected until they arrive to pick up the rental cars.

Self-defense: When you call to rent a car, or if you'll need to in the future, ask the agent what the rejection criteria are. Then ask the agent to run a driving report on you. If the agent can't run the report, contact your state's division of motor vehicles for the information.

Red flags: Most rental firms look for three driving infractions within the last three years. An infraction could be a suspended license or even a parking ticket.

Weekend Travel Bargains

Weekend car-rental rates usually start at noon on Thursdays. Rates can be up to 50% less than weekday rates.

Self-defense: If traveling on a Thursday, arrange to pick up a car after noon. If arriving earlier in the week but staying into the weekend, ask about returning the car you rented at weekday rates at noon on Thursday and exchanging it for a car at the lower rate.

Car-Rental Insurance Trap

Personal gold cards usually include collision insurance coverage automatically, but many corporate cards, including American Express, do not. Many non-gold cards also lack insurance provisions for car-renters.

Cancellation Charges

Car-rental companies are beginning to charge for no-shows. As travel picks up, firms are requiring reservations to be guaranteed with a credit card.

Reason: They can put through a charge even if the traveler fails to show. Cancellation policies at hotels are also being tightened. Some now require cancellation by noon on arrival day or they put through the charge. Some car-rental companies are experimenting with cancellation fees in the form of prepaid rentals, and some charge a cancellation fee, or the full amount, for no-shows.

Self-defense: Check all credit cards. Use only those offering collision coverage when renting. If you rent often but do not have any such card, consider getting one. The cost is far less than regularly buying Collision Damage Waivers (CDWs) at rental counters.

Before You Drive Away

Check out rental cars before driving away. You are not obligated to take any car that does not suit you. Have major dents and scratches noted on the rental contract. Make sure the car has a spare tire, jack and, in cold weather, a window scraper.

Better Car Renting In Europe

- Reserve a car through a U.S. travel agent who can offer better rates than a European agent.
- Ask for written confirmation of both the reservation and the rate in local currency.
- Make sure that either your credit card or personal auto insurance provides accident and liability coverage in foreign countries.
- Plan to pick up and return the car during business hours since European locations are likely to be closed at night and on weekends.
- Confirm with the rental agent that the car you're returning is not damaged, and request a final bill; disputing charges can be difficult after you return home.

SOURCES

Sources are listed in the order in which their contributions appear. A source may have contributed part or all of an article, or a series of articles.

Scott Ahlsmith, author of *The Complete Idiot's Guide to the Perfect Vacation*

Travel Holiday

Christopher Allen, author of *Passport to Discount Travel*

FreeFlier, Inc.

Gene Malott, editor of *The Mature Traveler*

David Keenan, Mastercard/Cirrus ATM Network

Herbert J. Teison, editor of *Travel Smart*

Condé Nast Traveler

Gerri Detweiler, author of *The Ultimate Credit Handbook*

Larry Ludmer, author of *The Great American Wilderness: Touring America's National Parks*

Catherine Fredman, travel editor of *New Choices*

Joan Rattner Heilman, author of *Unbelievably Good Deals & Great Adventures that You Absolutely Can't Get unless You're over 50*

Susan and Michael Fitzgerald, Frontiers International Travel

Laura Sutherland, author of *The Best Bargain Family Vacations in the U.S.A.*

Herbert J. Teison, editor of *Travel Smart*

Bruce Brumberg and Karen Axelrod, authors of *Watch It Made in the USA: A Visitor's Guide to the Companies that Make Your Favorite Products*

Earthwatch

Nadine Gordon Lee, Ernst & Young, LLP

Stanley Gillmar, Inversiones Metropolitanas, Inc.

USA Today

Runzheimer International

Jeffrey G. Saunders, Saunders Hotel Group

Herbert J. Teison, editor of *Travel Smart*

Josephine Kling, Landry and Kling Agency

Paul Grimes, editor at large in *Condé Nast Traveler*

Freighter Cruises

Lauretta Blake, Working Vacations, Inc.

Gene Malott, editor of *The Mature Traveler*

Bob Martin, author of *Fly There for Less*

Tom Parsons, editor of *Best Fares Discount Travel*

Donald Korn, author of *Retirement Angles: 1,001 Ways to Make Your Life Better Today and Tomorrow*

John E. Salak, editor of *The Best of New York*

Lynne Scanlon, author of *Overcoming Jet Lag*

Herbert J. Teison, editor of *Travel Smart*

Consumer Reports Travel Letter

William Bates, International Association of Air Travel Couriers

Jens Jurgen, editor of *Travel Companions*

Charles Leocha, author of *Travel Rights*

Randy Petersen, editor of *Inside Flyer*

Paul Grimes, editor at large in *Condé Nast Traveler*

Con Hitchcock, Public Citizen

Christopher McGinnis, Travel Skills Group

Bill Wood, U.S. Public Interest Research Group

The New York Times

Herbert J. Teison, editor of *Travel Smart*

Jens Jurgen, editor of *Travel Companions*

Donald L. Pevsner, Esq.

Herbert J. Teison, editor of *Travel Smart*

The Wall Street Journal

Much Better Business

Working For Yourself

Secrets of Starting a New Business

If you're thinking about starting a business, especially as a second career, consider a service business. As a rule, going into a service enterprise is easier, requires less investment, and is often more rewarding than other types of businesses.

SERVICE INDUSTRY ADVANTAGES

● **Up-front investment**. Though profits from retailing can be high, startup costs are usually much higher than they are for service companies.

Reason: Service companies generally have little or no merchandise in stock. They can be operated from a modest office or even from home. Bookkeeping is also simpler because service companies usually deal with a few high-paying clients instead of many customers who buy in low volume.

● **Direct customer contact**. Unlike retailing or manufacturing, a service business generally gives you a chance to deal directly with your customers. For many entrepreneurs, this is especially rewarding because they have an opportunity to see the influence of their work firsthand.

TODAY'S HOT SERVICES

Many service careers, like haircutting and accounting, have been around for ages and will be here for ages to come. Others are particularly suited to the 1990s, such as service companies that help clients cope with new technologies or the new demands of today's lifestyles.

Examples: businesses that train people to use computers and consultants who help companies write instruction manuals.

To find these lucrative niches, it pays to break out of your usual daily routine and examine today's trends. Watch TV shows you don't normally watch, read new publications and drive to different malls or shopping centers. Look for new things that are becoming important to today's busy consumers.

You'll probably discover some of the changes spotted by professional trend-watcher Faith Popcorn, who sells her advice to major international companies.

> **Small businesses are responsible for 54% of all sales in the U.S. and 50% of the private gross domestic product.**
>
> Source: U.S. Small Business Administration

New trends:
- **A growing desire for a simpler life.** This trend creates opportunities for such businesses as pet-sitting, home cleaning and shopping services.
- **Nostalgia for earlier decades.** Some entrepreneurs are capitalizing on this trend by designing retro fashions. Others have become consultants who help consumers find rare books and records.
- **Emphasis on children.** Today's entrepreneurs have gone far beyond child-care centers and tutoring. They now offer special training for children in fields such as computers, weight loss and even financial responsibility.
- **More travel.** This trend opens the doors for a wide variety of services for visitors who come to your city. In many areas, there's a growing demand for people who organize conventions and meetings. In places of historical interest, there's also often a demand for organized tours.

HOW TO MINIMIZE RISK

You can cut the risks of starting a new business by putting your ideas through rigorous testing before you invest in them.

Research your business idea thoroughly

Start by reading everything you can find about the business and going to conventions where you can talk with others in the field. Then visit a similar type of company. It's usually best to choose an out-of-town business so the owner will talk to you without fear of competition. Ask what problems, especially unexpected ones, the owner faced. Ask what he or she would do differently today in light of past experience.

Play the devil's advocate

Once you have an idea, think of as many reasons as you can why it might fail. Ask a friend who's knowledgeable in business to do the same. It's a good idea to know ahead of time what you're up against.

Crunch the numbers

If you don't know how to develop a business plan, hire an accountant or consultant who is an expert in the field or buy a book that will take you through it step by step.

TYPICAL COSTS OF STARTING A NEW BUSINESS

Stationery	$200 - $300
Fees and licences	$200 - $500
Advertising and promotions	$2,000 - $3,000
Computers, telephones and other office equipment	$3,000 - $5,000
Leased office space (small town)	$500 per month
Leased office space (large city)	$2,000 - $3,000 and up per month
Accountant, lawyer and clerical help	Varies

BIGGEST MISTAKES

Don't make the same mistakes that many other new business owners do.
- **Underestimating the indirect overhead.** Factor in hidden costs such as taxes, license fees and insurance, especially health insurance if you're no longer covered by the policy of your former employer.
- **Overestimating sales.** Ask owners of similar services to give you an honest estimate of how much business they think you'll do in the first three months, six months and one year. Then cut the lowest estimates by 50%.
- **Inadequate marketing.** Since advertising in the daily press and on television can be very expensive, consider weekly papers, radio and special-interest magazines. Also consider the Yellow Pages. Though not cheap in some areas, it's the first place many consumers turn for many services. If your service is unique, you might also get free

Legal Issues to Consider

Make sure you consider all the necessary legal aspects before you begin a new business, including the following.

- Licenses required.
- Zoning laws.
- Business- and state-specific regulations.
- Form of organization (corporation, partnership, limited liability company or sole proprietorship?).
- Tax status (Subchapter S?).

publicity by telling members of the local press about it. Another route to low-cost publicity is offering your service free to a local civic group that will spread the word.

- **Failing to give yourself a professional image.** Register a business name for your service, have a graphics designer assist you with brochures and get a separate telephone number that is answered in a professional manner.

How to Run a Successful Business

There is no perfect time to start a business. Success depends on the type of business you choose and the energy, vision, skills and capital you bring to the task.

THE MOST IMPORTANT STEPS

- **Do all you can in advance.** Once you start the business, you will be swamped and will need to devote

all your time and energy to generating revenue. Do everything you can before setting out on your own. That includes tasks such as developing a business plan, filing for incorporation and getting your bookkeeping in order.

- **Start your new business as a sideline.** Often, this isn't feasible. But if your business idea and your circumstances make it possible, you can test the waters by starting the venture part-time, or by gradually turning a hobby into a business.
- **Conserve your cash.** Don't pay outside consultants, such as market researchers, for information you can gather yourself.

  Exceptions: It's worth spending the money to hire a good lawyer and a good accountant. Don't try to handle these tasks on your own.

- **Be emotionally prepared.** Almost every successful entrepreneur goes through a period when failure appears imminent. A slow quarter is normal. If your business shows little sign of growth after two years, however, it's time to rethink your original assumptions.

BIGGEST TRAPS

- **Not having a competitive advantage.** Your product or service doesn't have to be unique, but there must be a compelling reason for people to buy from you rather than someone else.

  Warning: Never assume that just because you do something well business will come to you.

- **Waiting too long.** Don't put off planning a business until a downsizing eliminates your job. If you

Surprise Costs of Working For Yourself

Before quitting your job to work for yourself, take a hard look at the extra costs your business will incur.

Surprise: For the typical employee, an employer pays an amount equal to about 30% of salary to cover health and disability insurance, pension contributions, employment taxes and similar items. As a self-employed person, you'll have to make this up yourself.

Example: If you earn $50,000 in gross salary, you will have to net about $65,000 working for yourself to break even. In addition, you will not get paid sick leave or vacation.

Do Your Homework

Before leaving your job, list the various forms of insurance you'll have to replace and price them through trade groups you may be eligible to join.

313

expect to start your own business, start planning while you're still working for someone else.

● **Lacking essential skills.** An entrepreneur has to understand every part of the business, or team up with a partner who can supplement his or her knowledge.

Strategy: Before starting a business, improve your skills. Seek promotions or lateral moves that will increase your knowledge of marketing, finance, accounting and general management. If you can't do this at work, take courses at a local college.

● **Underestimating costs.** Entrepreneurs almost always underestimate the amount of capital they'll need and the hours they'll have to put in.

Rule of thumb: Estimate how much money and labor you think you'll have to invest. Doubling both numbers will result in amounts closer to what you'll actually need.

● **Assuming that traditional financing is available.** Don't assume you'll get a business loan from a bank. Banks don't like to lend to start-up businesses. You'll probably have to invest your savings, borrow against your home, borrow from family or friends, or tap a partner's capital.

● **Starting a business when your life is in turmoil.** Strange as it seems, that's when most people do it, and it's a very bad idea. Try not to start a business right after going through a divorce, a big move or a major health problem.

Be Your Own Boss

If you follow a few simple rules, starting your own business is not very costly. And it has some terrific advantages.

● **Extra income.** Five hundred dollars a day isn't an unreasonable amount to expect.

Reason: When you work for an employer, that company usually takes in at least $2 to $3 for every $1 it pays you in salary. When you work for yourself, the profits are all yours.

Moreover, by starting small—perhaps in your home—you can hold overhead to a minimum.

● **The chance to use your skills at something you truly enjoy.** Sadly, few regular jobs offer this opportunity. When you go into business for yourself, make sure you pick a field you like. You'll immediately be motivated, and the long hours won't seem like such a burden.

● **Control over your own time.** While starting a business is very demanding, you have more control over the hours you work. If you want to take off Thursday instead of Sunday, for example, you don't need anyone else's permission. Many businesses also offer the opportunity to travel abroad —and to deduct the cost on your tax return.

BEST BUSINESSES

Like any other enterprise, the best business to start is one that offers a product or service that you can produce cheaply for consumers who are eager to buy it. Finding that niche takes a lot of preliminary work, but there are more niches than you might imagine.

Exporting

Exporting is especially attractive today because American products have a cachet overseas and because many once-poor nations now have burgeoning economies and are eager for American goods.

Exporting is usually easier and more profitable than importing because it requires you to find only one overseas distributor to buy your products. When you import, on the other hand, you usually bear the entire burden of sales.

Note: Once you have experience at exporting, you can consider opportunities in importing.

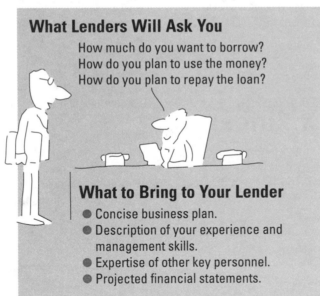

What Lenders Will Ask You

How much do you want to borrow?
How do you plan to use the money?
How do you plan to repay the loan?

What to Bring to Your Lender

● Concise business plan.
● Description of your experience and management skills.
● Expertise of other key personnel.
● Projected financial statements.

Brokering

What might sound like an esoteric niche is actually a straightforward business: bringing lenders together with other businesses. Nearly every company, from IBM to your local newsstand, needs cash at some point in its lifetime. Lenders have the money, but they don't always have time to look for all the potential borrowers in the business community. A financial broker charges a fee for helping them do that. Some business experience is needed, but you don't need a background in finance.

Mail order

You might think that the world can't sustain another mail-order company, but that's not the case. There's always room for a company with products people want, and there's no predicting what those products might be.

Who would have thought that putty in an egg-shaped container or pet rocks would be a hit? Today, the hot sellers include violet contact lenses and golf balls with more dimples.

Best bets: specialty foods, pet products, instruction courses and home needs—all of which require little capital to start up.

Aside from these opportunities, there are thousands of other business niches that creative entrepreneurs have started with almost no cash.

Examples: boarding pets, selling patterns for making stuffed animals, publishing political newsletters, locksmithing and making specialty home furniture.

SOLVING THE CASH PROBLEM

High-potential business ideas, especially in the technology area, can attract professional investors known as venture capitalists. You can find them through several directories located in public libraries. It also pays to contact local and state governments. Many have venture capital programs, some of which aren't widely publicized.

The Small Business Administration Can Help

The Small Business Administration (SBA) is the government agency that offers aid, counsel and protection for the interests of U.S. small businesses. The SBA provides a variety of loans and venture capital financing opportunities for small businesses that would otherwise be unable to secure financing. For more information, contact the SBA at 800-827-5722 or http://www.sba.gov/

Source: U.S. Small Business Administration

TIP — Before You Buy

Rather than immediately buying expensive equipment, consider leasing it or, in the case of manufacturing, farm out jobs to other companies. It may cost slightly more, but there's no point in investing in costly equipment until you have a steady stream of orders.

To make that happen, put money you might have invested in equipment into marketing and promotions, the activities that bring in orders.

LEASE ME

If you're willing to put up your own home or other asset as collateral, consider applying for a loan from the Small Business Administration.

OTHER NEEDS

Make sure you have the tools you need before you start your business.

Place of business and equipment

Don't splurge on an office. The object is to hold down overhead until you work up a healthy cash flow. A basement or den in your home is often a perfect site for the phone line, desk and office equipment you'll need to get started. Remember, Apple Computers started in a garage.

Merchant account

This enables you to accept credit card purchases. It isn't absolutely necessary, but it makes it easier to sell certain types of products.

Problem: Most large banks won't open merchant accounts for small businesses.

Solution: Contact an Independent Sales Organization (ISO) that acts as an intermediary between banks and small businesses. Most banks and chambers of commerce can tell you how to find an ISO. They are also frequently listed in the business pages of the telephone book.

Some small regional banks also set up merchant accounts for home-grown businesses, as do a few credit unions.

Be Your Own Bookkeeper

Keeping sufficient financial records should be one of your top priorities. Without them, you will be unable to run your business and increase your profits. In addition, records are needed to substantiate

1. Your tax returns under federal and state laws, including income tax and Social Security laws;
2. Your request for credit from vendors or a loan from a bank;
3. Your claims about the business, should you wish to sell it.

CEO — BOOKKEEPING — ACCOUNTING

Source: U.S. Small Business Administration

Professional services

It usually isn't necessary to pay big retainer fees to lawyers and accountants. Instead, use recommendations to find reliable professionals whom you can call on as needed.

Marketing plan

The biggest mistake is trying to force on the market something that you (and you alone) think is a great idea. Always let the market lead you. This usually means testing out ideas on a small scale before committing yourself to them in a big way.

Here's how: Try sending out a few direct mailings or putting a couple of modest ads in niche publications that cater to the market you're aiming at. Responses to inexpensive classified ads can often tell you if your product is mar-

ketable. If it is, consider other sales methods, such as regional distributors, display ads in national publications or a major direct mail campaign.

To keep up with consumer trends, study the ads in *Popular Science*, *Modern Franchising*, *Popular Mechanics* and similar publications. Also helpful are the auction and business opportunities columns in local papers, *The Wall Street Journal*, big-city newspapers and the new-product columns in magazines that interest you. All of these publications are available in most libraries.

Low-cost promotions

Try getting your product into the local press and the new-product columns in magazines that cover the field you're in. Niche publications thrive on telling their readers about new products and services. And there's no cost if they choose to write about you.

The local press is often hungry for business and feature articles about interesting products, so it pays to cultivate one or two people on the editorial staffs. Keep in mind that some types of businesses are easier to promote than others.

Examples: A new accounting service probably won't generate much media interest. A new sled will.

MARKETING: THE FOUR Ps

There is more to marketing than just advertising and selling. A major part of marketing involves researching your customers. You need to find out who they are, what they can afford, and how they think. Your ability to understand your clientele will be a major influence on the success or failure of your new business.

Here are four basic aspects of marketing, known as the Four Ps.

Product: the item or service you sell.

Price: the amount you charge for your product or service.

Promote: the ways you inform your market about who, what and where you are.

Provide: the channels you use to take the product to your customers.

Source: U.S. Small Business Administration

Biggest Mistakes for Retirees Starting Their Own Businesses

The average American can look forward to almost 20 active years after retirement, and many plan to spend these years pursuing the dream of running their own business.

Advantages: Retirees often have the benefits of superior skills and experience, coupled with a natural conservatism that develops with age.

Result: Mature entrepreneurship tends to be less risky than starting a business when you're young.

Most retirees don't have the time or the energy to recoup any serious mistakes or losses, so the key to success in later life is to work smarter. Avoid these pitfalls to make sure your second career is satisfying and prosperous.

BASING A BUSINESS ON YOUR HOBBY
You may have always dreamed of owning a bookstore or pet shop, but can you compete with the huge discount chain that just opened in the mall? You may love refinishing antiques, but can you find enough clients, charge enough and work rapidly enough to make a profit? It's great to be able to turn an avocation into a vocation, but do your market research first. Don't be afraid to enlist professional advice in this area.

OPENING A BUSINESS IN A LOCATION YOU DON'T KNOW WELL
Sure, you'd like to stay in the old neighborhood, or move to Florida. But will the location support the business you plan to open? Or does your dream location already have ten ice cream parlors? Can you afford to live there, is there adequate health care and can your children afford to visit? Spend time examining your proposed destination from a business and personal standpoint.

INEXPERIENCED MANAGEMENT
The primary cause of new business failures is not lack of money, as we see from the many million-dollar corporations that go bankrupt, but poor management of resources.

Rule of thumb: Don't get involved in any new venture without the right experience. Whether you are buying an existing business, a franchise or starting from scratch, take the time to learn the field. If you are unfamiliar with retailing or the food service business, work in a similar store or restaurant before going out on your own.

Helpful: business courses at community colleges and free or low-cost advice from the Small Business Administration.

SCORE Helps Small Businesses Win Big
The non-profit association, Service Corps of Retired Executives (SCORE), has 389 chapters and 12,500 volunteer members throughout the U.S. Trained members serve as counselors, advisors and mentors to small and aspiring business owners. Counselors have real-world experience in a wide variety of businesses and industries, and may be retired or working business owners, executives or operations managers. To find the SCORE chapter nearest you, contact The SCORE Association, 409 3rd St. SW, 4th Floor, Washington, DC 20024, 800-634-0245, 202-205-7630 or http://www.sba.gov

Source: The SCORE Association

INSUFFICIENT CAPITALIZATION AND CASH FLOW
This is the bane of all new businesses, not just retirement ventures. Many established businesses were started at a time when banks encouraged new enterprises, and money was easy to borrow.

Reality: Today, money is hard to get. Make sure you can arrange for sufficient funds, adequate cash reserves and an available line of credit before starting or expanding your business. Your business plan should include a safety cushion based on a worst-case scenario.

FAILURE TO ACCOMMODATE LIFESTYLE EXPECTATIONS

Younger people can afford to nurse a business along while it develops, which often means 14-hour days and several years of belt-tightening. But retirees seldom feel they can wait five years while their business grows. And they don't usually want to work twice as hard as they did before they retired for half the reward.

Self-defense: Make sure you and your spouse agree on your goals. Leave time for leisure activities when designing your plan. Choose a business that will allow you to work only as many hours as your energy level permits. If possible, presell to a targeted clientele to ensure your business will develop and stabilize quickly.

Example: Your dream may be to run a neighborhood bakery, but it takes a long time to find enough customers to support one. By securing a few contracts to supply local restaurants with home-baked pies, however, you would probably have enough business to survive the start-up period.

FAILURE TO NETWORK

The success of any business depends on the goodwill and help of others. But retirees may have grown out of touch with the mainstream business community or an important customer base, such as families with school-age children.

Self-defense: Before launching a new business, increase your visibility and social contacts by joining a wide range of groups, offering to give talks and participating in public relations activities.

AVOIDING NEW TECHNOLOGIES

Second-careerists may be unfamiliar with the latest electronic time-savers like computers and fax machines. Make sure you learn how to use anything that will make your job easier.

New Telemarketing Rules

For information on the government's new rules regarding the legal methods of telemarketing, request a free copy of *Telemarketing Sales Rules* from the Federal Trade Commission, Public Reference Branch at 202-326-2222.

High-Tech Money Saver

Fax letters long-distance instead of calling, to relay a message without expensive and time-consuming small talk.

Tip: Send your faxes late at night, when phone rates are lowest. Faxing a short letter long-distance is faster and cheaper than sending the letter by mail. And faxing local letters is the best bargain of all: Local phone calls are usually free, saving you 32¢ per letter.

Home Office Opportunities

The last half of the 1990s will offer a vast range of opportunities for working from home.

Changes in lifestyles have created the need for new types of businesses that can be run entirely from home. Inexpensive computer software now gives home businesses some of the advantages that once only large companies could afford.

Startup costs: usually $5,000 to $10,000 for computer equipment, a fax machine, stationery, a separate phone line, brochures and office furniture.

Here are some ideas for home businesses.

MYSTERY SHOPPER

A mystery shopper is the person retailers hire to tell them how shoppers are treated in their stores. As customer service has grown in importance, so have mystery shoppers (also called anonymous shoppers, silent shoppers or spotters).

Besides customer service, mystery shoppers check on employee honesty and monitor worker-training programs. Market research firms often provide this service, but many retailers prefer hiring individuals.

Most likely clients: stores whose owners cannot be on the premises to check on each of their local establishments.

Fees: $20 to $40 per visit.

To get into the business: A background in retailing is helpful as well as courses in customer service, usually available from local colleges.

Caution: Before you get started, check business

regulations in your state. A few states require mystery shoppers to be licensed as private investigators.

PUBLIC RELATIONS SPECIALIST

Today, even some large companies are looking for public relations specialists who work from their homes.

Reason: Individuals often have specialized product knowledge and valuable media contacts.

Requirements:
● Strong communications skills and the ability to write well.
● Creativity that will help a company develop ideas to market its products or services.
● Knowledge of the media.
Fees: The business is stimulating and pays well: $200 to $1,500 a day.

Most likely clients: small firms with low budgets, especially companies that are planning to introduce new products.

Helpful: The Public Relations and Marketing Forum on CompuServe (800-848-8900).

MEETING PLANNER

So much can go wrong with a meeting that companies and other organizations increasingly rely on planners.

Meeting planners select and reserve the meeting space, hire speakers and entertainers, set up promotions, arrange transportation and catering, and provide any special equipment that a given group will need.

Fees: $400 to $500 a day or around $40 to $60 an hour.

How to get business: Develop contacts among travel agents, hotels and people at the local convention bureau. Volunteering to plan a civic event can also be an effective way to get started.

Helpful: Meeting Professionals International offers a kit to people interested in a career as a meeting planner. Contact them at 4455 LBJ Freeway, Suite 1200, Dallas, TX 75244, 972-702-3000.

Instant Home Office

It's not difficult to create an office in your home. Here's all you need to get started.

● Separate telephone line.
● Fax machine.
● Computer.
● Stationery.
● Brochures.
● Furniture.

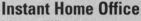

CLAIMS ASSISTANCE PROFESSIONAL

CAPs, as they're known, file private insurance company claims for people who have seen doctors. They then verify that the insurer or Medicare has paid the full amount and catch errors that can cost patients money. As a CAP you would also check to make sure that a doctor or clinic doesn't charge more than the amount allowed by the insurance company.

To find clients, it helps to cultivate lawyers, accountants and others who can give you referrals.

Fees: $20 to $75 an hour, or you can charge flat rates of $200 to $400 a client per year.

How to learn the business: Home-study courses are available through the Institute of Consulting Careers, 222 SE 16 St., Portland, OR 97214, 503-240-0931.

Also helpful:
● *Health Service Business on Your Home-Based PC* ($34.00) by Rick Benzel, McGraw-Hill, 1221 Avenue of the Americas, New York, NY 10020.

TEMPORARY-HELP PROVIDER

Since many temporary agencies can't keep up with the demand for specialized workers, the door is open for home businesses.

Fees: either a flat rate per day for placing a temp or a percentage of the salary. If you place as few as ten people a week, you may earn more than $50,000 a year.

Temporary specialties now in demand include social workers, musicians, librarians, insurance workers and convention help.

Caution: Depending how you run your service, you may need special liability insurance as well as professional help to keep up with tax and employment laws.

Helpful: The National Association of Temporary and Staffing Services, 119 S. Saint Asaph St., Alexandria, VA 22314, 703-549-6287.

TRANSCRIPT DIGESTER

Since transcripts of legal proceedings are often hundreds of pages long, lawyers rely on digesters to summarize the statements into concise, readable language.

Fees: from as low as 80¢ a transcript page when you get into the business, to $4 a page when you become experienced. A digester can usually handle up to 20 pages an hour.

Experience isn't necessarily needed to get into the business, but some paralegal training, available through many local schools, is an asset. Writing skills are a must. Personal contacts in law firms are essential for getting clients, and ads in legal publications can increase your name recognition.

Helpful:

- *The Transcript Digesting Manual*, Hillside Digesting Service, Box 2888, Fallbrook, CA 92088, 800-660-3376.
- Computer users can use the Working from Home Forum on CompuServe to download files that cover the basics of transcript digesting. There's no charge beyond the CompuServe fee.

PET SITTER

As pets increase in popularity, so will the need for people who care for them when their owners are away. Although the work does not require special skills, you should have an understanding of animals, including dogs, cats and tropical fish. In addition to just looking in on animals, a pet sitter must be able to handle emergencies, like taking a pet to the vet.

Fees: from about $7 a day per pet in small towns to $20 in big cities. Pet sitters can often get referrals from pet stores and veterinarians.

Helpful:

- The National Association of Professional Pet Sitters, 1200 G St. NW, Suite 760, Washington, DC 20005, 202-393-3317.

BUSINESS-PLAN WRITER

You might think that all company owners know how to write a business plan, but that just isn't the case. There are thousands of entrepreneurs who need plan writers when they start companies or need financing.

If you have a business background, this type of job could be a lucrative way to build on it. Nearly all business schools offer courses in business planning, and there are many helpful books, like *The Business Plan Writing Handbook* ($25) by Linda Elkins, Business Plan Writing, 3099 Friendship School Rd., Mechanicsville, MD 20659, 301-373-3745.

The best way to get business is to develop contacts who can refer clients to you. These include bank loan officers, trade associations and business organizations, business schools and lawyers who specialize in working with entrepreneurs.

Fees: $2,000 to $5,000, though a business plan writer with a proven track record can make far more.

HOME INSPECTOR

If you know about the construction business, you can often make close to $100,000 a year by inspecting property. Inspectors are hired by potential home buyers to find out whether property is sound. The result of your inspection is a report that spells out the condition of the house.

Fees: $150 to $400 per home.

Licensing isn't currently required, but it adds to your credibility to have a membership in the American Society of Home Inspectors, 85 W. Algonquin Rd., Arlington Heights, IL 60005, 800-743-2744.

How to get business: Solicit referrals from attorneys and Realtors.

NOT FOR MEN ONLY

In 1994, women owned one quarter of the companies in the U.S., over 7.7 million firms.

Source: The SCORE Association

From Idea To Reality

You need more than just a great idea to start a business. You need to be able to guide your idea carefully to the marketplace. Here's how.

PROTECT YOUR IDEA

Before you do extensive market research, it's wise to protect your idea. Begin by talking with a competent patent attorney.

How to find a patent attorney:

● Ask other inventors to recommend attorneys. To find other inventors, go to local, nonprofit inventor groups that can often be found in the Encyclopedia of Associations at the library.

● Get referrals from a trusted lawyer you're now using for other legal matters.

When you interview prospective patent attorneys, ask for referrals from several clients, including ones they've dissuaded from filing.

MARKET THE IDEA

The vast majority of inventors market their ideas by licensing them to established companies. In a typical licensing agreement, an inventor is paid a percentage of net sales, which means the company deducts its own costs before calculating royalties.

Since there are many other types of fee arrangements (including reimbursement for money you've already spent on the ideas), get advice from an attorney who's knowledgeable in the field.

Typical Patent Fees
The cost of attorney and filing fees.

A simple idea (like a new golf tee)	At least $2,000
More complex product ideas	$5,000 and up

More information: U.S. Patent and Trademark Office, 800-786-9199 or 703-308-4357.

Research companies fully before you approach them with your idea

Look for a growing business with an existing product line that will be enhanced by your invention.

Problem: Most companies are deluged with new product ideas. As a result, they're not eager to talk with inventors they don't know.

Solution: Get the name of the person in charge of new product development. If your call is given to the switchboard and you can't get the name, consult Standard & Poor's Register.

If you still can't find it, call any other executive's secretary and lead the person to think you're also a secretary who needs the new-product director's name for your boss. You'll usually get it. Make an appointment to see the executive in person. If you can't, write a detailed letter describing your idea.

Present your idea like a professional

Regardless of which type of presentation you make, be sure it gets these points across.

● There's a market for your idea. Tell the company who the typical customers will be and why they'll buy the product.

● Your product complements the company's existing product line.

● Manufacturing costs are low enough for the company to make large and long-term profits.

● Your product will put the company ahead of any actual or potential competitors.

Before showing your idea to anyone, consider asking him or her to sign a confidentiality agreement that makes it illegal to use the idea without your permission. Patent attorneys and other lawyers who work with inventors are familiar with these types of agreements.

Essential: Bring a prototype of your idea that can be used to show companies precisely how it works. Videos showing the product in use are also helpful.

If you don't have the skill to build a prototype, consider going to a friend who has a home shop or to a local school. High schools and junior colleges will often make prototypes as class projects. When you approach a school, go directly to a faculty member, not to the administration.

Caution: Many companies advertise services to help inventors get their products to market. Some charge high fees and perform negligible services.

Rule of thumb: Avoid inventors' services that ask for high up-front fees in exchange for patenting, producing and marketing your idea.

Weekend Entrepreneuring for a Big Boost in Income

End of the month and short of cash? Again? The easiest way to come up with an additional source of income is by becoming a weekend entrepreneur.

YOU'RE IN CONTROL

The advantage of being a weekend entrepreneur, rather than committing to a second job or putting in extra hours at your regular job, is that you control your own time. You can work a little or a lot.

Most part-time weekend jobs require very little initial investment, experience or overhead. All they take is a good idea, dedication and courage.

To generate extra income, you must be able to spot a trend and recognize what needs are currently unfulfilled.

Key: Find services or goods that you can provide that will make other people's lives easier.

Example: Two brothers in Oregon set up the adult equivalent of a weekend lemonade stand in the parking lot of a supermarket. Instead of lemonade, the brothers served fashionable gourmet coffee to weekend shoppers.

SAMS THAT WORK

SAM (Source of Additional Money) opportunities are everywhere. The key is to choose a weekend business that takes advantage of your interests, abilities, knowledge or skills.

Here are some SAMs that have paid off for other weekend entrepreneurs.

Car detailer

Clean and polish cars from top to bottom. Since their cars have to be immaculate, start with real estate brokers first. Go into an office, introduce yourself, drop off flyers and offer to do the first car for free. Charge a minimum of $40 per car.

Pet meals on wheels

Deliver cumbersome 20-pound bags of dry pet food and heavy cases of canned goods to pet owners' doors. Blanket a neighborhood with flyers and contact veterinarians and dog groomers to let them know you're in business. Don't charge a delivery fee, just mark up the pet food after negotiating a close-to-wholesale price with local distribution centers or retailers.

WANT TO START A SAM? THINK IT THROUGH!

Here are four questions to help you get your idea organized and launched.

1. How much time can you devote to launching a Source of Additional Money (SAM)?
Devote a consistent number of hours each week, whether it's for promoting your business, sending out bills or rolling up your sleeves and sewing quilts.

2. Will family members support and help you?
Get a commitment from them to help you in specific ways at specific times and hold them to it.

3. What are the insurance needs, licensing requirements and tax laws regarding your SAM?
You don't want surprises showing up from your insurance agent, the town or the IRS six months down the road.

4. Are you willing and able to take on the responsibility of customer satisfaction?
You will engender a great deal of goodwill among your customers if you act responsibly, but they will never forget it if you let them down.

Recycling pickup service

Save your neighbors the trouble of hand-feeding cans and bottles into recycling machines at the supermarket or loading their cars with recyclable material that must go to the dump. In exchange for keeping any cash refund, volunteer to recycle items that don't have a cash value, like newspapers in some states.

Special-occasion sign rentals

If you're handy with a jigsaw and have an artistic flair, create ready-to-rent yard cards for high-profile celebrations. Signs in the shape of bunny rabbits, teddy bears or carousel horses are great for kids' parties, while a humorous sign planted on a front lawn for a 40th birthday party will bring you $25 a day, $35 for three days or $50 for a week. You make the signs, install them and pick them up.

House portraits and custom stationery

People love to use portraits of their homes to create distinctive stationery, to send as holiday greeting cards, or simply to frame beautifully and hang in the house. If you're good with a camera or a sketch pad, show your portfolio to home owners in an upscale neighborhood and offer to photograph, sketch or paint their homes. Try charging from $85 for a pen-and-ink sketch to $150 for a color photograph. Adjust your prices depending upon the response.

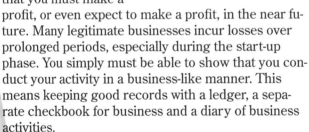

MAKE SURE THE PRICE IS RIGHT

The price of a service or item is based on the cost of producing it. Pricing can be very complicated, so beginners may want to seek expert advice.

> **Direct materials**
> **+ Labor costs**
> **+ Overhead**
> ---
> **= Total cost to produce the product**
> **+ Profit you desire**
> ---
> **= PRICE**

Make sure your price is competitive in the marketplace.

Sideline Businesses Are Tax-Saving Opportunities

Starting a sideline business is a great first step toward becoming your own boss on a full-time basis. But beware, sideline businesses face tax traps as well as opportunities.

STARTING UP

You can start your own sideline business by using your current business knowledge for endeavors such as consulting. It is also a great way to test a new business opportunity on a part-time basis, or to convert your favorite hobby, such as collecting, sailing or farming, into a business activity.

Key: In order to receive favorable tax status, you must be able to show the IRS that you have a profit motive behind your activity.

This does not mean that you must make a profit, or even expect to make a profit, in the near future. Many legitimate businesses incur losses over prolonged periods, especially during the start-up phase. You simply must be able to show that you conduct your activity in a business-like manner. This means keeping good records with a ledger, a separate checkbook for business and a diary of business activities.

It also includes advertising your product or service, having business cards and stationery, seeking advice from recognized professionals in your field, obtaining the permits or licenses required by local law, and, if you incur losses, modifying your practices to improve results.

The IRS is suspicious of loss deductions claimed from hobby-like activities, so you can expect such deductions to be scrutinized. However, even if the IRS concludes that you have no profit motive, you can deduct expenses to the extent that you have income from the activity. Only the deduction for a net loss would be disallowed.

For Profit or Pleasure?

When an activity earns a profit during three out of five consecutive years, it is presumed to have a profit motive, and loss deductions will be allowed for the years in which losses occurred.

Self-defense: If the IRS challenges the business status of your sideline activity, you can file **IRS Form 5213,** *Election to Postpone Determination as to whether the Presumption that an Activity is Engaged in for Profit Applies.* This delays the final determination of the activity's business status until after you've been in business five years. It also gives you extra time to qualify the activity as a business. In the meantime, you can claim business deductions. Some of your expenses, such as legal fees, may have to be capitalized and amortized over a five-year period.

IRS FORM 5213

Danger: If your activity fails to qualify as a business at the end of five years, you will owe back taxes and penalties.

Note: If you don't make a profit in three out of five years, you still may be okay. Business status may be upheld despite consecutive years of losses if you can show you have maintained a genuine profit motive for conducting the business.

TAX BENEFITS

A sideline business offers numerous tax-saving opportunities.

Keogh savings

Self-employment income can be used to make deductible contributions to a Keogh retirement plan, even if you are already covered by a pension plan at your regular job and thus are ineligible to make deductible IRA contributions. Keogh contributions are based on a percentage of net profit: up to 15% of your self-employment earnings can be deducted on up to $160,000 of self-employment income (in 1998) in a defined contribution plan. Other limits apply to more complicated plans.

Note: Even if you have a 401(k) at your full-time job, you can still have a Keogh plan.

Home-office deduction

You can deduct utilities, insurance, maintenance, rent or depreciation, and similar household expenses that are properly allocated to a home office. Converting personal expenses to business expenses gives you a tax deduction without incurring any additional cost.

To qualify for a deduction, a home office must be used exclusively for business and be the principal place where you conduct business or meet clients regularly. See **IRS Form 8829,** *Expenses for Business Use of Your Home,* regarding allocation of expenses to a home office.

Business-equipment deductions

You may already own a computer, fax machine, car phone or similar equipment that is used for your reg-

TAXING SIDELINE BUSINESSES

Advantages

- Business-equipment deduction.
- Deductible Keogh retirement plan.
- Family salary deduction.
- Home-office deduction.
- Local travel deduction.

Disadvantages

- Estimated income taxes.
- Higher risk of audit.
- Home office deduction may decrease your cost basis in your home.
- Must show genuine profit motive.
- Self-employment tax.

ular job. As an employee, however, it is difficult to deduct these items.

Problem: Such items can be used for personal reasons, so the IRS allows the deduction only if the equipment is acquired "for the convenience of the employer," meaning your boss requires you to buy it.

Moreover, employee business expenses are deductible only to the extent that they and other miscellaneous expenses total more than 2% of your Adjusted Gross Income (AGI). So even deductions that are allowed are cut back.

Loophole: These deduction restrictions do not apply to business owners. Owning a sideline business enables you to deduct the cost of business equipment in the year of purchase to the extent you have records that show you use the equipment for business and a portion of the expenses to the extent you can prove that they were for business.

Example: A phone bill for a car phone or fax machine may be deductible.

HOW TO GET AN EIN

Most small businesses (one-person operations may be exceptions) are required to obtain an employer identification number (EIN) from the federal government. Call the Internal Revenue Service at 800-829-1040 and request **Form SS4**. Mail the completed form to IRS, Attn: Entity Control, Philadelphia, PA 19255 or call 212-574-2400 to review the form by phone.

Source: The SCORE Association

In 1998 you can deduct up to $18,500 of office equipment purchases annually. Amounts in excess of $18,500 must be depreciated.

Family salaries

You can deduct payments made to family members who work in your business. If they are in a lower tax bracket than you, the family's tax bill will be reduced as a result.

In 1998, a child can earn up to $4,250 tax-free (the kiddie tax does not apply to earned income). The Tax Court has upheld the deduction of reasonable salaries paid to children as young as 7 years old for clerical and cleanup tasks. A child's salary can also support a deductible IRA contribution, obtaining an extra $2,000 deduction for family income and giving the child a start on tax-favored savings.

> **Loophole**
> Wages paid by a proprietorship (a self-employed individual's business) to a child under age 18 are not subject to Social Security tax.

Local travel deductions

The cost of traveling to a regular job is not deductible. But you can deduct the cost of commuting between two work sites and traveling between your home and work sites related to your home-based business. This may make commuting deductible all around.

TAX RISKS

There are drawbacks to operating a sideline business as well as benefits, however.

Audit risk

Business owners face a perceived greater audit risk than employees because of the perception that they have greater opportunity to hide income and exaggerate deductions. Audit risk rises especially if you claim deductions for red-flag items such as a home office or extensive business use of your car.

Self-employment taxes

If your annual salary and self-employment net income total less than the amount on which Social Security taxes are withheld, you owe 15.3% self-employment tax. On net income that exceeds the amount, you owe an additional 2.9%, the Medicaid portion of self-employment tax, with no income limit.

You don't owe self-employment tax if self-employment income is less than $400. Half the self-employment tax you pay is deductible.

Estimated taxes

Being self-employed doesn't increase the income tax you owe. But it makes you take on the cash-management responsibility of paying quarterly estimated taxes and payroll taxes for your employees, and of monitoring your income position to avoid underpayment penalties. Quarterly estimated taxes are paid with **IRS Form 1040-ES**, *Estimated Tax for Individuals*.

> IRS FORM
> **1040-ES**

Home office trap

When you sell your home, you can't use the home sale exclusion ($250,000 for singles; $500,000 on a joint return) for gain attributable to depreciation taken after May 6, 1998.

> IRS FORM
> **8829**

So the tax benefit you received with depreciation deductions taken in the past will be "recaptured" when you sell your home (taxed at 25%). This is so even if you're not using your home office in the year you sell your home.

All about Home-Based Franchises

A home business can be a great source of extra income, but it has two potential drawbacks. First, you need a considerable amount of business knowledge to turn a profit. Second, you must endure the solitude of working on your own.

Buying a franchise can be a solution to both problems: If you choose a franchise carefully, you can both work from home and as part of a team that gives you its business expertise.

No matter what your professional experience, there is nearly always a home-based franchise that can build on it.

Examples: consulting, home maintenance, marketing, education, designing, landscaping, construction, pet care and photography.

INSIDE FRANCHISING

The initial cost of starting a home-based franchise can be as low as $10,000 to $15,000, and run up to nearly $100,000. Profits may range from a few thousand dollars a month to more than $100,000 a year.

Besides money, you'll probably need a computer, business phone and other office equipment, typically running $6,000 to $15,000. Ideally, you should also have on hand one year's projected income, since new businesses always need ongoing investment.

What you get when you buy a franchise

A franchisor provides you technical and marketing

Where to Look for a Home-Based Franchise

Entrepreneur Magazine (12 issues for $19.97), 2392 Morse Ave., Irvine, CA 92714, 800-274-6229. This magazine runs an annual list of what its editors believe are the best of the home-based franchises.

Franchise Opportunities Guide ($15), International Franchise Association, 1350 New York Ave. NW, Suite 900, Washington, DC 20005, 800-543-1038.

The American Association of Franchisees and Dealers (AAFD) looks out for the rights and interests of U.S. franchisees and independent dealers. The AAFD's Trademark Chapters help franchise systems develop consensus decisions and promotes more equitable franchise relationships. In addition, the AAFD provides marketing, legislative, legal and financial support.

More information: AAFD, PO Box 8-887, San Diego, CA 92138-1887, 800-733-9858.

support, the right to use an established name and training in the business.

Downside: You have to give up part of your income, which must be paid in fees or royalties to the franchisor.

CHECKING OUT A FRANCHISE

When you spot a franchise business that you believe might be worth running from your home, ask the franchisor to send you more information, including a Uniform Franchise Offering Circular (UFOC).

This legal document discloses the history of the company and its managers, its financial status (including any bankruptcies), exclusive territories, trademark and copyright information, restrictions and obligations on the part of the franchisor and franchisees, names of franchisees, all fees and investments, and purchase requirements.

The UFOC is the only legal place for a franchisor to discuss earnings projections for franchisees, but there's no obligation on the part of the franchisor to include them. Never enter into a franchise when company representatives make earnings claims outside the UFOC. It's illegal for them even to hint at how much you might make or to disclose how much other franchisees make.

Instead, contact as many franchisees as you can. Ask them how much they've been making and how satisfied or dissatisfied they are with their franchisor.

Avoid franchisors who dispute or discount information that you've learned on your own from their franchisees you've talked with.

Next step: Find a franchisee who will let you spend some time watching the operation at his or her home. Not only are you likely to discover information the franchisor hasn't mentioned, but you will also learn firsthand about day-to-day business operation.

PROCEED WITH CAUTION
There are several signs that should alert you to stay away from a particular franchisor.

- Discrepancies between what a franchisor tells you and what you read in the UFOC.

- A history of numerous lawsuits.

- A company experienced in franchising but new to a particular business.

- A franchisor using a trademark similar to one that's better known.

- A franchisor who has saturated your area with similar businesses.

- A franchisor trying to pressure you, perhaps by claiming that someone else is on the verge of signing up for the same territory. (It's the oldest trick in the book. If it were true, why would the salesperson waste time with you?)

Once you've narrowed down the possibilities to two or three, retain a lawyer familiar with franchising to check out each one thoroughly. Though most franchisors operate honest businesses, some skirt the law in ways that only attorneys can spot.

How to Buy a Franchise

There are two ways to become your own boss: You can either start your own business or you can buy a piece of someone else's.

The second method is called franchising. There are about 650,000 owner-operated franchise units in the U.S., ranging from fast-food restaurants to educational services. Franchises make up 35% of the nation's total retail sales.

While buying a franchise may require less experience and knowledge than starting your own business from scratch, it demands the same drive and commitment, and there are just as many opportunities to make mistakes.

FINDING A HEALTHY FRANCHISE
Some franchises are much better than others, and some are much worse. Most people who become franchise owners think only of the money-making possibilities—not of the dangers and pitfalls.

Tip: Before becoming a franchise owner, read the franchise's Uniform Franchise Offering Circular (UFOC). The franchise company is legally obligated to give you the UFOC at least ten business days before you sign the franchise contract. Surprisingly, most franchise buyers never read this document carefully or even consult a lawyer.

Franchise contracts have specific territory rights, quality controls, performance obligations, and tough termination clauses. Review the UFOC with a franchise attorney to identify the negotiable areas. Ask your accountant to gauge the company's financial strength to make sure it has the resources to help you succeed in your endeavor.

The UFOC provides 20 categories of information about a company and its executives. The categories include background of management, information on lawsuits or bankruptcies, and details on any deals, such as discounts on franchise fees and financial interests in suppliers.

Red flags: numerous recent lawsuits, very few written obligations for the company, many obligations for the franchise buyer, no franchise fee refunds and no franchisee rights to end the contract.

Talk to between five and ten of the company's current franchise owners to find out if the company is dedicated to helping them succeed. Franchise owners' names are listed on the back of the UFOC.

Healthy signs: Current franchise owners say they're meeting or exceeding revenue and profit projections, have numerous two-way communications, have an active Franchisee Advisory Council (FAC) with decision-making power, receive help promptly when they ask for it, and receive new marketing programs and products frequently.

Bad signs: Franchise owners complain about sales and profits, tell horror stories about lack of support from the company, know of other owners who have failed and express negative attitudes toward the franchisor. If you find more than one or two out of ten or 20 franchise owners have had bad experiences, be wary about your choice.

Tip: Check the UFOC for the annual turnover rate. Only about 5% of franchise owners fail outright, but many leave the business for other reasons. An annual turnover rate of 3% or less is outstanding, 3% to 5% is satisfactory, and more than 5% signals trouble.

MAKING THE DEAL

Out of ignorance, most people choose to handle the research and dealing involved in buying a franchise themselves.

Strategy: Have an experienced accountant review the franchisor's financial reports, which must be placed at the back of the UFOC. If the reports are outdated, call the company for interim reports.

Good news: There are no secrets to the numbers. Any good CPA can figure them out.

A franchise lawyer, not a regular attorney, should review the fine print of your franchise agreement. To find a qualified franchise attorney in your area, consult *Franchise Update's Directory of Franchise Attorneys, 1997 Edition* ($9.95), Box 20547, San Jose, CA 95160-0547, 800-289-4232.

Have your lawyer negotiate any onerous provisions of the franchise agreement. Be prepared to find that, because the franchise contract applies to many people, you have little leeway on major issues such as franchise fees and quality standards. But you have room to bargain on some issues.

Examples: You can try to eliminate some ancillary fees, like additional training costs. You may also be able to defer royalty fees until you reach a certain sales level. You may be able to defer some advertising fees until a certain number of franchises open in your area, and you might water down default or termination clauses.

Caution: Most agreements allow franchise companies to terminate a contract with just 30 days' notice for a variety of franchisee transgressions, such as nonpayment of royalties or failure to meet quality standards. Most franchisees, however, can't cancel an agreement unless the company commits a gross violation, such as filing for bankruptcy or being found guilty of a felony.

WHAT IT TAKES TO SUCCEED

Owning a franchise is not like being an employee. At the start, the work is a lot more demanding. To make the business take off, you may have to be willing to put in six ten- or 12-hour days per week for several years. After that, you can expect to work fairly normal hours.

Many corporate refugees aren't aware that they, and not someone from the franchisor, have to pick up the slack if anything goes wrong.

Examples: If the bathrooms have to be cleaned and there's no one there to do it, it's your job. If an important employee calls in sick or makes a last-minute decision to go to the prom, you may have to work from 8 a.m. to midnight.

You also have to be willing to follow the franchise company's guidelines, even if you disagree with its latest marketing efforts. Extremely opinionated or stubborn people may not enjoy being franchisees. Even a high quality franchise may not turn a quick profit, so don't expect a windfall overnight. Ideally, you should have enough cash in the bank to carry you for six to 12 months if the early stages are rough. Budget for unexpected costs.

Examples: You may have to pay hefty legal fees to get a zoning variance. Giving away coupons to attract business in your first few months may also reduce your initial revenues.

SOURCES

Sources are listed in the order in which their contributions appear. A source may have contributed part or all of an article, or a series of articles.

Ben Chant, author of *How to Start a Service Business*

Scott Shane, PhD, DuPree Center for Entrepreneurship and New Venture Development at Georgia Institute of Technology

Joseph Martingale, Towers Perrin

Tyler G. Hicks, author of *How to Start Your Own Business on a Shoestring*

Gustav Berle, PhD, SCORE, the Small Business Administration's Service Corps of Retired Executives

Andy Dappen, author of *Cheap Tricks*

Paul Edwards, coauthor of *The Best Home Businesses for the 90s*

Judy Ryder, World Inventors Network

Jennifer Basye, author of *How to Become a Successful Weekend Entrepreneur*

Laurence I. Foster, KPMG Peat Marwick

Gregory Matusky, franchise consultant

Robert L. Perry, Enterprise Unlimited

Index

J

K

L

M

T